Robert Keating O'Neill is Director of the John J. Burns Library and Part Time Faculty, Political Science, at Boston College, Chestnut Hill, Massachusetts. He has been Burns Librarian since 1987. He holds both a PhD in History and an MA in Library Science from the University of Chicago. Previously he was Director of the Indiana Historical Society Library in Indianapolis and Head of Special Collections at Indiana State University, where he was also Associate Professor of Library Science in the College of Arts and Sciences.

His many publications include: *Irish Libraries, Museums, Archives and Genealogical Centres: A Visitors' Guide* (2002); *Management of Library and Archival Security: From the Outside Looking In* (1998), co-published simultaneously as *Journal of Library Administration* (volume 25, number 1, 1998); *Ulster Libraries, Archives, Museums and Ancestral Heritage Centres: A Visitors' Guide* (1997); and *English-Language Dictionaries, 1604–1900: The Catalog of the Warren N. and Suzanne B. Cordell Collection* (1988). He co-edited *The Art of the Book from the Early Middle Ages to the Renaissance: A Journey through a Thousand Years* (2000). He has written numerous articles, reviews and prefaces.

O'Neill is a former president of the Manuscript Society (1992–1994), and the Éire Society of Boston (1995–1997). He continues to serve as a member of the board of directors of both these organisations. He also serves on the board of the Charitable Irish Society of Boston and is a past member of the boards of Bookbuilders of Boston and the Madame C.J. Walker Urban Life Center, Indianapolis. He is a fellow of the Massachusetts Historical Society in Boston, and a member of the Grolier Club in New York, the Club of Odd Volumes in Boston, and the Royal Dublin Society, Dublin, Ireland. He is also a fellow of the Manuscript Society, and received the Society's Award of Distinction.

He was honoured by the Irish and American governments for his role in the recovery of stolen Irish artefacts in 1991. In 2003 he received the Éire Society of Boston's Gold Medal and was named to *Irish America* magazine's 'Top 100 Irish Americans'. O'Neill is also the 2004 recipient of the Ambassador's Award, established by the St Patrick's Committee of Holyoke, Massachusetts in conjunction with the Irish Ambassador to the United States.

O'Neill is married to the former Helen Ann Parke. The couple have six grown-up children and live in Holliston, Massachusetts.

A VISITORS' GUIDE

IRISH LIBRARIES

ARCHIVES, MUSEUMS &
GENEALOGICAL CENTRES

Robert K. O'Neill

ULSTER HISTORICAL
FOUNDATION
2007

Published 2007
by Ulster Historical Foundation
Cotton Court, Waring Street, Belfast BT1 2ED
www.ancestryireland.com

Ulster Historical Foundation is pleased to acknowledge
support for this publication from the Belfast Natural History
and Philosophical Society.

© R.K. O'Neill
ISBN: 978-1-903688-69-4

Printed by Lightning Source
Typeset by December Publications
Design by Dunbar Design

CONTENTS

ACKNOWLEDGEMENTS

In compiling this guide, I have had the indispensable help of numerous librarians, archivists, genealogy centre managers, coordinators and researchers throughout the island of Ireland. Their names can usually be found as the contact persons in the entry for their respective institutions, but this is not always the case, as a number of people who were very helpful preferred not to have a specific contact person listed or recommended another name. Surveys and follow-up enquiries were no doubt unwelcome intrusions into the already overcrowded schedules of these professionals, yet their generous and gracious gifts of knowledge and time gave proof to the adage that if you want a job done well, give it to a busy person. Users of this guide can be assured that the level of professionalism, courtesy and assistance they will find in Ireland will be second to none.

A number of individuals in Ireland provided helpful advice and assistance in the compilation of this work. I am particularly grateful to Mario Corrigan, Jack Gamble, Aoife McBride, Wesley McCann, Fergus O'Donoghue SJ, Colette O'Flaherty and Evan Salholm. Professor Kevin Whelan, former Burns Library Visiting Scholar in Irish Studies at Boston College and current Director of the University of Notre Dame's Keough-Naughton Institute in Dublin, graciously read over the glossary and contributed a number of helpful improvements and clarifications. Ulster Historical Foundation Executive Director Fintan Mullan and Director Dr Brian Trainor encouraged me to undertake this work and provided support throughout this project. I wish to acknowledge in particular the assistance of Dr Trainor. His enthusiasm, energy and help have been a constant source of inspiration. He not only read the entire manuscript, but also identified those institutions whose resources, especially in the area of genealogy, merited expanded treatment. He also prepared the valuable appendix, 'Tithe and Valuation Records for Ireland, *c.* 1823–*c.* 1930', an expanded version of the appendix he initially prepared for my *Ulster Guide* (1997) and which subsequently appeared in the 2002 edition of *Irish Libraries*. I am grateful to the Public Record Office of Northern Ireland and to the National Archives of Ireland for their permission to list, as an appendix to this book, the references to their tithe and valuation holdings for the parishes of Ireland. I wish also to thank Karel Kiely for permission to reprint her article, 'Tracing Your County Kildare Ancestors', which offers helpful advice to all interested in tracing their roots anywhere in Ireland. Karel also helped with the updating of the piece on the Irish Genealogical Project. Wendy Dunbar lent her award-winning design talent and expertise to this work, and her contributions made this book a more aesthetically pleasing as well as user-friendly one.

On this side of the Atlantic, Dennis Ahern, who was so extraordinarily helpful to me in the compilation of the first edition of this guide, was always available whenever I had specific questions, especially of a genealogical nature. That I was able to bring this work to a timely conclusion is due in no small measure to the support of my employer, Boston College. I am especially grateful to University Librarian Jerome Yavarkovsky and to my Administrative Secretary Mary Lafferty for their support and encouragement. Burns Library colleague John Atteberry was always available to read over material and offer valuable suggestions. The Irish American Partnership generously provided a grant to help with the costs associated with an undertaking of this magnitude. For the past two decades, the Partnership has been an inspiration and a source of hope to thousands in Ireland who have benefited directly or indirectly from its educational and economic programmes and grants. Joseph F. Leary Jr, President of the Partnership since its founding in 1987, has championed library services in Ireland, especially at the rural primary school level.

No acknowledgement would be complete, however, without recognising the deep debt I owe to my wife, Helen, whose love, patience and understanding made frequent absences from home and late nights at the computer tolerable. I want also to thank our children – Kathleen, Kevin, Kerry, Daniel, MaryAnn and Timothy – for their support and love. Since the first edition of this work was published in 2002 the O'Neill family has grown by three – my daughter-in-law Sandra O'Neill (wife of Daniel), my son-in-law Alex Southworth (husband of Kerry), and my first grandchild, Sebastian John Southworth, born 3 September 2006, to whom I dedicate this book.

INTRODUCTION

In 2002, the Ulster Historical Foundation published the first edition of my *Visitors' Guide to Irish Libraries, Archives, Museums and Genealogical Centres*. This work grew out of an earlier guide I had compiled on research resources available in nine county historic Ulster, entitled *A Visitor's Guide: Ulster Libraries, Archives, Museums and Ancestral Heritage Centres*. The 2002 guide not only expanded to include all 32 counties in Ireland, but also reflected, to a significant extent, the rapid integration and delivery of new and improved services, especially electronic services, and the expansion of resources offered by many Irish libraries and archives between 1997 and the end of 2002. This expansion of services and resources has continued apace, with many institutions now offering remote access to their catalogued holdings and some offering remote access to their information databases.

As with the previous guides, the primary target of this guide is the visitor to Ireland, chiefly the North American visitor, who may be travelling or contemplating a trip to Ireland for the first time. In most instances this visitor will be primarily interested in family history, and this guide is consciously orientated towards the needs of the genealogist. Nevertheless, it is hoped that all researchers, including serious academic researchers, will find it useful. That they do so will be due in no small measure to the incredible support I have received from colleagues in libraries, archives and genealogical centres throughout the island of Ireland. These good people have been very generous with their time, contributions and advice, and the extensive information that they have unselfishly made available has made this guide possible.

I started this project by sending request letters to each of the institutions that agreed to participate in the 2002 guide. I included a copy of the 2002 entry for each, and asked the contact person to update the entry, with careful attention to remote access options, including any digitisation or web based projects released since the autumn of 2002 or scheduled to be released any time until spring 2006. Visitors, I noted, would be especially interested to learn if free internet access is available in a particular institution. It would also be useful, I suggested, to mention any active friends groups or local/family history groups that operate through the library or archive, with contact information. I also contacted a number of institutions that did not appear in the 2002 guide, and I am pleased to report that this edition contains a small but important number of new entries.

The initial response was strong and encouraging, as many responders noted how helpful the first edition of the guide had been and how pleased they were that I was updating it. In addition to personal visits to a number of institutions, I sent scores of e-mails and faxes and made dozens of telephone calls. I compiled the entries relying chiefly on the amended entries submitted by responders, institutional publications (including historical monographs, brochures, leaflets and pamphlets), institutional websites and telephone calls. I then e-mailed, posted or faxed drafts of these revised entries to the various institutions. The response was gratifying, and I tried to incorporate all the amendments that were provided to me, making some allowances for consistency of format. In those cases where I was not able to get through to the institution either by fax, e-mail or post, I telephoned. The final product represents a sincere effort to reflect the information provided to me as accurately and as fully as possible. If I have failed to do so, I apologise and accept full responsibility for any errors or misunderstandings that may appear in this guide.

This is not intended to be a comprehensive guide to libraries, archives and genealogical centres in Ireland. Rather, it is an effort to include those institutions that are likely to be most attractive to and welcoming of visitors, with a focus on local and family history. No doubt some will find institutions that they believe should have been listed here but are not. Some institutions specifically asked not to be included, some simply did not respond to repeated efforts to solicit their participation, and still others may simply have been overlooked. There are other very helpful and valuable reference sources that readers may want to consult. I recommend in particular the *Directory of Irish Archives*, fourth edition, edited by Seamus Helferty and Raymond Refaussé (Dublin: Four Courts Press, 2004). This work includes many of the religious and specialised archives that are not included in this guide, primarily because access to visitors is limited or because holdings fall outside the guide's scope. Between 1983 and 1996, the Library Association of Ireland, in cooperation with the Library Association Northern Ireland Branch, published five editions of its *Directory of Libraries and Information Services in Ireland*. In 1999, however, the decision was made to discontinue the printed version in favour of an online version that is currently available at http://www.libraryassociation.ie/directory. RASCAL (Research and Special

Collections Available Locally), hosted by Queen's University Belfast, provides online access to information resources held in local libraries and archives in Northern Ireland. The RASCAL project has identified over 400 collections in some 70 institutions, including libraries, museums and archives. The RASCAL Directory is accessible at www.rascal.ac.uk.

In compiling this guide I was struck both by the wealth of resources available in Ireland and by the warm welcome extended to me and to all visitors. Naturally, in doing research, especially family history research, the reader will be drawn in particular to the large repositories in Dublin, such as the National Archives, the National Library of Ireland, the General Register Office Research Room and the Valuation Office, or the Public Record Office and the General Register Office in Belfast. But one should not overlook the bounty to be found in the local history collections of city, county and even some branch libraries, which often contain important local resources, including databases for church and civil records, copies of *Griffith's Valuation*, Ordnance Survey maps and local newspapers. The entries for the Centre for Dublin and Irish Studies and the Belfast Central Library, for example, reveal an exceptional wealth of materials that visitors too often overlook. Many of the county libraries, such as Westmeath and Kildare, also offer rich and varied resources, and competition for mircrofilm readers may be less intense. Staff in local libraries are also very knowledgeable and helpful. Two new local library acquisitions clearly emphasise the importance of considering resource collections outside the large metropolitan areas. These are the Jackie Clarke Collection in Ballina, County Mayo and the Aidan Heavey Collection in Athlone, County Westmeath. These are exceptionally rich collections. The Clarke Collection is still being organised, but it has already yielded a treasure trove of Irish historical materials, especially on the 1798 and 1916 Rebellions. The Heavey Collection is especially strong in the field of Irish literature, but also solid on the subjects of history, Irish language, Irish printing and binding, and politics.

Though this publication is aimed primarily at a North American audience, it is being published in Belfast; hence; orthography practice follows the British English rather than American English model. Examples include: acknowledgements (acknowledgments), artefacts (artifacts), catalogue (catalog), centre (center), colour (color), defence (defense), favour (favor), judgement (judgment), kilometre (kilometer) and labour (labor).

ENTRY FORMAT

ARRANGEMENT

Entries are arranged alphabetically by city or town within county. This arrangement, in addition to providing a 32 county organisational structure with which most visitors are familiar, also offers a convenient and easy way to get around to institutions that are grouped together within a relatively small geographical area, especially in the cities of Dublin, Belfast and Cork. To assist visitors who might be uncertain or even confused about geographical location, I have made generous use of 'See' references.

County Dublin, in particular, offers some interesting challenges to those unfamiliar with its administrative divisions. In 1994, County Dublin was divided into three separate administrative units, South Dublin, Dún Laoghaire/Rathdown and Fingal. Nevertheless, all listings here are under the single county of Dublin, subdivided alphabetically by city or town in the following order: Dublin City, Dún Laoghaire, Killiney and Swords, with 'See' references under Dublin City to avoid possible misunderstanding. The entries for Fingal County Libraries, Local Studies Department, and for Fingal County Archives are to be found alphabetically among the listings for the City of Dublin within the County of Dublin, as they are both located at the end of O'Connell Street on the north side of Dublin city centre. But the headquarters for this library system is located in the town of Swords, the administrative seat of Fingal, which embraces the area of County Dublin north of the River Liffey. Fingal Genealogy is also located in Swords.

Belfast presents yet another interesting problem, as it is actually located within two counties, Down and Antrim. But since every entry but one in this guide for Belfast City is geographically located within the borders of County Antrim, Belfast is listed under County Antrim, with a note to this effect in the heading.

While this arrangement may cause some confusion, especially to those accustomed to thinking of County Dublin and Dublin City as one, the alternative of listing institutions alphabetically by county, without regard to city or town, would present, I believe, even more confusion in certain cases, especially in Counties Antrim and Londonderry (Derry).

Elsewhere, the geographical listings are fairly uncomplicated. However, it might be helpful to note that Galway Family History Society West Ltd precedes East Galway Family History Society because the former is located in Galway City while the latter is located in the town of Woodford. To make finding institutions even easier, an alphabetically arranged listing by type of institution is provided in the appendix under the following categories:

I.   Academic Libraries;

II. Special Libraries;
III. Public Libraries;
IV. Archives;
V. Genealogical and Heritage Centres.

While visitors may be familiar and comfortable with the county system, it should be noted that the county system was gradually introduced into Ireland by the Anglo-Normans from the end of the twelfth century but completed in the north only in the seventeenth century with the Flight of the Earls (1607) and the establishment of the Ulster Plantation. Hence, there never was officially a County Derry. It was named Londonderry from the start, and County Londonderry is therefore used as the geographical designation. But within County Londonderry, entries are arranged under the City of Derry, as this is both the historic name of the city founded as a monastic site in the sixth century by St Columcille (St Columba), and the name officially adopted by the Derry City Council, though the British Government has not officially recognised this name change. Two more points on counties. County Laois was initially called Queen's County, and County Offaly was King's County. 'See' references are provided for each of these former names. These were changed to their present names following Ireland's independence. Visitors should also be aware that two of the important ports from which many Irish emigrated also underwent name changes with Ireland's independence: Kingstown in County Dublin became Dún Laoghaire and Queenstown in County Cork became Cobh.

'See' references are also used wherever there might be confusion about the official name of an institution. Trinity College Dublin (TCD) is also the University of Dublin, and University College Dublin (UCD) is also the National University of Ireland, Dublin. The Historical Library, Religious Society of Friends, in Dublin, is more popularly known either as The Friends' Historical Library or the Quaker Library. The official name of the institution, as preferred by the institution itself, is the name used as the heading in this guide, with 'See' references to other names by which the institution might be known.

TELEPHONE AND FAX NUMBERS
Telephone and fax numbers are given as if you were calling from within Ireland or from within Northern Ireland. The international code for Ireland is 353 and for Northern Ireland it is 44. For direct dialled calls from Canada and the United States, first dial 011, then the country code, the local code (dropping the 0) and the telephone number. Thus, if you were calling the National Archives of Ireland in Dublin from the United States, you would dial 011 353 1 407 2300. If you were calling the General Register Office in

Belfast, you would dial 011 44 28 9025 2000, again dropping the 0 before the local code of 028. To call Northern Ireland from within Ireland, dial 0801 before the local code, dropping the 0; hence, the GRO in Belfast would be: 0801 28 9025 2000. The international code for the UK (44) is not needed, but again you drop the 0 in the local code (028). To call Ireland from Northern Ireland, however, the international code for Ireland is needed, preceded by 00; hence, to call the National Archives in Dublin from Belfast, you would dial 00 353 1 407 2300, again dropping the 0 from the Dublin code (01). Remember, there is a five to eight hour time difference between the United States and Ireland. When it is noon in Boston, it is 5.00pm in Ireland.

E-MAIL ADDRESSES AND WEBSITES
These are perhaps the two areas most subject to change. The information given is as current as the printed format will allow. Indeed, in more than a few cases, changes occurred between the time the information was originally collected and the time the final copy was sent to the institution for editing. Some website addresses were given even though they are currently not accessible. In these cases, it was believed that these sites would be operational by the time this publication appears in print, but there are no guarantees.

HOURS
Opening hours are also subject to change, and it is wise to contact institutions in advance to be sure that the hours are as indicated. All libraries and archives are closed on Sundays unless otherwise noted. Please note in particular that many of the smaller institutions have limited staffing, and vacations and illness may affect announced operating hours. One major difference that may be noted between this edition and the first, however, is the significant expansion of library and archival hours, especially for county libraries. Whereas it was common for many libraries, even large ones, to close for lunch between 1.00pm and 2.00pm, this is now less often the case. More libraries are also offering evening and Saturday hours. I was especially impressed on a visit to the small and beautiful West Waterford town of Cappoquin in June 2006 to find the library open on Saturdays until 6.00pm, with free internet access.

ACCESS AND SERVICES
Information here is provided with the visitor chiefly in mind. Access is treated broadly, encompassing not only physical access (e.g. wheelchair access; reader's card, advance notice, letter of recommendation required, etc) but also fax or e-mail services and online access to the institution's OPAC (Online Public Access Catalogue). Services include reference, borrowing privileges, photocopying, microfilm reader/printer access, internet access, exhibits and

publications. Fees, if applicable, are provided, but only as a guideline, as they are subject to change. Note: Ireland adopted the euro in January 2002, but Northern Ireland, as part of the United Kingdom, continues to use the pound sterling, and there are no immediate plans to convert to the euro.

CONTACT

In most instances, a specific person is listed to give visitors the name of the person most likely to be able to help with his or her question. But please keep in mind that personnel may change or may be away on holiday or leave. In certain cases, institutions have asked that an individual not be listed as the contact; rather, that a title only be listed (e.g. Archivist). Academic titles, such as Dr, and degrees, such as PhD, for contact persons, are not given, as most did not supply them and I wanted to be consistent. It can be assumed, however, that most of the contact persons, especially in academic settings, have advanced degrees, many of them holding the doctorate. Titles are, however, provided in the case of clerical, military or police personnel.

DESCRIPTION

This area is used to provide the visitor with some understanding of the history and place of the institution within a broader context. It is helpful to know, for example, the origin of the name 'Linen Hall Library' or the source of financial support for institutions so that visitors may have a better appreciation of the demands that they may be making on them. Many institutions in Ireland, even government supported ones, are hard pressed to serve their principal clientele because of staff shortages and limited resources. It is important for visitors to understand this and to be patient, polite, courteous and considerate. I am always surprised as the director of a private American academic research library how demanding some enquirers can be. I have received requests from people with absolutely no ties to the institution demanding that the library provide them with answers to a long list of research questions and that we do so promptly. Such impolite demands are invariably filed away in the wastebasket, without the courtesy of a reply: visitors take heed! If you find institutions especially helpful, a note of appreciation is always welcome. For those wishing to express their appreciation to a library or archive in more tangible ways, financial contributions may be sent directly to the institution or channeled through several not for profit organisations based in America, such as the Irish American Partnership, which has made the funding of libraries in Ireland a priority.

HOLDINGS

This is the most important element of this guide. Despite the devastation wrought by the destruction of the Public Record Office in 1922 during the Civil War, Ireland is still rich in resources. Many of these repositories are well kept secrets, even among the Irish. A quick perusal of the breadth and depth of holdings to be found in Irish libraries and archives should impress even the most seasoned researcher. The holdings statement, however, is not intended to be comprehensive. Rather, it is meant to highlight the strengths of an institution's collection, with a particular focus on local studies and genealogy. Even in the areas of local history and genealogy, there is a good deal more depth and breadth to the collections than may be indicated by the information provided. I was heavily dependent on the information that institutions made available to me, and, frankly, some were rather modest in describing their holdings. I was often able to collect additional material through personal contacts or from institutional publications, but this could not be done in every case.

LOCATION

Brief directions are given to each entry's location, often with information on parking or access by public transportation. Public transportation in Ireland is very good, and constantly improving. Virtually every entry in this guide can be reached by rail or bus, with perhaps no more than a ten to fifteen minute walk from the station or depot. The rail service between Dublin and Belfast is especially good, taking only two hours along a scenic route, and significant upgrades of other rail services have either been made since 2002 or are in the works. Taxi fares in Ireland and Northern Ireland are fairly reasonable, though the weak dollar and higher petrol (gasoline) prices have made all forms of transportation significantly more expensive for the North American visitor since 2002. As a concession to this guide's primary audience, distance is given in miles, not kilometres, even though Ireland has officially adopted the metric system. A kilometre is roughly equal to 0.6 miles. Thus, 100 kilometres is equal to 60 miles. The mile is still the standard in Northern Ireland.

THE IRISH GENEALOGICAL PROJECT,
THE IRISH FAMILY HISTORY FOUNDATION
AND IRISH GENEALOGY LTD

The Irish Genealogical Project was established in 1988 as a joint private/public venture to computerize all the major Irish genealogical resources. The project's goal was to establish a network of 35 genealogical centres, with at least one for each county in Ireland, linked by a central or 'signposting' agency that would refer enquirers to appropriate local centres and provide uniform indexing, servicing and fee schedule guidelines. These centres would create computerized databases of genealogical records to offer a fee-based genealogical research service to those interested in tracing their family roots. Starting in 1990, a Digital VAX system was set up to computerize births, marriages, deaths, Griffith's Valuation, Tithe Applotment Books, graveyard inscriptions, and census records. Some centres subsequently indexed additional types of records, including directories, school rolls, hearth money rolls, and information specific to their locale, such as newspaper indexes. In 1990 this became a cross-border effort, and both the Irish government and the Northern Ireland Office provided financial support for the project for the purposes of creating jobs and promoting tourism.

A number of genealogical centres had been operating successfully before this island-wide project was launched. The Ulster Historical Foundation, for example, was founded in 1956 to promote interest in Ulster history and genealogy. But these centres operated on an *ad hoc* basis, and a more coordinated island-wide project seemed warranted; hence the creation of IGP. However, the project initially failed to fulfil expectations. For a start, the central agency never materialized as planned. To fill this void, the Irish Family History Foundation (IFHF) was established in 1990 by the local centres to set standards for indexing records, genealogical research services, and fees. While IFHF provided an umbrella organization of sorts, facilitating access to websites and establishing recommended fee schedules, it lacked the authority and resources needed to address some of the serious concerns that were surfacing. Furthermore, it did not enjoy the support of all the centres. Participation was voluntary, and several major centres opted to go it alone.

Originally the project was to have been completed by 1993, but this target date proved unrealistic. To begin with, government assistance largely took the form of employment training grants. Young, unemployed people were hired to do the indexing, but they first required training in office and computer skills. At least half their time was spent on non-genealogical-related work, such as gaining marketable skills and looking for employment. This continues to be the case today, and certification of trainees in all skills takes precedence over the indexing of genealogical records. While the governments, with the help of grants from the International Fund for Ireland and the European Union, did initially fund equipment purchases, including the VAX, a photocopier and microfilm reader, they subsequently restricted their funding to training grants, leaving the centres to fall back on their own and/or local resources. Some centres were more successful than others in developing these resources. Several were forced to close, while others were able to offer only partial services.

In 1993 Irish Genealogy Ltd (IGL) was formed to coordinate the activities of the IGP and to oversee its completion. A lack of resources initially limited its effectiveness, but since 1996 adequate funding has enabled IGL to carry out its original mission successfully. IGL is composed of representatives of all the Irish groups interested in the development of genealogy as a business, including IFHF, the Association of Professional Genealogists in Ireland (APGI), the Association of Ulster Genealogists and Record Agents (AUGRA), and government departments, north and south. Although it is intended to be independent of any particular group of stakeholders, it clearly has a mandate to promote tourism. To achieve this end, IGL recognized that it needed to provide tourists and professional genealogists with a network of centres that offers a reliable, comprehensive, computerised database of genealogical records, excellent customer service, and a central referral or 'signposting' agency that will direct customers to one of the IFHF centres or to appropriate professional genealogists. Since 1996 it has made substantial progress towards these goals. All but a few of the heritage centres have now come under IFHF and IGL's umbrella. While these centres continue to maintain absolute autonomy, they recognize the value of acting collectively on many issues. This partnership has resulted in some impressive achievements, some of which are enumerated below. For further information on IGL, contact: Eamonn Rossi, Chief Executive Officer, IGL, 7–9 Merrion Row, Dublin 2; tel. (01) 661 7334; e-mail eamonn.rossi@irishgenealogy.ie. For further information on IFHF, contact: Pat Stafford, Secretary, IFHF, Yola Farmstead, Tagoat, Co. Wexford; tel. (053) 32610; e-mail wexgen@iol.ie.

This Guide makes no effort to evaluate the services offered by individual centres. Readers are advised instead to consult in particular the findings of a survey of Irish Heritage Centres conducted by The Irish Ancestral Research Association, which can be found on its website: http://tiara.ie/results.htm. This survey, as well as surveys or audit reports conducted by *Irish Roots*, by IGL and by the Comptroller and Auditor General of Ireland in the late 1990s, revealed significant inconsistencies in the quality of services offered. These surveys, however, may not accurately reflect the current status of individual centres, and it should be noted that many centres have made a concerted effort to address the failings pointed out in the surveys and/or audits, particularly in the areas of delivery time and customer relations. Improvements in funding and premises have also been made. For example, the 'signposting' service has now been fully developed, with a Central Signposting Index launched on the web at www.irishgenealogy.ie. The Kerry centre will shortly reopen with modern systems and a strong management team. Perhaps most important, the databases themselves have been significantly enhanced, both in terms of the quantity, depth and breadth of the records they contain and in terms of the quality and reliability of these records. Some 16,493,000 records have been indexed in the IFHF centres as of October 2002, and an Accuracy Audit by Eneclann in 2000, using a more statistically reliable sample, found a far lower error rate among centres than that reported two years earlier by the Comptroller and Auditor General. IGL is also replacing the antiquated and cumbersome VAX computer system with a modern server/client IT system with a common software platform. This will secure records onto modern media for posterity.

One last note. Genealogists often complain that they do not have direct access to the databases of these heritage centres: only staff researchers at the various centres are allowed to search the databases. While this may seem frustrating, it should be noted that all centres have signed an agreement with their local bishop/archbishop and his individual parish priests governing the access and use of parish records, which in most cases make up the largest part of any centre's database. This agreement provides for strict controls on the access to and publishing, reproduction and copying of these records to preserve their confidential nature. Some parishes have yet to cooperate with these centres, and no parish priest is required to do so. Making the databases directly accessible to the public is, therefore, not currently an option.

CLASSIFIED LIST OF INSTITUTIONS

1

ACADEMIC LIBRARIES AND ARCHIVES

DUBLIN CITY UNIVERSITY LIBRARY, Dublin City, County Dublin

EDGEHILL THEOLOGICAL COLLEGE, Belfast, County Antrim

HISTORY AND FAMILY RESEARCH CENTRE – LOCAL STUDIES DEPARTMENT, Newbridge, County Kildare

NATIONAL UNIVERSITY OF IRELAND, CORK (UCC) – BOOLE LIBRARY, Cork City, County Cork

NATIONAL UNIVERSITY OF IRELAND, GALWAY – JAMES HARDIMAN LIBRARY, Galway City, County Galway

NATIONAL UNIVERSITY OF IRELAND, MAYNOOTH – JOHN PAUL II LIBRARY, Maynooth, County Kildare

QUEEN'S UNIVERSITY BELFAST LIBRARY, Belfast, County Antrim

RUSSELL LIBRARY. *See* ST PATRICK'S COLLEGE MAYNOOTH ARCHIVES, Maynooth, County Kildare

ST MARY'S UNIVERSITY COLLEGE LIBRARY, Belfast, County Antrim

ST PATRICK'S COLLEGE – CREEGAN LIBRARY, Dublin City, County Dublin

ST PATRICK'S COLLEGE, MAYNOOTH – RUSSELL LIBRARY, Maynooth, County Kildare

STRANMILLIS UNIVERSITY COLLEGE LIBRARY, Belfast, County Antrim

TRINITY COLLEGE LIBRARY, Dublin City, County Dublin

UCD SCHOOL OF HISTORY AND ARCHIVES, Dublin City, County Dublin

UNION THEOLOGICAL COLLEGE – GAMBLE LIBRARY, Belfast, County Antrim

UNIVERSITY COLLEGE DUBLIN LIBRARY, Dublin City, County Dublin

UNIVERSITY OF LIMERICK LIBRARY AND INFORMATION SERVICES, Limerick City, County Limerick

UNIVERSITY OF ULSTER LIBRARY, BELFAST CAMPUS, Belfast, County Antrim

UNIVERSITY OF ULSTER LIBRARY, COLERAINE CAMPUS, Coleraine, County Londonderry

UNIVERSITY OF ULSTER LIBRARY, JORDANSTOWN CAMPUS, Newtownabbey, County Antrim

UNIVERSITY OF ULSTER LIBRARY, MAGEE CAMPUS, Derry City, County Londonderry

2
ARCHIVES

BANTRY HOUSE, Bantry, County Cork

CARDINAL TOMÁS Ó FIAICH LIBRARY AND ARCHIVE, Armagh City, County Armagh

CASHEL AND EMLY ARCHDIOCESAN ARCHIVES (ROMAN CATHOLIC), Thurles, County Tipperary

CLARE COUNTY ARCHIVES SERVICE, Ennis, County Clare

CORK ARCHIVES INSTITUTE, Cork City, County Cork

CORK PUBLIC MUSEUM (MÚSAEM POIBLÍ CHORCAÍ), Cork City, County Cork

DIOCESAN ARCHIVE, DROMORE (ROMAN CATHOLIC), Newry, County Down

DIOCESE OF CLONFERT ARCHIVE, Loughrea, County Galway

DONEGAL COUNTY ARCHIVES SERVICE, Lifford, County Donegal

DOWN AND CONNOR DIOCESAN ARCHIVES, Belfast, County Antrim

DUBLIN CITY ARCHIVES, Dublin City, County Dublin

DUBLIN DIOCESAN ARCHIVES, Dublin City, County Dublin

FINGAL COUNTY ARCHIVES, Dublin City, County Dublin

THE GAA MUSEUM, Dublin City, County Dublin

GALWAY CITY LIBRARY – LOCAL HISTORY DEPARTMENT AND ARCHIVES, Galway City, County Galway

GARDA MUSEUM/ARCHIVES, Dublin City, County Dublin

GRAND LODGE OF FREEMASONS OF IRELAND: LIBRARY, ARCHIVES AND MUSEUM, Dublin City, County Dublin

GUINNESS ARCHIVE, Dublin City, County Dublin

IRISH ARCHITECTURAL ARCHIVE, Dublin City, County Dublin

IRISH FILM ARCHIVE OF THE IRISH FILM INSTITUTE, Dublin City, County Dublin

IRISH JESUIT ARCHIVES, Dublin City, County Dublin

IRISH JEWISH MUSEUM, Dublin City, County Dublin

IRISH THEATRE ARCHIVE, Dublin City, County Dublin

IRISH TRADITIONAL MUSIC ARCHIVE, Dublin City, County Dublin

JAMES HARDIMAN LIBRARY. *See* NATIONAL UNIVERSITY OF IRELAND, GALWAY – JAMES HARDIMAN LIBRARY – DEPARTMENT OF SPECIAL COLLECTIONS AND ARCHIVES, Galway City, County Galway

KERRY LOCAL HISTORY AND ARCHIVES COLLECTION, Tralee, County Kerry

LIMERICK ARCHIVES, Limerick City, County Limerick

LONGFORD COUNTY LIBRARY – ARCHIVES AND LOCAL STUDIES, Longford Town, County Longford

LOUTH COUNTY ARCHIVES SERVICE, Dundalk, County Louth

MICHAEL DAVITT MUSEUM, Foxford, County Mayo

THE MILITARY ARCHIVES, Dublin City, County Dublin

NATIONAL ARCHIVES OF IRELAND, Dublin City, County Dublin

NATIONAL GALLERY OF IRELAND RESEARCH SERVICES, Dublin City, County Dublin

NATIONAL PHOTOGRAPHIC ARCHIVE, Dublin City, County Dublin

NATIONAL UNIVERSITY OF IRELAND, GALWAY – JAMES HARDIMAN LIBRARY – DEPARTMENT OF SPECIAL COLLECTIONS AND ARCHIVES, Galway City, County Galway

PUBLIC RECORD OFFICE OF NORTHERN IRELAND, Belfast, County Antrim

ST PATRICK'S COLLEGE MAYNOOTH ARCHIVES, Maynooth, County Kildare

UCD SCHOOL OF HISTORY AND ARCHIVES, Dublin City, County Dublin

ULSTER FOLK AND TRANSPORT MUSEUM, Holywood, County Down

WATERFORD CITY ARCHIVES, Waterford City, County Waterford

WATERFORD COUNTY ARCHIVES SERVICE, Dungarvan, County Waterford

WICKLOW COUNTY LIBRARY – LOCAL HISTORY COLLECTION AND ARCHIVES, Bray, County Wicklow

3

GENEALOGICAL AND HERITAGE CENTRES AND SERVICES

ARMAGH ANCESTRY, Armagh City, County Armagh

ASSOCIATION OF PROFESSIONAL GENEALOGISTS IN IRELAND, Dublin City, County Dublin

BRÚ BORÚ HERITAGE CENTRE, Cashel, County Tipperary

CLARE HERITAGE AND GENEALOGICAL CENTRE, Corofin, County Clare

CORK CITY ANCESTRAL PROJECT, Cork City, County Cork

COUNTY CAVAN GENEALOGICAL RESEARCH CENTRE, Cavan Town, County Cavan

COUNTY DERRY OR LONDONDERRY GENEALOGY CENTRE, Derry City, County Londonderry

COUNTY ROSCOMMON HERITAGE AND GENEALOGY COMPANY, Strokestown, County Roscommon

COUNTY SLIGO HERITAGE AND GENEALOGY SOCIETY, Sligo Town, County Sligo

COUNTY WEXFORD HERITAGE AND GENEALOGY CENTRE, Rosslare, County Wexford

DONEGAL ANCESTRY, Ramelton, County Donegal

DÚN LAOGHAIRE-RATHDOWN HERITAGE CENTRE, Dún Laoghaire, County Dublin

DÚN NA SÍ HERITAGE CENTRE, Moate, County Westmeath

EAST CLARE HERITAGE COMPANY, Tuamgraney, County Clare

EAST GALWAY FAMILY HISTORY SOCIETY, Woodford, County Galway

FINGAL GENEALOGY, Swords, County Dublin

GALWAY FAMILY HISTORY SOCIETY WEST LTD, Galway City, County Galway

THE HERITAGE CENTRE, Monaghan Town, County Monaghan

HERITAGE WORLD (formerly IRISH WORLD FAMILY HISTORY SERVICES), Donaghmore, County Tyrone (closed in February 2002)

IRISH MIDLANDS ANCESTRY (LAOIS AND OFFALY FAMILY HISTORY RESEARCH CENTRE), Tullamore, County Offaly

KERRY GENEALOGICAL RESEARCH CENTRE, Killarney, County Kerry

KILDARE HERITAGE AND GENEALOGY COMPANY LTD, Newbridge, County Kildare

KILKENNY ARCHAEOLOGICAL SOCIETY, Kilkenny City, County Kilkenny

KILLARNEY GENEALOGICAL CENTRE. See KERRY GENEALOGICAL RESEARCH CENTRE, Killarney, County Kerry

LAOIS AND OFFALY FAMILY HISTORY RESEARCH CENTRE. See IRISH MIDLANDS ANCESTRY, Tullamore, County Offaly

LEITRIM GENEALOGY CENTRE (SINSEARLANN LIATROMA), Ballinamore, County Leitrim

LONGFORD RESEARCH CENTRE, Longford Town, County Longford

MALLOW HERITAGE CENTRE, Mallow, County Cork

MAYO NORTH FAMILY HERITAGE CENTRE, Ballina, County Mayo

MEATH HERITAGE AND GENEALOGY CENTRE, Trim, County Meath

MEATH–LOUTH FAMILY RESEARCH CENTRE. See MEATH HERITAGE AND GENEALOGY CENTRE, Trim, County Meath

MONAGHAN ANCESTRY, Monaghan Town, County Monaghan

OFFALY HISTORICAL AND ARCHAEOLOGICAL SOCIETY, See IRISH MIDLANDS ANCESTRY, Tullamore, County Offaly

OFFICE OF THE CHIEF HERALD/GENEALOGICAL OFFICE, Dublin City, County Dublin

ORDNANCE SURVEY OF NORTHERN IRELAND, Belfast, County Antrim

SOUTH MAYO FAMILY RESEARCH CENTRE, Ballinrobe, County Mayo

TIPPERARY FAMILY HISTORY RESEARCH CENTRE, Tipperary Town, County Tipperary

TIPPERARY NORTH GENEALOGY AND HERITAGE SERVICES, Nenagh, County Tipperary

ULSTER HISTORICAL FOUNDATION, Belfast, County Antrim

WATERFORD HERITAGE SERVICES, Waterford City, County Waterford

WICKLOW FAMILY HISTORY CENTRE, Wicklow Town, County Wicklow

4
GOVERNMENT ORGANISATIONS AND OFFICES

GENERAL REGISTER OFFICE, Belfast, County Antrim

GENERAL REGISTER OFFICE, Roscommon Town, County Roscommon

NATIONAL ARCHIVES OF IRELAND, Dublin City, County Dublin

NATIONAL LIBRARY OF IRELAND, Dublin City, County Dublin

NORTHERN IRELAND ASSEMBLY LIBRARY, Belfast, County Antrim

OFFICE OF THE CHIEF HERALD/GENEALOGICAL OFFICE, Dublin City, County Dublin

ORDNANCE SURVEY OF NORTHERN IRELAND, Belfast, County Antrim

POLICE MUSEUM, Belfast, County Antrim

PUBLIC RECORD OFFICE OF NORTHERN IRELAND, Belfast, County Antrim

REGISTRY OF DEEDS, Dublin City, County Dublin

VALUATION OFFICE, Dublin City, County Dublin

5
PUBLIC LIBRARIES

AIDAN HEAVEY PUBLIC LIBRARY ATHLONE, Athlone, County Westmeath

ARMAGH PUBLIC LIBRARY, Armagh City, County Armagh

BAILIEBORO LIBRARY, Bailieboro, County Cavan

CAVAN COUNTY LIBRARY, Cavan Town, County Cavan

BALLYMONEY LIBRARY, Ballymoney, County Antrim

BANGOR LIBRARY, Bangor, Co Down

BELFAST CENTRAL LIBRARY, Belfast, County Antrim

CARLOW CENTRAL LIBRARY, Carlow Town, County Carlow

CENTRAL LIBRARY, Derry City, County Londonderry

CENTRE FOR DUBLIN AND IRISH STUDIES, Dublin City, County Dublin

CLARE COUNTY LIBRARY – LOCAL STUDIES CENTRE, Ennis, County Clare

CORK CITY LIBRARIES, Cork City, County Cork

CORK COUNTY LIBRARY, Cork City, County Cork

DONEGAL COUNTY LIBRARY, Letterkenny, County Donegal

DUBLIN CITY PUBLIC LIBRARIES AND ARCHIVE, Dublin City, County Dublin

DUBLIN CITY PUBLIC LIBRARIES – CENTRAL LIBRARY, Dublin City, County Dublin

DÚN LAOGHAIRE LIBRARY – LOCAL HISTORY DEPARTMENT, Dún Laoghaire, County Dublin

ENNISKILLEN LIBRARY, Enniskillen, County Fermanagh

FINGAL COUNTY LIBRARIES, Dublin City, County Dublin

GALWAY CITY LIBRARY, Galway City, County Galway

GALWAY CITY LIBRARY – LOCAL HISTORY DEPARTMENT AND ARCHIVES

HISTORY AND FAMILY RESEARCH CENTRE – LOCAL STUDIES DEPARTMENT, Newbridge, County Kildare

HOLYWOOD BRANCH LIBRARY, Holywood, County Down

THE JACKIE CLARKE LIBRARY, Ballina, County Mayo

KERRY LOCAL HISTORY AND ARCHIVES COLLECTION, Tralee, County Kerry

KILKENNY COUNTY LIBRARY, Kilkenny City, County Kilkenny

LAOIS COUNTY LIBRARY – LOCAL STUDIES COLLECTION, Portlaoise, County Laois

LEITRIM COUNTY LIBRARY (LEABHARLANN CHONTAE LIATROMA), Ballinamore, County Leitrim

LIMERICK CITY PUBLIC LIBRARY, Limerick City, County Limerick

LIMERICK COUNTY LIBRARY – LOCAL STUDIES COLLECTION, Limerick City, County Limerick

LOCAL STUDIES DEPARTMENT, SEELB LIBRARY HEADQUARTERS, Ballynahinch, County Down

LONGFORD COUNTY LIBRARY – ARCHIVES AND LOCAL STUDIES, Longford Town, County Longford

LOUTH COUNTY LIBRARY – REFERENCE AND LOCAL HISTORY LIBRARY, Dundalk, County Louth

MAYO COUNTY LIBRARY, Castlebar, County Mayo

MEATH COUNTY LIBRARY HEADQUARTERS, Navan, County Meath

MONAGHAN BRANCH LIBRARY, Monaghan Town, County Monaghan

M'SKIMIN ROOM, Carrickfergus, County Antrim

NEWCASTLE BRANCH LIBRARY, Newcastle, County Down

NEWRY BRANCH LIBRARY, Newry, County Down

NEWTOWNARDS BRANCH LIBRARY, Newtownards, County Down

NORTH-EASTERN EDUCATION AND LIBRARY BOARD – LIBRARY SERVICE HEADQUARTERS, Ballymena, County Antrim

OFFALY COUNTY LIBRARY – LOCAL STUDIES AND ARCHIVES SERVICE, Tullamore, County Offaly

OMAGH LIBRARY, Omagh, County Tyrone

ROSCOMMON COUNTY LIBRARY, Roscommon Town, County Roscommon

SELB IRISH AND LOCAL STUDIES LIBRARY, Armagh City, County Armagh

SLIGO COUNTY LIBRARY, Sligo Town, County Sligo

TIPPERARY LIBRARIES – TIPPERARY STUDIES, Thurles, County Tipperary

WATERFORD COUNTY LIBRARY HEADQUARTERS, Lismore, County Waterford

WESTMEATH COUNTY LIBRARY HEADQUARTERS – LOCAL STUDIES COLLECTION, Mullingar, County Westmeath

WEXFORD COUNTY LIBRARY, Ardcavan, County Wexford

WICKLOW COUNTY LIBRARY – LOCAL HISTORY COLLECTION AND ARCHIVES, Bray, County Wicklow

6
SPECIAL LIBRARIES

ARMAGH COUNTY MUSEUM, Armagh City, County Armagh

ARMAGH OBSERVATORY, Armagh City, County Armagh

ARMAGH PUBLIC LIBRARY, Armagh City, County Armagh

AUSTIN CLARKE LIBRARY. *See* POETRY IRELAND/ÉIGSE ÉIREANN, Dublin City, County Dublin

CARDINAL TOMÁS Ó FIAICH LIBRARY AND ARCHIVE, Armagh City, County Armagh

CENTRAL CATHOLIC LIBRARY, Dublin City, County Dublin

CENTRE FOR MIGRATION STUDIES, Omagh, County Tyrone

CHESTER BEATTY LIBRARY, Dublin City, County Dublin

CORK PUBLIC MUSEUM (MÚSAEM POIBLÍ CHORCAÍ), Cork City, County Cork

CRAIGAVON MUSEUM SERVICES – PHILIP B. WILSON LIBRARY, Craigavon, County Armagh

DONEGAL COUNTY MUSEUM, Letterkenny, County Donegal

FRANCISCAN LIBRARY KILLINEY, Killiney, County Dublin

GLENSTAL ABBEY LIBRARY, Murroe, County Limerick

GPA BOLTON LIBRARY, Cashel, County Tipperary

HERITAGE AND MUSEUM SERVICE, Derry City, County Londonderry

HISTORICAL LIBRARY, RELIGIOUS SOCIETY OF FRIENDS, Dublin City, County Dublin

HISTORY AND FAMILY RESEARCH CENTRE – LOCAL STUDIES DEPARTMENT, Newbridge, County Kildare

THE HONORABLE SOCIETY OF KING'S INNS, Dublin City, County Dublin

IRISH LINEN CENTRE AND LISBURN MUSEUM LIBRARY, Lisburn, County Antrim

IRISH JEWISH MUSEUM, Dublin City, County Dublin

THE JESUIT LIBRARY, Dublin City, County Dublin

LIFFORD OLD COURTHOUSE, Lifford, County Donegal

LINEN HALL LIBRARY, Belfast, County Antrim

MARSH'S LIBRARY, Dublin City, County Dublin

MICHAEL DAVITT MUSEUM, Foxford, County Mayo

MONAGHAN COUNTY MUSEUM, Monaghan Town, County Monaghan

MUSEUM OF ARCHAEOLOGY AND HISTORY. See NATIONAL MUSEUM OF IRELAND, Dublin City, County Dublin

MUSEUM OF COUNTRY LIFE. See NATIONAL MUSEUM OF IRELAND, Dublin City, County Dublin

MUSEUM OF DECORATIVE ARTS AND HISTORY. See NATIONAL MUSEUM OF IRELAND, Dublin City, County Dublin

MUSEUM OF NATURAL HISTORY. See NATIONAL MUSEUM OF IRELAND, Dublin City, County Dublin

NATIONAL GALLERY OF IRELAND RESEARCH SERVICES, Dublin City, County Dublin

NATIONAL LIBRARY OF IRELAND, Dublin City, County Dublin

NATIONAL MUSEUM OF IRELAND, Dublin City, County Dublin

NORTHERN IRELAND ASSEMBLY LIBRARY, Belfast, County Antrim

NORTHERN IRELAND HOUSING EXECUTIVE – LIBRARY INFORMATION SERVICES, Belfast, County Antrim

POLICE MUSEUM, Belfast, County Antrim

REPRESENTATIVE CHURCH BODY LIBRARY, Dublin City, County Dublin

ROYAL COLLEGE OF PHYSICIANS OF IRELAND, Dublin City, County Dublin

ROYAL DUBLIN SOCIETY, Dublin City, County Dublin

ROYAL IRISH ACADEMY, Dublin City, County Dublin

ROYAL SOCIETY OF ANTIQUARIES OF IRELAND, Dublin City, County Dublin

SELB IRISH AND LOCAL STUDIES LIBRARY, Armagh City, County Armagh

ULSTER AMERICAN FOLK PARK, Omagh, County Tyrone

ULSTER FOLK AND TRANSPORT MUSEUM, Holywood, County Down

ULSTER MUSEUM LIBRARY, Belfast, County Antrim

LOCATION
Town centre. Parking to the rear of the library building.

NORTH-EASTERN EDUCATION AND LIBRARY BOARD – LIBRARY SERVICE HEADQUARTERS

Local Studies Service, Demesne Avenue
BALLYMENA, COUNTY ANTRIM, BT43 7BG
Northern Ireland

TELEPHONE: (028) 2566 4121
E-mail: yvonne.hirst@ni-libraries.net
Website: www.ni-libraries.net

HOURS
M–W, F–Sa, 9.00am–5.00pm; Th, 9.00am–8.00pm

ACCESS AND SERVICES
Visitors welcome, but advance notice preferred. Collection for reference only.
Disabled access facilities. Fees for photocopying and microfilm prints. Internet access
for local studies research only.

CONTACT
Yvonne Hirst, Local Studies Development Officer

DESCRIPTION
Local Studies Service oversees local study collections at the various libraries within
the 28 member network of the North-Eastern Education and Library Board Library
Service, established in 1973. In addition to local collections in most of these
libraries, there are a number of important special collections. These include the
Langford Lodge Collection, Ballymena; the Hugh Thomson Collection at Coleraine,
County Londonderry; the M'Skimin Room, Carrickfergus; and the George Shiels
Collection at Ballymoney Library. It is the goal of the Library Service to collect,
record, organise and conserve all appropriate material documenting the life and
history of the area it serves.

HOLDINGS
The Local Studies Service, in addition to coordinating local studies collections
throughout the NEELB Library Service area, maintains a reference only local studies
collection in Ballymena. This collection includes *Griffith's Valuation* for County
Antrim and part of County Londonderry; the 1901 census for Counties Antrim and
Londonderry and parts of Belfast; and Ordnance Survey maps.

School records: it is not generally known that the Public Record Office of Northern
Ireland has redistributed considerable parts of its holdings of records of public
elementary schools. These are mainly post-1945 school roll books but some earlier
roll books and daily report books are included. These records were distributed to the
Area Library Boards with coverage for their area of responsibility. This means that
the collection of records for over 80 schools now held in the library at Ballymena
includes records for Draperstown and Magherafelt schools in the southern part of
County Londonderry and also for schools in Coleraine and District. Samples of
these records include: Ballynagashel (Loughguile) roll books 1875–80, 1895–9,
1938–51, 10 vols; Cranny (Desertmartin, County Londonderry) roll books 1875–8,

1887–90 and 1893–9. For half of the schools, records transferred include pupil registers dating from *c.* 1940.

LOCATION
Demesne Avenue, near town centre.

BELFAST CENTRAL LIBRARY

Royal Avenue
BELFAST, BT1 1EA
Northern Ireland

TELEPHONE: (028) 9050 9150; FAX: (028) 9033 2819
E-mail: belb.info@ni-libraries.net
Website: www.belb.org.uk

HOURS
General Library: M, W, Th, 9.00am–8.00pm; Tu, F, 9.00am–5.30pm; Sa, 9.00am–4.30pm
Newspaper Library: M, Th, 9.00am–7.30pm; Tu–W, F, 9.00am–5.00pm; Sa, 9.00am–12.30pm (Note: access to Newspaper Library is in Library Street)

ACCESS AND SERVICES
Flagship library of the Belfast Education and Library Board, Belfast Central Library is open to visitors for reference services but borrowing privileges for non-residents may be restricted. Free internet access for all Northern Ireland public library members. One membership card valid for all libraries. Charge of £1.50 per half hour for non-members; ID required. Membership open to anyone living, working or studying in the area. Disabled access facilities. Closed stacks. Photocopying and microform prints available for a fee. Computerised, printed and card catalogues. Linked to emigration database of Ulster American Folk Park. The library offers various leaflets, brochures and guides to its holdings, including a *Guide to Irish and Local Studies Department*. Other publications of interest are: *Annual Reports: Catalogue of Books and Bound Manuscripts of the Irish Historical, Archaeological and Antiquarian Library of the Late Francis Joseph Bigger* (Belfast, 1930); and Thomas Watson, *Natural History: a Select List of Fine Books from the Stock of Belfast Central Library* (Belfast, 1988).

CONTACT
Katherine McCloskey, Chief Librarian
David Jess, Assistant Chief Librarian

DESCRIPTION
The Central Library, opened in 1888, is a major research and reference library. It is part of the Belfast Education and Library Board, which operates another 20 branch libraries throughout the city. In addition to maintaining a strong general collection and several major research collections, the library seeks to provide an up to date reference and information service to the general public.

The collection includes some 1,000,000 volumes, plus the largest newspaper collection in Northern Ireland. In addition, the library maintains significant collections of periodicals, maps, microforms, music scores, pamphlets, photographs, postcards, music recordings, theatre materials and government documents for

Northern Ireland, the Republic of Ireland and the UK. Special collections include the 10,000 volume Natural History Collection; a rare book collection, including incunabula and pre-1701 English printed books; a pamphlet collection, especially of those dealing with the 'Popish Plot'; the Fine Press Collection, including a complete run of Cuala Press, and the Irish Collection. The last of these is the largest in Northern Ireland, anchored by the 4,000 volume Francis Joseph Bigger Collection. The Bigger Collection is complemented by the Bigger Archive, with 10,000 items of archaeological, historical and biographical interest. This archive also includes a significant body of correspondence with notable local, national and international figures. Bigger (1863–1926), the grandson of United Irishman David Bigger, was a successful lawyer and member of the Gaelic League who assembled an impressive collection of books, pamphlets and bound manuscripts of Irish historical, archaeological and antiquarian interest. Frederic Bigger, the collector's brother, donated the collection in 1927, and a catalogue of 3,000 entries was published in 1930. Other major Irish holdings include some 800 pre-1851 Belfast imprints, an extensive collection of printed maps of Ireland and several author collections, including books and manuscripts, e.g. Forrest Reid, Amanda McKittrick Ros, Lynn Doyle and Sam Thompson. Complementing the Irish Collection is the Newspaper Collection, which contains virtually complete runs of the *Belfast Telegraph*, *News Letter*, *Irish News* and *Northern Whig*, plus extensive holdings of provincial papers from Ireland, north and south. The library has a newspaper cuttings index covering the eighteenth and nineteenth centuries that may provide a short cut to finding information in the papers. The library also houses the Deposit Collection of UK patents, a superb music library, and strong holdings in the humanities, local history, business information, fine arts and literature and science and technology. The library does not offer genealogical services *per se*, but its holdings in this area are extensive and staff are willing to assist researchers as far as possible.

LOCATION
City centre, a few blocks north of Belfast City Hall. Public car parks nearby.

BUSINESS INFORMATION SERVICES AND EURO INFO CENTRE
See INVEST NORTHERN IRELAND, Belfast

DIOCESAN LIBRARY OF DOWN, DROMORE AND CONNOR

Note: This Church of Ireland library no longer exists. Books were split between the Representative Church Body Library, Dublin, and the Armagh Public Library, Armagh. Some manuscript material was sent to the Public Record Office of Northern Ireland, Belfast.

DOWN AND CONNOR DIOCESAN ARCHIVES

73a Somerton Road
BELFAST, BT15 4DJ
Northern Ireland

TELEPHONE: (028) 9077 6185

HOURS
By appointment

ACCESS AND SERVICES
Privately funded archives of the Roman Catholic Diocese of Down and Connor, which includes Belfast. Advance notice required. Apply to Archivist. Photocopying available for a fee.

CONTACT
Diocesan Archivist

DESCRIPTION
Archives for the largest Roman Catholic diocese in Northern Ireland, which historically embraces Belfast, County Antrim, most of County Down and the Liberties of Coleraine in County Londonderry.

HOLDINGS
Houses the official records of the Roman Catholic see of Down and Connor. Of special interest are the correspondence files of various bishops of the diocese dating back to 1803.

LOCATION
In the Fortwilliam section of north-east Belfast, between Antrim Road and Shore Road.

EDGEHILL THEOLOGICAL COLLEGE

9 Lennoxvale
BELFAST, BT9 5BY
Northern Ireland

TELEPHONE: (028) 9068 6935; FAX: (028) 9068 7204
E-mail: librarian@edgehillcollege.org
Website: www.edgehillcollege.org

HOURS
Term time: M–F, 9.00am–5.00pm
Vacation period: by appointment

ACCESS AND SERVICES
Theological library primarily for the faculty and students of this Methodist college. Visitors welcome but restrictions may apply. Photocopying available for a fee.

CONTACT
Stephen Edgar, College Librarian

DESCRIPTION
Private religious library run by the Methodist Church in Ireland.

HOLDINGS
Library of some 10,000 volumes, with special emphasis on Methodism and theology. Includes some rare material. Note: some older material has been transferred to the WESLEY HISTORICAL SOCIETY IN IRELAND, Belfast.

LOCATION
3.5 acre campus located about 1.5 miles south of the city centre, between Malone Road and Stranmillis Road, near Stranmillis University College and Queen's University.

GAMBLE LIBRARY
See UNION THEOLOGICAL COLLEGE, Belfast

GENERAL REGISTER OFFICE

Northern Ireland Statistics and Research Agency,
Oxford House, 49–55 Chichester Street
BELFAST, BT1 4HL
Northern Ireland

TELEPHONE: (028) 9025 2000; FAX: (028) 9025 2044
E-mail: gro.nisra@dfpni.gov.uk (birth, death and marriage certificate enquiries),
groreg.nisra@dfpni.gov.uk (marriage, re-registration and adoptions),
grostats.nisra@dfpni.gov.uk (statistical queries)
Website: www.groni.gov.uk

HOURS
M–F, 9.30am–4.00pm; closed public holidays

ACCESS AND SERVICES
Open to the general public, but application forms required. Disabled access facilities.
General searches and index searches may be made by any member of the public over
16 years of age. Fees charged for searches and extracts. Current (December 2005)
fees: full certified birth, death, marriage and adoption certificates, £11; short birth
certificate, £11; staff search for each five year period, £5.50; general searches, £24
per hour; index searches, £10 (up to six hours or part thereof). Further verifications
£2.50 each.
    The GRO now offers an online certificate ordering service (www.groni.gov.uk).
The following public search facilities are available for anyone interested in tracing
ancestors:

- Assisted searches. General search of records assisted by members of GRO
  staff for any period of years and any number of entries. Children cannot be
  admitted to the search room.
- Index search. Volumes of indexes are available for searching with limited
  verification of entries by staff. Children cannot be admitted to the search
  room.

Note: To book the above services, telephone (028) 9025 2000. Appointments should
be made up to two weeks in advance, but are not compulsory. Access can be gained
if the facility is not fully booked.

CONTACT
Customer Services Manager

DESCRIPTION
The GRO is part of the Northern Ireland Statistics and Research Agency and is
primarily concerned with the administration of the registration of births, deaths and
marriages. The main records held are statutory registers of births, deaths, marriages,
still births and adoptions. The registers themselves are not open to inspection, but
the information from them is supplied in the form of certificates. The GRO,
formally established in 1922 following partition, stores vital records of Northern
Ireland for issue of certified copies to the public. Birth, death and Roman Catholic

marriage registrations date from 1864 to present; non Roman Catholic marriages date from 1845 to present; adoptions date from 1930 to present; still-births date from 1961 to present.

HOLDINGS
The GRO holds paper indexes for births from 1864 onwards, deaths from 1922 onwards and marriages from 1922 onwards. It holds computerised indexes for births from 1864 onwards, deaths from 1864 onwards and marriages from 1845 onwards.

LOCATION
City centre, on the street extending from City Hall to Law Courts and Waterfront Hall.

INVEST NORTHERN IRELAND – BUSINESS INFORMATION SERVICES AND EURO INFO CENTRE

Bedford Square, Bedford Street
BELFAST, BT2 7EH
Northern Ireland

TELEPHONE: (028) 9023 9090; FAX: (028) 9043 6536
E-mail: bis@investni.com
Website: www.investni.com

HOURS
By appointment

ACCESS AND SERVICES
Visitors welcome but by appointment only. Advance notice and ID required. Disabled access facilities. Library information resources and services available to any company trading or wishing to trade in Europe, but services not exclusive to Europe. Entire collection catalogued online; printed finding aids available. Focus on electronic information services, including CD-ROMs and databases. Invest Northern Ireland has published guides to EU funding in Northern Ireland and to business websites. Charges for photocopying and research.

CONTACT
Librarian

DESCRIPTION
Established in 1989 to provide small businesses with access to a unified European market, Invest Northern Ireland offers entrepreneurs information resources and services through its library division. Invest Northern Ireland maintains a wide variety of resources, including trade directories, environmental rules and regulations and information on standards to encourage small business development.

HOLDINGS
The library emphasises access to electronic data, but it does maintain a reference collection of some 2,000 printed books and 200 journals. Strengths of the collection include market information and European legislative sources.

LOCATION
City centre.

LINEN HALL LIBRARY

17 Donegall Square North
BELFAST, BT1 5GD
Northern Ireland

TELEPHONE: (028) 9032 1707; FAX: (028) 9043 8586
E-mail: info@linenhall.com
Website: www.linenhall.com

HOURS
M–F, 9.30am–5.30pm; Sa, 9.30am–1.00pm

ACCESS AND SERVICES
Independent subscribing research library with some public funding. Open to the
public free of charge for reference services. Advance notice for research use advised.
Borrowing privileges restricted to members. General stacks and modern Irish interest
material are open access; otherwise stacks are closed access. Access to research
resources in the Northern Ireland Political Literature Collection requires a written
letter of introduction from a university or research institute. Disabled access
facilities. Houses the city's largest general lending collection at one location.
Photocopying and microform prints available for a fee. Laptops and cameras can be
used by arrangement. Immediate membership available. Leaflets for membership and
for collections available. Other publications include the annual report and library
newsletter. *See also* John Killen, *History of the Linen Hall Library* (Belfast, 1990).

CONTACT
John Gray, Librarian

DESCRIPTION
The Linen Hall Library was founded in 1788 as the Belfast Reading Society and is
the oldest library in Belfast. It is also the last surviving subscribing library in Ireland.
The library recently opened a spacious and attractive addition to its historic
nineteenth century headquarters, formerly a warehouse in the linen district.

HOLDINGS
The library houses more than 250,000 volumes, 75,000 pamphlets, plus significant
holdings of periodicals, newspapers, manuscripts, maps, microforms, photographs,
films and recordings. It maintains a general lending and reference collection, the
latter being especially strong in genealogy, heraldry, history and travel. Its great
strength, however, is the Irish and Local Studies Collection, with particularly strong
material on Belfast and Counties Antrim and Down. The library seeks to collect in
all Irish interest areas. The Northern Ireland Political Literature Collection,
1968–present, contains some 250,000 items relating to the Troubles, including runs
of about 2,000 periodical titles, 11,500 books, 5,000 posters, 55,000 photographs,
significant archives and extensive ephemera. The Genealogical Collection includes
some 5,000 volumes, mainly of Ulster interest and Scottish and American
connections, plus army, church and educational lists. Other significant collections
include the Kennedy Collection of Ulster Poetry and the Theatre and Performing
Arts Collection.

LOCATION
City centre, facing the front of Belfast City Hall. Main entrance on Fountain Street.

METHODIST HISTORICAL SOCIETY
See WESLEY HISTORICAL SOCIETY IN IRELAND, Belfast

NORTHERN IRELAND ASSEMBLY LIBRARY

Parliament Buildings, Stormont
BELFAST, BT4 3XX
Northern Ireland

TELEPHONE: (028) 9052 1250; FAX: (028) 9052 1922
E-mail: issuedesk.library@niassembly.gov.uk

HOURS
M–F, 9.00am–5.00pm (and until half hour after completion of Assembly sittings if after 4.30pm)

ACCESS AND SERVICES
Usually limited to members and staff of the Northern Ireland Assembly and to government personnel. Referrals made to other appropriate sources. Some exceptions may be made. Appointment required. Apply in writing to Librarian, preferably with sponsorship of an academic institution. Short extracts may be copied. Loans may not be made to visitors. Card catalogue available; a retrospective cataloguing project is under way to transfer card records to machine readable form.

CONTACT
George Woodman, Reader Services Librarian. E-mail: george.woodman@niassembly.gov.uk

DESCRIPTION
Established in 1921 to serve members and staff of the Parliament of Northern Ireland, and from 1973 the Northern Ireland Assembly. Also acts as a reference library for government departments.

HOLDINGS
The collection includes some 17,500 books, 70,000 official publications, 150 journals, 2,000 microforms and three photograph albums. In addition to collecting Northern Ireland official publications and legislation, the library focuses on Irish history and Northern Ireland history, government and politics. The Northern Ireland Collection emphasises public administration, ethnic/religious conflict and constitutional law. Collections of special note include a collection of eighteenth century and earlier historical and topographical materials, eighteenth century journals, acts of parliament and other Irish parliamentary material. There is also access to about 45 electronic services, both online and CD-ROM.

LOCATION
Parliament Buildings, Stormont, east of Belfast city centre. Approach from either Massey Avenue or the Upper Newtownards Road. Limited parking available.

NORTHERN IRELAND HOUSING EXECUTIVE – LIBRARY INFORMATION SERVICES

The Housing Centre, 2 Adelaide Street
BELFAST, BT2 8PB
Northern Ireland

TELEPHONE: (028) 9031 8022; FAX: (028) 9031 8024
E-mail: library@nihe.gov.uk
Website: www.nihe.gov.uk

HOURS
M–Th, 10.00am–5.00pm; F, 10.00am–4.00pm

ACCESS AND SERVICES
Library primarily for use of staff. Visitors welcome to consult for reference purposes, but by appointment only. Advance notice required. Laptops permitted. Open stacks. Collection catalogued on computer. Disabled access facilities. Short extracts may be copied. Restricted city centre parking.

CONTACT
Margaret Gibson, Library Information Services Manager. E-mail:
margaret.a.gibson@nihe.gov.uk

DESCRIPTION
The Housing Executive administers a vast network of public housing throughout Northern Ireland. Its library serves the reference and research needs of staff.

HOLDINGS
The library's collection includes some 12,000 volumes and pamphlets, plus some 200 periodical titles gathered to meet staff reference and research needs. Special interests include architecture and planning, construction, landscape design, housing, the public sector, management, finance and the social sciences, especially sociology. The library also archives Housing Executive publications.

LOCATION
City centre.

ORDNANCE SURVEY OF NORTHERN IRELAND

Colby House, Stranmillis Court
BELFAST, BT9 5BJ
Northern Ireland

TELEPHONE: (028) 9025 5755; FAX: (028) 9025 5700
E-mail: osni@osni.gov.uk
Website: www.osni.gov.uk

HOURS
M–F, 9.15am–4.30pm; closed public and bank holidays

ACCESS AND SERVICES
For old maps and aerial photographs, telephone (028) 9025 5743 (voice mail); e-mail: oldmaps@osni.gov.uk. Appointment necessary to search for archive maps and aerial photographs. Search fee applies. Copies of maps and aerial photographs

available for purchase. See website for current costs of maps and photographs.

CONTACT
Director

DESCRIPTION
OSNI is an executive agency with the Department of Culture, Arts and Leisure for Northern Ireland.

HOLDINGS
The archive houses significant holdings of maps and aerial photographs and films: six inch scale series maps, 1830–1900; six and 25 inch scale series maps, 1830–1900; six and 25 inch scale series maps, 1900–50; Irish Grid maps 1959–present; aerial films 1959–present. The archive also houses many original copies of the earlier county series maps.

LOCATION
Off Stranmillis Road, about 1.5 miles south of city centre, near Stranmillis University College.

POLICE MUSEUM

PSNI Headquarters
'Brooklyn', 65 Knock Road
BELFAST, BT5 6LE

TELEPHONE: (028) 9065 0222; FAX: (028) 9070 0124
E-mail: museum@psni.police.uk
Website: www.psni.police.uk/museum

HOURS
M–F, 10.00am–12.30pm; 2.00pm–4.30pm

ACCESS AND SERVICES
Visitors welcome, but prior appointment preferred. Parking for disabled available and wheelchair access to some public areas. Brochure/leaflet and guide to the collection available. Study space can be made available. Groups should book in advance. A genealogical search service is available for constabulary service records, 1822–1922. Museum may also be viewed on the internet.

CONTACT
Hugh Forrester, Curator

DESCRIPTION
The museum includes displays of uniforms and equipment, photographs and memorabilia relating to the Irish Constabulary since its formation in 1822. The prefix 'Royal' was added in 1867 and in 1922 the Royal Ulster Constabulary was created. In November 2001, the RUC became the Police Service of Northern Ireland (PSNI).

HOLDINGS
The museum houses a unique collection of material ranging over the 200 years of organised policing in Ireland. The collection contains an extensive range of uniforms and associated 'appointments', firearms, medals, badges and trophies and other

material relating generally to policing. There is an archive of photographic material
and documents dating back to the early nineteenth century. The museum also
includes a reference library and research facility containing personnel records of the
early constabulary.

LOCATION
East Belfast, off Upper Newtownards Road.

PRESBYTERIAN HISTORICAL SOCIETY

Room 218, Church House, Fisherwick Place
BELFAST, BT1 6DW
Northern Ireland

TELEPHONE: (028) 9032 2284
Website: www.presbyterianireland.org

HOURS
M–Tu, Th–F, 10.00am–12.30pm, W, 1.15pm–3.30pm

ACCESS AND SERVICES
Visitors welcome, appointments preferred. Photocopying available for a small fee.
Publications include: *A History of Congregations in the Presbyterian Church in Ireland,
1610–1982.*

CONTACT
Assistant Secretary

DESCRIPTION
The Presbyterian Historical Society was created in 1906 to promote public awareness
of the history of the Presbyterian Churches in Ireland. It is largely supported by the
Presbyterian Church of Ireland.

HOLDINGS
The Society possesses a library of some 12,000 books and pamphlets. These are
mainly concerned with ecclesiastical history and in particular Presbyterian history.
The collection includes a large number of congregational histories. A set of *The
Witness*, a Presbyterian newspaper covering the period 1874–1941, is also available
for consultation, as are the printed minutes of the General Assembly beginning in
1840.

Manuscript material includes session minutes, baptisms and marriages from
individual churches as well as some presbytery minutes. These include session
accounts for Armagh Presbyterian Church for 1707–32, session minutes for
Aghadowey Presbyterian Church for 1702–61 and baptisms from Cullybackey
(Cunningham Memorial) Presbyterian Church covering the period 1726–1815. The
Guide to Church Records produced by the Public Record Office of Northern Ireland
(Belfast, 1994) indicates which congregational records are available at the
Presbyterian Historical Society. The society also has a duplicate set of the microfilm
copies of Presbyterian Church registers held by PRONI covering the vast majority of
Presbyterian congregations in Ireland.

Of particular interest is the large amount of biographical data on Presbyterian
ministers. This material can be accessed through a card index, while there are also
handwritten and printed *fasti* providing information on clergymen. A small

collection of private papers of Presbyterian ministers is available in the Presbyterian Historical Society. These include some of the papers of the most distinguished nineteenth century Presbyterian minister, Rev Henry Cooke.

LOCATION
City centre, just west of Belfast City Hall, close to the offices of the Ulster Historical Foundation.

PUBLIC RECORD OFFICE OF NORTHERN IRELAND

66 Balmoral Avenue
BELFAST, BT9 6NY
Northern Ireland

TELEPHONE: (028) 9025 5905; FAX: (028) 9025 5999
E-mail: proni@dcalni.gov.uk
Website: www.proni.gov.uk

HOURS
M–W, F, 9.15am–4.45pm; Th, 10.00am–8.45pm

ACCESS AND SERVICES
A publicly funded executive agency within the Department of Culture, Arts and Leisure (DCAL), open to the general public. ID required for first time users to register. Advance notice required for groups but not individuals. Laptops permitted at selected points in Reading Room. Photocopying and microfilming services available; carried out by staff. Public areas accessible to those with a disability, and sign reading and a loop hearing system available. There is no single guide to the records of PRONI but there are exceptionally detailed catalogues, indexes and finding aids to individual collections. Details of the acquisitions can be found in annual *Deputy Keeper's Reports* up to 1989, indexed under personal names, places and subjects. Summary of more recent acquisitions can be found in *Annual Report and Accounts*. By 2007 all of PRONI's catalogues will be available online. Though PRONI is the major resource for genealogical information in Northern Ireland, it cannot provide a comprehensive research service. However, it can undertake paid searches in response to specific requests for information and staff offsite will give guidance to visitors. Records of government departments, courts, local authorities and other public bodies not yet open to the public are subject to the Freedom of Information Act (2000). This provides general access rights but also includes provisions that may exempt information from release for extended periods – for example, sensitive personal data. Applications for access should be made in writing. Publications include: *Annual/Statutory Report of the Deputy Keeper of Records, Guide to Sources for Women's History, Guide to Educational Records*, plus a range of leaflets on the records available for tracing family trees, for local history and on different topics such as the Famine, the Act of Union and the Titanic. A full list of publications available appears on the PRONI website.

CONTACT
Offsite services: Readers' Services (Readers)
Written and e-mail enquiries: Access to Information Unit
Group visits and publications and leaflets: Education, Learning and Outreach

DESCRIPTION
PRONI was established in 1923 following partition and opened in 1924 as the official repository for public records in Northern Ireland, but it also houses the largest collection of private records in Northern Ireland.

HOLDINGS
PRONI has more than 53 shelf kilometres of records. The bulk of its public records deal with Northern Ireland since the early 1920s. The archive also includes older documents from private sources, some dating back to the fourteenth century, with strong holdings of material from the 1600s. PRONI's holdings can be divided into a number of categories: public records which include tithe applotment records, valuation books and maps, Poor Law records and school records, private archives which include church records (mostly available in the Self Service Microfilm Room), landed estate records, business records, solicitors' records, records of private individuals and families and photographs. PRONI also holds copies of the 1901 census for the six counties of Northern Ireland, which are available in the Self Service Microfilm Room.

PRONI on the Web
Introductions to the major private collections can be read on the PRONI website (www.proni.gov.uk). Most relate to the archives of the great landed estates, but there are some introductions to business records, including the shipbuilding firm, Harland and Wolff. Introductions to government and non-departmental records are currently being compiled in conjunction with the electronic cataloguing project; those for all classes of records in the Ministry/Department of Education are already available on the website. PRONI also has several useful indexes on its website. The Geographical Index lists counties, parishes, townlands, baronies, Electoral Divisions and Poor Law Unions. The Prominent Person Index lists all the occurrences of a name in the PRONI catalogues together with all the reference numbers to the archive collections relevant to that individual. The Presbyterian Church Index gives the name, county and reference number of all those Presbyterian Church records that have been microfilmed by PRONI. A similar index is available for Church of Ireland records. The website also includes copies of PRONI's information leaflets that describe the content of different types of records and how to access them. The most recent additions to the website include digitised images of archives including fully searchable indexes which may be accessed free of charge. It is possible to search for a name and/or place among the signatures of half a million people who signed the Ulster Covenant in 1912 and to view the page where the signature occurs. It is also possible to search for a name and/or place in the pre-1840 freeholders' registers, which contain lists of people who were entitled to vote or who actually voted at elections and then to view the pages where the name occurs. Further online digital archives are planned – the wills of Northern Ireland testators, 1858–c. 1900 will be the next to appear.

LOCATION
Approximately three miles south-west of city centre, between Lisburn and Malone Roads. Metro buses 8 or 9 from the city centre take passengers to within walking distance of PRONI. The Balmoral railway halt is also close by.

QUEEN'S UNIVERSITY BELFAST LIBRARY

University Road
BELFAST, BT7 1LS
Northern Ireland

TELEPHONE: (028) 9097 5023; FAX: (028) 9032 3340
E-mail: library@qub.ac.uk, or use website for contact
Website: www.qub.ac.uk/lib

HOURS
Main Library
Term time: M–Th, 8.30am–10.00pm; F, 8.30am–8.30pm; Sa, 9.00am–12.30pm
Vacation period: 8.30am–5.30pm
Special Collections
Term time: M–Th, 9.00am–9.30pm; F, 9.00am–8.00pm
Vacation period: M–F, 9.00am–5.00pm; Sa, 9.00am–12.30pm

ACCESS AND SERVICES
Queen's University Belfast Library is a publicly funded academic research library open to the general public for reference purposes where material may not be readily accessed elsewhere. Researchers welcome but intending visitors should provide advance notification detailing the collections they wish to consult and dates of intended visit. ID required. Laptops permitted. Photocopying restricted. Digital cameras permitted. Digital copies can be provided when photocopying is not permitted; this is a fee based service. The library, including the Special Collections Department, is wheelchair accessible. All books and journals listed on online catalogue and classified according to Library of Congress classification. Printed guide to manuscript collections available for consultation; guides to manuscript collections may also be accessed electronically from Special Collections Department web pages. See library website: www.qub.ac.uk/lib.

RASCAL
Research and Special Collections Available Locally, hosted by Queen's University Belfast, is a web based directory of special collections available for consultation in Northern Ireland. It provides online access to collection descriptions and contact details to resources held in local libraries, museums and archives. Over 400 collections in almost 70 institutions are listed. The RASCAL Directory is accessible at www.rascal.ac.uk.

Queen's University Branch Libraries
Branch libraries are not listed separately in this guide. These are located outside the Main Library and may be contacted directly as follows:
  Agriculture and Food Science Library, Agriculture and Food Science Centre, Newforge Lane, Belfast, BT9 5PX. Telephone: (028) 9025 5227; fax: (028) 9025 5400;
  Biomedical Library, Medical Biology Centre, Lisburn Road, Belfast BT9 7BL. Telephone: (028) 9032 9241, extension 2797/(028) 9026 3913; fax: (028) 9031 5560;
  Medical Library, Mulhouse Building, Mulhouse Road, Belfast BT12 6DP. Telephone: (028) 9063 2501;
  Science Library, Lennoxvale, Belfast BT9 5EQ. Telephone: (028) 9097 4302;

Veterinary Sciences Library, Veterinary Research Laboratories, Stormont, Belfast, BT4 3SD. Telephone: (028) 9052 5622.

CONTACT
Elizabeth Traynor, Assistant Director of Information Services
Deirdre Wildy, Senior Subject Librarian (Arts and Humanities). Telephone: (028) 9097 3607; e-mail: d.wildy@qub.ac.uk

DESCRIPTION
Queen's College Belfast was established in Ireland by Queen Victoria in 1845, along with colleges in Cork and Galway. In 1908 it was elevated to university rank with its own charter and statutes. Today the university enrols more than 20,000 full and part time students. Recently two colleges were added to the university: Stranmillis University College and St Mary's University College. Adjacent to the Main Library is the Seamus Heaney Library, designed as a multidisciplinary study centre for students. It provides students with study space, computer services and easy access to recommended textbooks and course readings. Access to the Seamus Heaney Library is restricted to students and staff of Queen's University. For more information on the university, see W.T. Moody and J.C. Beckett, *Queen's Belfast* (1959) and B.M. Walker and A. McCreary, *Degrees of Excellence* (1994).

HOLDINGS
The library houses the largest collection in Northern Ireland. The QUB Library alone contains more than 1,000,000 volumes, plus significant holdings of pamphlets, periodicals and manuscripts. The collection is quite diverse, representing the teaching and research interests of the curriculum and faculty. The Special Collections Department houses some 50,000 volumes, including 20 incunabula, manuscript collections and the archives of the university. Major collections include the Hibernica Collection, a collection of books and pamphlets relating to the literature, politics and social history of Ireland; the Percy Collection, the eighteenth century library of the Church of Ireland Bishop of Dromore; the Bunting Collection, eighteenth century music manuscripts; the Andrews and Thomson Collections of early scientific papers; the Somerville and Ross Collection, consisting of diaries, correspondence and manuscripts; the Hart Collection, the diaries and personal papers of Sir Robert Hart, Inspector General of the Chinese Imperial Maritime Customs, 1868–1907; and the Cardinal Cahal Daly Collection, the private library of the former Roman Catholic Archbishop of Armagh and Primate of All Ireland, formerly housed in the library of the recently closed Queen's University Armagh Campus.

LOCATION
One mile south of city centre, near Botanic Gardens and the Ulster Museum.

ST MARY'S UNIVERSITY COLLEGE LIBRARY

191 Falls Road
BELFAST, BT12 6FE
Northern Ireland

TELEPHONE: (028) 9032 7678; FAX: (028) 9033 3719
E-mail: library@stmarys-belfast.ac.uk
Website: www.stmarys-belfast.ac.uk

HOURS
Term time: M–Th, 9.00am–9.00pm; F, 9.00am–5.00pm; Sa, 9.00am–1.00pm
Vacation period: M–F, 9.00am–1.00pm, 2.00pm–5.00pm
Closed St Patrick's Day, Easter Week, 12 and 13 July, Christmas–New Year period

ACCESS AND SERVICES
One of two publicly funded university colleges of Queen's University Belfast. Library open to visiting staff and students from other higher education establishments for reference purposes. Open stacks. ID required, as is signing of visitor's book. Disabled access facilities. Library has a printed guide, photocopying facilities and internet access.

CONTACT
John Morrissey, Librarian. E-mail: j.morrissey@stmarys-belfast.ac.uk
Felicity Jones, Assistant Librarian. E-mail: f.jones@stmarys-belfast.ac.uk

DESCRIPTION
St Mary's University College was founded in 1900 by the Dominican Sisters to educate young women for the Roman Catholic school system. In 1985 St Mary's amalgamated with St Joseph's, its male counterpart, to form the present St Mary's College. While maintaining its independence, the college has a special relationship with Queen's University, which validates St Mary's degrees. The purpose of the college has expanded with the introduction of a BA degree in Liberal Arts and the education and training of teachers for Irish language schools.

HOLDINGS
The collection includes 100,000 items, some 300 direct subscription journals and access to a large range of remote databases. There is also a substantial range of non-book materials and teaching and learning resources. Areas of chief curriculum interest include: education, Irish language, religious education and theology, business studies, European studies, human development, philosophy, physical education, design and technology, English, art, history, geography and science.

LOCATION
One mile west of Belfast city centre, on Falls Road, close to Royal Victoria Hospital.

SEAMUS HEANEY LIBRARY
See QUEEN'S UNIVERSITY BELFAST LIBRARY

STRANMILLIS UNIVERSITY COLLEGE LIBRARY

Stranmillis Road
BELFAST, BT9 5DY
Northern Ireland

TELEPHONE: (028) 9038 4310; FAX: (028) 9066 3682
E-mail: library@stran.ac.uk
Website: www.stran.ac.uk

HOURS
Term time: M–Th, 9.00am–9.00pm; F, 9.00am–4.30pm
Vacation period: M–Th, 9.00am–5.00pm; F, 9.00am–4.30pm

ACCESS AND SERVICES
One of two publicly funded education colleges in Northern Ireland, integrated academically with Queen's University Belfast. Library open to general public for reference purposes. Visitors welcome, especially out of term, but borrowing privileges may be restricted. ID required. Open stacks. Access for those with disabilities by arrangement. Library offers photocopying and microform prints, computerised databases, finding aids and a printed guide.

CONTACT
Wesley McCann, Librarian

DESCRIPTION
Stranmillis was founded in 1922 as a training college for teachers. Today it concentrates on preparing teachers who work with children of ages three to thirteen. Its library supports the learning, teaching and research needs of staff and students.

HOLDINGS
The collection includes some 90,000 volumes and 400 journals. Areas of chief curriculum interest are: education, English, religious studies, history, art, design and technology, science, geography, physical education, music and drama. Among special collections of interest are: the Ulster Collection of books relating to the northern counties of Ireland, a modest collection of nineteenth century Irish school books, a microfilm copy of the *News Letter* 1737–1925 and a microfilm copy of the Lawrence Collection of Irish photographs 1880–1914 (the original is located at the National Library of Ireland, Dublin).

LOCATION
Two miles south of city centre, on Stranmillis Road. Spacious, beautifully landscaped campus. Parking available by arrangement.

ULSTER HISTORICAL FOUNDATION

Balmoral Buildings, 12 College Square East
BELFAST, BT1 6DD
Northern Ireland

TELEPHONE: (028) 9033 2288; FAX: (028) 9023 9885
E-mail: enquiry@uhf.org.uk
Website: www.ancestryireland.com

HOURS
By appointment, M–F, 9.00am–5.00pm; preliminary enquiry in writing preferred

ACCESS AND SERVICES
Publicly and privately funded, not for profit, fee based genealogical research centre and publisher, open to the public. Research consultancy provided for a fee. Preliminary search assessments to establish whether research is feasible also carried out for a charge of £20/US$31. For schedule of research fees, contact Executive Director or see website. Full report averages £150–£250. UHF has undertaken over 10,000 searches for clients throughout the world and each year answers over 3,000 genealogical enquiries. Also publishes a wide range of materials, primarily in the areas of Irish, local and family history. For a current listing consult website.

CONTACT
Fintan Mullan, Executive Director

DESCRIPTION
The Ulster Historical Foundation is the principal genealogical research centre in Ireland, with a concentration on the province of Ulster (six counties of Northern Ireland, plus Counties Cavan, Donegal and Monaghan in the Republic of Ireland). Founded in 1956 to promote interest in Ulster history and genealogy, it provides a professional and comprehensive research service, publishes books and pamphlets and organises annual family history and heritage conferences. It is a member of the Irish Genealogical Project, an island-wide effort to computerise all the major Irish genealogical sources. To this end, it has been at work for years compiling a comprehensive computerised database of genealogical records for Ulster, principally for Counties Antrim and Down, including Belfast. The database is used as a tool, in conjunction with other documentary sources, to provide a comprehensive ancestral research service.

HOLDINGS
The UHF's database contains: pre-1900 church and civil records 1845–1921 for counties Antrim and Down, including Belfast, plus gravestone transcripts for most of Northern Ireland and calendars of flax growers in Ireland in 1796. It also houses a collection of some 10,000 family history reports, which it has been compiling since 1956.

LOCATION
City centre, Great Victoria Street, two blocks west of Belfast City Hall.

ULSTER MUSEUM LIBRARY

Botanic Gardens
BELFAST
BT9 5AB

TELEPHONE: (028) 9038 3000

Note: The Ulster Museum is closed from autumn 2006, for approximately two years, to undergo major redevelopment. Researchers wishing to consult published material, including books, should contact the relevant curator. Updated contact details for curatorial staff can be found on the museum's website at www.ulstermuseum.org.uk.

UNION THEOLOGICAL COLLEGE – GAMBLE LIBRARY

108 Botanic Avenue
BELFAST, BT7 1JT
Northern Ireland

TELEPHONE: (028) 9020 5093
E-mail: librarian@union.ac.uk
Website: www.union.ac.uk/library

HOURS
M–Th, 9.00am–5.00pm; F, 9.00am–4.30pm; closed Easter Week, Twelfth Fortnight (July) and Christmas–New Year period (two weeks)

ACCESS AND SERVICES
Visitors welcome; advance notice preferred. Borrowing privileges available to members, who may join for a current fee of £30 per year. Card catalogue represents approximately 40 per cent of book collection; computer catalogue for books received since 1993. Photocopying available for a fee. The college publishes an annual calendar and a students' handbook.

CONTACT
Stephen Gregory, Librarian

DESCRIPTION
Union Theological College was established by the Presbyterian Church in Ireland. The library supports the work of the faculty, students of the college and ministers.

HOLDINGS
The library houses more than 50,000 books, with a heavy emphasis on theology and Irish church history. A separate collection of rare books features works on theology and church history. Special collections of note include the Magee College Pamphlets Collection and the Assembly's College Pamphlets Collection. There is also a collection of record books of genealogical interest.

LOCATION
One mile south of Belfast city centre, immediately behind main buildings of Queen's University.

UNIVERSITY OF ULSTER LIBRARY, BELFAST CAMPUS

York Street
BELFAST, BT15 1ED
Northern Ireland

TELEPHONE: (028) 9026 7268; FAX: (028) 9026 7278
E-mail: m.khorshidian@ulster.ac.uk
Website: library.ulster.ac.uk

HOURS
Term time: M–Th, 8.45am–10.00pm; F, 8.45am–6.00pm; Sa, 10.00am–5.00pm
Vacation period: M–Th, 8.45am–5.00pm; F, 8.45am–4.00pm

ACCESS AND SERVICES
Visitors welcome but ID required. Campus undergoing major refurbishment due to be completed in 2010, so previous notice needed. Disabled access facilities with some restrictions. Borrowing privileges not extended to visitors on this campus. Entire University of Ulster library system shares a common catalogue database, available free from library website. Visitors may also wish to consult RASCAL website at www.rascal.ac.uk, a web based gateway to research and special collections in Northern Ireland.

CONTACT
Marion Khorshidian, Campus Library Manager

DESCRIPTION
The Belfast campus originated as a technical college in 1849 and was established as a university campus in 1984. It is traditionally considered the home of the School of

Art and Design, though other humanities subjects are taught also, mainly at undergraduate level. The campus is part of the four campus University of Ulster system, which includes Coleraine, County Londonderry, Jordanstown, County Antrim, and Magee, Derry.

HOLDINGS
The library contains some 62,000 volumes and more than 90,000 slides in support of the campus's curriculum, with strengths in the areas of fine art, design, graphics, fashion, textiles, ceramics, jewellery, metalwork, architecture, film, photography and print-making. The library holds occasional exhibitions relating to its holdings/interests, e.g. The Wood Engravings of Robert Gibbings (1988), Illustrated by Hugh Thomson, 1860–1920 (1989), The Dolmen Press, 1951–87 (1991) and Wendy Dunbar: Book Designer (1994). An illustrated catalogue was produced for each of these exhibitions.

LOCATION
City centre, about one mile north of Belfast City Hall. Royal Avenue becomes York Street just past the Belfast Central Library.

WESLEY HISTORICAL SOCIETY IN IRELAND

Edgehill College, 9 Lennoxvale
BELFAST, BT9 5BY
Northern Ireland

TELEPHONE: (028) 9181 5959
E-mail: robin@roddie.plus.com

HOURS
M–Th, 9.00am–12.30pm

ACCESS AND SERVICES
Appointment in advance with Archivist advisable. Photocopying facilities available on request. Alphabetical name, geographical and keyword card catalogues to periodicals and journals available offsite for consultation. Shelf list in manuscript detailing archival holdings also available.

CONTACT
Rev Robin P. Roddie, Honorary Archivist

DESCRIPTION
The Wesley Historical Society in Ireland administers and maintains an archive and reading room in Belfast with a comprehensive and unrivalled collection of works on or relating to Methodism in Ireland. It was founded in 1926 to promote the study of the Methodist Church in Ireland.

HOLDINGS
The collection comprises over 8,000 items and is particularly strong in the works of John and Charles Wesley and Adam Clark. It contains extensive runs of Methodist journals and periodicals, including the *Irish Evangelist* (1859–83), the *Christian Advocate* (1883–1923), the *Irish Christian Advocate* (1923–71) and the *Methodist Newsletter* (1973–present). Other series include the Dublin edition of the *Methodist Magazine* (1801–23) and the *Primitive Wesleyan Methodist Magazine* (1823–45),

which was unique to Ireland. The collection also includes a range of original and printed manuscript materials. These comprise the archives of the Irish Branch of the Wesley Historical Society from 1926 onwards, original diaries and journals of Irish preachers such as Rev Adam Averell (1754–1847), founder of the Irish Primitive Wesleyans in 1818, a complete series of minutes of the Irish Conference from 1752, Methodist church registers, photographs and other ephemera relating to Methodism in Ireland. Of major interest is the biographical information that has been collected on Methodist preachers and ministers in Ireland.

LOCATION
South Belfast, close to Malone Road.

M'SKIMIN ROOM

Carrickfergus Library, 2 Joymount Court
CARRICKFERGUS, COUNTY ANTRIM, BT38 7DQ
Northern Ireland

TELEPHONE: (028) 9336 2261; FAX: (028) 9336 0589
E-mail: carrickfergus.library@ni-libraries.net
Website: www.neelb.org.uk

HOURS
M, W, F, 9.30am–8.00pm; Tu, Th, 9.30am–5.30pm; Sa, 9.30am–5.00pm

ACCESS AND SERVICES
Visitors welcome. Borrowing privileges available. Disabled access facilities. Free internet access for all Northern Ireland public library members. One membership card valid for all libraries. Charge of £1.50 per half hour for non-members; ID required. Membership of library open to anyone living, working or studying in the area.

CONTACT
Dawn Young, Branch Manager

DESCRIPTION
A special local collection held in the Carrickfergus Library, named after an eighteenth century historian of Carrickfergus, Samuel M'Skimin. The library is part of the North-Eastern Education and Library Board, which oversees 28 libraries in the north-eastern region of Northern Ireland.

HOLDINGS
The collection focuses on Carrickfergus and the surrounding area. It houses nearly 1,000 volumes, with a special emphasis on county histories and Irish literature. The collection includes journals, maps, microforms, newspapers and newspaper cuttings. The library's general collection exceeds 30,000 volumes.

LOCATION
Close to town centre and near Carrickfergus Castle, one of the best preserved Norman castles in Ireland. Carrickfergus is situated on the coast just north of Belfast.

IRISH LINEN CENTRE AND LISBURN MUSEUM LIBRARY

Market Square
LISBURN, COUNTY ANTRIM, BT28 1AG
Northern Ireland

TELEPHONE: (028) 9266 3377; FAX: (028) 9267 2624
E-mail: irishlinencentre@lisburn.gov.uk
Website: www.lisburncity.gov.uk/irish_linen_centre_and_lisburn_museum/library

HOURS
Museum: M–Sa, 9.30am–5.00pm; closed public holidays
Library: M–F, 9.30am–4.30pm

ACCESS AND SERVICES
Museum: open to public free of charge. Access for disabled persons. Car parking for disabled badge holders available. Shop and cafe offsite.
Library: appointment required. There are no lending facilities. Photocopying service possible, subject to discretion of staff officer in charge. No charge for use of study facilities; however, photocopying is chargeable.

CONTACT
Brenda Collins, Research Officer. E-mail: brenda.collins@lisburn.gov.uk

DESCRIPTION
The Irish Linen Centre and Lisburn Museum is financed and managed by Lisburn City Council. Its aim is to collect, safeguard and interpret artefacts and information relating to the Irish linen industry and the history of Lisburn and the Lagan Valley, making them accessible now and preserving them for the future. The Museum's Research Library contains a range of resources in relation to the Museum's main areas of interest, especially textiles and art in relation to linen, and Irish history, particularly the history of Ulster, Lisburn and the Lagan Valley.

HOLDINGS
The library houses some 2,000 books and approximately 20 journals; a collection of nineteenth and twentieth century Ordnance Survey maps for the district; original copies of the two local newspapers, *Lisburn Herald* and *Lisburn Standard* for many years from the 1890s until the 1950s (also a complete microfilm run for the *Lisburn Standard* from which copies can be printed); microfilm copies of the 1901 census schedules for Lisburn and the surrounding district; and a collection of audio and video tapes relating to the museum's areas of interest. In addition, the library houses the collection of the former Lambeg Industrial Research Association, which closed in 1993. LIRA was originally founded in 1919 as the Linen Industry Research Association and the library collection reflects its research work into a range of aspects of flax and linen production. The library comprises over 6,000 books, journals and research reports. The majority of the material was published between 1900 and 1970; there are also some rare books, pamphlets and journals dating from the eighteenth century.

LOCATION
Town centre. Only 300 metres from rail and bus stations. Disabled parking possible at museum and public car parks within 50 metres. 24 hour interactive tourist information point outside the building.

THE SOCIETY OF FRIENDS LIBRARY

Meeting House, Railway Street
LISBURN, COUNTY ANTRIM, BT28 1XG
Northern Ireland

ACCESS AND SERVICES
The library deals with postal enquiries only.

CONTACT
Librarian

DESCRIPTION
The archive of the Religious Society of Friends in Ulster.

HOLDINGS
The Religious Society of Friends, or Quakers as they are commonly known, kept amazingly detailed records, many of which date back to the nineteenth century. The library in Lisburn holds all the original surviving records of the Ulster Province Meeting and its constituent meetings with the sole exception of the first minute book of the Ulster Province Meeting. This is in the Historical Library of the Religious Society of Friends in Dublin. These minute books begin in 1674. A large amount of additional documentary source material is also available, including, for the Ulster Province/Quarterly Meeting, copies of marriage certificates (1731–86), a Book of Sufferings (1748–1809) and a register of births and burials (1841–58). Material from the local meetings survives for Antrim, Ballyhagen, Cootehill, Grange (near Charlemont), Lisburn, Lurgan and Richhill. For the Lisburn and Lurgan meetings there are minute books from 1675. Of particular interest from the Ballyhagen meeting is a collection of wills with detailed inventories dating from the late seventeenth and early eighteenth centuries. There are also family lists from c. 1680. Copies of these records are available in the Public Record Office of Northern Ireland (T/1062 and MIC/16). A list of the Ulster material, compiled by B.G. Hutton, can be found in the *Guide to Irish Quaker Records, 1654–1860* published by the Irish Manuscripts Commission in 1967.

LOCATION
Town centre.

UNIVERSITY OF ULSTER LIBRARY, JORDANSTOWN CAMPUS
(Sir Derek Birley Learning Resource Centre)

Shore Road
NEWTOWNABBEY, COUNTY ANTRIM, BT37 0QB
Northern Ireland

TELEPHONE: (028) 9036 6964; FAX: (028) 9036 6849
E-mail: m.mccullough@ulst.ac.uk
Website: www.ulster.ac.uk/library

HOURS
Term time: M–F, 8.45am–10.00pm; Sa, 1.00pm–5.00pm; Su, 1.00pm–5.00pm
Vacation period: M–Th, 9.00am–5.00pm; F, 9.00am–4.00pm

ACCESS AND SERVICES
Visitors welcome but advance notice preferred. Borrowing privileges and database
searching not usually extended to external visitors. Application preferred for access to
special collections. Disabled access facilities. University of Ulster shares a common
catalogue database. Fees apply for photocopying and microform print services;
advance notice preferred.

CONTACT
Mary McCullough, Campus Library Manager

DESCRIPTION
The Jordanstown campus is part of the four campus University of Ulster system,
which also includes Belfast, Coleraine, County Londonderry and Magee, Derry.
Jordanstown is the largest of the four campus libraries in the University of Ulster
system. In October 2002, the university formally opened the Sir Derek Birley
Learning Resources Centre, a state of the art facility with 1,200 study spaces, of
which 900 have network connections. There are 380 networked desktop computers
available.

HOLDINGS
The library houses a collection of 280,000 volumes, plus significant holdings of
journals (2,000 titles), microforms, newspapers, pamphlets and recordings. It also
provides access to over 4,000 online electronic journals. Its special subject areas are
business and management, social services, health sciences, informatics and
engineering. Special collections include the Irish Travellers Collection and a
collection of radical English language newspapers and journals on microfilm. The
library does not house any genealogical sources of note.

LOCATION
Seven miles north of Belfast, along the coast.

COUNTY ARMAGH

ARMAGH ANCESTRY

40 English Street
ARMAGH, BT61 7BA
Northern Ireland

TELEPHONE: (028) 3752 1802; FAX: (028) 3751 0180
E-mail: ancestry@armagh.gov.uk
Website: www.visitarmagh.com

HOURS
By appointment: details will be taken at any time and replied to by Researcher.

ACCESS AND SERVICES
Privately and publicly funded genealogical service centre open to the public. Visitors welcome but advance notice preferred. Disabled access facilities. No fee for access to library. The centre offers fee based, professional genealogical research services. Fees vary depending on service and time involved.

CONTACT
Genealogical Researcher

DESCRIPTION
Armagh Ancestry, established in 1992, participates in the Irish Genealogical Project (IGP), an effort to create a comprehensive genealogical database for all Ireland from a wide variety of sources, including church and state records, tithe applotment books, *Griffith's Valuation*, the 1901 census and gravestone inscriptions. For a list of other participants in the IGP, *see* index. Armagh Ancestry offers a genealogical research service for County Armagh. Computerisation of genealogical records for County Armagh has been under way since 1985. Complete records include: all the County Armagh Roman Catholic registers dating up to 1900; civil births, 1864–1922; marriages, 1845–1922; and some Protestant registers up until 1900. Currently, the centre is inputting civil deaths, 1864–1922, and pre-1900 church registers of all denominations. In 1997 the Armagh Records Centre was transferred to Armagh Ancestry. The Records Centre had computerised pre-1900 Catholic parish registers of the Archdiocese of Armagh, covering 60 parishes spread over three counties: most of Armagh, a large part of east and central Tyrone and all of Louth.

Armagh Ancestry also offers a PRONI (Public Record Office of Northern Ireland) outreach facility.

HOLDINGS
The centre offers a small genealogical library for consultation, with special emphasis on County Armagh. Items of special interest include: computerised database of County Armagh church and civil records, CD-ROM of *Griffith's Valuation* and tithe applotment books.

LOCATION
City centre, within St Patrick's Trian Visitor Complex behind the Tourist Information Centre. Public car parks nearby.

ARMAGH CITY LIBRARY

Market Street
ARMAGH, BT61 7BU
Northern Ireland

TELEPHONE: (028) 3752 4072
E-mail: helen.grimes@ni-libraries.net
Website: www.selb.org

HOURS
M, W, F, 9.30am–5.30pm; Tu, Th, 9.30am–8.00pm; Sa, 9.30am–5.00pm

ACCESS AND SERVICES
Spread over two floors with disabled access. First floor has large reference area with study facilities and 22 computers with internet access. Use of these free to members; visitors charged a small fee. Photocopying and fax facilities available. Membership of the library open to anyone living, working or studying in the area.

CONTACT
Helen Grimes, Library Manager

DESCRIPTION
This is one of the Southern Education and Library Board's larger branch libraries. It is housed in the Market House, which dates from 1815, on a site where the gaol and sessions house once stood. It has access to material throughout Northern Ireland via the five Education and Library Boards' library network.

HOLDINGS
The collection, which encompasses reference, educational and leisure material, comprises over 24,000 books and 3,000 videos, compact discs and cassettes.

LOCATION
City centre.

ARMAGH COUNTY MUSEUM

The Mall East
ARMAGH, BT61 9BE
Northern Ireland

TELEPHONE: (028) 3752 3070; FAX: (028) 3752 2631
E-mail: acm.info@magni.org.uk
Website: www.armaghcountymuseum.org.uk

HOURS
M–F, 10.00am–5.00pm; Sa, 10.00am–1.00pm, 2.00pm–5.00pm; closed bank
holidays

ACCESS AND SERVICES
Publicly funded museum whose library and exhibits are open to the public free of
charge. Disabled access facilities; library stacks closed. At least two weeks' advance
notification by letter preferred for access to research collections. Laptops permitted;
pencils only in library. Photocopying available; free public parking. The library issues
leaflets and brochures. Copies of its publication, *Harvest Home: the Last Sheaf, a
Selection of the Writings of T.G.F. Paterson Relating to County Armagh* (1975), are still
available in the museum shop.

CONTACT
Catherine McCullough, Curator

DESCRIPTION
Armagh County Museum is a branch of the Museums and Galleries of Northern
Ireland (MAGNI). *See also* Ulster American Folk Park, Omagh; Ulster Folk And
Transport Museum, Holywood; and Ulster Museum Library, Belfast. A community
museum focusing on County Armagh, it contains one of the finest county
collections in Ireland. The museum is housed in a distinctive classical revival
building, which first opened in 1834 as a school.

HOLDINGS
Museum holdings include artworks, archaeological objects, local and natural history
specimens, textile, railway and military artefact collections. Paintings of note include
John Luke's *The Old Callan Bridge* and many works by George Russell (Æ). The
library houses approximately 10,000 volumes and 48 linear feet of manuscripts, plus
a small collection of photographs. The holdings are especially strong in local history,
with important collections of maps and prints. Subject areas include: archaeology,
history, folk and rural life, fine arts and crafts, natural history, military history and
costume relating to County Armagh. Among special collections of note are: the
T.G.F. Paterson Manuscript Collection (300 bound volumes), including working
papers with notes on local families and buildings; a collection of Paterson's journal
Armachiana, vols 1–24, including Paterson's typed notes with indexes; the journals
(7 vols) of William Blacker (1777–1855), including local notes and jottings with an
account of the Battle of the Diamond (1795); and manuscripts and illustrated
poems of George Russell (Æ, 1867–1935). Of special genealogical interest are the
Ordnance Survey maps (1834) for Counties Tyrone and Armagh, a printed copy of
Griffith's Valuation for County Armagh and the Paterson Collection.

LOCATION
On the Mall, an urban parkland in the centre of Armagh.

ARMAGH DIOCESAN ARCHIVES
See CARDINAL TOMÁS Ó FIAICH MEMORIAL LIBRARY AND ARCHIVE, Armagh

ARMAGH OBSERVATORY

College Hill
ARMAGH, BT61 9DG
Northern Ireland

TELEPHONE: (028) 3752 2928; FAX: (028) 3752 7174
E-mail: jmf@srm.ac.uk
Website: star.arm.ac.uk, climate.arm.ac.uk
HOURS
M–F, 9.00am–5.00pm; closed bank holidays

ACCESS AND SERVICES
Publicly funded, non-circulating library and archives open to researchers by
appointment; advance notice to Librarian required. Stacks open except for special
collections. Collection catalogued on cards; printed catalogue for part of collection
also available. Textbook collection of some 3,000 books listed in Microsoft Access
database for in-house use. Access to library free, but charges may be made for use of
library or services at Librarian's discretion. See website for activities and programmes.

CONTACT
John McFarland, Librarian

DESCRIPTION
The Armagh Observatory was founded in 1790 by Archbishop Richard Robinson,
Church of Ireland Primate, who also founded the Armagh Public Library. It
continues to function as an important player in astronomical research, and its library
and archives, housed in the observatory's original Georgian mansion, seek to
maintain a centralised Northern Ireland collection of astronomical works.

HOLDINGS
The library and archives hold approximately 3,000 books, 5,000 photographs, 200
linear feet of manuscripts, 50 periodical subscriptions and a very strong collection of
some 20,000 journal volumes. In addition to astronomy, the library has strong
holdings in mathematics, physics, astrophysics, climate and climate change. The
archives contain documents relating to the administration of the observatory,
observations, meteorological records, personal papers and astronomical drawings.
Among special collections of significance are: a collection of historical instruments,
the manuscripts of J.L.E. Dreyer, the papers of J.A. Hamilton, the papers of T.R.
Robinson and the T.R. Robinson (1792–1882) Collection of Rare and Antiquarian
Books (200 vols). A more detailed list of holdings can be found on the RASCAL
(Research and Special Collections Available Locally) website: www.rascal.ac.uk.

LOCATION
Close to city centre, in main observatory building. Limited free parking.

ARMAGH PUBLIC LIBRARY

43 Abbey Street
ARMAGH, BT61 7DY
Northern Ireland

TELEPHONE: (028) 3752 3142; FAX: (028) 3752 4177
E-mail: armroblib@aol.com
Website: www.armaghrobinsonlibrary.org

HOURS
M–F, 10.00am–1.00pm, 2.00pm–4.00pm; or by appointment; closed bank holidays

ACCESS AND SERVICES
Private, non-circulating library, open to the public. No fee for casual visits, but donations appreciated. Fee applies for guided tours as follows: 1–24 people, £2 per head; 25 or more people, set fee of £50. Disabled access facilities available. Advance notice for specific research requests preferred. Fees for photocopying services. Pencils only; laptops and cameras with permission of the Keeper. No bags allowed. Computer catalogue for book collection; printed catalogue for manuscript collection. Publications of interest include: James Dean, *Catalogue of Manuscripts in the Public Library of Armagh* (1928) and Colin McKelvie, 'Early English Books in Armagh Public Library: a Short-Title Catalogue of Books Printed Before 1641', *Irish Booklore* 3, 91–103.

CONTACT
Keeper (position currently vacant)
Ms Carol Conlin, Assistant Keeper

DESCRIPTION
The Armagh Public Library, also known as the Robinson Library, was founded in 1771 by Archbishop Richard Robinson, Church of Ireland Primate, who also founded the Armagh Observatory. It is housed in a late eighteenth century classical revival building.

HOLDINGS
The library houses some 35,000 volumes, including Archbishop Robinson's personal collection of early printed books on history, canon and civil law, heraldry, literature, medicine, philosophy, religion, theology and travel. The Robinson Collection is fully integrated into the main collection, which has been enhanced over the past two centuries chiefly by other clerical collections. In recent times the library has concentrated on ecclesiastical history, St Patrick and Jonathan Swift. Book highlights include incunabula, Colgan's *Acta Sanctorum Hiberniae* (1645), a 'Breeches Bible' and a first edition of *Gulliver's Travels*, with marginal emendations in Swift's own hand. The Manuscript Collection includes medieval and early modern European items, many of Irish interest, especially concerning lands and tithes records. Other collection highlights include: a fine map collection, a collection of engravings known as the Rokeby Collection and Archbishop Marcus Gervais Beresford's collection of Irish artefacts.

LOCATION
Near city centre, close to St Patrick's Church of Ireland Cathedral. Ample free parking available at cathedral.

CARDINAL TOMÁS Ó FIAICH MEMORIAL LIBRARY AND ARCHIVE

15 Moy Road
ARMAGH, BT61 7LY
Northern Ireland

TELEPHONE: (028) 3752 2981; FAX: (028) 3751 1944
E-mail: eolas@ofiaich.ie, kieran.mcconville@ni-libraries.net
Website: www.ofiaich.ie

HOURS
M–F, 9.30am–5.00pm; closed bank holidays

ACCESS AND SERVICES
Free and open to public with full disabled access facilities. Laptops permitted. Free
internet access. Library hosts annual series of lectures and seminars relating to Irish
history, literature and Church history. Also hosts Armagh Diocesan Historical
Society, whose journal, *Seanchas Ard Mhacha* (1954–present), is published annually.
COFLA holds digitised Roman Catholic church records for the Archdiocese of
Armagh and offers an expert genealogy service. It also offers a limited Irish language
service.

CONTACT
Kieran McConville MA, Librarian

DESCRIPTION
The Ó Fiaich Library opened in 1999 and is named in memory of the late Cardinal
Tomás Ó Fiaich (1923–90), churchman and scholar, who was Archbishop of
Armagh and Catholic Primate of All Ireland (1977–90). It seeks to collect and
promote research in areas that were of special academic and cultural interest to the
late Cardinal. COFLA is in partnership with UCD SCHOOL OF HISTORY AND
ARCHIVES, Dublin, and the Ó Cleirigh Institute.

HOLDINGS
The library houses a collection of some 20,000 books, 450 journal titles,
manuscripts, photographs, recordings, art and artefacts. Among its major archives
are: the personal library and papers of Cardinal Tomás Ó Fiaich; the papers of the
Archbishops of Armagh from Richard Reilly (1786–1818) to John D'Alton
(1946–63); Roman Catholic parish registers for Armagh Archdiocese (all of County
Armagh and parts of Counties Tyrone, Louth and Londonderry); the Micheline
Kearney Walsh Overseas Archive; the papers of Fr Laurence P. Murray (d. 1941); the
papers of Fr Louis O'Kane (d. 1973); the papers of Sister Sarah Clarke; and the
papers of Mgr Raymond Murray.

LOCATION
Library entrance located on Moy Road (A29), to the rear of St Patrick's Roman
Catholic Cathedral, within easy walking distance of that building. Parking available.

ARMAGH RECORDS CENTRE

See CARDINAL TÓMAS Ó FIAICH MEMORIAL LIBRARY AND ARCHIVE,
Armagh

IRISH AND LOCAL STUDIES LIBRARY
See SELB IRISH AND LOCAL STUDIES LIBRARY, Armagh

QUEEN'S UNIVERSITY BELFAST LIBRARY, ARMAGH CAMPUS
Note: The Armagh campus was closed in August 2005, and its library, including the extensive private library of Cardinal Cahal Daly, was transferred to Queen's University Belfast Library.

ROBINSON LIBRARY
See ARMAGH PUBLIC LIBRARY, Armagh

SELB IRISH AND LOCAL STUDIES LIBRARY

39c Abbey Street
ARMAGH, BT61 7EB
Northern Ireland

TELEPHONE: (028) 3752 7851; FAX (028) 3752 7127
E-mail: irishandlocalstudies.selb@ni-libraries.net
Website: www.selb.org

HOURS
(under review)
M, W, F, 9.30am–1.00pm, 2.00pm–5.00pm; Tu, 2.00pm–5.00pm; Th, 9.30am–1.00pm, 2.00pm–8.00pm

ACCESS AND SERVICES
Shares accommodation with Armagh Integrated College, the Centre for Cross Border Studies and the Secretariat for North–South Ministerial Council at old Armagh City Hospital site. Entrance at rear of car park and access to Reading Room via lift or stairs. Visitors welcome. A section of material most used is on open access in Reading Room; remainder held in adjoining rooms and on floor below. There are five reader/printers for viewing microforms collection, housed in designated room. Photocopying facilities and ten PCs with internet access available for public use. Individual study carrels can be booked for specified periods.

CONTACT
Mary T. McVeigh, Irish and Local Studies Librarian. E-mail: mary.mcveigh@ni-libraries.net

DESCRIPTION
Established by the Southern Education and Library Board in the late 1970s, the library's policy has been to collect material on all aspects of Irish life and learning from earliest times to the present day, with particular emphasis on the area covered by the Southern Board (i.e. County Armagh, South Down and East Tyrone) and neighbouring counties (Louth, Cavan and Monaghan) in the Republic.

HOLDINGS
The library holds an extensive collection of books, journals, maps, photographs and microforms. Its newspaper collection includes local, provincial and national papers as well as some devoted to specific interests, e.g. *The Irish Builder* and *The Irish Citizen* (a women's suffrage paper). Its microforms include Board of Guardian minutes for Armagh, Banbridge, Cookstown and Newry; the 1901 census for County Armagh; the Linen Hall Collection of political periodicals, 1966–89; reports of the Commissioners of National Education in Ireland, 1834–1920; a selection of Dublin Castle records including those on anti-government organisations, 1882–1921; and some county inspectors' monthly reports for the same period. It also holds the Francis Crossle manuscripts relating to local families and the history of the Newry area, plus a collection of eighteenth and early nineteenth century pamphlets devoted primarily to contemporary economic, political and religious issues.

LOCATION
Near city centre, at old City Hospital site. Entrance from main car park.

CRAIGAVON MUSEUM SERVICES – PHILIP B. WILSON LIBRARY

Waterside House, Oxford Island, Annaloiste Road
CRAIGAVON, COUNTY ARMAGH, BT66 6NJ
Northern Ireland

TELEPHONE: (028) 3834 1635; FAX: (028) 3834 1331
E-mail: museum@craigavon.gov.uk
Website: www.craigavonmuseum.com

HOURS
By appointment

CONTACT
Paul Henry, Library/Administrative Officer

DESCRIPTION
Craigavon Museum Services reflects the history of the South Lough Neagh area, where the new city of Craigavon is situated, along with the towns of Portadown and Lurgan. The museum collection is based on the social, economic and industrial heritage of the area, and in particular the local canal systems and inland waterways. The museum runs the Philip B. Wilson Library.

HOLDINGS
The Philip B. Wilson Library houses three main reference collections totalling around 4,000 volumes. Topics included are agriculture, military history, crafts, architecture, transportation and church history. The library also holds the collections of the Ulster Quarterly Meeting of the Religious Society of Friends, which dates from the mid-1600s to the late 1900s and includes obituaries, journals, biographies and travels in ministry. In addition, there is a Methodist book collection containing volumes relating to the history of Methodism in Ireland and the writings and teachings of John Wesley.

LOCATION
Off junction 10 on the MI motorway.

COUNTY CARLOW

CARLOW CENTRAL LIBRARY

Tullow Street
CARLOW
Ireland

TELEPHONE: (059) 917 0094; FAX: (059) 914 0548
E-mail: library@carlowcoco.ie
Website: www.carlow.ie

HOURS
M–F, 9.45am–5.30pm and Tu, Th, 6.30pm–8.30pm; Sa, 9.45am–1.00pm

ACCESS AND SERVICES
Visitors welcome. Membership required for borrowing privileges. ID required for application. Photocopying services available for a modest fee. Free internet access.

CONTACT
Thomas King, County Librarian

DESCRIPTION
Carlow County Library operates branches in Carlow, Muine Bheag (Bagenalstown) and Tullow.

HOLDINGS
The Local Studies Collection is housed in the Carlow branch. This collection includes the Jackson, Bruen and Tyndall Collections, and the Baggot Papers, Burton Papers and Vigors Papers. It also includes an extensive newspaper collection on microfilm and/or hard copy. Newspapers held include: *Nationalist and Leinster Times*, September 1883–December 2004 (microfilm), 1981–present (hard copy); *Carlow People*, 1997–present (hard copy); *Carlow Sentinel*, 1832–1920 (microfilm); *Carlow Morning Post*, 1818–November 1822, 1828–January 1835 (microfilm); *Carlow Post*, 1853–78 (microfilm); *Carlow Independent*, 1879–June 1882 (microfilm); *Leinster Independent*, 26 December 1834–18 April 1840 (microfilm); *Leinster Reformer*, 1840–1 (hard copy); *Carlow Standard*, 2 January–19 April 1832 (microfilm); *Carlow Vindicator*, 1892 (microfilm); *Carlow Weekly News*, 27 March 1858–24 October 1863 (microfilm); *Finn's Leinster Journal*, 1767–1806 (microfilm); *Leinster Journal*, 1807–12 (microfilm); *Irish Times*, 1965–August 2005 (microfilm),

May 2002–present (hard copy). Map holdings include: Down Survey barony and civil parish maps with terriers of County Carlow, 1654; Ordnance Survey six inch maps for County Carlow, 1840 and 1879; Ordnance Survey large scale (five foot) town maps: Carlow, Muine Bheag, Tullow, Leighlinbridge, 1873; Archaeological Survey maps with index volume of County Carlow (Office of Public Works), 1986. Other sources, especially of genealogical interest, include: tithe applotment books for County Carlow (*c.* 1830); *Griffith's Valuation* for County Carlow and valuation maps, 1853; Carlow Poor Law Union minute books, 1845–1923; census of population for30 County Carlow, 1901 (complete records); census of population for County Carlow, 1911 (complete records); folklore – Carlow Schools Folklore Manuscripts on microfilm 1937–8; and local directories, including a range of *Thom's Directory* and others.

Please note that microfilm resources can also be consulted by prior arrangement at the new branch library in Tullow: Tullow Civic Offices and Library, The New Link Road, Tullow, County Carlow. Telephone: (059) 913 6299; fax (059) 915 2156.

LOCATION
Town centre.

CARLOW GENEALOGY PROJECT
Note: Closed since early 2005. Future unknown at time of publication.

COUNTY CAVAN

BAILIEBORO LIBRARY

Market Square
BAILIEBORO, COUNTY CAVAN
Ireland

TELEPHONE: (042) 966 5779
E-mail: bailieborolibrary@hotmail.com, cavancountylibrary@eircom.net
Website: www.iol.ie/~libcounc/cavan

HOURS
M, W, F–Sa, 10.30am–5.15pm; Tu, Th, 1.30pm–8.30pm

ACCESS AND SERVICES
Visitors welcome. Free membership. Advance notice preferred and ID required.
Disabled access facilities on ground level, with immediate plans to install a lift to
make library fully accessible. No borrowing privileges for non-members. Photocopier
available. Free access to internet and computer facilities. Entire collection automated
and catalogued. Planned activities throughout the year, including art and creative
writing workshops, lectures, exhibitions, readings and annual Children's Book
Festival in October.

CONTACT
Fiona Burke, Senior Library Assistant. E-mail: fburke@cavancoco.ie

DESCRIPTION
Former market house converted to a library in 1992. The system is operated by
Cavan County Council Library Services.

HOLDINGS
The library houses a book stock of some 9,000 volumes, with a good local history
collection, including a copy of *Griffith's Valuation* for most of County Cavan, and an
extensive reference service.

LOCATION
Town centre.

CAVAN COUNTY LIBRARY

Central Library and Heritage Centre, Farnham Street
CAVAN
Ireland

TELEPHONE: (049) 433 1799; FAX: (049) 433 1384
E-mail: cavancountylibrary@eircom.net
Website: www.iol.ie/~libcounc/cavan

HOURS
M, W, F–Sa, 10.30am–5.15pm; Tu, Th, 10.30am–8.30pm

ACCESS AND SERVICES
Visitors welcome. Disabled access. Photocopiers, microform readers/printers and free
internet access available. Coffee shop.

CONTACT
Josephine Brady, County Librarian

DESCRIPTION
The library is the central library in the county's 12 library system. Of these, the
Cavan, Cootehill and Bailieboro libraries operate six days per week. The system is
operated by Cavan County Council Library Services.

In autumn 2003 construction started on a new purpose built library and
heritage centre on Farnham Street that is scheduled to open in 2006. The ground
floor will offer the spacious, state of the art Central Library, which will include a
local studies section designed to ensure controlled access and long term conservation
of the collection. Integral to the new library will be an events space measuring more
than 65 square metres to cater for art exhibitions, recitals, concerts, dance
workshops, lectures and readings. The new building is designed to centralise and
integrate delivery of key research services. In addition to the Central Library, it will
accommodate the Local Authority Staff and Elected Members Library, the County
Arts Office, the County Heritage Office and the Cavan County Archive. The
County Cavan Genealogical Research Centre will also be integrated into the new
facility, though it will continue to use its existing facility at Cana House for some
services (*See* following entry). Tourist information for County Cavan will also be
provided as part of the one stop service offered by the new library and heritage
centre.

HOLDINGS
The library houses a strong local history collection, approaching 4,000 volumes,
including many eighteenth and nineteenth century books on Cavan Town and
County Cavan; maps, including the 1835 Ordnance Survey for County Cavan, the
Cavan–Leitrim Railway and the south-western section of Farnham Estate; important
holdings of social and genealogical concern, including Cavan Assizes, 1807–51,
which record individuals charged with crimes and the verdicts rendered; eighteenth
and nineteenth century legal documents, such as leases, rentals and wills for County
Cavan, account and fee books and inspectors' reports from Bailieboro Model School,
1860s–1900s; minute books for the Board of Guardians (1839–1921) and the Rural
District Council (1899–1925); diaries, including the diary of Randal McCollum,
Presbyterian minister, Shercock, County Cavan, describing social conditions in

Cavan, 1861–71; photographs and postcards; and the correspondence and papers of various local personages. There is an extensive microfilm and photocopy collection of materials relating to County Cavan, especially rich in family history sources, newspaper holdings and directories. Genealogical sources also include the 1821, 1901 and 1911 censuses, *Griffith's Valuation* and tithe applotment books. Recently the former Catholic Bishop of Kilmore, Dr Francis J. McKiernan, donated to Cavan County Council his entire book collection, which is particularly strong in the area of local history. The library also acquired the Farnham Archive Collection, which will become available to the public in the near future.

A digitisation project to scan photographs and historical journals is under way.

LOCATION
Town centre. Limited on-street parking available; car parks nearby.

COUNTY CAVAN GENEALOGICAL RESEARCH CENTRE

Cavan Central Library, Farnham Street
CAVAN
Ireland

TELEPHONE: (049) 436 1094; FAX: (049) 433 1494
E-mail: canahous@iol.ie
Website: www.irishroots.net

HOURS
M–F, 9.00am–5.00pm; closed Christmas, Easter and public holidays

ACCESS AND SERVICES
Building of database is continuing at Cana House, while reception, gift shop and research service will be moving to first floor of new Central Library (due to open in 2006). Visitors welcome and disabled facilities available. Enquiries also welcome by telephone, fax, e-mail or post. Admission free but fees payable for genealogical research.

Fees
Single search. A search will be made for one or more baptism/birth, marriage, census record or whatever source is requested. Photocopy of the record provided, if available. Fee €25.

Assessment report. Enquirers can become registered clients for whom an assessment is carried out, which involves thorough examination of database along with research of non-computerised sources in order to discover all information held in library regarding their ancestor or ancestors. When assessment is complete, they will receive a report detailing all information that has been located and fees involved, based on single/source prices listed hereunder. Fee €45.

Partial report. On receipt of assessment report clients may decide to purchase none, some or all records located, or to purchase some immediately and others at a later stage. Photocopies of records provided, if available. Having purchased some records, research results may trigger more information requests or clients may be able to supply more information to enable further research.

Full bound report. If sufficient information is located a bound report may be recommended, which includes analysis of all information discovered, photocopies of all entries where available and a short history of area or areas involved. Bound reports vary in price depending on extent but generally start at €300 and are usually 50 to over 100 pages long.

Single Source Price List
The following fees apply for the major sources as laid down by the Irish Family History Foundation. Cheques, bank drafts, Visa and Mastercard accepted.

Civil Records
Single birth, marriage or death record, €25; birth records per household, €50.

Church Records
Single baptism record, €25; baptism records per household, €50; single marriage or death record, €25.

Census Records
1821 census per household, €25; 1901 census per household, €25; 1911 census per household, €25.

Land Records
Griffith's Valuation per townland, €15; Griffith's maps, €7; tithe applotment books per townland, €20.

CONTACT
Mary Sullivan, Manager
Concepta McGovern, Senior Researcher

DESCRIPTION
County Cavan Genealogical Research Centre was established in 1988 to build a database of all sources of a genealogical nature that are known to exist for County Cavan. The centre is the Irish Family History Foundation's designated family history centre for County Cavan and is part of the Irish Genealogical Project, an island-wide project to computerise all the major Irish genealogical sources.

HOLDINGS
There are now over one million records in the Cavan database, mostly pre-1920, and the earliest church records date from 1702. The database, which is growing daily, comprises church records of baptisms, marriages and burials; civil records of births, deaths and marriages, which commenced for the whole country in 1864; 1821, 1841, 1901 and 1911 census records; pre- and post-Famine land records, occupational and commercial directories; some military records; gravestone inscriptions; and numerous other sources of a genealogical nature applicable to County Cavan. There is no uniform starting date for church records. Each parish and denomination has different starting dates depending on the history and circumstances of each. For example, the records of the Church of Ireland parish of Kilmore begin in 1702 but the records for the Roman Catholic parish of Larah do not commence until 1876. The centre also holds parish histories, journals, microfilm copies of newspapers, some school registers, rent rolls and other genealogical sources. The information that the centre can provide depends on what information enquirers can provide and what records survive for the particular parish/area. For example, the 1821 census of Ireland, which, for most of the country, was destroyed in the Public Records Office fire in 1922, survives for 16 County Cavan parishes. The centre has a small reference library, which includes books, journals, manuscripts and maps.

LOCATION
Town centre. Car parks and limited on-street parking nearby. Cana House dates
back to around 1810 and is located at the back of St Felim's Boys' School on
Farnham Street. It is a five minute walk from the town's main street, and the centre
is signposted at the gateway entrance, which it shares with the school.

COUNTY CLARE

CLARE HERITAGE AND GENEALOGICAL RESEARCH CENTRE

Church Street
COROFIN, COUNTY CLARE
Ireland

TELEPHONE: (065) 683 7955; FAX: (065) 683 7540
E-mail: clareheritage@eircom.net
Website: www.clareroots.com

HOURS
M–F, 9.00am–5.30pm

ACCESS AND SERVICES
Clare Heritage is a not for profit, fee based genealogical research centre offering a professional service to persons wishing to trace their Clare ancestry. A fee of €165 (or equivalent) covers a preliminary report and administrative costs and includes an initial search of the source material that the centre holds, e.g. parish registers, land records, Census returns, civil records. Fee of €385 (or equivalent) may be required to complete a full search and covers all expenses and time expended by the centre. Fee will not exceed €385 (or equivalent) without prior consultation and advice as to probability of positive results. Application can be made online with a credit card.

CONTACT
Antoinette O'Brien, Coordinator

DESCRIPTION
The Clare Heritage and Genealogical Research Centre was founded in 1982 by the late Dr Ignatius (Naoise) Cleary. It is a member of the Irish Family History Foundation, the coordinating body for a network of government approved genealogical research centres in the Republic of Ireland and Northern Ireland, which have computerised tens of millions of Irish ancestral records of different types. The Clare centre now holds data on just over 500,000 people born in County Clare during the nineteenth century and into the middle of the twentieth century. Common surnames in County Clare include: McMahon, McNamara, O'Brien, Moloney, Ryan, Kelly, McInerney, O'Connor, Keane, O'Halloran, Hogan, Burke, Murphy, Lynch and Walsh. The main towns and villages include: Ennis, Kilrush, Kilkee, Miltown Malbay, Ennistymon, Ballyvaughan, Corofin, Sixmilebridge,

Newmarket-on-Fergus, Killaloe, Tulla, Scariff, Feakle, Quin, Kilfenora, Lisdoonvarna, Liscannor, Broadford, Kildysart, Mullagh and Quilty.

HOLDINGS
The centre has indexed all available Roman Catholic parish registers (pre-1900 baptismal and marriage records) for the 47 Clare parishes. The age and condition of these records vary from parish to parish; some records date back to 1802. Because civil recording of births, marriages and deaths does not begin until 1864, parish records remain the main source of genealogical data in Ireland. Also available are: all available Church of Ireland records; tithe applotment books, 1820s; *Griffith's Valuation*, 1855; 1901 census; civil records – marriages and deaths, 1864–1995, and births, 1900–50; New South Wales archives, 1848–69 (6,000 assisted emigrants entries, R. Reid); *Clare Journal*, 1779–1900; birth, marriage and death notices; and tombstone inscriptions from approximately 80 Clare graveyards. Access is also available to: nineteenth century workhouse records; reports on some convict trials; many Clare wills; Ordnance Survey maps showing parish and townland boundaries; and a reference library which includes publications and lists on landed gentry, Irish surnames, histories of County Clare and its parishes and various family histories.

LOCATION
In the village of Corofin, eight miles north of Ennis.

CLARE COUNTY ARCHIVES SERVICE

Clare County Council, 1 Bindon Court, Harmony Row
ENNIS, COUNTY CLARE
Ireland

TELEPHONE: (065) 684 6414; FAX: (065) 682 0882
E-mail: archivesrecords@clarecoco.ie
Website: www.clarelibrary.ie/eolas/archives/archives_index

HOURS
By appointment: contact Archivist

ACCESS AND SERVICES
Visitors welcome. Material can be requested and will be made available to researchers through Clare County Library's Local Studies Centre. One day's notice required for production of material. As material is processed and listed it will be made available for public inspection.

CONTACT
Róisín Berry, Archivist

DESCRIPTION
Clare County Archives was established in 1999 and provides an integrated cultural and information service to researchers at home and abroad. The service seeks to maintain the highest preservation standards possible for the collections in its care while seeking to maximise public knowledge of and access to archives.
The Archives Service is county-wide and in addition to local authority records, it collects other material relating to the county including: private papers; solicitors' papers; architectural drawings, maps and plans; estate papers; photographic collections; and records of academic, social and economic institutions.

HOLDINGS
Local Authority Archives
The service is custodian of a wide range of archival series and includes the records of a number of predecessor groups of the present local government system including the Grand Juries, Poor Law Unions, Rural District Councils and Boards of Public Health and Assistance.

The Archives Service currently holds the archives of Clare County Council, Kilkee Town Commissioners and Kilrush Urban District Council. It contains Board of Guardian minute books for Ennis, Ennistymon, Kilrush and Corofin Unions and Rural District Council minute books for Corofin, Ennis, Ennistymon, Kildysart, Tulla and Scariff Rural District Councils.

Non-Local Authority Archives
Clare County Archives Service is also committed to collecting archival material of private origin thus enriching knowledge of the history of the county. The archives of Our Lady's Hospital, Ennis, were acquired in 2002 in a joint project with the Mid-Western Health Board. The hospital records reveal a microcosm of the social and economic conditions pertaining in Ennis and in County Clare and for this reason the archives are a valuable part of the county's history.

The papers of Roger Casement were transferred to the archives in October 2003. The collection contains mainly correspondence as well as receipts, essays, leaflets and newspaper cuttings. Of particular interest, however, are his letters, which provide us with a glimpse of the Irish-German background to the Easter Rising and Ireland's claim to political independence.

The Griffith Family Papers document the lives of the family of Rev Julius Henry Griffith, who served as Rector of Drumcliffe Union (Killaloe) from 1884. The family lived in the Rectory at 1 Bindon Street in Ennis, County Clare. The papers include correspondence, birth and marriage certificates, financial material, diaries, photographs and press cuttings, and include a family member's eyewitness account of the sinking of the battleship HMS *Victoria* in the Lebanon on 22 June 1893, with the loss of hundreds of lives.

LOCATION
Access through Local Studies Centre. *See* following entry.

CLARE COUNTY LIBRARY – LOCAL STUDIES CENTRE

The Manse, Harmony Row
ENNIS, COUNTY CLARE
Ireland

TELEPHONE: (065) 684 6271; FAX: (065) 684 2462
E-mail: mailbox@clarelibrary.ie
Website: www.clarelibrary.ie/eolas/library/local-studies/locstudi1.htm

HOURS
M, 9.30am–1.00pm, 2.00pm–5.30pm; Tu–F, 9.30am–1.00pm, 2.00pm–5.00pm; Sa, 10.00am–2.00pm

ACCESS AND SERVICES
Visitors welcome. Disabled access, though public restroom is not wheelchair accessible. Fees for photocopying and microfilm prints. Entire collection catalogued

online. In addition, there is a separate, extensive card index (not online) arranged by subject, people and place. Free internet access.

Publications programme of Clare County Library and Clasp Press has issued more than a dozen titles since 1995. These are still available in print and available from Clasp Press, Library Headquarters, Mill Road, Ennis, County Clare. Titles include: *Folklore of Clare*, *Archaeology of the Burren*, *The Clare Anthology*, *The Stranger's Gaze*, *A Handbook to Lisdoonvarna*, *The Antiquities of County Clare*, *Kilrush Union Minute Books*, *Sable Wings Over the Land*, *County Clare: a History and Topography*, *Two Months at Kilkee*, *Poverty Before the Famine*, *Memories of an Islander: a Life on Scattery and Beyond* and *Family and Community in Ireland*, 3rd edition.

CONTACT
Local Studies Librarian

DESCRIPTION
The Local Studies Centre is part of Clare County Library and focuses on material of Irish interest in all subject areas, with special reference to County Clare. There is a separate archives department, Clare County Archives Service. *See* preceding entry.

HOLDINGS
The Irish Collection houses books (some 8,000) and periodicals relating to Ireland. A separate Clare Collection (some 2,000 titles) contains newspapers, photographs, manuscripts, microfilm and maps relating specifically to County Clare. Journals of specific relevance to Clare include *The North Munster Antiquarian Journal*, *Dal gCais*, *The Other Clare*, *Molua*, *The Clare Association Yearbook* and *Sliabh Aughty*. Local parish and sporting magazines are also collected. The following local newspapers are available: Dunboyne Collection of newspaper clippings, 1824–73; *Ennis Chronicle and Clare Advertiser*, 1788–1831 (incomplete); *Clare Freeman and Ennis Gazette*, February 1853–January 1884; *Clare Journal and Ennis Advertiser*, 1778–1917 (incomplete); *Limerick Reporter*, 1845–52; *Celtic Times*, 1887; *Clare Champion*, 1903–present; *Clare People*, 1977–80; *County Express*, 1979–present; *Ennis Express*, 1979–82; *Sunday Tribune*, 1983–7; *Irish Times*, 1859–70, 1916–22, 1987–present; *Saturday Record*, July 1898–September 1936; *Clare Independent and Tipperary Catholic Times*, 1877–85. A recent newspaper acquisition is the *Freeman's Journal* (1763–1805). Newspaper holdings are added to each year as resources permit. A new current newspaper, the *Clare People*, was launched in 2005.

The collection of photographs contains approximately 4,000 prints of Clare scenes. The Lawrence Collection (1870–1914) is the largest in the archive. Other collections include the Westropp Collection (1900), the McNamara Collection (1910), Irish Tourist Association Survey (1943), and the Bluett (1940s–1960s) and O'Neill (1950s) Collections. Among the special collections are: Schools Folklore Scheme, Twigge Manuscripts; Ordnance Survey field name books; Petworth House Archive (Clare material); Dorothea Lange contact prints; and some estate papers on microfilm. Of special genealogical interest are *Griffith's Valuation*, the 1901 and 1911 censuses; tithe applotment books; first and second editions of Ordnance Survey six inch maps (complete for County Clare) and voter lists. *See also* holdings of Clare County Archives Service. Consult website for a more detailed list of holdings. Two recent microfilm additions are the Church of Ireland parish of Drumcliffe (Ennis) parochial register, 1744–1870 (incomplete) and the old age pension search forms for County Clare from the 1841 and 1851 censuses.

Clare County Library is actively digitising the patrimony of County Clare and making it freely available to all on the internet. Useful links on its website include 'Genealogy', 'Places' and 'History'. The website is a virtual resource which complements the work of the Local Studies Centre and Clare County Library.

LOCATION
Turn left at the end of Abbey Street. Located on the left, beside De Valera Library.

EAST CLARE HERITAGE COMPANY

St Cronan's Church
TUAMGRANEY, COUNTY CLARE
Ireland

TELEPHONE: (061) 921 351, (086) 874 9710
E-mail: eastclareheritage@eircom.net
Website: www.eastclareheritage.com

HOURS
M–F, 10.00am–5.00pm

ACCESS AND SERVICES
Totally voluntary and community based company with charitable status formed in 1989. In 1991 it opened a heritage centre in a tenth century church at Tuamgraney. Entry fees: adults, €4; children, €2, families, €10.

Centre offers fee based genealogical research service for persons interested in tracing East Clare family roots. Fee of €75 for preliminary search of records. In most cases this is all that will be charged. Enquirers notified of any additional costs. Advice freely given on availability of records and possibility of positive results. Applications available through website. The company publishes local histories and newsletters that include genealogical material. Some of the families covered to date in publications are Woods, Reades, Tandys, Logans, Bourchiers, Allens, Tiernans, Huleatts and Bloxams of Mountshannon; Reids, Ringroses, Walnutts and Davises of Scariff; O'Gradys, Bradys, Drews, Parkers and Crottys of Tuamgraney; Goonanes of Whitegate. The company has also set up an O'Grady website at www.gradyhistory.com.

The company provides boat trips and guided tours to Holy Island on Lough Derg from April to September, seven days a week, weather permitting. First crossing 10.00am, last crossing 6.00pm. Duration of tour: one hour. Rates: adults, €8; children, €4; group rates by appointment.

East Clare Heritage has published to date the following books and journals, most of which still available in print and can be ordered directly from the centre or from Gerard Madden at Scariff, County Clare: *Holy Island, Jewel of the Lough* (1990, reprinted 1997, 2003), €7; *For God or King: the History of Mountshannon County Clare 1742–1992* (1993, reprinted 1997), €15; *The Famine Memorial Park, Tuamgraney County Cleer* (1997); *A History of the Great Hunger in the Scariff Workhouse Union from 1839 to 1853*, €10; *A History of Tuamgraney and Scariff since Earliest Times* (2000), €15; *History of the O'Maddens of Hy–Many* (2004), €15; *History of the O'Grady's of County Limerick and County Clare* (2006), €15; and 12 editions of the annual journal *Sliabh Aughty*, containing numerous articles on genealogy and local history, average price €8. DVD on history, folklore, culture and traditions of North-East Clare also available, €20.

CONTACT
Gerard Madden, Secretary

DESCRIPTION
East Clare Heritage Company provides a comprehensive family research facility for East Clare and encourages the publication of family history in its annual journal *Sliabh Aughty*. This journal also contains a brief history and the gravestone inscriptions of an East Clare graveyard. To date most of the graveyards are indexed. The tenth edition of this publication is now being published and all ten editions will be available in disk form soon. The company is headquartered in a church built around 950AD, which is claimed to be the oldest church in continuous use in Ireland, England, Scotland and Wales. This tradition is being maintained and service is held here on the last Sunday of each month throughout the year. The church is built on the site of an earlier monastery founded by St Cronan in the seventh century. The Vikings raided the monastery in 886 and again in 949. Cormac Uí Cillín, the Abbot of Tuamgraney, rebuilt the church and erected a round tower prior to his death in 964. Although no trace of the round tower remains, it has the distinction of being the earliest for which there is a written record. Brian Boru, High King of Ireland (1002–14), repaired the round tower and repaired and enlarged the church. The building operates as a visitor centre during the summer months. It also houses a folk museum. Dr Edward McLysaght, Ireland's foremost family historian, is interred in the grounds of the church. Tuamgraney is also the home town of the novelist Edna O'Brien.

HOLDINGS
In addition to gravestone inscriptions noted above, the company has access to all the standard genealogical reference sources for East Clare, including: *Griffith's Valuation*; tithe applotment books; church and civil records; the 1901 census; Ordnance Survey maps; school registers; numerous deeds and other legal documents. It also has a number of family histories and continues to compile information on families with East Clare connections.

LOCATION
Near the western edge of Lough Derg in County Clare, a 40 minute drive from Shannon Airport.

COUNTY CORK

BANTRY HOUSE

BANTRY, COUNTY CORK
Ireland

TELEPHONE: (027) 50047; FAX: (027) 50795
E-mail: info@bantryhouse.com
Website: www.bantryhouse.com

HOURS
March–October: Su–Sa, 10.00am–6.00pm

ACCESS AND SERVICES
Open to the public for an admission charge. Fee schedule: house, gardens and
French Armada Centre, €10 per person (accompanied children up to 14 years of age
who are not part of a school group admitted free); students and seniors, €8; groups
of 20 or more, €8; school groups, €6; admission to gardens and French Armada
Centre only, €5. Admission to house and grounds free to residents. Accommodation
available (consult website). Archive has been deposited at the Boole Library,
University College Cork.

CONTACT
Bantry House: Egerton Shelswell-White, Owner
Archives: Carol Quinn, Archivist, University College Cork. E-mail: c.quinn@ucc.ie

DESCRIPTION
Bantry House has been in the possession of the White family since 1739 and was the
seat of the four Earls of Bantry (1816–91). The house contains furniture, paintings
and other *objets d'art* collected for the most part by the Second Earl of Bantry, who
was also responsible for laying out the formal gardens.

HOLDINGS
This archive contains the formal records of the legal, financial and general
administration of Bantry House and Estate, and also the more personal records
relating to the lives and personalities of the White family who have lived in Bantry
House for over 200 years. These documents contain much invaluable social
information about the White family and the circles in which they moved, as well as
records relating to the tenants who occupied and worked the estate. For further

details, consult UCC Archives website. Please note that this collection is not yet fully processed and is, therefore, not currently accessible.

LOCATION
In Bantry Town, overlooking Bantry Bay, 60 miles south-west of Cork City.

CORK ARCHIVES INSTITUTE

City Archives Building, Great William O'Brien Street, Blackpool
CORK
Ireland

TELEPHONE: (021) 427 7809; FAX: (021) 427 4668
E-mail: archivist@corkcity.ie
Website: www.corkarchives.ie

HOURS
Tu–F, 10.00am–1.00pm, 2.30pm–5.00pm

ACCESS AND SERVICES
By appointment only, with at least one week's notice if possible. Application form for permission to read records is available in PDF format on the institute's website. Photocopying service available. The institute is unable to undertake genealogical research on behalf of the public.

CONTACT
Brian McGee, Archivist

DESCRIPTION
Cork Archives Institute is the official repository for the local authority records of Cork City and County and is co-funded by Cork City Council, Cork County Council and University College Cork. The institute acquires, preserves and makes available local archives including those from local private sources such as societies, businesses, families and individuals. Contents are related mainly to the history of Cork and consist of records, manuscripts, plans and drawings and photographs, identified as worthy of permanent preservation because of their historical or evidential value.

HOLDINGS
Cork Archives Institute holds one of the finest collections of local archives in Ireland. Collections include the archives of current and former local authorities such as Cork City Council, Cork County Council, Town Government for Youghal 1609–1965, Poor Law Unions for most of County Cork, and Rural and Urban District Councils.

As well as complete sets of Boards of Guardian minute books of for most of the Poor Law Unions in the county, 1839–1924 (except Fermoy and Schull), the archive has the most complete collection of workhouse admission registers in the Republic of Ireland. Some of these archives also include pupil registers for the workhouse 'national' school (in the case of Cork) and books recording deaths and births in workhouses. A selective list of holdings by category follows:

Poor Law Unions
Cork Poor Law Union: workhouse 'indoor relief' or admission registers, 1840–1920 with indexes from 1853; record of death books, 1853–1931; pupil registers (male)

for workhouse 'national' school, 1873–1904. Kinsale Poor Law Union: indoor registers, 1841–1917; admission and discharge books, 1845–1925; pauper discharge books, 1855–84; death record book, 1842–99; register of patients in Fever Hospital, 1849–50. Midleton Poor Law Union: indoor registers, 1841–1923; birth register, 1844–1930. Youghal Poor Law Union: indoor register, 1848–51; poor rate books, 1852–1900. For Youghal there are also town rate books, 1833 and voter registers for parts of the county from 1858.

School Records
There are holdings for Crosshaven and Templebreedy National Schools, 1880–1972, Ballyphehane National School, 1959–95, and a massive collection of approximately 120 volumes for Cork District Model School including registers and roll books, 1865–1988.

Business, Estate and Society Records
Business records include those of Beamish and Crawford Brewery, Cork Distillers, Cork Butter Market, Cork Gas Company, R. and H. Hall corn merchants, Sunbeam Wolsey textile manufacturers, Cork Steam Ship Company, Ogilvie and Moore provisioners and Hickey and Byrne printers. Personal papers include those of politicians, soldiers, civic leaders and literary figures such as Richard Dowden, Mayor of Cork; Liam de Roiste, TD; Seamus Fitzgerald, politician; Liam Ó Buachalla, cultural activist; Geraldine Cummins, author and playwright; Siobhán Lankford, soldier; and Denny Lane, patriot, poet and businessman. There is a wide variety of landed estate papers, such as those of: the Colthurst family, Blarney; the Newenham family, South Cork; the Courtenay family, Midleton and the Earls of Bandon. The Ryan-Purcell Collection is of particular interest because as well as being a land owner, the person for whom it is named acted as agent for a number of estates in North Cork. Also held are records of some trade unions, clubs, societies, religious organisations and schools, including Cork Workers' Council, Cork Typographical Union, Cork Presbyterian Congregation, Cork Grafton Club, the Sick Poor Society, Cork Theatre and Cork District Model School.

LOCATION
In Blackpool, about a 20 minute walk from the city centre. Parking not provided. Bus services to Blarney from the city centre stop at the nearby Watercourse Road. There are currently 12 buses per day within relevant hours.

CORK CITY ANCESTRAL PROJECT

Cork County Library, Model Farm Road
CORK
Ireland

TELEPHONE: (021) 434 6435
E-mail: corkancestry@ireland.com
Website: www.irishroots.net/cork

HOURS
To be confirmed

ACCESS AND SERVICES
Project still in development. Indexing of records only ongoing at present. However,

enquiries may be telephoned or posted to the above number/address. On completion of its indexing project, the centre will offer fee based genealogical research service to persons interested in tracing Cork City family roots.

CONTACT
Karen O'Riordan

DESCRIPTION
The centre is a member of the Irish Genealogical Project, an effort to create a comprehensive genealogical database for all Ireland from a wide variety of sources, including church and state records, vital records, tithe applotment books, *Griffith's Valuation*, the 1901 census and gravestone inscriptions.

HOLDINGS
Indexing of church records for Cork City ongoing.

LOCATION
Cork County Library, near County Hall.

CORK CITY LIBRARIES

Headquarters (Central Library), 57–61 Grand Parade
CORK
Ireland

TELEPHONE: (021) 492 4900; FAX: (021) 427 5684
E-mail: libraries@corkcity.ie
Website: www.corkcitylibraries.ie

HOURS
M–Sa, 10.00am–5.30pm

ACCESS AND SERVICES
Visitors welcome, but borrowing privileges may be restricted. Membership available for a fee. No membership required for use of reference or information facilities: these services provided free of charge except photocopying. Photocopying, fax and public internet workstations available. Exhibitions a regular feature in Central Library and at all local libraries. Cork City Libraries hosts a number of national exhibitions and also exhibitions involving local organisations and groups.

CONTACT
Liam Ronayne, Cork City Librarian
Tina Healy, Assistant Librarian, Reference Library
Kieran Burke/Lucy Stewart, Assistant Librarians, Local Studies Department
Kitty Buckley, Assistant Librarian, Music Library

DESCRIPTION
Cork City Libraries, the library service of Cork City Council, is a resource for all of the people of Cork: a resource for children and young people, a resource for life and learning, a resource for culture and the imagination.
The Central Library, situated on the Grand Parade, houses Adult Lending services, the Children's Library, Music Library, Reference Library and Local Studies Library. Library members can borrow books, audio books on tape and CD, sound recordings of plays, poetry, prose and language learning tapes and CDs. Music

Library members can also borrow music on cassette and CD. The Central Library is open six days per week including lunchtime.

Cork City Library's catalogue of books, CDs and other items in stock is available on the internet at www.corkcitylibraries.ie. Internet access is available to members of the public at a nominal charge in the Central Library and local libraries. The most recent innovation is the 'Cork Past and Present' element of the website, which features digitised images, plans and maps, the history of Patrick Street, bilingual list of street names and place names and much more. Users can access 'Cork Past and Present' directly at www.corkpastandpresent.ie, as well as by going through www.corkcitylibraries.ie.

The library also provides a network of five local libraries around the city – three on the north side of the city, in Hollyhill, Mayfield and at St Mary's Road/Cathedral Cross, and two on the south side, in Douglas and Tory Top (Ballyphehane). A sixth library is expected to open in Bishopstown in 2006.

HOLDINGS
The reference library houses 32,000 books, including directories, encyclopaedias, government publications, yearbooks and dictionaries, Irish interest material, journals, periodicals and Sunday and daily newspapers. Access to the newspaper and journal collection is enhanced by an index, created and added to on a daily basis by library staff, and by online information from databases and the internet and CD-ROMs. The Local Studies Department or Cork Collection contains some 5,700 books on the history, geography, antiquities, archaeology, folklore and culture of Cork City and County. The collection also contains microfilm, a comprehensive local newspaper archive, journals, periodicals, manuscripts, maps and photographs. The Music Library has a stock of 20,000 CDs, DVDs, vinyl records and tapes, in addition to 2,500 scores and 3,000 books. The collection caters for all musical tastes including classical, jazz, light opera, folk, choral, military band music, rock and popular. Audio art tapes, including plays, poetry, prose and audio books, are available. Free membership of the music library is available for registered visually impaired citizens. Listening facilities are available in the library. The lending library contains 45,000 adult books and 14,000 children's books.

LOCATION
City centre.

CORK COUNTY LIBRARY

Library Headquarters, Model Business Park, Model Farm Road
CORK
Ireland

TELEPHONE: (021) 454 6499; FAX: (021) 434 3254
E-mail: corkcountylibrary@corkcoco.ie
Website: www.corkcoco.ie

HOURS
Reference/Local Studies Department: M–F, 9.00am–5.30pm; closed bank holidays
Lending Department: M–F, 9.00am–5.30pm

ACCESS AND SERVICES
Visitors welcome, but appointment recommended for those wishing to avail of

microfilm viewers. Photocopying (subject to copyright regulations), advice and guidance on research available; telephone enquiries welcome, but staffing levels limit ability to engage in correspondence on queries. Public internet workstation available.

CONTACT
Kieran Wyse
Niamh Cronin

DESCRIPTION
The headquarters of Cork County Library provides a public library service throughout the county via a network of 27 branches and five mobile libraries. The Local Studies Department offers a wide range of resources reflecting a broad definition of Cork local studies, which includes areas such as local history, natural history, social studies, planning and genealogy. The department's collection reflects an understanding of local history as encompassing all aspects of life in County Cork, past and present.

HOLDINGS
There is a large collection of printed books in the Local Studies Collection and the Irish Studies Collection. Microfilm holdings include 1901 census returns (Cork City and County), tithe applotment books (Cork) and nineteenth and twentieth century Cork newspapers. Other holdings include *Griffith's Valuation* for Cork City and County.

Primary Sources for Cork Local Studies
Cork County Library's Local Studies Collection includes a number of primary and secondary sources that are key resources for those engaged in local history and genealogical research. In most cases, these resources are available only for consultation at the Model Farm Road Reference Department. Sources are divided into two categories:

Land Tenure and Occupancy
Civil Survey, 1654: survives only for the Barony of Muskerry and for Cork. Provides a description of parishes, quality of soils and names of landed proprietors. Published by the Irish Manuscripts Commission (IMC) in 1942.

Census of Ireland, 1659: This document, edited by Seamus Pender and published by the IMC in 1939, under the headings of County, Baronies and Parishes, gives the names of townlands, tituladoes or principal residents and population figures.

Book of Survey and Distribution, c. 1670: records details of distribution of forfeited lands under the Acts of Settlement and Explanation and gives the names of the landed proprietors in 1641 and 1670. A facsimile copy is held by the library.

Tithe applotment books: comprise a survey of the titheable land in each parish and were compiled between 1823 and 1838. They list only land occupiers; labourers and other landless rural residents are not recorded. In some instances, they include occupiers of small plots on the edges of towns. Microfilm copies of the tithe applotment books for County Cork are held by the library. An index of surnames for each parish is the only finding aid.

Primary Valuation of Tenements (*Griffith's Valuation*), c. 1850: a popular source for local historians and genealogists, these volumes list occupiers of land and houses with acreage in the case of land and valuation in the case of both land and houses. They are published by barony and are further subdivided by parish and townland. A surname index identifying those listed and the townland and parish of occupancy is the principal finding aid. A complete set of the printed volumes is available for reference at the County Library Local Studies Department.

Devon Commission Report: the report of the Commissioners of Inquiry into the state of the law and practice in respect of the occupation of land in Ireland, with minutes of evidence, was published in 1845. A microfiche copy is available at the library.

Miscellaneous
1901 census: the earliest Irish census for which the original household returns survive. It is an invaluable source for the family and social historian. It is arranged by District Electoral Divisions and by townlands or streets within these divisions. The 1901 census returns for Cork City and County are held on microfilm at the County Library (Cork City Library holds microfilm copies of the only other complete census, that of 1911). A fragment of the 1851 census for County Cork survives and covers an area around Kilworth in north-east Cork. Cork County Library holds a copy of the surviving returns.

Census data: though the original returns do not survive, the statistical data derived from censuses from 1813 onwards are accessible and are a useful source of information. The 1871 census statistics for County Cork, for example, give the comparative population figures for each townland and parish in the county for 1841, 1851, 1861 and 1871. These can be used to illustrate the effects of the Famine and emigration at townland and parish level. Cork County Library holds copies of these from 1851 onwards.

Schools Manuscripts Folklore Collection: this collection of material was collected for the Irish Folklore Commission from 1937 to 1939 through the national schools. The material included consists of local folklore and historical traditions collected by schoolchildren from their parents, grandparents and neighbours and written up in copybooks. The quality and value of the material varies from school to school, but it is nevertheless a fascinating and valuable record. The collection for County Cork is available on microfilm at the Reference Department.

A.E. Casey, (compiler), *O'Kief, Coshe Mang, Slieve Lougher and Upper Blackwater in Ireland* (15 vols, 1952–1971): this unique compilation of original sources, newspaper abstracts and other records contains a wealth of useful material, relating primarily to the Blackwater Valley and north Cork region, but also relating to the county at large. Care should be taken in using it, as much of the material was transcribed and is prone to errors in transcription.

Irish Tourist Association (ITA) files for County Cork: around 1939, the ITA commissioned researchers to compile files of local historical material at town and parish level that would be of interest to visitors. Each file contains a synopsis of local history, local tourist attractions, local industries and so forth. Much of the material is copied from secondary sources, but some original material is included. The manuscript collection is accompanied by a collection of 269 photographs, mostly of historic buildings.

LOCATION
Western suburbs of the city.

CORK PUBLIC MUSEUM (MÚSAEM POIBLÍ CHORCAÍ)

Fitzgerald Park
CORK
Ireland

TELEPHONE: (021) 427 0679; FAX: (021) 427 0931
E-mail: museum@corkcity.ie
Website: www.corkcity.ie

HOURS
M–F, 11.00am–1.00pm, 2.15pm–5.00pm (September–May)/2.15pm–6.00pm
(June–August); Sa, 11.00am–1.00pm, 2.15pm–4.00pm
April–September: Su, 3.00pm–5.00pm
Closed bank holiday weekends

ACCESS AND SERVICES
Visitors welcome. Admission free. Museum offers exhibitions and programmes to
the public. Exhibition themes include prehistory Cork and Cork crafts, including
Cork glassware and silverware. The museum also houses an important archives
collection anchored by the Michael Collins Collection. A project to create a
computer database of the museum's collections has been completed and to date over
26,000 objects have been input. Work to create a database of digital images of the
museum's collections is under way. The museum now holds a large archive covering
the 1916–21 War of Independence period, with particular emphasis on County
Cork native Michael Collins and on Thomas MacCurtain and Terence MacSwiney,
first and second Republican Lord Mayors of Cork (both died in office – MacSwiney
by hunger strike in Brixton Prison; MacCurtain killed by police).

CONTACT
Curator

DESCRIPTION
Cork Public Museum has been preserving and exhibiting the region's cultural
heritage since 1910. Recently it expanded its exhibition and storage areas. It is
funded by Cork City Council.

HOLDINGS
The museum houses artefacts and archival material that document the history,
archaeology and industrial life of Cork City and the surrounding area. Of special
interest is the museum's collection of the correspondence of Michael Collins,
donated in July 2000 by Mr Peter Barry, former TD and Minister for Foreign
Affairs. The correspondence between Michael Collins and Kitty Kiernan forms the
largest body of the collection. The collection also contains letters from Harry
Boland, another leading figure in the fight for independence, a friend of Collins and
unsuccessful suitor of Kiernan. There are a small number of letters to Collins from
various individuals, from Collins to Cumann na mBan and to Kiernan from other
individuals.

LOCATION
Fitzgerald Park, off Western Road, along the River Lee.

NATIONAL UNIVERSITY OF IRELAND, CORK (UCC) – BOOLE LIBRARY

University College Cork, College Road
CORK
Ireland

TELEPHONE: (021) 490 2281; FAX: (021) 427 3428
E-mail: library@ucc.ie
Website: booleweb.ucc.ie

HOURS
Consult website for full details of opening hours.
First term
Reading: M–Th, 8.30am–9.45pm; F, 8.30am–8.45pm; Sa, 10.00am–12.45pm
Second and third terms
Reading: M–Th, 8.30am–10.15pm; F, 8.30am–9.15pm; Sa (second term only),
10.00am–5.45pm; Sa (third term only), 10.00am–9.45pm; Su (March–May only),
10.00am–5.45pm
Vacation period (July–mid-September)
Lending: M–F, 9.15am–4.15pm; reading: M–F, 8.30am–4.15pm; Sa,
10.00am–12.45pm

ACCESS AND SERVICES
Visitors admitted at Librarian's discretion. Annual membership fee for borrowing
privileges. Disabled access facilities. Photocopying and microform prints available for
a fee. Internet access available. Leaflets and booklets describing services available.
Consult website for special regulations governing external users and user fees.
External readers may choose to: (a) consult library collection; (b) use information
services; and (c) borrow library material. Eligibility: (a) graduates of UCC; (b)
members of Graduates Associations of some Irish universities; (c) persons engaged in
scholarly research who are not eligible to use the library through membership of the
College.

For access to special collections and archives *see* separate entry below.

Brookfield Health Sciences Library is located opposite security desk and next to
nursing and midwifery studies reception desk within the Brookfield complex. It is
on two floors (ground floor and lower ground) and houses the main nursing and
midwifery collections for UCC. Along with the Nursing and Midwifery Studies
Collection, Brookfield Library holds the Clinical Therapies, Epidemiology and
Public Health, Pharmacy and General Practice Collections.

The Medical Library, located at Cork University Hospital, is jointly funded by
UCC and the Southern Health Board. Staff and students of UCC, as well as
healthcare professionals working in the University Hospital, St Finbarr's Hospital
and Erinville Hospital, may consult in, and borrow from, the Medical Library. Other
healthcare professionals may apply to Librarian for consultation or borrowing
facilities as external readers, on payment of appropriate fee. One fee covers the Boole
Library, the Medical Library and the Brookfield Health Sciences Library.

CONTACT
Information desk. Telephone: (021) 490 2794; e-mail: informationdesk@ucc.ie

DESCRIPTION
The Boole Library is the main library for University College Cork, part of the National University of Ireland system that also includes campuses in Dublin, Galway, Limerick and Maynooth. Its first purpose is to serve the university by 'supporting study, teaching and research as efficiently as possible'. The Boole Library brings together in one large centre many sources of information not readily available elsewhere in Munster. They include books, periodicals, audiovisual materials, a European Community Documentation Centre, online searching and inter-library loans, together with the professional expertise to interpret the collections to its users. The Boole Library is named after George Boole, first Professor of Mathematics at Queen's College, Cork (now UCC). He developed Boolean algebra, which led to the creation of computer science.

HOLDINGS
Subjects of concentration include: humanities, law, medicine (CUH), medicine (UCC), official publications, European Documentation Centre, science and social sciences. The library houses a collection of 600,000 books, 4,000 periodicals (including national and foreign newspapers), an expanding collection of electronic resources covering all disciplines, the European Documentation Centre, which receives most of the basic documents of the European Communities and those of some international organisations, all Irish Government publications, a representative collection of British official publications, tapes, LPs, CDs, videos and slides. Special collections and archives are treated separately: *See* following entry.

LOCATION
The university is located one mile west of city centre. Follow signs to the library.

NATIONAL UNIVERSITY OF IRELAND, CORK (UCC) – SPECIAL COLLECTIONS AND ARCHIVES

Boole Library, University College Cork
CORK
Ireland

TELEPHONE: (021) 425 0001 (Special Collections), (021) 425 0003 (Archives);
FAX: (021) 427 3428 (Special Collections), (021) 427 3428 (Archives)
E-mail: h.davis@ucc.ie, specialcollections@ucc.ie (Special Collections);
c.quinn@ucc.ie (Archives)
Website: booleweb.ucc.ie/search/subject/speccol/speccol.htm (Special Collections);
booleweb.ucc.ie/search/subject/archives/archives2.htm (Archives)

HOURS
Special Collections
Term time: M–F, 9.30am–4.45pm
Vacation period (July–September): M–F, 9.30am–4.15pm.
Please telephone or e-mail to make arrangements at least 24 hours prior to arrival.

Archives
By appointment only
Term time: M–F, 9.30am–12.30pm, 2.15pm–4.45pm
Vacation period (July–September): M–F, 9.30am–12.30pm, 2.15pm–4.15pm

ACCESS AND SERVICES
Visitors welcome but advance notice and ID required. Wheelchair access. Pencils
only; laptop facilities available. Photocopying and microfilm printing facilities
available by arrangement with Special Collections Librarian (or Archivist for archival
material) and are subject to copyright and other restrictions. All material is for
consultation only and may not be removed from the library. Printed and electronic
guides available, viz. *Special Collections Boole Library University College Cork: an
Introduction*; *Primary Sources for Medieval Studies in the Boole Library Special
Collections*; *Sources for Seventeenth to Nineteenth Centuries Historical Studies in the
Boole Library Special Collections*. The library's website gives detailed descriptions of
holdings.

CONTACT
Crónán Ó Doibhlin, Sub-Librarian, Head of Division
Helen Davis, Special Collections Librarian
Carol Quinn, Archivist
Emer Twomey, Assistant Archivist. E-mail: emer.twomey@ucc.ie

DESCRIPTION
Special collections of the Boole Library consist of primary source materials in a
variety of formats (book, manuscript, map, newspaper, microform, electronic) which
support research and teaching in the humanities and social sciences, spanning all
periods from classical and early Christian to modern, with a particular emphasis on
Ireland (especially Munster) and the Irish diaspora. Private libraries donated by
individuals are sometimes maintained as discrete units by special arrangement. Since
1997 the section has acquired archival collections relating primarily, but not
exclusively, to Munster families and businesses.
    The Boole Library Archives Service is an active repository, collecting and
administering archival collections generated from outside of UCC which
complement the research and teaching needs of University College Cork.

HOLDINGS
Holdings include archives, books, manuscripts, facsimiles of manuscripts, maps,
microforms, newspapers, pamphlets, journals, theses, photographs and recordings.
These collections are divided into three main categories: manuscripts, printed books
and archives. For more detailed information, consult website.

Manuscripts
Highlights from the Manuscript Collections include Gaelic manuscripts, divided
into two main series. (1) the Tórna Collection, containing manuscripts which
belonged to Professor Tadhg Ó Donnchadha, Professor of Irish at University College
Cork, 1916–44, and catalogued by Professor Pádraigh de Brún of the Dublin
Institute for Advanced Studies, Clár Lámhscríbhinní Gaeilge Choláiste Ollscoile
Chorcaí: Cnuasach Thórna (TR 017 DEBR). Tórna manuscripts are identified
numerically with a 'T' prefix. (2) Other Gaelic Manuscript Collections consists of
over 200 manuscripts purchased by or donated to the library. Seventy-seven of these
belonged to Professor James E.H. Murphy, Professor of Irish at Trinity College
Dublin, 1896–1919. A catalogue of this collection has been compiled by Dr
Breandán Ó Conchúir, Department of Modern Irish at University College Cork,
and published by the Dublin Institute for Advanced Studies (1991), Clár
Lámhscríbhinní Gaeilge Choláiste Ollscoile Chorcaí: Cnuasach Uí Mhurchú (TR

017 OCON). Most of the remainder belonged to Canon Power, lecturer in and later Professor of Archaeology at University College Cork, 1915–32. The catalogue of these and the other Gaelic manuscripts in the collection has been prepared by Dr Breandán Ó Conchúir and is currently in press. A list is available at the enquiry desk in the research room. Non-Gaelic manuscripts are grouped as 'manuscripts in English and/or bilingual'. These include the papers of various eminent professors, including George Boole, Tadhg Ó Donnchadha (Tórna), Daniel Corkery and Cormac Ó Cuilleanáin, and reflect part of the intellectual history of the college; they constitute a large portion of this collection. Archival descriptive lists of the Boole, Corkery and Ó Cuilleanáin collections are available, as are several other such lists. These are available for consultation at the enquiry desk in the Research Room. Please note that Tórna's papers are entirely independent of the Tórna Collection. Also included in this category are documents belonging to and relating to individuals or enterprises, e.g. William O'Brien and Kinsale Manorial Records. An archival finding list is available for the William O'Brien papers; all access is through the list at the enquiry desk in the Research Room and requires 24 hours' notice for retrieval.

The Manuscript Collection also includes several manuscript estate maps, music scores and minor manuscripts from the Middle East and Far East. In addition, there are manuscripts on microfilm, which include a large collection of manuscripts of Gaelic and historical interest, such as the Gaelic manuscripts in the Royal Irish Academy, the Folklore Collections at University College Dublin, manuscripts in the National Archives, Public Records Offices in London and Belfast and other institutions in Ireland and abroad. List of holdings is available at the enquiry desk. Of special genealogical interest are microfilm copies of Petty's parish maps for most of Munster, the originals of which are in the National Library of Ireland; the 1901 census returns for most of Munster; and all published censuses up to and including 1911.

There was no census between 1901 and 1911. The Special Collections Department does not have the 1911 census returns: but it does have nineteenth century published censuses. Twentieth century published censuses from 1926 (there was no census in 1921) are held by the Official Publications Section in the Boole Library. (Owing to a one hundred year embargo on census returns after 1911 no access will be allowed to the returns in the National Archives, Dublin.)

Holdings of manuscripts in facsimile are quite extensive. Among these are: *the Book of Kells, Book of Durrow* and *Book of Lindisfarne*; those published by the Irish Manuscripts Commission and the Royal Irish Academy; the *Domesday Book*; the *Utrecht Psalter*; and several Books of Hours. Early English manuscripts in facsimile series are also available, as are modern manuscript facsimiles, including the works of John Milton and James Joyce and the letters of Paul Valéry.

Printed Books

Major collections of printed books include: Pre-1850 Books – some 13,000 books and pamphlets published before 1850. St Fin Barre's Cathedral Library, which consists of some 3,000 books and pamphlets, mostly pre-1850, of theological, political and general interest; the Tórna Collection of books and journals belonging to the late Professor Tadhg Ó Donnchadha, which forms the nucleus of a research collection for Celtic studies; Munster Printing – a collection of books, pamphlets and ephemera printed in Munster irrespective of date.

Special collections of individual donors include the Arnold Bax Collection of Memorabilia. Bax (1883–1953) was Master of the King's Musick, 1941–53. This collection consists of a small number of his own compositions, a portion of his library, some of his letters and some personal effects. Other collections include the Corkery Collection, containing a portion of the library of Daniel Corkery (1878–1964), whose papers are also available in the Special Collections Department; the de Courcy Ireland Collection, containing a wide range of books, periodicals and ephemera dealing with maritime history and travel, acquired from Dr John de Courcy Ireland (1911–present); and the Friedlander Collection, named in memory of Elizabeth Friedlander (1903–84), German artist and designer who lived in Kinsale, County Cork, and designed covers for Penguin books, the Nonesuch Press and many other prestigious publishing houses during her long life. Within this collection are books from Penguin and other publishers on a wide variety of subjects, including book design, layout, calligraphy and the arts, and printing in general. These books and some of her papers were donated to University College Cork by Mr Gerald Goldberg. Another collection of importance is the Ó Ríordáin Collection.

Archives Service
Major archival collections include: Attic Press/Róisín Conroy Collection, generated and collected by Róisín Conroy as co-founder and publisher of Attic Press and as an activist in the Irish Women's Movement; family papers belonging to the Grehan family; estate collections – Bantry House Collection; Seward Estate, Youghal, County Cork; Ryan of Inch Family Papers; political papers – Thomas MacDonagh Collection, Neville Keery Papers (unprocessed); literary papers – John Montague Papers (unprocessed); correspondence of Frank O'Connor and Sean O'Faolain; Nancy McCarthy Papers (unprocessed). Other collections include the Peters Photographic Collection (World War II), Papers of George Boole, Papers of Daniel Corkery and the Seán Ó Riada Collection. Please note that access to unprocessed collections is not permitted.

LOCATION
Temporarily located at Youngline Industrial Estate, Pouladuff Road, Cork, for the duration of the new postgraduate library building project. A shuttle bus runs to and from the main campus every 20 minutes. It is expected the service will have returned to the Boole Library by 2008.

MALLOW HERITAGE CENTRE

27–28 Bank Place
MALLOW, COUNTY CORK
Ireland

TELEPHONE: (022) 50302; FAX: (022) 20276
E-mail: mallowhc@eircom.net
Website: www.mallowheritagecentre.com

HOURS
M–F, 10.30am–1.00pm, 2.00pm–4.00pm; closed religious and bank holidays

ACCESS AND SERVICES
Fee based organisation offering genealogical research services to those interested in

tracing their roots in County Cork, especially in East and North Cork. Enquiries
welcome. Application form can be found on the centre's website. Initial search fee of
€63.50 (or equivalent) per family must accompany applications. Priority/next day
search, €90; single search, €30. Delay of four weeks can be expected for a reply to
an initial enquiry. Chief surnames in rural Cork include: McCarthy, O'Callaghan,
McAuliffe, Fitzgerald, Sullivan, Murphy, Walsh, O'Connor and O'Connell.

CONTACT
Martina Aherne

DESCRIPTION
Mallow Heritage Centre is the designated heritage centre for the Diocese of Cloyne.
It is a member of the Family History Foundation, the coordinating body for a
network of government approved genealogical research centres in the Republic of
Ireland and in Northern Ireland, which have computerised tens of millions of Irish
ancestral records of different types. It is also a member of the Irish Genealogical
Project.

HOLDINGS
The centre holds baptismal and marriage records for 46 out of the 120 parishes
within the County of Cork, totalling 1,000,000 entries on its database, the third
largest record database in Ireland. Main records include: Roman Catholic baptismal
and marriage records, a few dating from 1757, and Church of Ireland records for the
North Cork area only, the earliest dating from 1730. A variety of the main
genealogical sources are currently being computerised and tombstones from several
cemeteries have been transcribed.

LOCATION
On the main Cork to Limerick Road, half an hour's drive north of Cork City. The
Heritage Centre is next to the Hibernian Hotel, just west of the town centre.

COUNTY DONEGAL

DONEGAL ARCHAEOLOGICAL SURVEY
See DONEGAL COUNTY MUSEUM, Letterkenny

DONEGAL COUNTY LIBRARY

Central Library and Arts Centre, Oliver Plunkett Road
LETTERKENNY, COUNTY DONEGAL
Ireland

TELEPHONE: (074) 912 1968; FAX: (074) 912 1740
E-mail: central@donegallibrary.ie
Website: www.donegallibrary.ie

HOURS
M, W, F, 10.30am–5.30pm; Tu, Th, 10.30am–8.00pm; Sa, 10.30am–1.00pm

ACCESS AND SERVICES
Visitors welcome. Disabled access. Photocopying, printouts from the internet and
microfilm reader available for a modest fee. Public internet access in Central Library
and 12 other service points. County Library has developed a WebOPAC facility, and
its catalogue, with all the library's holdings, including local material, is available
online at www.donegallibrary.ie.

CONTACT
Maureen Kerr, Assistant Librarian, Central Library. Telephone: (074) 912 4950; fax:
(074) 912 4950

DESCRIPTION
Main library of the county's 17 member library network, with library administration
located at Rosemount, close to the Central Library in Letterkenny.

HOLDINGS
The library houses more than 40,000 volumes, with access to the system's some
400,000 volumes, including significant holdings of early printed books (some 300
pre-1851 volumes). Local authors collections include: Patrick MacGill, Peadar
O'Donnell, Seumas MacManus and John Kells Ingram. These collections consist
mostly of printed editions of their works, plus a small amount of original papers and
illustrative matter. The Collection of Personal Papers includes: Cathal Ó Searcaigh's

personal archive – manuscripts of his poetry and other writings, original editions of his published work in monograph and journal form, videos and tapes of his broadcast work, and other relevant papers and materials that are currently being deposited with Donegal County Library. Cathal Ó Searcaigh's own library of poetry and other literature will be housed in his house in Mín a'Leagha, Gort a'Choirce, and will be catalogued by Donegal County Library and maintained by Donegal County Library *in situ*.

LOCATION
Housed in three storey building on the corner of Lower Main Street and Oliver Plunkett Road, in the town centre.

DONEGAL COUNTY MUSEUM

High Road
LETTERKENNY, COUNTY DONEGAL
Ireland

TELEPHONE: (074) 912 4613; FAX: (074) 912 6522
E-mail: museum@donegalcoco.ie
Website: www.donegal.ie

HOURS
M–F, 10.00am–12.30pm, 1.00pm–4.30pm; Sa, 1.00pm–4.30pm

ACCESS AND SERVICES
Visitors welcome, but at least two weeks' advance notice required if a researcher desires to view a particular artefact or group of artefacts. Access also depends on availability of staff. ID required. Wheelchair access. Fax and photocopying services available. Museum contains two exhibition galleries: one for temporary exhibitions, the other for permanent exhibition telling the story of Donegal from the Stone Age to the twentieth century. Collections catalogued manually and electronically.

CONTACT
Curator or Assistant Curator

DESCRIPTION
Donegal County Museum was first opened to the public in 1987 and is housed in what was once the Warden's house of the Letterkenny Workhouse, built in the 1840s. Several renovations and an extension to the museum were carried out between 1990 and 2000. The role of the museum is to collect, record, preserve, communicate and display for the use and enjoyment of the widest community possible the material evidence and associated information of the history of Donegal.

HOLDINGS
The museum develops and cares for a comprehensive collection of over 6,000 original artefacts relating to the County of Donegal in the areas of archaeology, geology, natural history, social and political history and folklife. It also houses the archives of the Donegal Archaeological Survey, consisting of maps, plans, drawings, slides and files relating to the Survey. The Survey was published in book form and contains a description of the field antiquities of County Donegal from the Mesolithic period to the seventeenth century.

LOCATION
Signposted in Letterkenny, a five minute walk from the town centre or bus station.

DONEGAL COUNTY ARCHIVES SERVICE

Donegal County Council, Three Rivers Centre
LIFFORD, COUNTY DONEGAL
Ireland

TELEPHONE: (074) 917 2490; FAX: (074) 914 2290
E-mail: archivist@donegalcoco.ie
Website: www.donegal.ie/dcc/arts/archive.htm

HOURS
M–F, 9.00am–12.30pm, 1.15pm–4.30pm

ACCESS AND SERVICES
Public access by advance appointment only, by arrangement with Archivist. Service offers small permanent exhibition area with regularly changing exhibitions; research room; photocopying facilities; occasional joint exhibitions with other organisations; lectures and talks; liaison with local schools; and events for Heritage Week (last week in August or first week in September) and other local festivals.

CONTACT
Niamh Brennan, Archivist. E-mail: archivist@donegalcoco.ie

DESCRIPTION
Donegal County Archives holds the archives of Donegal County Council, its predecessor bodies, schools, railways and private historical collections of local interest. The priorities of the service include the listing and conservation of archival materials to make them accessible to the public, and the general development of the Archives Service.

HOLDINGS
Poor Law Unions
Donegal County Council has some of the finest surviving local archives in Ireland, including one of the nation's best county collections of records of Boards of Guardians of the Poor Law Unions in the county. The principal function of the Boards of Guardians was to supervise and run workhouses where the destitute were accommodated. Workhouses in Donegal were in Letterkenny, Ballyshannon, Stranorlar, Dunfanaghy, Carndonagh (run by the Inishowen Board), Donegal, Glenties and Milford. The collection includes:

an almost complete set of minute books, *c.* 1840–*c.* 1923, for all Poor Law Unions in the county except Donegal Town (where minutes only survive for the years 1914–23);

a considerable number of indoor relief registers and workhouse admission and discharge registers, which give very detailed information about destitute persons entering or leaving the workhouses, covering:

Dunfanaghy Poor Law Union, 1891–1915,
Glenties Poor Law Union, 1851–1922 (incomplete),
Inishowen Poor Law Union, 1844–59, 1899–1911,
Letterkenny Poor Law Union, 1864–78,

Milford Poor Law Union, 1855–1922;
outdoor relief registers for Letterkenny Union, 1855–99, and Milford Union, 1847–99;
minute books for the dispensaries at Killygordon and Stranorlar, 1852–99;
other records, including records of deaths for Milford (1899–1917) and Letterkenny Unions (1910–21), and some financial and administrative correspondence and documentation for some of the unions.

Grand Jury

The Archives Service holds significant records relating to the Grand Jury of Donegal, a local authority responsible for services including making and repair of roads and bridges, construction of courthouses, levying for support of district hospitals, schools and prisons. The Grand Jury's administrative functions were taken over by the newly established Donegal County Council in 1899. Grand Jury records include: 34 volumes of Spring and Summer and Lent Assizes 1754–1898 (with many gaps in years); accounts and correspondence, 1816 – 1901; and a Grand Jury map, 1801.

Rural District Councils

The Rural District Councils were set up under the 1898 Local Government (Ireland) Act. Functions included local housing, sewerage, water and public health services. They were abolished in 1925. Records include minutes of meetings for the councils of:
Ballyshannon (19 volumes of minutes, 1899–1925);
Donegal (11 volumes of minutes, 1914–25);
Dunfanaghy (volumes of minutes for the period 1899–1918 and 13 folders of correspondence, 1909–18);
Glenties (14 volumes of minutes, 1899–1925);
Inishowen (13 volumes of minutes, 1899–1925);
Letterkenny (18 volumes of minutes, 1899–1925);
Londonderry No. 2 (volumes of minutes, 1899–1925);
Milford (26 volumes of minutes, 1899–1925);
Strabane No. 2 (15 volumes of minutes, 1899–1922);
Stranorlar (8 volumes of minutes, 1899–1925).

Donegal County Council, 1899–present

Records of the County Council, formed under the 1899 Local Government Act, and still in existence today, include:
minutes including Committee minutes, 1899–1975 (77 volumes);
County Manager's Orders, 1942–75;
finance material including abstracts of accounts, secretary's statements and General Ledgers, 1914–67;
motor tax registers, 1903–23, 1951–92;
housing records including housing of 'working classes' and 'labourers': plans, correspondence, reports etc, 1890–1940;
County Library archives, including reports and minutes of meetings, 1928–87;
electoral material, including registers of electors from the county, summaries of registers, 1920–1980s (incomplete);
notices of elections, correspondence, 1920s–1980s;
local and general election campaigning material, generally from the 1970s;
planning: applications, registers and development plans, 1934–72;
environmental services, plans and maps;

roads: plans, drawings and maps;
legal deeds.

Private Records
Records of administration for landed estates include: some rentals and maps for the
Murray Stewart Estate, Killybegs and other areas in South-West Donegal,
1749–1880; administrative records and maps for the Cochranes of Redcastle and
Edward Harvey of Ballyliffin Estate, both in Inishowen, c. 1860–1900, and one
Harvey rental, c. 1900 including lands at Inch; the Hamiltons of Fintown, 1818–49,
and the Boytons and Montgomerys of Convoy, 1890s–1920s.

Other privately acquired archives include the papers of: Irish speaking poet
Cathal Ó Searcaigh and the manuscripts of other local authors; papers relating to the
history and culture of Donegal in the nineteenth and twentieth centuries, collected
by Fr Patrick Gallagher of the Donegal Historical Society; and the historical lecture
notes taken by Dr Maureen Wall. Also included are photographs of various towns;
oral history interviews; and archives relating to the Groves of Castle Grove House,
Letterkenny.

School Records
Pupil registers and roll books for public elementary/primary or 'national' schools, c.
1880–c. 1990 are available for 80 schools (some no longer in existence), including
schools at Dunfanaghy, Donegal, Mountcharles, Lettermacaward, Burtonport,
Dunkineely, Fintown, Letterkenny, Buncrana, Ballyshannon, Ramelton, Fanad,
Newtowncunningham, Creeslough, Churchill, Bunbeg, Kilmacrenan, Liscooley and
Ray. The archive also holds rollbooks, registers and financial and administrative
papers relating to the Lifford Endowed (Secondary) Schools.

Petty Sessions
Very rare court records (19 vols) for local petty sessions, mainly at Ballyshannon
1828–55. These include:

Registry of Criminal Proceedings at Ballyshannon Petty Sessions, 1828–48,
1849–51, 1851–53 – details include date, informant's name and address, name and
residence of person charged, offence (e.g. 'waylaying and assault', 'entering his
orchard and stealing apples', 'stealing three bricks'); witnesses sworn; and
determination (e.g. 'fined', 'committed to gaol');

Registry of Civil Proceedings at Ballyshannon Petty Sessions, 1828–48, 1848–50,
1851–56 – details include date; complainant's name and address; defendant's name
and address; complaint (e.g. 'non payment of county cess', 'having a quantity of flax
on the public road', 'wilfully driving your mare into his grazing land'); witnesses
sworn; and adjudication (e.g. 'dismissed', 'no appearance', 'postponed', 'settled',
'fined');

Registry of Summons issued from Ballyshannon Petty Sessions, 1828–33, 1831–9,
1833–7, 1844–8, 1848–50 – details include name and address of complainant;
name of person summoned; date; offence (e.g. 'assault and forcibly carrying away
turf', 'house breaking'); and decision (e.g. 'dismissed', 'no jurisdiction', 'conviction',
'fined').

Railways
The railways of Donegal were closed down by 1960. The Archives Service holds
some of the records relating to the railways, including:
Letterkenny and Lough Swilly railway records: accounts, personnel documents (with
restricted access);
West Donegal Railway Drawings (1880);
Finn Valley Railway plans (1860);
prints of Great Northern Railway Company (1956–60);
prints of Lough Swilly Railway trains (1951–9);
prints of Letterkenny and Burtonport Extension Railway (1951–9);
prints of trains, stations and lines of County Donegal Railways Joint Committee
(1951–61);
bye-laws, accounts, legal documents, timetables, leaflets and tickets, 1880–1960;
posters and flyers relating to railways, c. 1900–50.

LOCATION
First floor, Three Rivers Centre.

LIFFORD OLD COURTHOUSE

The Diamond
LIFFORD, COUNTY DONEGAL
Ireland

TELEPHONE: (074) 914 1733; FAX: (074) 914 1228
E-mail: info@liffordoldcourthouse.com
Website: www.liffordoldcourthouse.com

HOURS
M–F, 9.00am–4.30pm; Su, 12.30pm–4.30pm

ACCESS AND SERVICES
Formerly called 'Seat of Power Visitor Centre', centre's full name now 'Lifford Old
Courthouse, Donegal's Amazing 18th Century Court, Jail and Asylum'. Visitors
welcome; admission fee for exhibitions. Current (2006) fees: adults, €6; children,
€3; students and seniors, €4; families, €15. Advance notice required for large
groups. Late openings can be arranged in advance. Historic Courthouse Restaurant
open all day below courtroom adjoining the cells. Free brochures available. Access to
archives by appointment.

CONTACT
Gillian Graham, Manager

DESCRIPTION
The old courthouse was built in 1746 by Dublin architect Michael Priestly and
functioned as a courthouse until 1938. It was restored and reopened as a heritage
centre in 1994. It traces the history of Lifford, especially its struggle for 'seat of
power' status in Donegal, and the history of the O'Donnell dynasty, using
audiovisual aids and displays. In addition, there are audiovisual displays of famous
trials held in the courtroom and of the prisoners and inmates held in the original
underground cells and lunatic asylum. Lifford was also the administrative centre for
the Plantation. The building is believed to have been built on the foundation of
Lifford Castle, a sixteenth and seventeenth century O'Donnell stronghold.

HOLDINGS
The courthouse houses the Rupert Coughlan Collection of documents, manuscripts and charts on the O'Donnell family and chieftains; and historic local artefacts, letters and photographs relating to the old courthouse and gaol. The building houses the Lifford branch of the County Donegal Library Service.

LOCATION
Located in the Diamond, Lifford, one mile west of Strabane, County Tyrone, and 14 miles from Derry City.

DONEGAL ANCESTRY

The Quay
RAMELTON, COUNTY DONEGAL
Ireland

TELEPHONE: (074) 915 1266; FAX: (074) 915 1702
E-mail: info@donegalancestry.com, donances@indigo.ie
Website: www.donegalancestry.com

HOURS
Genealogy Centre: M–Th, 9.30am–4.30pm; F, 9.30am–3.30pm; or by appointment
Heritage Centre: M–Sa, 10.00am–5.30pm; Su, 2.00pm–5.30pm; weekend opening hours during summer season only

ACCESS AND SERVICES
Visitors welcome. Donegal Ancestry offers fee based genealogical research service and consultation service for anyone wishing to discuss family history query with centre's trained researchers. Consultation fee applies; appointment not necessary. Computerisation of church records ongoing. Types of research report include: location search; search of specific sources; preliminary report (this involves initial search, full assessment of all relevant sources and advice on the feasibility of conducting further research); staged report (to facilitate customers who want to spread the cost of research over time); and full report. Last of these an exclusive and individually designed full family history report, explaining sources available for research, administrative geography, family names, local history and maps, transcripts or copies of records uncovered (when appropriate, certificates may also be included). Research fees: preliminary report costs minimum of €76 (or equivalent). Follow-on research fees may vary with time involved and length of report; full costing prepared for all research and furnished to customers before any research is undertaken. Enquiries dealt with in rotation and, due to the large volume of work currently on hand, it may take up to 8 weeks for new research to be undertaken. Every effort is made to facilitate customers where possible.

CONTACT
Joan Patton, Manager
Susan McCaffrey and Kathleen Gallagher, Researchers

DESCRIPTION
Donegal Ancestry is the Irish Family History Foundation's designated genealogical research centre for County Donegal. The centre provides a fee based family history research service using computerised and non-computerised records and covers the

geographic area of County Donegal. Principal towns and villages in County Donegal include: Ballyshannon, Donegal, Bundoran, Ballybofey, Lifford, Raphoe, Letterkenny, Dunfanaghy, Buncrana, Carndonagh, Greencastle and Moville.

HOLDINGS
Sources available to Donegal Ancestry for consultation include: pre-1900 parish registers; civil birth, marriage and death records; *Griffith's Valuation*; tithe applotment books; 1901 and 1911 census returns; graveyard inscriptions; hearth money rolls; passenger list extracts; 1630 muster rolls; estate records; school roll books; poll of electors extracts, mid-1700s; Ordnance Survey memoirs; and other miscellaneous sources.

LOCATION
Seven miles north of Letterkenny (the largest commercial centre in County Donegal). The main road from Letterkenny leads directly onto the Mall in Ramelton; turn right at the bottom of the hill and follow the road to the left, which runs parallel to the Leannan River. The genealogy centre is located in one of the two restored warehouses on the quayside; the adjoining building has a heritage exhibition that outlines the path of Ramelton's development from its origins at the time of the Plantation of Ulster in the seventeenth century up to the present. Guided tours available. Ramelton sometimes appears as Rathmelton (the historic spelling), especially on maps and road signs (but it is pronounced locally as Ramelton).

COUNTY DOWN

LOCAL STUDIES DEPARTMENT

SEELB Library Headquarters, Windmill Hill
BALLYNAHINCH, COUNTY DOWN, BT24 8DH
Northern Ireland

TELEPHONE: (028) 9756 6400, extension 235/236/237; FAX: (028) 9756 5072
E-mail: seelb.localstudies@ni-libraries.net
Website: www.seelb.org.uk

HOURS
M–F, 9.00am–5.00pm

ACCESS AND SERVICES
Visitors welcome, but owing to space restrictions appointment is recommended to
ensure that all the relevant material can be made available. Disabled access.
Microfilm reader/printer available. Free internet access for all Northern Ireland
public library members. One membership card valid for all libraries. Charge of
£1.50 per half hour for non-members; ID required. Membership of library open to
anyone living, working or studying in the area.

   Local Studies can send out Ordnance Survey maps, street directories and old
newspapers in bound volumes to be consulted at any of the South Eastern Education
and Library Board's libraries. Some member libraries (Downpatrick, Colin Glen,
Lisburn and Bangor) also have microfilm reader/printers to which microfilm copies
can be sent. Most books from Local Studies Collection can be borrowed through
local branch library, but rare works of local or special interest available for
consultation in Ballynahinch only. Library Service does not conduct genealogical
searches but is happy to assist and advise users seeking genealogical information.

CONTACT
Deirdre Armstrong, Local Studies Librarian
Mary Bradley, Local Studies Librarian

DESCRIPTION
Local Studies is located at the Library Headquarters of the South Eastern Education
and Library Board in Ballynahinch, County Down, which serves County Down and
South County Antrim.

HOLDINGS

The Local Studies Collection contains books, maps, newspapers and illustrations on the history, topography, industry, transport, literature and culture of County Down and South County Antrim, the area served by the SEELB Library Service. Local Studies also collects information and cultural materials on the rest of Ulster and the whole island of Ireland.

There are also 30,000 books, including 4,500 fiction titles, covering all aspects of Irish life, with special emphasis on Ulster in general and Counties Down and Antrim in particular. It also includes over 3,000 maps covering Counties Antrim and Down; Ordnance Survey parish memoirs; and a collection of postcards and photographs, mostly Victorian and Edwardian, relating to County Down, South County Antrim and Belfast. The library holds the Lawrence Collection (*See* National Library of Ireland, Dublin for originals) on microfilm, with indexes to the Welch and Lawrence Collections. Other important resources include a range of Irish periodical titles, local newspapers, including newspaper indexes (e.g. *County Down Spectator*) and the Irish Emigration Database.

Of special importance is the indexing of local newspapers project. Since 1973 staff in the Local Studies Department have been preparing an index from the local newspapers in County Down and South County Antrim and other newspapers such as the *Belfast Telegraph* and *Irish Times*. The index currently contains more than 250,000 entries and is available as an online database. Specific newspaper indexes are available for purchase. These include *County Down Spectator* (1904–64), £1.50; *Down Recorder* (1836–86), £5; *Mourne Observer* (1949–80), £2; *Newtownards Chronicle* (1871–1900), £3; *Newtownards Chronicle* (1901–39), £5; *Northern Herald* (1833–6), £1.50; *Northern Star* (1792–7), £3.50. These papers are held on file on microfilm. For a nominal fee, photocopies of newspaper articles can be supplied. Payments can be made by international reply coupon or by sterling cheque. Visitors also have free access to the Ulster American Folk Park's Emigration Database.

LOCATION

Town centre, at the eastern end of Windmill Street near the intersection of Crossgar Road, on a historic 1798 battle site.

BANGOR LIBRARY

80 Hamilton Road
BANGOR, COUNTY DOWN, BT20 4LH
Northern Ireland

TELEPHONE: (028) 9127 0591; FAX: (028) 9146 2744
E-mail: bangorlibrary@ni-libraries.net
Website: www.seelb.org.uk

HOURS

M, W, 9.30am–8.00pm; Tu, F, 9.30am–5.00pm; Sa, 10.00am–1.00pm, 2.00pm–5.00pm

ACCESS AND SERVICES

Visitors welcome, but ID required to join and have borrowing privileges. Borrowing privileges for visitors may be restricted. Consult Librarian. Disabled access. Photography by arrangement with Branch Library Manager. Fees for photocopying and microform prints. Free internet access for all Northern Ireland public library members. One membership card valid for all libraries. Charge of £1.50 per half hour for non-members; ID required. Membership of library open to anyone living, working or studying in the area. Library's centre of excellence offers access to 20 PCs, including adaptive technology.

CONTACT
Stephen Hanson, Branch Library Manager. E-mail: stephen.hanson@ni-libraries.net

DESCRIPTION
Established in 1910 with financial assistance from the Carnegie Trust, Bangor is a busy branch library serving the needs of some 21,000 registered clients in this historic community, site of one of Ireland's great early monastic establishments.

HOLDINGS
The library houses a general educational and recreational collection of some 37,000 volumes, with access to the 341,000 volumes held by the combined libraries of the South Eastern Education and Library Board, headquartered in Ballynahinch. In addition to its print collection, the library offers a local studies database, which gives access to over 3,500 journal and newspaper articles indexed online. Of genealogical interest is the library's printed copy of *Griffith's Valuation* and a 3,000 volume reference collection. Available on microfilm is the *County Down Spectator* from 1904 to the present.

LOCATION
Hamilton Road runs between High Street and Upper Main Street in Bangor town centre. The library moved to temporary premises in mid-2006 to allow a full refurbishment and extension to the original 1910 building. Work is expected to take 18 months.

HOLYWOOD BRANCH LIBRARY

Sullivan Building, 86–88 High Street
HOLYWOOD, COUNTY DOWN, BT18 9AE
Northern Ireland

TELEPHONE: (028) 9042 4232; FAX: (028) 9042 4194
E-mail: holywoodlibrary@ni-libraries.net
Website: www.seelb.org.uk

HOURS
M, W, F, 9.30am–5.00pm; Tu, Th, 9.30am–8.00pm; Sa, 10.00am–5.00pm

ACCESS AND SERVICES
Visitors welcome. Borrowing privileges for visitors may be restricted. Disabled access. Fees for photocopying and fax services. Free internet access for all Northern Ireland public library members. One membership card valid for all libraries. Charge of £1.50 per half hour for non-members; ID required. Membership of library open to anyone living, working or studying in the area.

CONTACT
Josephine Quinn, Branch Library Manager. E-mail: josephine.quinn@ni-libraries.net

DESCRIPTION
Attractive, inviting facility housed in a renovated 1862 building. Part of the South Eastern Education and Library Board, headquartered in Ballynahinch.

HOLDINGS
The library houses a general educational and recreational collection of some 25,000 books, with access to the combined resources of the South Eastern Education and Library Board. It houses a small but good local studies collection, with some standard genealogical reference sources for the local area, including *Griffith's Valuation*. Ordnance Survey maps of the area may be requested from the central Local Studies Collection.

LOCATION
Town centre.

ULSTER FOLK AND TRANSPORT MUSEUM

Cultra
HOLYWOOD, COUNTY DOWN, BT18 0EU
Northern Ireland

TELEPHONE: (028) 9042 8428; FAX: (028) 9042 8728
E-mail: uftm@nidex.com
Website: www.uftm.org.uk, www.magni.org.uk

HOURS
March–June: M–F, 10.00am–5.00pm; Sa, 10.00am–6.00pm; Su, 11.00am–6.00pm
July–September: M–F, 10.00am–6.00pm; Sa, 10.00am–6.00pm; Su, 11.00am–6.00pm
October–February: M–F, 10.00am–4.00pm; Sa, 10.00am–5.00pm; Su, 11.00am–5.00pm
Closed for several days at Christmas

ACCESS AND SERVICES
Museum
Open to general public. Separate admission charges to Folk Museum and Transport Museum (adults, £5; children (5–16 years), £3; reduced rates for seniors, students, families, groups, etc; children under five free). Combined visit to both Folk Museum and Transport Museum: adults, £6.50; children, £3.50. Disabled access to most of site. Museum publishes a wide range of material, including the journal *Ulster Folklife*, exhibition catalogues, educational study packs and worksheets for schools.
Library and Archive
Appointment required. Library offers reference assistance, photocopying, microfilm reader/printer, photographic reproductions and database searching.

CONTACT
Roger Dixon, Librarian

DESCRIPTION
The museum occupies 177 acres just east of Belfast in northern County Down. It is devoted to preserving the ways things were in the north of Ireland, especially around the turn of the twentieth century. While your primary purpose in visiting the museum may be to conduct research in its library and archives, it would be

worthwhile to take time to explore the Folk Museum's exhibitions and reconstructed farms, houses, workshops, mills, schools, churches and other facilities that take you back in time. The Transport Museum also offers an array of distractions, from old railway engines and cars to the modern De Lorean automobile, which was manufactured in Belfast. The museum is part of the Museums and Galleries of Northern Ireland (MAGNI) service, which also includes the Ulster American Folk Park, Omagh, County Tyrone; the Ulster Museum, Belfast; and its branch, the Armagh County Museum, Armagh. The museum has been voted Irish Museum of the Year and ranks among Ireland's most important cultural, educational and tourist facilities.

HOLDINGS
The library and archive collections support the various interests of the museum, especially folk life, social history and transport. The book collection, which exceeds 25,000 volumes, and an extensive range of periodicals, are available for reference purposes only. The archive boasts an extensive collection of photographs from the late nineteenth century to the present. The largest collection of photographs is the 70,000 item archive of Harland and Wolff Ltd, which records the shipping activity of the company from 1895 to the mid-1980s. Harland and Wolff built the Titanic, and the museum's archive houses what is probably the world's largest and most important collection of photographic negatives and ship plans relating to this ill fated liner and other famous ships built by the yard. The museum also houses Ireland's largest collection of Lloyd's shipping and yacht registers along with an extensive collection of sound recordings documenting stories, language, music, customs, beliefs and traditions, including the BBC (Northern Ireland) Archive and the tape recorded survey of Hiberno-English. The most important recent addition is the Living Linen Archive, which has recorded the knowledge and experience of people associated with the linen industry. The museum also maintains an Ulster Dialect Archive, and has compiled an Ulster Dictionary onto a computer database.

LOCATION
About ten miles east of Belfast on the A2 Belfast to Bangor Road, 2.5 miles outside Holywood.

NEWCASTLE BRANCH LIBRARY

141–143 Main Street
NEWCASTLE, COUNTY DOWN, BT33 0AE
Northern Ireland

TELEPHONE: (028) 4372 2710; FAX: (028) 4372 2710
E-mail: info@seelb.org.uk
Website: www.seelb.org.uk, www.ni-libraries.net

HOURS
(Subject to change) M, Tu, 9.30am–8.00pm; W, F, 9.30am–5.00pm; Sa, 10.00am–1.00pm, 2.00pm–5.00pm

ACCESS AND SERVICES
Visitors welcome, but ID required. Visitors can join if they need to borrow materials but ID showing proof of address required. Visitors entitled to nine items, which can be returned to any other public library in Northern Ireland. Free internet access for

all Northern Ireland public library members. One membership card valid for all libraries. Charge of £1.50 per half hour for non-members; ID required. Membership of the library open to anyone living, working or studying in the area. Disabled access. Photocopying and fax services available.

CONTACT
Corwyn Rogers, Branch Library Manager. E-mail: corwyn.rogers@ni-libraries.net

DESCRIPTION
Small branch library, part of the South Eastern Education and Library Board system, headquartered in Ballynahinch.

HOLDINGS
Houses a collection of more than 10,000 volumes, with access to the system's larger collection, including the Local Studies Department in Ballynahinch. Modest local studies collection focusing on Newcastle and South County Down.

LOCATION
Beside the Shimna Bridge on Newcastle's main street.

DIOCESAN ARCHIVE, DROMORE (ROMAN CATHOLIC)

44 Armagh Road
NEWRY, COUNTY DOWN, BT35 6PN
Northern Ireland

TELEPHONE: (028) 3026 2444; FAX: (028) 3026 0496
E-mail: bishopofdromore@btinternet.com
Website: www.dromore.org (in development)

HOURS
By appointment

ACCESS AND SERVICES
Enquiries welcome, but advance notice required. Researchers asked to know exactly what they are looking for, as archive not fully processed.

CONTACT
Most Rev John McAreavey

DESCRIPTION
Small Roman Catholic diocesan archive. The Diocese of Dromore is part of the Archdiocese of Armagh and includes portions of Counties Down, Armagh and Antrim.

HOLDINGS
The archive comprises the written materials handed down by diocesan bishops from approximately 1850. The volume of material is very uneven. The archive is in the process of being reorganised following its removal from the Bishop's House while this was being refurbished.

LOCATION
Bishop's House, Newry.

NEWRY BRANCH LIBRARY

79 Hill Street
NEWRY, COUNTY DOWN, BT34 1DG
Northern Ireland

TELEPHONE: (028) 3026 4683/4077; FAX: (028) 3025 1739
E-mail: selb.hq@selb.org
Website: www.selb.org

HOURS
M, F, 9.30am–6.00pm; Tu, Th, 9.30am–8.00pm; W, Sa, 9.30am–5.00pm

ACCESS AND SERVICES
Visitors welcome, but ID required. Borrowing privileges for visitors may be
restricted. Consult Librarian. Disabled access. Photocopying, fax and internet
services available. Free internet access for all Northern Ireland public library
members. One membership card valid for all libraries. Charge of £1.50 per half hour
for non-members; ID required. Membership of library open to anyone living,
working or studying in the area.

CONTACT
Frances Lynch, Senior Assistant
Rosemary Loughran, Senior Assistant

DESCRIPTION
Branch library of the Southern Education and Library Board system.

HOLDINGS
Houses a general educational and recreational collection of more than 40,000
volumes, with access to the system's larger collection. Strong reference collection,
including local history of Newry and surrounding areas.

LOCATION
City centre.

NEWTOWNARDS BRANCH LIBRARY

Queen's Hall, Regent Street
NEWTOWNARDS, COUNTY DOWN, BT23 4AB
Northern Ireland

TELEPHONE: (028) 9081 4732; FAX: (028) 9081 0265
E-mail: info@seelb.org.uk
Website: www.seelb.org.uk

HOURS
M–W, F, 10.00am–8.00pm; Sa, 10.00am–1.00pm, 2.00pm–5.00pm

ACCESS AND SERVICES
Visitors welcome, but ID required. Borrowing privileges for visitors may be restricted.
Consult Librarian. Disabled access. Photocopying and fax services available. Free
internet access for all Northern Ireland public library members. One membership card
valid for all libraries. Charge of £1.50 per half hour for non-members; ID required.
Membership of the library open to anyone living, working or studying in the area.

CONTACT
Elizabeth Consiglia, Branch Library Manager
Irene Costley, Branch Library Manager

DESCRIPTION
Branch library of the South Eastern Education and Library Board system.

HOLDINGS
Houses a collection of more than 20,000 volumes, with access to the system's larger collection. Modest local studies collection focusing on Newtownards and North County Down.

LOCATION
Town centre.

COUNTY DUBLIN

BLACKROCK LIBRARY, Michael Smurfit Graduate School of Business
See UNIVERSITY COLLEGE DUBLIN LIBRARY, Dublin

ASSOCIATION OF PROFESSIONAL GENEALOGISTS IN IRELAND

Honorary Secretary, 30 Harlech Crescent, Clonskeagh
DUBLIN 14
Ireland

E-mail: apgi@dublin.com
Website: www.apgi.ie

DESCRIPTION
APGI is an association of individual professional genealogical researchers who subscribe to a strict code of practice. APGI acts as a regulating body to maintain high standards among its members and to protect the interests of clients. Members act as advisers in the National Library's Genealogy Advisory Service and a similar service at the National Archives, both in Dublin. There are currently 25 members, all of whom are accredited by an independent board of assessors. Some offer special areas of interest, e.g. 'research within Ulster only'. A brochure listing members and their addresses with telephone numbers, e-mail addresses and websites, where applicable, is available through the Honorary Secretary or through the website. Fees apply for research undertaken at the request of clients.

AUSTIN CLARKE LIBRARY
See POETRY IRELAND/ÉIGSE ÉIREANN

CENTRAL CATHOLIC LIBRARY

74 Merrion Square
DUBLIN 2
Ireland

TELEPHONE: (01) 676 1264; FAX: (01) 678 7618
E-mail: catholicresearch@eircom.net
Website: www.catholiclibrary.ie

HOURS
M–F, 11.00am–6.00pm; Sa, 11.00am–5.00pm

ACCESS AND SERVICES
Visitors and enquiries welcome, but advance notice preferred. Membership fees
apply: general public, €25 per year; students and seniors, €10. No disabled access
facilities. Open and closed collections; closed collection accessible only on request.
Sheaf and card catalogues available. Printed catalogue of older books available.
Photocopying (excludes early printed books) available for a fee at Librarian's
discretion. Staff carry out any photocopying. Laptops and photography permitted
with Librarian's approval. Series of four lectures held each spring and autumn.
Copies of library brochures available on request. Borrowing privileges limited to
members. Library regularly holds book sales.

CONTACT
Teresa Whitington, Librarian

DESCRIPTION
The library is a voluntary subscription library founded by Fr Stephen Brown SJ in
1922 to provide reading matter and reference services on church and religious affairs.
It is entirely self-funded, relying on membership fees, donations and bequests.

HOLDINGS
The collection totals more than 100,000 volumes dealing with all branches of
human knowledge with which religion is concerned. It also includes journals and
pamphlets. Though its focus is Catholic, the library's holdings vary widely and
include an important reference collection. Closed collections include: the Art Library
– a small archive dealing with the work of the Academy of Christian Art, a
collection on European art, including Celtic art, and a non-European art collection
donated by Sir John Galvin, a member of the board of the Chester Beatty Library;
the Irish Room – journals, books on Irish history and nineteenth century Irish
fiction; the Leo Room – sociology, politics and international affairs; the Carnegie
Collection – philosophy, religion and sociology (many dealing with non-Catholic
and non-Christian traditions); the Periodicals Collection; and some 1,200 older
printed books (1541–1850), mostly of a Catholic interest. Among the reference
books are several standard works on genealogy.

LOCATION
Nearly halfway along the south side of Merrion Square from the Upper Merrion
Street end. The south side is the side running from Upper Merrion Street to Upper
Mount Street and the Pepper Canister Church (St Stephen's). Bus 7 stops about five
minutes' walk from the library. From the north side of the city, bus 13 stops nearby.
The library is a ten minute walk from Pearse DART station.

CENTRAL LIBRARY
See DUBLIN CITY PUBLIC LIBRARIES, Dublin

CENTRE FOR DUBLIN AND IRISH STUDIES

Dublin City Library and Archive, 138–144 Pearse Street
DUBLIN 2
Ireland

TELEPHONE: (01) 674 4999; FAX: (01) 674 4879
E-mail: dublinstudies@dublincity.ie
Website: www.dublincity.ie/living_in_the_city/libraries/heritage_and_history

HOURS
M–Th, 10.00am–8.00pm; F–Sa, 10.00am–5.00pm; closed bank holidays, including
Saturdays of bank holiday weekends

ACCESS AND SERVICES
The Centre for Dublin and Irish Studies and Dublin City Archives share facilities at
Dublin City Library and Archive. Visitors welcome. The library is intended for
serious students and researchers as well as the general public. Facilities include the
Research Reading Room, conference rooms and exhibition rooms. All readers need a
reference readers' ticket to use the collections. Readers need to bring personal ID
and tickets will be issued without delay. No admission fees. Fees charged for
photocopying and photography. Facilities provided for laptops; pencils only. No
photography in Research Reading Room or in collections. Part of library catalogue
accessible online. All items published before 1801 included in the English Short
Title Catalogue (ESTC). Parts of collection accessible through printed *Catalogue of
the Library of Sir John T. Gilbert* (Dublin, 1918) and on card catalogue in Research
Reading Room. Conferences, seminars and single lectures held regularly.
Information can be found on the website.

Library has compiled and published a *Directory of Dublin for 1738* (Dublin,
2000). This replicates the eighteenth century directories, but information drawn
from legal recognisances, parish cess books, newspaper advertising and other sources.
Laid out in alphabetical order by surname, in street order and by occupation or
trade, and accompanied by fold out map based on maps of the period. This has
proved quite useful for family and historical research. Annual lecture held in January
to commemorate the life and works of Sir John T. Gilbert, and first eight of these
lectures published as separate booklets. All publications available for purchase
through website.

CONTACT
Máire Kennedy, Divisional Librarian. E-mail: maire.kennedy@dublincity.ie

DESCRIPTION
The Centre for Dublin and Irish Studies houses the special collections of the city's
public library system, most especially the valuable collection of books on early
Dublin contained in the library of Sir John T. Gilbert, the Dix Collection, the Yeats
Collection, the Swift Collection and the Dublin and Irish Collections. It also houses
one of the strongest genealogical collections in Ireland.

HOLDINGS
The Dublin Collection
The Dublin Collection comprises a number of special collections relating to Dublin
and Dubliners. New material is acquired as it becomes available, including second
hand and antiquarian books, newspapers, periodicals, photographs, maps, prints,

drawings, theatre programmes, playbills, posters, ballad sheets, audiovisual materials and ephemera, as resources allow. The collection includes the following special collections.

The Gilbert Library

The most extensive of the special collections, the Gilbert Library is made up of the manuscripts, books and other printed materials collected by Sir John T. Gilbert (1829–98), historian and archivist. The collection reflects Gilbert's interest in the social, political and cultural history of Ireland, particularly of Dublin. Notable features include early Dublin newspapers, fine Dublin bookbindings of the eighteenth century, Dublin almanacs and directories. Of special interest are the manuscripts of the municipal records of the city of Dublin and records of the Dublin guilds. A printed catalogue of the Gilbert Library compiled by Douglas Hyde and D.J. O'Donoghue is available. John T. Gilbert's many original historical works and his edited volumes are prominent in the library. He is perhaps best known for his three volume *History of the City of Dublin*. He compiled and edited the *Calendar of Ancient Records of the Corporation of Dublin*, the first seven volumes of which were published during his lifetime. His widow (the novelist Rosa Mulholland) continued the work, and 19 volumes of the *Calendar* were published from 1889 to 1944. The *Calendar* comprises a record of the muniments in the possession of Dublin City Council and is an extremely valuable source for the history of the city.

The Dix Collection

The gift of Irish bibliographer E.R. McClintock Dix, this collection contains some 700 Dublin and Irish imprints, mainly from the seventeenth and eighteenth centuries, and a number of eighteenth century fine bindings.

The Yeats Collection

This consists mainly of first editions of Yeats works, including those from the Dun Emer Press founded by Lilly and Lollie Yeats.

The Swift Collection

Consisting of books, manuscripts, periodicals and ephemera, this contains an extensive collection of rare and valuable items and is growing annually.

The Directories Collection

This is one of the most heavily used collections and includes an almost complete set of Dublin directories from 1751 to the present. Specific holdings include: *Watson's Almanack*, 1729–1837; *Wilson's Dublin Directories*, 1751–3; 1761–1837; *Pettigrew and Oulton's Dublin Directories*, 1834–47; *Thom's Irish Almanac and Official Directories*, 1844–present. The early directories, from 1751 to 1833, are in surname order only, and from 1834 street listings are available as well as the name sequence. *Pigot's Directory of Ireland 1822–4* on microfiche is the earliest directory in the collection to cover all of Ireland, followed by *Slater's Directory of Ireland*, published in the years 1846, 1856, 1870, 1881 and 1894. The 1894 edition has a very useful general directory of private residents of Ireland.

The Newspaper Collection

The newspaper collection covers a range of titles published from the 1700s to the present. The early Dublin newspapers, including rare and some unique items dating from 1700 to 1750, form an important part of the collection. Current and recent issues of the newspapers are not available for viewing for a period of six months, as all newspapers are sent out for binding. (Daily newspapers are available for reading

in the Business Information Centre, Dublin City Public Libraries – Central Library,
Ilac Centre, Dublin 1.)

The Family History Collection
The library has a strong collection of source materials for family history. These
include: *Griffith's Valuation* 1847–64, held on microfiche and covering 32 counties;
tithe applotment books 1823–38, held on microfilm and covering 32 counties;
Ordnance Survey first edition six inch maps; Ordnance Survey letters, held in
typescript copies and arranged by county; and census returns of 1901 and 1911. The
1901 and 1911 returns have been microfilmed and the library holds a full set for
Dublin City and County. Church of Ireland registers of Dublin parishes from the
Representative Church Body Library, Dublin, have been microfilmed and purchased
for the library. Many date from the seventeenth to the end of the nineteenth century.
Selected Dublin parish registers were published in book form and are held in the
library: those of St John's, Dublin, 1619–99, baptisms, marriages, burials; St
Michan's, Dublin, 1636–85, baptisms, marriages, burials; St Catherine's, Dublin,
1636–1715, baptisms, marriages, burials; Monkstown, County Dublin, 1669–1786,
baptisms, burials; St Nicholas Without, 1694–1739, baptisms, marriages, burials; St
Andrew's, St Anne's, St Audoen's, St Bride's, 1632–1800, marriages; St Marie's, St
Luke's, St Catherine's, St Werburgh's, 1627–1800, marriages; St Patrick's,
1677–1800, baptisms, marriages, burials; the register of the parish of St Thomas,
Dublin, 1750–1791, edited by Raymond Refaussé, Representative Church Body
Library, 1994. Also available are: the registers of the French Conformed Churches of
St Patrick and St Mary, Dublin (1893); and a set of Huguenot records relating to
Ireland on microfiche. There are a number of publications that may be of special
interest to genealogists. These include: shipping indexes of persons who left Ireland
for America during the nineteenth century; *The Famine Immigrants 1846–51*,
covering those arriving at the port of New York during the Famine; *Memorials of the
Dead*, a series of volumes compiled by Richard Flatman, and another series by Brian
Cantwell listing gravestone inscriptions in cemeteries in Dublin, Wicklow and
Wexford (these are not published but are available in bound typescripts); and *First
World War Memorial Records*, published in 1923 in eight volumes listing the Irish
soldiers who died in World War I. The names are in alphabetical order. Other
helpful standard reference sources include: *Who's Who* (1897–1998 is available on
CD-ROM), *Burke's and Lodge's Peerages*; biographical dictionaries; indexes to wills
(published indexes compiled before the destruction of the Public Record Office);
King's Inns Admission Papers; *Alumni Dublinensis*, containing a list of students of
Trinity College Dublin from 1593 to 1860; Civil Survey for Dublin and other
counties, seventeenth century; and *Palmer's Index to The Times 1790–1905* on CD-
ROM. There are also General Register Office indexes to births, marriages and deaths
(on microfilm from the Church of Jesus Christ of LDS) 1864 to the 1950s, with
some gaps, and marriages from 1845; microfilm copies (from the LDS) of cemetery
records from Deansgrange and Mount Jerome cemeteries; a Microsoft Access
database in the Research Reading Room of baptisms, marriages and burials from
Dublin parishes, containing some 160,000 records.

The Irish Collection
The Irish Collection is made up of about 90,000 items: books and other materials
relating to Ireland, by Irish authors, or in the Irish language. A comprehensive
collection of material of Irish interest published outside Ireland is also available, as

well as a considerable amount of material of genealogical interest. This general collection gives a national context to the Dublin special collections.

LOCATION
The library is situated on Pearse Street, two blocks eastwards from Pearse DART station. Bus 3 from O'Connell Street to Ringsend stops across the street.

CHESTER BEATTY LIBRARY

Dublin Castle
DUBLIN 2
Ireland

TELEPHONE: (01) 407 0750; FAX: (01) 407 0760
E-mail: info@cbl.ie
Website: www.cbl.ie

HOURS
Exhibitions
May–September: M–F, 10.00am–5.00pm
October–April: Tu–F, 10.00am–5.00pm
All year: Sa, 11.00am–5.00pm, Su, 1.00pm–5.00pm
Closed Good Friday, 24–26 December, 1 January and public holiday Mondays.
Research
Reading Room reference: M–F, 10.00am–1.00pm, 2.15pm–5.00pm
Access to manuscript collections: by written arrangement, M–F, 10.00am–12.45pm, 2.15pm–4.45pm

ACCESS AND SERVICES
Free admission to exhibition galleries. Access to Reading Room by appointment. Photocopier and microfilm reader available. Online access to reference and early printed book collections available at www.opac.cbl.ie. Laptops permitted; pencils only; gloves may be required for use in the Reading Room. Photography not permitted. Photographs, microfilms, transparencies and digital images to order.

CONTACT
Reference Library: Celine Ward, Reference Librarian. E-mail: reference@cbl.ie
Manuscript research: write to Director or Specialist Curator (consult website for details)
Friends of the Chester Beatty Library: Janet Sheahan. E-mail: jsheahan@cbl.ie
Photographic services: Sinead Ward. E-mail: sward@cbl.ie

DESCRIPTION
The library was formed by the American born mining engineer and philanthropist Chester Beatty (1875–1968), who moved his priceless collections of artworks, manuscripts and illustrated printed books to Dublin in 1950. The library relocated to its current premises in 1999. Beatty bequeathed his library to a trust for the benefit of the public. It is now supported by the Government of Ireland. The library boasts a state of the art exhibition gallery in a modern addition to the renovated and redesigned eighteenth century clock tower building in the grounds of Dublin Castle. Facilities include a restaurant, gift and bookshop, audiovisual presentations, roof garden, wheelchair access and baby changing facilities. Free brochures are available in

eight languages. The Chester Beatty Library is a 'must see' even if you have no plans to research its rich collections. The exhibitions alone are worth a visit. The Chester Beatty Library was named European Museum of the Year 2002.

HOLDINGS
The library houses one of the world's finest collections of manuscripts, prints, icons, paintings, early printed books and *objets d'art*, with special strengths in the areas of the Middle East and Asia. Items from the collection date back to 2700 BC. Among the highlights of the collection are: Egyptian papyrus texts, exceptional early Biblical papyri, illuminated copies of the Koran, the Bible and European medieval and renaissance manuscripts.

LOCATION
In the garden behind the main buildings of Dublin Castle, off Dame Street. There is also an entrance on Ship Street. It is a ten minute walk from Trinity College. The library is on bus routes 13, 16, 19 and 123 (from O'Connell Street).

DUBLIN CITY ARCHIVES
(*See also* IRISH THEATRE ARCHIVE, Dublin)

Dublin City Library and Archive, 138–144 Pearse Street
DUBLIN 2
Ireland

TELEPHONE: (01) 674 4996/7; FAX: (01) 674 4879
E-mail: cityarchives@dublincity.ie
Website: www.dublincity.ie

HOURS
M–Th, 10.00am–8.00pm; F–Sa, 10.00am–5.00pm; closed Sundays, bank holidays and bank holiday weekends

ACCESS AND SERVICES
Visitors welcome. ID required to facilitate registration on first visit. Disabled access facilities. Laptops permitted; pencils only. Photocopying and microform prints available for a fee. Publications specifically relating to the holdings of the archives include: Sir John T. and Lady Gilbert (eds), *Calendar of Ancient Records of Dublin*, 19 vols (Dublin, 1889–1944); Mary Clark, *The Book of Maps of the Dublin City Surveyors* (Dublin, 1983); Niall McCullough, *A Vision of the City: Dublin and the Wide Streets Commissioners* (Dublin, 1991); Philomena Connolly and Geoffrey Martin, *The Dublin Guild Merchant Roll* (Dublin, 1992); Mary Clark and Raymond Refaussé, *Directory of Historic Dublin Guilds* (Dublin, 1993); Mary Clark and Gráinne Doran, *Serving the City: the Dublin City Managers and Town Clerks* (Dublin, 1996); Colm Lennon and James Murray, *The Dublin City Franchise Roll* (Dublin, 1998); and Jane Ohlmeyer and Éamonn Ó Ciardha, *The Irish Statute Staple Books* (Dublin, 1998).

CONTACT
Mary Clark, City Archivist

DESCRIPTION
Dublin City Archives houses the historic records of the municipal government of

Dublin from the twelfth century to the present. On 1 January 2002 Dublin
Corporation changed its name to Dublin City Council.

HOLDINGS
The Dublin City Archives contain a wealth of published and unpublished records,
including City Council and committee minutes, account books, correspondence,
reports, court records, charity petitions, title deeds, maps and plans, photographs
and drawings, all of which document the development of Dublin over eight
centuries. Among the principal civic collections are: royal charters of the city of
Dublin, 1171–1727; medieval cartularies, including two important bound
manuscripts, one written on vellum, the *White Book of Dublin* (also known as the
Liber Albus) and the *Chain Book of Dublin*; Dublin City assembly rolls, 1447–1841;
Board of Dublin Aldermen, 1567–1841; journals of sheriffs and commons,
1746–1841; Tholsell Court of Dublin, sixteenth–eighteenth centuries; Dublin city
treasurer's accounts, 1540–1841; freedom records, 1468–1918; City Surveyor's
maps, 1695–1928; minutes and reports of Dublin City Council, 1841–present;
photographic collection, including Liffey Bridges and North Strand bombing;
records of Dublin Corporation departments, nineteenth and twentieth century.

LOCATION
The archives are situated on Pearse Street, two blocks eastwards from Pearse DART
station. Bus 3 from O'Connell Street to Ringsend stops across the street.

DUBLIN CITY PUBLIC LIBRARIES AND ARCHIVE

Library Headquarters, 138–144 Pearse Street
DUBLIN 2
Ireland

TELEPHONE: (01) 674 4800; FAX: (01) 674 4879
E-mail: dublinpubliclibraries@dublincity.ie
Website: www.dublincitylibraries.ie

HOURS
See separate listings for Dublin City Public Libraries – Central Library, Centre for
Dublin and Irish Studies and Dublin City Archives. Call or visit website for hours of
branch libraries listed below. Library Headquarters is not open to visitors.

CONTACT
Deirdre Ellis-King, Dublin City Librarian
Margaret Hayes, Deputy City Librarian

DESCRIPTION
The Headquarters Library is responsible for the overall administration of library
services in a network of 31 libraries and service points. These include: Ballyfermot
Library (telephone (01) 626 9324/5); Ballymun Library (telephone (01) 842 1890);
Cabra Library (telephone (01) 869 1414); Central Library (telephone (01) 873
4333); Charleville Mall Library (telephone (01) 874 9619); Coolock Library
(telephone (01) 847 7781); Dolphin's Barn Library (telephone (01) 454 0681);
Donaghmede Library (telephone (01) 848 2833); Drumcondra Library, telephone
(01) 837 7206); Finglas Library (telephone (01) 834 4906); Inchicore Library
(telephone (01) 453 3793); Kevin Street Library (telephone (01) 475 3794); Marino

Library (telephone (01) 833 6297); Pembroke Library (telephone (01) 668 9575); Phibsborough Library (telephone (01) 830 4341); Raheny Library (telephone (01) 831 5521); Rathmines Library (telephone (01) 497 3539); Ringsend Library (telephone (01) 668 0063); Terenure Library (telephone (01) 490 7035); Walkinstown Library (telephone (01) 455 8159); Children's and Schools (telephone (01) 475 8791); Community and Youth Information Centre (telephone (01) 878 6844); Mobile Libraries (telephone (01) 869 1415); Civic Museum (telephone (01) 679 4260); and City Archives (telephone (01) 677 5877).

HOLDINGS
See separate listings for Central Library, Centre for Dublin and Irish Studies and Dublin City Archives.

LOCATION
Headquarters is situated on Pearse Street, two blocks eastwards from Pearse DART station. Bus 3 from O'Connell Street to Ringsend stops across the street.

DUBLIN CITY PUBLIC LIBRARIES – CENTRAL LIBRARY

Ilac Centre, Henry Street
DUBLIN 1
Ireland

TELEPHONE: (01) 873 4333; FAX: (01) 872 1451
E-mail: dublincitylibraries@dublincity.ie
Website: www.dublincitylibraries.ie

HOURS
M–Th, 10.00am–8.00pm; F, Sa, 10.00am–5.00pm

ACCESS AND SERVICES
Open to the public. For those wishing to borrow material, full membership available on production of ID and proof of address. Visitors welcome to use all other facilities but will need to provide personal ID when using some services.

CONTACT
Michael Molloy, Divisional Librarian. E-mail: michael.molloy@dublincity.ie

DESCRIPTION
Located within a shopping centre in Dublin's city centre, the Central Library is the largest in a network of 31 libraries and service points administered by the Dublin City Public Libraries.

HOLDINGS
The Central Library offers a wide range of services in addition to its extensive collection of adult and junior material for lending. These include: internet access, photocopying, computerised catalogue, newspapers, periodicals, exhibitions, lectures and tours. The Central Library also offers a Business Information Centre, Open Learning Centre and specialist Music Library.

Business Information Centre
The Business Information Centre is a reference service and a key information source for those starting a business or conducting research. It holds sample business plans, journals and newspapers, company information, market research and financial

markets information and national and international statistics. It also offers reference books, national and international directories, journals, databases, newspaper cuttings and an extensive collection of company reports.

The Open Learning Centre

This offers a wide range of self-learning opportunities in language and computers. Courses in audio and video are available in approximately 80 different languages. Courses are available in basic computer skills, wordprocessing, spreadsheets, databases and use of the internet. All courses must be booked in advance and a certificate is awarded to students who complete 50 hours of study using the learning facilities. The centre also facilitates conversation exchange in Italian, Spanish, French, German, Irish, Japanese and Russian.

Music Library

The Music Library is a valuable resource for anyone with an interest in music. The library offers a lending and reference service, including music CDs, cassettes and videos for lending. It also stocks literature on all aspects of music, sheet music including vocal scores, songbooks, tutor books and orchestral sets. In addition, the library provides listening facilities for leisure or study purposes and a wide range of music periodicals. A number of computer databases have been produced including a tracks index, a sheet music index and databases of music and choral societies in Dublin.

LOCATION
In the Ilac Shopping Centre, between Henry Street and Parnell Street, in the city centre.

CREEGAN LIBRARY
See ST PATRICK'S COLLEGE – CREEGAN LIBRARY, Dublin

DUBLIN CITY UNIVERSITY LIBRARY

Dublin City University
DUBLIN 9
Ireland

TELEPHONE: (01) 700 5212; FAX: (01) 700 5602
E-mail: infodesk@dcu.ie
Website: www.dcu.ie/~library

HOURS
Term time: M–Th, 8.30am–10.00pm; F, 8.30am–9.00pm; Sa, 9.30am–5.00pm
Vacation period: consult library website

ACCESS AND SERVICES
Visitors welcome, but must apply for a non-graduate external membership to gain access to collections and services. Annual fee charged. Accessible to persons with a disability. All locally held material can be found by using library catalogue (OPAC), available online. Library also provides access, via its website, to an extensive collection of online information resources including full text journals and newspapers. Reciprocal arrangements with other university libraries are in place and visiting facilities can be arranged. Users can also avail of photocopying/printing/

scanning facilities, read microforms, watch videos and access the internet. DCU shares an integrated OPAC with Mater Dei Institute of Education (Clonliffe Road, Dublin 3; telephone (01) 874 1680; fax (01) 836 8920) and St Patrick's College, the first system in Ireland to provide full web search facilities in both English and Irish. Catalogues of the three libraries provide single search point for over 350,000 book titles. DCU is also a member of ALCID (Academic Libraries Cooperating in Dublin), giving students and faculty access to the libraries of: Mater Dei; NUI Galway; NUI Maynooth; Royal College of Surgeons in Ireland; Royal Irish Academy; St Patrick's, Drumcondra; Trinity College Dublin; University College Cork; University College Dublin; and University of Limerick.

CONTACT
Paul Sheehan, Director of Library Services. Telephone: (01) 700 5211; e-mail: paul.sheehan@dcu.ie
Ellen Breen, Sub-Librarian, Information and Public Services. Telephone: (01) 700 5210; e-mail: ellen.breen@dcu.ie

DESCRIPTION
Dublin City University was established as the National Institute of Higher Education, Dublin, in 1980, to respond to the challenges being set for higher education by rapidly diversifying industrial and business sectors in Ireland and in the European Union. It gained univesity status in 1989. The university currently enrols more than 9,000 students. In 2000, it opened its new state of the art library building, designed to facilitate all forms of research and learning. The university includes St Patrick's College, Drumcondra; and Mater Dei Institute of Education, each with separate libraries, but linked by the same library management system. *See* separate listing for St Patrick's College.

HOLDINGS
The library's collection contains approximately 180,000 volumes, 1,100 print subscriptions and over 21,000 electronic subscriptions, and mirrors the academic programmes offered by DCU. These include: business; education; computing and mathematical sciences; engineering and design; humanities; applied language and intercultural studies; communications; and science and health, including nursing and sport.

LOCATION
The university is located on an 85 acre campus in the northern suburbs of Dublin, near Glasnevin cemetery and the Botanic Gardens. It is served by buses 11, 11A, 13, 13A, 19A and 60.

DUBLIN COUNTY ARCHIVES
See FINGAL COUNTY ARCHIVES, Dublin

DUBLIN DIOCESAN ARCHIVES

Archbishop's House, Drumcondra
DUBLIN 9
Ireland

TELEPHONE: (01) 837 9253, extension 183; FAX: (01) 836 8393

E-mail: archives@dublindiocese.ie (this e-mail address is protected from spam and requires Javascript enabled)
Website: www.dublindiocese.ie

HOURS
M–F, 9.30am–1.00pm, 2.00pm–4.45pm; closed religious and bank holidays; appointment essential to guarantee access to collections: contact Diocesan Archivist

ACCESS AND SERVICES
Visitors welcome; appointment in advance highly recommended. Please contact Diocesan Archivist. Pencils only; laptops permitted with Archivist's permission. Photocopying by staff only for a modest fee. Microfilm reader/printer available.

CONTACT
Noelle Dowling, Diocesan Archivist

DESCRIPTION
The Dublin Diocesan Archives exists to preserve the records of the Roman Catholic Archdiocese of Dublin and has operated as an archival repository on a full time basis since 1984. The Diocesan Archives has three functions:
to preserve the records of central diocesan administration;
to provide services to the secretariats and agencies at Archbishop's House and to the clergy and the laity of the Archdiocese of Dublin;
to make the archives of the Archdiocese of Dublin available to researchers.

HOLDINGS
The Dublin Diocesan Archives preserves records documenting the history of the Archdiocese of Dublin down through the centuries. It possesses a few items dating back to the fifteenth and sixteenth centuries but essentially its holdings date from the eighteenth, nineteenth and twentieth centuries. The holdings comprise collections of the papers of archbishops and bishops of Dublin, priests and lay persons, and the records of Catholic colleges and lay organisations. The Diocesan Archives does not hold the registers of baptisms and marriages for the 200 parishes of the Dublin Archdiocese. These are still held in local parish custody.
    The two oldest items held by the Diocesan Archives are vellum manuscripts. The first of these is a foundation charter of the Guild of St Sythe given in 1476 under the seal of King Edward IV (see Colm Lennon, 'The Foundation charter of St. Sythe's Guild, Dublin, 1476,' *Archivium Hibernicum* xlviii, 1994). The second is a papal bull dated 1555 from the pontificate of Pius IV, providing Hugh Curwen to the See of Dublin. This document is believed to be the oldest bull of appointment of a bishop currently preserved in Ireland.
    The core of the collections consists of the surviving papers of eight successive archbishops of Dublin covering the period 1770–1972. These collections include the papers of such significant historical figures as John Thomas Troy (1784–1823), builder of the Pro Cathedral, Paul Cullen (1852–78), Ireland's first cardinal, and John Charles McQuaid (1940–72). These collections are currently open to researchers.
    The Diocesan Archives also holds the combined surviving records of the Catholic Association and the Loyal National Repeal Association, 1806–50 (see Fergus O'Higgins, 'Catholic Association Papers in the Dublin Diocesan Archives', *Archivium Hibernicum* xxxix, 1984). Another important collection is the Papers of Bartholomew Woodlock (1860–79), who succeeded John Henry Newman, a rector of the Catholic University of Ireland.

LOCATION
Archbishop's House is a prominent landmark overlooking Drumcondra Road. The
archives are located to the rear of Archbishop's House in a wing of the former
diocesan seminary, Holy Cross College. Visitors should enter the campus via the
main entrance on Drumcondra Road and follow the blue signs directing them to the
Diocesan Archives. The 3, 11, 11A, 13, 13A, 16, 16A, 33 and 41 buses from the
city centre stop on Lower Drumcondra Road close to Archbishop's House. Trains
on the Dublin–Maynooth (Sligo) line stop at Drumcondra Station on Lower
Drumcondra Road.

DUBLIN UNIVERSITY
See TRINITY COLLEGE DUBLIN

DÚN LAOGHAIRE LIBRARY
See DÚN LAOGHAIRE LIBRARY – LOCAL HISTORY DEPARTMENT, Dún
Laoghaire

DÚN LAOGHAIRE-RATHDOWN HERITAGE CENTRE

The Courtyard, Marlay Park, Rathfarnham
DUBLIN 16
Ireland

TELEPHONE: (01) 205 4700
E-mail: heritage@dlrcoco.ie

HOURS
M–Th, 9.00am–5.00pm

ACCESS AND SERVICES
Dún Laoghaire-Rathdown Heritage Centre offers a fee based, partial genealogical
service to persons wishing to trace their roots in South County Dublin. In addition,
centre holds a large collection of archival material covering area's archaeology,
geology and ecology, with illustrations, photographs and maps, plus files on area's
maritime history. Fees vary depending on amount of time and research required.
Typically, initial enquiry receives reply within two weeks. Visitors welcome and given
immediate service. Publications include: *In the Mind's Eye: Memories of Dun
Laoghaire*; *Dalkey: St Begnet's Graveyard*; and *Dalkey: Medieval Manor and Seaport*.

CONTACT
Catherine Malone

DESCRIPTION
Dún Laoghaire-Rathdown Heritage Centre is the Irish Family History Foundation's
designated genealogical centre for South County Dublin. IFHF is the coordinating
body for a network of government approved genealogical research centres in the
Republic of Ireland and in Northern Ireland that have computerised tens of millions
of Irish ancestral records of different types. The centre focuses on Roman Catholic
and Church of Ireland parish registers for South County Dublin. The area covered
by this centre now lies in the hinterland of Dublin city but was, in the nineteenth
century, a collection of rural towns and villages. The centre's archival holdings are an

important research source for the history of this area. Chief surnames of South Dublin include: Byrne, Doyle, Kelly, Murphy, Kavanagh, O'Neill, O'Brien, O'Connor, O'Farrell and O'Toole.

HOLDINGS
The centre has computerised over 145,000 records. The main records include: Roman Catholic records (baptismal and marriage) 1755–1900; Church of Ireland records, which include burial records as well as baptismal and marriage records, starting in 1694; and Presbyterian records that date from 1843. Also computerised are the pre-1900 gravestone inscriptions at the extensive Deansgrange Cemetery (from 1868) and St Begnet's Cemetery in Dalkey. The Centre has compiled an inventory of war memorials, listing all wars memorialised in the Dún Laoghaire-Rathdown area, and has also collated the names of the men from area who fought in World War I. Main towns in the Dún Laoghaire-Rathdown Heritage Centre's area include: Booterstown, Cabinteely, Dundrum, Dún Laoghaire (formerly Kingstown), Blackrock, Dalkey, Glasthule, Monkstown and Donnybrook.

LOCATION
Bus 16 from O'Connell Street stops at the main gate.

FINGAL COUNTY ARCHIVES

11 Parnell Square
DUBLIN 1
Ireland

TELEPHONE: (01) 872 7968; FAX: (01) 878 6919
E-mail: archives@fingalcoco.ie
Website: www.fingalcoco.ie (follow links to 'Archives')

HOURS
M–F, 10.00am–1.00pm, 2.00pm–4.30pm

ACCESS AND SERVICES
Visitors welcome. Research facilities provided free of charge. Advance appointment required. In order to facilitate researchers, appointments outside normal hours may be arranged if sufficient notice given. Archives for reference purposes only; materials not available for loan. Access to storage area not permitted. Depending on age and condition of material, photocopying services may be provided. Please note: some records may have to be withdrawn for conservation treatment and may not always be available for consultation.

CONTACT
Archivist

DESCRIPTION
Under the terms of the 1993 Local Government Act, Dublin County Council was replaced by the three new Councils of Fingal, South Dublin and Dún Laoghaire-Rathdown. The archives of Dublin County Council were transferred to Fingal County Archives, which is now located within the former headquarters of Fingal County Libraries, 11 Parnell Square. All material relating to the former Dublin County Council and its predecessor bodies including Boards of Guardians and Grand Juries is housed here.

HOLDINGS
Fingal County Archives contains a small number of manuscript Grand Jury minute books and a more extensive collection of printed Presentment Books for the period 1818–98, when most of the Grand Juries' functions were transferred to the newly established County Councils. The Grand Juries were responsible for setting up Boards of Trustees to supervise and maintain the turnpike (toll) roads system. Fingal County Archives contains the records of a number of these boards for roads leading out of County Dublin north and south. The collection of records of the Board of Trustees for the turnpike road between Dublin and Dunleer, County Louth, is one of the most complete in the country, covering the period 1775–1856. Fingal County Archives also contains material for the Boards of Guardians and Rural District Councils of Balrothery, Dublin North, Dublin South and Rathdown and the Rural District Council of Celbridge.

The Dublin County Council records constitute the largest body of material in the archives. Dublin County Council was established under the 1898 Local Government Act. In the early years of its existence its main functions were the maintenance of roads and mental hospitals and the raising of rates. In 1930 it took over the functions of the Boards of Guardians and Rural District Councils and as the century progressed its functions expanded to include the provision of roads, planning, libraries, community and environmental services. Fingal County Archives contains a large number of collections dealing with the establishment and provision of these services. There are also collections of records of some Urban District Councils and Town Commissioners such as Balbriggan and Howth, and the Dublin Board of Assistance/Dublin Board of Public Health. Fingal County Archives also contains a small number of collections of private individuals and organisations connected with the County of Dublin, including the Fingal Estate Papers, 1685- –1969, the Butler Estate Papers and a small collection of correspondence belonging to Miss Brigid Connolly, a member of Cumann na mBan, 1914–36.

LOCATION
Dublin city centre, at the north end of O'Connell Street, opposite the entrance to the Garden of Remembrance.

FINGAL COUNTY LIBRARIES

Local Studies Department, 11 Parnell Square
DUBLIN 1
Ireland

TELEPHONE: (01) 878 6910; FAX: (01) 878 6919
E-mail: fincolib@iol.ie
Website: www.fingalcoco.ie (follow links to 'Local Studies')

HOURS
By appointment

ACCESS AND SERVICES
Visitors welcome. Photocopying and microfilm print services available for a modest fee. Local Studies produces publications and exhibits to promote the collection. In addition to publishing a series of seven different posters of old picture postcards (relating to the towns of Balbriggan, Howth, Skerries, Rush, Malahide,

Portmarnock, Baldoyle and Sutton), Local Studies has published several books, including: *Discovering Fingal: a Photographic Tour*, vol. 1 (1997); *Discovering Fingal: a Photographic Tour*, vol. 2 (2002); *Swords: Monastic Foundation to Modern Town*, by the Transition Year students of Loreto College, Swords (2001–2); Aine Shields, *Swords in the 19th Century* (2003); Sean Lennon, *Dublin Writers and Their Haunts* (2003); and Petra Skyvova, *The Holy Wells of Fingal* (2005).

CONTACT
Jeremy Black, Local Studies Librarian

DESCRIPTION
Part of the Fingal County Libraries system, headquartered at County Hall Main Street, Swords, County Dublin (telephone (01) 890 5524; fax (01) 890 5599) under the sponsorship of Fingal County Council. Fingal County Council was established on 1 January 1994 following the dissolution of Dublin County Council and the Corporation of Dún Laoghaire and their replacement with three new administrative counties, South Dublin, Dún Laoghaire-Rathdown and Fingal.

HOLDINGS
A comprehensive collection of material relating to the Fingal area has been assembled since 1994 and is currently housed at Parnell Square. Items contained in the collection include: antiquarian and new books covering standard reference texts, history, topography, ecclesiastical matters, transport, maritime matters, postal matters and many more; periodicals, including older standard research titles and those with specific local history interest; prints, focusing on sketches of the archaeological and architectural views of Fingal; photographs, including copies of the relevant Fingal subjects taken from the primary collections of the National Library of Ireland, with some private photographic material also available; postcards (800 items capturing scenes of Fingal from the early part of the twentieth century); pictures (watercolour, oil and ink drawings by local artists and some original paintings); maps (Ordnance Survey, townland, Down Survey and contemporary development items); videos (copies of videos produced within the Fingal area by various groups); newspapers (bound editions of the *Fingal Independent*, 1994–present); and ephemera (material including pamphlets, letters, coins, posters, postal items, memorabilia and curiosities makes up a growing portion of the collection).

LOCATION
Dublin city centre, at the north end of O'Connell Street, opposite the entrance to the Garden of Remembrance.

FINGAL GENEALOGY
See under SWORDS, County Dublin

FRANCISCAN LIBRARY
See under KILLINEY, County Dublin

THE FRIENDS' HISTORICAL LIBRARY
See HISTORICAL LIBRARY, RELIGIOUS SOCIETY OF FRIENDS, Dublin

THE GAA MUSEUM
(Gaelic Athletic Association)

St Joseph's Avenue, Croke Park
DUBLIN 3
Ireland

TELEPHONE: (01) 819 2323; FAX: (01) 819 2324
E-mail: gaamuseum@crokepark.ie
Website: www.gaa.ie/museum

HOURS
September–June: M–Sa, 9.30am–5.00pm; Sundays and bank holidays,
12.00pm–5.00pm
July–August: M–Sa, 9.30am–6.00pm
Closed 1 January, Good Friday, eve of All Ireland hurling and football finals, 24–27
and 31 December. On match days the museum is open to Cusack Stand ticket
holders only and regular museum admission rates apply.

ACCESS AND SERVICES
Located under Cusack Stand in Croke Park. Access via St Joseph's Avenue off
Clonliffe Road. Group bookings welcome. Guided tours of Croke Park Stadium
depart daily, except on match days, from museum. For up to date information on
stadium tour times, consult website. Museum is self-guided and includes a 'test your
skills in hurling and gaelic football' games area. Facilities include gift shop, café,
toilets, baby changing facilities and ample car parking. Disabled access.

CONTACT
Joanne Clarke, Museum Manager
Tony McGuinness, Assistant Manager

DESCRIPTION
The GAA Museum opened to the public in 1998 and was established to
commemorate, recognise and celebrate the GAA's enormous contribution to Irish
sporting, cultural and social life since its foundation in 1884. The museum looks at
the birth and growth of the GAA at home and abroad and its unique role in the
national movement and cultural revival in Ireland.

Over 40 audiovisual presentations bring to life the players, matches, unique
moments and countless memories of the past. Film presentations include topics such
as the GAA's role in the struggle for independence and the excitement of All Ireland
Final Day. Touch screen technology enables the visitor instantly to recall historic
moments, great players and great games. Specially designed interactive displays allow
visitors to test their own skills in hurling and Gaelic football.

Guided tours of Croke Park Stadium offer an in-depth, behind the scenes look
at one of the most historic and modern sporting arenas in the world.

HOLDINGS
The museum houses a vast collection of sports memorabilia, including hurleys,
jerseys, trophies, medals, programmes and photographs. On permanent display is the
original All Ireland Football Championship trophy, the Sam Maguire (1928) and the
original All Ireland Hurling Championship trophy, the Liam MacCarthy (1923).
Medal collections belonging to legendary players such as Christy Ring, Jack Lynch,
Jimmy Doyle, Noel Skehan and Peter McDermott are also on display.

The GAA Museum has an extensive archive collection consisting of a range of artefacts including programmes, yearbooks, annuals, medals, photographs, posters, tickets and various GAA related memorabilia.

LOCATION
In Croke Park, Drumcondra, on the north side of the Liffey, *en route* to Dublin Airport. It is located under the Cusack Stand, which is accessible via St Joseph's Avenue, just off Clonliffe Road. It is a 15 minute walk from O'Connell Street (city centre). Buses from O'Connell Street are: 3, 11, 11A, 16, 16A, 123; bus 51A runs from Lower Abbey Street to Clonliffe Road. By rail, the museum is a 15 minute walk from Connolly station; it is less than ten minutes from Drumcondra station.

GARDA MUSEUM/ARCHIVES
Record Tower, Dublin Castle
DUBLIN 2
Ireland

TELEPHONE: (01) 666 9998; FAX: (01) 666 9992
E-mail: gatower@iol.ie
Website: www.garda.ie (follow links to 'Historical Society')

HOURS
M–F, 9.00am–5.00pm; Sa–Su, by appointment

ACCESS AND SERVICES
Visitors welcome but advance notice preferred, especially for use of archives or library. No admission charge. Disabled access facilities, but only to ground floor. Pencils only when using original material. Laptops and photography permitted. Printed finding aids available.

CONTACT
Inspector Patrick McGee, Archivist

DESCRIPTION
An Garda Síochána Museum/Archives collects and preserves archival material and artefacts relating not only to An Garda Síochána, but also to the Irish Constabulary, the Royal Irish Constabulary and the Dublin Metropolitan Police. It serves both as a support service within the Police Force, with a primary responsibility to provide a records management service, and as an outreach resource for the general public.

HOLDINGS
The Historical Library houses a collection of police related publications, including monthly Garda publications from 1922 to the present. The book collection numbers approximately 1,000 catalogued bound volumes. The archives contain photographs, sound recordings and documents outlining the history and development of policing in Ireland in the nineteenth and twentieth centuries. The sound recordings are of retired RIC/DMP and Garda members. In addition to documenting policing in Ireland, the collection seeks to document the impact of Irish policing on the English speaking world and the British colonies. Of special interest is the large genealogical collection on policing from 1822 to 1922. The archives also contain the Dublin Metropolitan Police personnel register for the period 1836–1925.

LOCATION
The museum/archive is located at the Record Tower of Dublin Castle, off Dame
Street, next to City Hall and diagonally opposite Christchurch Cathedral. There is
also an entrance on Ship Street.

GENEALOGICAL OFFICE
See OFFICE OF CHIEF HERALD/GENEALOGICAL OFFICE

GENERAL REGISTER OFFICE
Note: The General Register Office was relocated from Joyce House, 8–11 Lombard
Street East, Dublin 2 to Government Offices, Convent Road, Roscommon, on 11
April 2005. *See* current listing under Roscommon Town, County Roscommon, for
details.
   The Research Room, however, continues to be located at Joyce House, 8–11
Lombard Street East, Dublin, approximately two minutes' walk from Pearse station.
Exiting the station entrance, turn right, cross Pearse Street (at the traffic lights) and
continue straight ahead. Joyce House is a four storey red brick building on the right.
Website: www.groireland.ie. Opening hours: M–F, 9.30am–4.30pm; closed bank
holidays. Contact Declan Roche, Manager, Research Room.

GILBERT LIBRARY
See CENTRE FOR DUBLIN AND IRISH STUDIES, Dublin

GRAND LODGE OF FREEMASONS OF IRELAND: LIBRARY, ARCHIVES AND MUSEUM

Freemasons' Hall, 17 Molesworth Street
DUBLIN 2
Ireland

TELEPHONE: (01) 676 1337; FAX: (01) 662 5101
E-mail: hayesr@freemason.ie
Website: www.irish-freemasons.org

HOURS
Museum: M–F, 9.30am–5.00pm
Library and Archive: by appointment

ACCESS AND SERVICES
Visitors welcome, but by appointment only; advance notice and ID required. No
disabled access facilities. Laptops permitted; pencils only. No access charges to
library, but fees charged for postal and e-mail queries. Printed finding aids available;
approximately half the 12,000 volume book collection catalogued on cards.
Descriptive lists available for some correspondence files and minute books. General
readers may consult all published works, while only members may borrow books. *See*
holdings for further restrictions. Access to archival material also limited. Records
prior to 1975 available to the general public, but Grand Secretary's permission
required for access to post-1975 material. Records of current Lodges and other
Masonic bodies deposited with the archives may only be consulted with permission

of bodies concerned. Photocopying available but with some restrictions. Microfilm
reader available.

CONTACT
Librarian and Archivist

DESCRIPTION
The Library, Archives and Museum of the Grand Lodge of Ireland serves as the
repository for the history of Irish Freemasonry in Ireland and abroad. Started in the
1730s, the purpose of the library/archives is to collect, preserve and exhibit items
and information relating to the development of the Masonic Order. The collection is
funded by the Grand Lodge, and acquisitions come primarily as gifts from members
and the public.

HOLDINGS
The collection houses approximately 12,000 volumes. The Chetwode Crawley
Library contains books printed between 1527 and 1851 and these volumes can be
neither lent nor photocopied. Books printed since 1851 form the modern section
and members may borrow recently published books or older books from this section
that are available in duplicate. The library contains books on all Grand Lodges,
organised geographically. The archives, consisting of some 800 boxes of material,
house the records of the Governing Bodies of the Order, as well as representative
collections from Lodges and Chapters. Membership registers date from 1760 and the
correspondence files date from the 1820s. The latter include some 100,000 pieces
from the Secretaries of Irish Lodges from around the world to the Grand Secretary.
Pre-1975 records of schools and other charities supported by the Masons are
available for research, but with restrictions.

LOCATION
City centre, opposite Buswell's Hotel, near Kildare Street, close to the National
Library and the National Museum.

GUINNESS ARCHIVE

Guinness Storehouse, St James's Gate
DUBLIN 8
Ireland

TELEPHONE: (01) 471 4557; FAX: (01) 408 4737
E-mail: guinness.archives@diageo.com
Website: www.guinness-storehouse.com

HOURS
By appointment, M–F, 9.30am–5.00pm

ACCESS AND SERVICES
Visitors welcome by appointment. Disabled access. Laptops permitted; pencils only.
Photocopying available for a fee. Archive service very recent and collections largely
uncatalogued. Access may be restricted to parts of the collection that are
uncatalogued at discretion of Archivist.

CONTACT
Eibhlin Roche, Guinness Archivist

DESCRIPTION
The archive is the only corporate archive in Ireland fully open to the public. It serves as an information resource for Diageo Ireland and globally as well as for the researching public. The archive supports the Guinness Storehouse as a whole in providing artefacts for exhibition.

HOLDINGS
The collection includes books and journals relating to brewing and brewery history; maps, plans, photographs, film, brewing ledgers relating to the Guinness company history; records from all brewery departments; artefacts and Guinness memorabilia. Major collections include: correspondence with Lord Iveagh; brewery memoranda, 1802–25, 1869–97; Board orders, 1909–15; Head Brewers' desk diaries, 1881–1993; Brewery Annual Reports; Hains and Shands Reports on Overseas Trade, 1906–25; Brewery Guide Books, 1888–1955; Guinness posters, bottles, dripmats and labels; minute books of the Brewers' Guild of Dublin, minute books of the Coopers' Guild of Dublin and minute books from Robert Perry and Sons Ltd. Of special genealogical interest are employee ledgers and personnel files.

LOCATION
The archive is located in Guinness Storehouse at St James's Gate.

HISTORICAL LIBRARY, RELIGIOUS SOCIETY OF FRIENDS

Quaker House Dublin, Stocking Lane, Rathfarnham
DUBLIN 16
Ireland

TELEPHONE: (01) 495 6890; FAX: (01) 495 6890
E-mail: qhist@eircom.net
Website: www.quakers-in-ireland.ie

HOURS
Th, 10.30am–1.00pm

ACCESS AND SERVICES
Visitors welcome and no prior appointment required; however, it can be helpful to know in advance visitors' particular area of interest. Library open only for short while on Thursdays, but exceptions sometimes made to allow researchers access to materials on Thursday afternoons, staff permitting. Library staffed entirely by volunteers. Photocopying and microfilm reader available. Fee for postal queries. Library maintains card indexes to holdings including separate indexes for photographic archive and museum collection. These indexes have been computerised. Library offers recent publications for sale.

CONTACT
Rachel M. Bewley-Bateman, Curator. E-mail: bewleyrm@gofree.indigo.ie

DESCRIPTION
The library is supported by the Religious Society of Friends, the Quakers, who arrived in Ireland in the seventeenth century.

HOLDINGS
The Quakers have kept excellent records ever since their arrival in Ireland, and the library is therefore an especially rich repository of information for Irish social,

political, religious and genealogical studies. The collections include books, pamphlets, photographs, recordings and museum pieces, such as examples of Quaker embroidery and bonnets. Records generally reflect the concerns of Quakers through the centuries, and subject interests include famine relief, the anti-slavery campaign, care of the mentally ill, education, temperance, peace, prison reform, refugees and commercial interests. Of special interest to genealogists is that each meeting kept minutes, and from these minutes were transcribed registers of birth, marriages and deaths, that are available in the library. Microfilm copies of these registers are available at the National Library of Ireland, Dublin, and the National Archives of Ireland, Dublin. The library also houses tapes of Quaker lectures and addresses and tapes of reminiscences by elderly Irish Quakers.

LOCATION
In the South Dublin suburb of Rathfarnham, an easy commute by taxi from Nutgrove Shopping Centre or Tallaght Shopping Centre. The Luas red line serves Tallaght Shopping Centre. Taxi telephone numbers: Tallaght Taxis: (01) 451 0000, (01) 459 9444; Orchard Taxis (from Rathfarnham): (01) 493 8888. The nearest bus stop to Quaker House is the terminus of buses 15 and 15X (The 15X is a Monday–Friday service only, excluding bank holidays). Both buses will leave the traveller on the Scholarstown Road, a 12 minute walk up Stocking Lane to Quaker House, part of which requires walking on the road. For this reason, it is not advisable to walk at night. Ample parking nearby if arriving by car.

THE HONORABLE SOCIETY OF KING'S INNS

Henrietta Street
DUBLIN 1
Ireland

TELEPHONE: (01) 878 2119; FAX: (01) 874 4846
E-mail: library@kingsinns.ie
Website: www.kingsinns.ie

HOURS
By appointment

ACCESS AND SERVICES
Visitors welcome, but by appointment only; advance notice, references and ID required. No disabled access facilities. Laptops permitted; pencils only. Charges for genealogical and other research undertaken vary by category of user. Registered members of the society (Category A) exempted from search fees but pay reduced photocopying and facsimile charges and normal postage charges. Academics (Category B) may be charged a search fee depending on length of time involved in search, and pay a slightly higher charge for photocopying and facsimile services and normal charges for postage. All others granted permission to use the library facilities (Category C) required to pay minimum fee of €14 per search plus normal charges for photocopying, facsimiles and postage. Photocopying carried out by staff; 12c per page surcharge for all users. Consult library staff for fee schedule.
    Publications available at the library for consultation include: Wanda Ryan-Smolin (cataloguer), *King's Inns Portraits*, Daire Hogan, *The Honorable Society of King's Inns* and various accession lists. Visitors may purchase *King's Inns Barristers*

1868–2004, price €30. Several leaflets, including *Library Guide* and *How to Find Irish Cases*, are available free of charge.

CONTACT
Jonathan Armstrong, Librarian. E-mail: jonathan.armstrong@kingsinns.ie

DESCRIPTION
The library was founded in 1787. The society itself dates from 1541. King's Inns trains students wishing to become barristers (lawyers), and the focus of its collection is on the law, with history, literature, classics, biography, typography, science and natural history also well represented.

HOLDINGS
In addition to its book collection, the library houses architectural drawings, art and artefacts, manuscripts, maps, microforms, newspapers and pamphlets. Of special interest are the holdings of: British parliamentary papers; Irish appeals to the House of Lords; the pamphlet collection; the papers of John Patrick Prendergast, Irish language manuscripts and rentals under the 1849 Encumbered Estates Act. Of special genealogical interest are the King's Inns admission papers, 1607–1867 (abstracts published by Irish Manuscripts Commission), plus a printed copy of *Griffith's Valuation* and a collection of Ordnance Survey maps.

LOCATION
Off Bolton Street, almost directly opposite Dublin Institute of Technology Bolton Street, on the north side of the Liffey, west of Parnell Square. King's Inns can also be approached via Constitution Hill, opposite Broadstone Bus Garage.

IRISH ARCHITECTURAL ARCHIVE

45 Merrion Square
DUBLIN 2
Ireland

TELEPHONE: (01) 663 3040; FAX: (01) 663 3041
E-mail: info@iarc.ie
Website: www.iarc.ie

HOURS
Tu–F, 10.00am–5.00pm

ACCESS AND SERVICES
Visitors and enquiries welcome. No appointment necessary. Readers required to register when using the archive for the first time. Disabled access facilities. Laptops permitted; pencils only. Photocopying available for a fee of 25c–50c; photographic prints, €20–€140, depending on size and nature of print required. Card catalogue available. See D. Griffin and S. Lincoln, *Drawings from the Irish Architectural Archive* (Dublin, 1993). See website for updated lists of collections.
Archive has moved to new premises (formerly 73 Merrion Square). New premises contain a larger reading room (seating approximately 20 readers), a lecture room, meeting room and an exhibition gallery.

CONTACT
Colum O'Riordan, Archive Administrator
David Griffin, Archive Director

DESCRIPTION
The Irish Architectural Archive is a charitable company established in 1976 to collect, preserve and make available the records of Ireland's architectural heritage. The archive is a non-confrontational body, which does not involve itself in any way in matters of planning or conservation controversy. The archive also pursues an active publications policy and outreach programme, including exhibitions to bring the riches of its collections to as wide an audience as possible.

HOLDINGS
The Irish Architectural Archive collects, preserves and makes available records of every type relating to the architecture of Ireland. The holdings date from the 1690s to the 1990s and comprise in excess of 250,000 architectural drawings, 400,000 photographs, 20,000 items of printed matter and several dozen architectural models. The collections include information, primary or secondary, on every notable Irish architect, on every important Irish building period or style and on most significant holdings in the 32 counties of Ireland. Major collections include: Ashlin and Coleman Collection, Boyd Barrett Murphy O'Connor
Collection, Burgage Collection, Rudolf Maximillian Butler Collection, Charleville Forest Collection, Cullen and Co. Collection, C.P. Curran Collection, Dublin Artisans Dwellings Co. Collection, Emo Court Collection, Desmond FitzGerald Collection, Charles Geoghan Collection, Guinness Drawings Collection, Alan Hope Collection, Brendan Jeffers
Collection, Alfred Jones Biographical Index, McCurdy and Mitchell Collection, Raymond McGrath Collection, Munden and Purcell Collection, Donal O'Neill Flanagan Collection, Patterson Kempster Shortall Collection, Anthony Reddy Associates Collection, Fred Rogerson Collection, RIAI Murray Collection, Royal (Collins) Barracks Collection, Royal Institute of the Architects of Ireland Archives, Robinson Keefe and Devane Collection, Scott Tallon Walker Collection, Michael Scott Collection, Sibthorpe Collection, Stephenson Gibney Collection, Townley Hall Collection, Tyndall Hogan Hurley Collection and the Workhouse Collection.
    The archive's photograph collection is one of the largest in Ireland. Aside from ongoing photographic survey work carried out by the archive, photographic collections include Automobile Association Photographs, BKS Aerial Photographs, Buildings of Ireland Photographs, Alec R. Day ARPS Collection, J.V. Downes Slide Collection, Kieran Clendining Collection, Green Studio Collection, Thomas Gunn Collection and the Westropp Albums.

LOCATION
Halfway along the eastern side of Merrion Square, the largest of the terraced houses. Bus 7 stops about five minutes' walk away. From the north side of the city, bus 13 stops near the archive. It is a ten minute walk from Pearse DART station.

IRISH FILM ARCHIVE OF THE IRISH FILM INSTITUTE

6 Eustace Street
DUBLIN 2
Ireland

TELEPHONE: (01) 679 5744; FAX: (01) 677 8755
E-mail: *see* contact
Website: www.irishfilm.ie

HOURS
Film and tape viewing: M–F, 10.00am–1.00pm, 2.00pm–6.00pm
Tiernan MacBride Library: M, Th, 2.00pm–5.30pm; Tu, 10.30am–1.00pm,
2.00pm–5.30pm; W, 10.30am–1.00pm, 2.00pm–7.00pm

ACCESS AND SERVICES
Visitors and enquiries welcome. Appointment necessary for paper archive, film and
tape viewing but not for access to library. Booking should be made with Irish Film
Archive staff by phone at least 48 hours in advance. Archive staff must be informed
of cancellations at least 24 hours in advance of appointment. Information relating to
film, tape, stills, posters and library holdings held on computer database. Limited
access to these databases available via website. Archive staff facilitate public enquiries
relating to content of any aspect of collections. Access to collections may be
restricted owing to donor stipulations or preservation concerns. Tiernan MacBride
Library accessible for reference purposes only, but all materials may be photocopied.
Use and access charges apply, except access to Paper Archive Collection. Currently
(2006), charges are as follows: film, €15 per hour; tape, €6.50 per hour. There is a
daily tape rate of €20 per visit per day, €75 per week. Access charges to Tiernan
MacBride Library are: students, €1.50 per visit or €15.00 per annual membership;
general public, €2 per visit or €20 per annual membership.

CONTACT
Kasandra O'Connell, Head of Archive. E-mail: koconnell@irishfilm.ie
Sunniva O'Flynn, Archive Curator. E-mail: soflynn@irishfilm.ie
Orna Roche, Librarian. E-mail: oroche@irishfilm.ie

DESCRIPTION
The Irish Film Archive, which includes the Tiernan MacBride Library, is part of the
Film Institute of Ireland and is funded by the Arts Council of Ireland and by user
charges. It acquires, preserves and provides access to the national audiovisual
heritage. The archive holds collections of film and videotape made in and about
Ireland and documents relating to the history of film in Ireland.

HOLDINGS
The film collection now numbers more than 15,000 cans, reflecting the history of
professional and amateur production in Ireland from 1897 to the present. Much of
the collection has been transferred to videotape for reference purposes, totalling over
2,000 VHS tapes of Irish material. The paper collection of the Irish Film Archive
includes stills, posters and document collections relating to Irish cinema. Still and
poster collections include: 1,193 stills, 453 posters, 288 transparencies and 21 video
prints.
    The Tiernan MacBride Library is the most comprehensive collection of film
related publications in Ireland. It contains approximately 2,300 books covering all

aspects of national and international cinema. The library also subscribes to a wide range of film journals and readers have access to film related CD-ROMS. The library holds a valuable collection of material relating to all elements of Irish cinema. Files of clippings on Irish film production are maintained and updated on a daily basis. Collections of special note include: Lord Killanin Collection, Pat Murphy Collection, Tiernan MacBride Collection and Gael Linn Collection.

LOCATION
The archive is located in the Temple Bar area of Dublin, off Dame Street, opposite Dublin Castle, a few blocks west of Trinity College.

IRISH JESUIT ARCHIVES

35 Lower Leeson Street
DUBLIN 2
Ireland

TELEPHONE: (01) 647 1099; FAX: (01) 676 2984
E-mail: archives@jesuit.ie
Website: www.jesuit.ie/irl/history

HOURS
By appointment

ACCESS AND SERVICES
Advance notice required. Disabled access facilities; laptops permitted; pencils only. No photocopier, microfilm/microfiche reader/printer or other electronic aids available and none may be brought in. Printed finding aids available.

CONTACT
Fergus O'Donoghue SJ, Province Archivist

DESCRIPTION
The Irish Jesuit Archives are the official repository for the records of the Irish Jesuits from the sixteenth to the twentieth centuries. They are part of the central administration of the Irish Jesuit Province, though located some distance from the Provincialate. The major part of the holdings represents the concerns of central administration, but there are extensive holdings of the papers of individual Jesuits.

HOLDINGS
The archives house the Irish Jesuit papers relating to work in Ireland, Australia, Hong Kong and Zambia. Earliest papers date back to 1577. In addition, the archives include the MacErlean transcripts of Irish Jesuit material in European archives from 1527 to 1774. The collection includes over 1,000 photographs.

LOCATION
Close to the city centre, a five minute walk from the south-eastern corner of St Stephen's Green. Entrance by 35 or 36 Lower Leeson Street.

IRISH JEWISH MUSEUM

3–4 Walworth Road, South Circular Road
DUBLIN 8
Ireland

TELEPHONE: (01) 453 1797 (Museum Office); (01) 490 1857 (Curator); FAX: (01) 490 1857 (Curator)

HOURS
May–September: Su, Tu, Th, 11.00am–3.30pm
October–April: Su, 10.30am–2.30pm

ACCESS AND SERVICES
Visitors welcome. No admission charge. Access to manuscripts and photographs requires Curator's permission. Adult and school tours available by request.

CONTACT
Curator

DESCRIPTION
The museum seeks to document the religious, historical and cultural life of the Jewish people in Ireland, most especially the communities of Belfast, Cork, Derry, Dublin, Limerick and Waterford. Though the collection focuses on the past 150 years, there have been Jews in Ireland since 1492. The museum is located in a former synagogue, which consisted of two adjoining terraced houses. The original synagogue, with all its fittings, can be viewed upstairs. The home of Rabbi Isaac Herzog, first Chief Rabbi of Ireland and father of Dr Chaim Herzog (1918–97), the Irish born President of Israel, is nearby. President Herzog officially opened the Museum on 20 June 1985 during a state visit to Ireland. The fictional boyhood home of Leopold Bloom, the hero of Joyce's Ulysses, is also close by, at 52 Upper Clanbrassil Street. There are some 1,400 Jews living in Ireland today: 1,200 in the south, 200 in the north.

HOLDINGS
The Jewish Museum contains a substantial collection of memorabilia relating to Ireland's Jewish communities, whose commercial and social life is documented in photographs, paintings and other displays. A feature of particular interest is a kitchen depicting a typical Sabbath/Festival meal setting in Jewish home at the turn of the twentieth century. The museum also contains a collection of material on Judaism in general.

LOCATION
In Portobello, off Victoria Street, just south of the city centre, an area that once had a sizeable Jewish population. Buses include: 16, 19 and 122 to Victoria Street, South Circular Road and 14, 15, 65 and 83 to Lennox Street, off South Richmond Street.

IRISH THEATRE ARCHIVE

Dublin City Library and Archive, 138–144 Pearse Street
DUBLIN 2
Ireland

TELEPHONE: (01) 674 4996/4997; FAX: (01) 674 4879
E-mail: cityarchives@dublincity.ie
Website: www.dublincity.ie

HOURS
M–Th, 10.00am–8.00pm; F–Sa, 10.00am–5.00pm

ACCESS AND SERVICES
Visitors welcome. ID required to facilitate registration on first visit. Disabled access
facilities. Laptops permitted; pencils only. Photocopying and microfilm prints
available for a fee. No borrowing privileges permitted. Publication: *Prompts: Bulletin
of the Irish Theatre Archive.*

CONTACT
Mary Clark, Honorary Archivist

DESCRIPTION
The Irish Theatre Archive is operated by Dublin City Council under the auspices of
Dublin City Archives. Its mission is to collect and preserve materials relating to the
history of theatre in Ireland.

HOLDINGS
The archive houses an impressive array of materials relating to theatre in Ireland.
Types of material include: programmes, posters, photographs, press cuttings, prompt
books, costume and stage designs, together with plays in typescript and manuscript.
Theatre collections include: An Damer; Cork Theatre Company; Dublin Masque
Theatre Guild; Dublin Theatre Festival; Gaiety Theatre, Dublin; Irish Theatre
Company; Olympia Theatre, Dublin; Rough Magic Theatre Company; Brendan
Smith Academy; and Theatre Royal, Dublin. There are also the collections of actors,
costumiers and designers, including: P.J. Bourke, Eddie Cooke, Ursula Doyle,
Donald Finlay, James N. Healy, Eddie Johnston, Nora Lever, Micheál Mac
Liammóir, Dennis Noble, Jimmy O'Dea, Shelah Richards and Cecil Sheridan.

LOCATION
On Pearse Street, two blocks eastwards from Pearse DART station. Bus 3 from
O'Connell Street to Ringsend stops across the street.

IRISH TRADITIONAL MUSIC ARCHIVE

73 Merrion Square
DUBLIN 2
Ireland

TELEPHONE: (01) 661 9699; FAX: (01) 662 4585
Website: www.itma.ie

HOURS
M–F, 10.00am–1.00pm, 2.00pm–5.00pm; closed Christmas–New Year period and
bank holidays

ACCESS AND SERVICES
Visitors welcome. Advance notice preferred; ID and references required; no access
charge. No disabled access facilities. Book collection fully catalogued on computer
and most of collection of sound recordings catalogued on computer and indexed;

non-circulating collection. Archive offers listening, viewing and reading facilities; photocopying and faxing available for a fee; laptops permitted.

CONTACT
Róisín Ní Bhriain, Secretary

DESCRIPTION
The archive was established in 1987 as a multimedia reference and resource centre for the collection, preservation and promotion of the traditional song, music and dance of Ireland. Dedicated to the promotion of public education in Irish traditional music, it is a public, not for profit institution supported by the Arts Council of Ireland, the Arts Council of Northern Ireland and private donations. It boasts the largest collection in existence of the materials of Irish traditional music.

HOLDINGS
The archive collects comprehensively and broadly all materials, including sound recordings, books, photographs and videos, for the appreciation and study of Irish traditional music. Its collections extend beyond Ireland to include areas of Irish settlement abroad, especially in Britain and North America. The archive also includes a representative collection of traditional music of other countries. The collection includes some 8,000 volumes of books, 750 films, 130 journals, ten linear feet of manuscripts, 1,200 pamphlets, 5,500 photographs, 18,000 recordings and 6,400 pieces of sheet music.

LOCATION
Halfway along the south side of Merrion Square, which is the side running from Upper Merrion Street to Upper Mount Street and the Pepper Canister Church (St Stephen's). Bus 7 stops about five minutes' walk from the archive. From the north side of the city, bus 13 stops near the archive. It is a ten minute walk from Pearse DART station.

THE JESUIT LIBRARY

Milltown Park, Sandford Road
DUBLIN 6
Ireland

TELEPHONE: (01) 218 0285; FAX: (01) 260 0371
E-mail: jeslib@eircom.net
Website: www.milltown-institute.ie

HOURS
M–F, 9.00am–5.00pm

ACCESS AND SERVICES
Visitors welcome, but by appointment. Advance notice and references required. Library services leased on annual basis to Milltown Institute of Theology and Philosophy, a third level college located in the same building. See website above. Books may be borrowed by members of the Jesuit order and by registered students and staff of the Institute of Theology and Philosophy. Photocopying services available. Approximately 95 per cent of the collection catalogued on computer and can be browsed on OPAC in library. Catalogue not yet available through internet, however, and no printed catalogue exists.

CONTACT
Patricia Quigley, Librarian

DESCRIPTION
The Jesuit Library, Milltown Park, is the library of the Irish Province of the Society
of Jesus. It is a private library specialising in theology (including scripture and
spirituality) and philosophy.

HOLDINGS
The library houses a collection of some 130,000 bound volumes, which mainly
cover theology, church history, philosophy, the human sciences, scripture and Irish
material. It is strongest in theology, scripture, patristic studies, spirituality and
medieval and modern European philosophy. It receives more than 265 current
periodicals, the principal areas covered being theology, church history, scripture,
spirituality and philosophy. The library also contains a collection of rare and Irish
books. Access to the Irish Collection is strictly closed.

LOCATION
In Milltown, south-west of Donnybrook, about two miles south-east of St Stephen's
Green through Ranelagh. From city centre or Lower Baggot Street, take buses 11,
44, 44A or 48A.

MACBRIDE LIBRARY (TIERNAN MACBRIDE LIBRARY)
See IRISH FILM ARCHIVE OF THE IRISH FILM INSTITUTE, Dublin

MARSH'S LIBRARY

St Patrick's Close
DUBLIN 8
Ireland

TELEPHONE: (01) 454 3511; FAX: (01) 454 3511
E-mail: keeper@marshlibrary.ie
Website: www.marshlibrary.ie

HOURS
M, W–F, 10.00am–1.00pm, 2.00pm–5.00pm; Sa, 10.30am–1.00pm

ACCESS AND SERVICES
Visitors welcome. Admission fees: general public, €2.50; students and seniors,
€1.50; children free. Researchers admitted free but required to make application in
advance to the Keeper of the Library. Consult website for details. No disabled access
facilities but special arrangements can be made for researchers; laptops permitted;
pencils only. Marsh's Library offers impressive exhibitions programme; catalogues
available for purchase, if still in print. Consult website for listing. To commemorate
its 300th anniversary, the library produced an exhibition and accompanying
illustrated catalogue: Muriel McCarthy and Caroline Sherwood-Smith (compilers),
This Golden Fleece: Marsh's Library, 1701–2001: a Tercentenary Exhibition (Dublin,
2001). The proceedings of a tercentenary conference have been published: Muriel
McCarthy and Ann Simmons (eds), *The Making of Marsh's Library: Learning, Politics
and Religion in Ireland, 1650–1750* (Dublin, 2004). See also Muriel McCarthy,
Marsh's Library, Dublin: All Graduates and Gentlemen (Dublin, 2003).

CONTACT
Muriel McCarthy, Keeper of the Library

DESCRIPTION
Marsh's Library was founded in 1701 by Narcissus Marsh, Archbishop of Dublin
and a deeply religious and scholarly man. The first public library in Ireland, it
contains some 25,000 volumes, largely reflecting its founder's sophisticated interest
in the full spectrum of seventeenth century knowledge. The library remains virtually
the same as it was 300 years ago, and it is one of the cultural treasures of Ireland,
used by luminaries from Jonathan Swift to James Joyce. It is cited in *Ulysses*. Some
modern physical additions have been made to the library, including a conservation
bindery and seminar room, but without altering its appearance. Visitors to Marsh's
Library can step three centuries back in time.

HOLDINGS
The library was built on four major acquisitions. The first was the 10,000 volume
personal library of Bishop Stillingfleet, covering a variety of subjects, including
theology, science, mathematics, history, medicine, lexicography and witchcraft. The
Stillingfleet Collection occupies the first gallery. The second acquisition was the
library of a French Huguenot medical doctor, Elias Bouhéreau, whose interests
included Protestantism, theology and medicine. The third collection was the library
of Archbishop Marsh himself. Marsh was particularly interested in science,
mathematics and music, but he was also interested in oriental languages and
rabbinical and medieval writers. He collected books in Hebrew, Arabic, Turkish and
Russian. The fourth major collection was bequeathed to the library in 1745 by
Bishop Stearne, whose collecting interests closely paralleled those of Stillingfleet,
Marsh and Bouhéreau. Exhibitions at Marsh's Library have drawn heavily on the
collection's rich holdings, especially in the areas of Bibles, music, medicine, natural
science, botany, religious controversy, orientalia and travel. The library also houses
early manuscripts and printed books in the Irish language.

LOCATION
Discreetly tucked away behind St Patrick's Cathedral. Entry is through a stone
archway in St Patrick's Close. It is near the National Archives, within easy walking
distance (10–15 minutes) of St Stephen's Green.

MATER DEI INSTITUTE OF EDUCATION LIBRARY
See DUBLIN CITY UNIVERSITY LIBRARY

THE MILITARY ARCHIVES

Cathal Brugha Barracks, Rathmines
DUBLIN 6
Ireland

TELEPHONE: (01) 804 6457; FAX: (01) 804 6237

HOURS
Tu–Th, 10.00am–4.00pm; closed public and defence force holidays and
Christmas–New Year period

ACCESS AND SERVICES
By appointment only. ID and advance notice required. References required for academic researchers. Access limited to five persons at a time; hence, appointment well in advance by letter or phone is mandatory. No disabled access facilities. Laptops permitted; pencils only. Photography with permission only.

CONTACT
Officer in Charge/Military Archivist

DESCRIPTION
The Military Archives is the place of deposit for the records of the Department of Defence, the Defence Forces and the Army Pensions Board. The function of the archives is to collect, preserve and make available material relating to the history of the development of the Irish Defence Forces from the formation of the Irish Volunteers in November 1913 to the present day, inclusive of overseas service with the United Nations since 1958.

HOLDINGS
The archive houses approximately 32,000 linear shelf feet of archival material, including department files, military documents, records and some related photographs/films. Major collections include the Bureau of Military History (1913–21), which includes 1,773 witness statements, 334 sets of contemporaneous documents, photographs (including action sites of the 1916 Easter Rising), press cuttings and voice recordings; Collins papers 1919–21; liaison documents (British evacuation and truce); Civil War operations and intelligence reports; internment camps and some prison records 1922–4; captured documents (IRA) 1922–4; the army crisis 1924; military mission to the United States 1926–7; Irish Volunteer Force files; emergency defence plans 1939–46; military intelligence and Directorate of Operation files 1939–46; Office of the Controller of Censorship files; internment camp records and Department of Defence files for the 1939–46 period; as well as Air Corps and Naval Service material and records. Other collections of special interest include bound volumes of *An tÓglach* (1918–33) and *An Cosantóir* (1940–present), plus other military periodicals and newspapers; the National Army Census, 1922; records and history of units that served overseas on United Nations peacekeeping missions; and 800 personal papers collections.

LOCATION
At Cathal Brugha Barracks, Rathmines, Dublin, adjacent to Portobello Bridge, approximately three miles from the city centre on the south side of the Liffey. Served by buses 14A or 15 from the city centre.

MILLTOWN PARK LIBRARY
See THE JESUIT LIBRARY, Dublin

NATIONAL ARCHIVES OF IRELAND

Bishop Street
DUBLIN 8
Ireland

TELEPHONE: (01) 407 2300; FAX: (01) 407 2333

E-mail: mail@nationalarchives.ie
Website: www.nationalarchives.ie

HOURS
M–F: 10.00am–5.00pm; closed St Patrick's Day, Good Friday, Easter Monday, 25 December–2 January, bank and public holidays, and for media previews in December (consult website).

ACCESS AND SERVICES
Visitors welcome; disabled access facilities; ID and reader's ticket required (reader's ticket can be applied for on day of first visit); no access charge; laptops permitted; pencils only; photocopies and microform printouts available for a modest fee. There are 26 microform readers in Bishop Street, including eight reader/printers, available on a first come, first served basis. The NAI publishes *Reports of the Director* and *Reports of the National Archives Advisory Council*. Also available are helpful leaflets, including *Reading Room Information* (2004), *Some Facts about the National Archives* (2004) and *Sources for Family History and Genealogy* (2004). All leaflets are also printed in Irish.

For up to date research guides and information consult website; especially helpful for genealogical researchers. Website also offers access to online exhibitions, e.g. the 2005 Condolences and Funerals exhibition, featuring documents relating to two key national events – the visit of the Taoiseach, Eamon de Valera, to Eduard Hempel, German Minister to Ireland, to present condolences on the death of Adolf Hitler in 1945; and the repatriation of the remains of Sir Roger Casement, followed by his state funeral, in 1965. Click on 'What's New' section.

CONTACT
Director

DESCRIPTION
The National Archives was formally established in 1988 with the amalgamation of the Public Record Office of Ireland and the State Paper Office. It is a government agency, open free of charge to the public.

HOLDINGS
The NAI is the official depository for the records of the Irish government. All government departments and state agencies are required to deposit their papers with the National Archives, although the Minister for Arts, Sport and Tourism may approve places other than the National Archives as places of deposit for specified departmental records. Exceptions include military documents (*see* Military Archives, Dublin) and the Geological Survey records, located at Beggar's Bush, Haddington Road, Dublin 4.

In addition to government records, the archives include private and business collections. Types of record include architectural records, manuscripts, maps, microforms and photographs. The archives of the following government departments and state agencies are held at the Bishop Street location: Agriculture, Food; Arts, Heritage, Gaeltacht and the Islands; Education and Science (in part); Enterprise, Trade and Employment; the Environment, Heritage and Local Government; Finance; Foreign Affairs; Health and Children; Justice, Equality and Law Reform; the Marine; Public Enterprise; Social and Family Affairs; Transport.

Also at Bishop Street are the archives of the Offices of the Attorney General, the Comptroller and Auditor General, Public Works and the Secretary to the President.

In addition, the records of the following government agencies are to be found at Bishop Street: Fair Trade Commission, Government Information Services, Labour Court, Ordnance Survey (in part), Patents Office, Registry of Friendly Societies, Valuation Office and Boundary Survey and the Department of the Taoiseach. The following archives at Bishop Street are among the most consulted records: 1901 census; 1911 census; cholera papers (Board of Health); Customs and Excise; Famine Relief Commission; national school applications, registers and files; Valuation Office and Boundary Survey; archives salvaged from the Four Courts fire in 1922 (in part); Chancery pleadings; Church of Ireland parish registers; Ferguson manuscripts; genealogical abstracts (Betham, Crosslé, Groves, Grove-White and Thrift); Irish Record Commission; O'Brien set of encumbered/landed estates court rentals; will books and grant books.

Bishop Street also houses archives acquired from private sources (M, D, T, 975–999, 1000– series, etc), as well as trade union archives.

Archives from the State Paper Office in Dublin Castle and now at Bishop Street include: Rebellion papers; State of the Country papers; official papers; outrage papers; convict reference files; Privy Council Office; Chief Crown Solicitor's Office; Dáil Éireann Records, government and cabinet minutes; and the Office of the Governor General and General Prisons Board.

The following archives are available only in microform at Bishop Street: tithe applotment books; *Griffith's Valuation*; 1821–51 census (fragments); *Books of Survey and Distribution*; Lodge's Records of the Rolls; and the shipping agreements and crew lists, pre-1922.

Note: some archives remain at offsite storage and may eventually be transferred to Bishop Street. These include: court records; wills, 1900–78; administration papers, 1900–78; Schedules of Assets (Principal Registry), 1922–78; archives salvaged in 1922 (in part); Companies Registration Office; national school salary books; Office of Public Works (in part); Taxing Master of the High Court; Quit Rent Office (in part); Royal Hospital, Kilmainham; shipping agreements and crew lists, post-1922; business records; hospital records, with prior permission. Requests for these records require advance notice (at least one day) and they are made available at Bishop Street. It is advisable to telephone several days in advance to check on exact position of archives to be consulted, as the above location list is subject to change.

Some records are stored in a warehouse behind Bishop Street and may require up to an eight week delay before they can be retrieved. These include: Ordnance Survey (in part) and Quit Rent Office (in part).

LOCATION
A few blocks west of St Stephen's Green and south of Dublin Castle, near St Patrick's Cathedral. The National Archives is on the west end of Bishop Street, at the corner of Bride Street.

NATIONAL GALLERY OF IRELAND RESEARCH SERVICES

Merrion Square West
DUBLIN 2
Ireland

TELEPHONE: (01) 663 3546; FAX: (01) 661 5372
E-mail: *see* contact
Website: www.nationalgallery.ie

HOURS
M–F, 10.00am–5.00pm; closed Christmas, Easter and bank holidays

ACCESS AND SERVICES:
For Fine Art Library, NGI Archive, ESB Centre for the Study of Irish Art, Yeats
Archive and Diageo Print Room. Visitors welcome, but by appointment only.
Advance notice required. Applications can be made by phone, e-mail or in writing.
Wheelchair access. Laptops permitted. Photocopying facilities available.

CONTACT
Archives: Leah Benson, Archivist. E-mail: lbenson@ngi.ie
Diageo Print Room: Anne Hodge, Curator of Prints and Drawings. E-mail:
ahodge@ngi.ie
ESB Centre for the Study of Irish Art: Dr. Brendan Rooney, CSIA Administrator. E-
mail: brooney@ngi.ie
Fine Art Library: Andrea Lydon, Librarian. E-mail: alydon@ngi.ie
Yeats Archive: Leah Benson, Archivist. E-mail: lbenson@ngi.ie

DESCRIPTION
The National Gallery is Ireland's major museum of art. In addition to offering
visitors celebrated exhibitions of Irish and world art, the National Gallery provides
five separate research service centres.

Archives
The Archives contain the official records of the institution, reflecting the history of
the gallery from the 1850s to the present day. They are a valuable source for those
interested in the development of the institution since its foundation and its
involvement in Irish cultural affairs.

Diageo Print Room
The Diageo Print Room provides researchers and the general public with supervised
access to the National Gallery of Ireland's wide-ranging collection of prints and
drawings. Works range from simple pencil sketches, preparatory studies for
paintings, finished landscape watercolours, portraits in all media and architectural
and topographical drawings. Highlights include Irish and British landscape and old
master drawings from the Italian, French and Dutch schools.

ESB Centre for the Study of Irish Art
The ESB Centre for the Study of Irish Art facilitates study and research into Irish
art. The collection consists of primary and secondary material relating to individual
artists, groups and institutions from the eighteenth century to the present.

Fine Art Library
The Fine Art Library's specialist collection comprises over 50,000 publications
relating to art from the fifteenth century to the present. Areas and artists that feature
in the gallery's collection are especially well represented. Many of the library's
holdings, particularly older publications, are unavailable elsewhere in Ireland. The
collection also covers related areas such as museology, architecture, history and
biography.

Yeats Archive
The Yeats Archive consists of a prestigious collection of material, primarily donated by Anne Yeats, relating to Jack B. Yeats and members of the Yeats extended family.

HOLDINGS
The library houses a collection of some 50,000 volumes and includes exhibition catalogues from galleries and museums worldwide. It maintains research level collections on European Art from the Middle Ages to the 1950s and on Irish Art from the Middle Ages to the present. It maintains study level holdings in the areas of general art, museum studies, education in art, architecture, Irish history, conservation and the decorative arts. The archives house the gallery's minute books and documents relating to its history and foundation. In addition, the archives include the papers of various individuals connected with the gallery, including some Irish artists. *See* above for additional information on holdings.

LOCATION
At the northern end of Merrion Square West, near Clare Street, next to Leinster House (the seat of the Irish parliament). The library is located near the main entrance, one flight down. There is also an entrance on Clare Street to the new Millennium Wing of the National Gallery where the Diageo Print Room, Centre for the Study of Irish Art and Yeats Archive are located.

NATIONAL LIBRARY OF IRELAND

Kildare Street
DUBLIN 2
Ireland

TELEPHONE: (01) 603 0200; FAX: (01) 676 6690
E-mail: info@nli.ie
Website: www.nli.ie

HOURS
Main Reading Room: M–W, 10.00am–9.00pm; Th–F, 10.00am–5.00pm; Sa, 10.00am–1.00pm; closed Christmas, Easter and public holidays
Manuscripts Reading Room: M–W, 10.00am–8.30pm; Th–F, 10.00am–4.30pm; Sa, 10.00am–12.30pm; closed Christmas, Easter and public holidays

ACCESS
Visitors welcome; ID required. Students must have letter from academic supervisor. Advance notice for group visits required. Non-circulating collection. Certain collections or partial collections are held offsite and a 24 hour call-up applies for some material – other offsite material is retrieved on Tuesdays and Thursdays only. Wheelchair access. Pencils only; laptops permitted. Photocopying available for a fee, with restrictions for age and condition of material and for copyright. Library website carries information on exhibitions programme. Published histories of the library include, *The National Library of Ireland: One Hundred and Twenty Five Years* (Dublin, 2002); Noel Kissane (ed.), *Treasures from the National Library of Ireland* (Drogheda, 1994); Noel Kissane, *The National Library of Ireland* (Dublin, 1984), vol. 42 of Irish Heritage series; Patrick Henchy, *The National Library of Ireland, 1941–1976* (Dublin, 1986) and Gerard Long, 'The Foundation of the National Library of Ireland, 1836–1877', in *Long Room* 36 (1991), 41–58. A full listing of

the library's publications can be found on website. Online catalogue holds records of greater part of printed books collection; prints, drawings and photographs (some 30,000 of which have digitised images attached); and manuscripts catalogued since 1990. There is a printed catalogue of manuscripts entitled *Manuscript Sources for the History of Irish Civilisation*, which, with its three volume supplement, lists manuscript material catalogued prior to 1976; card catalogue covers the period 1976–90. Also online are detailed special lists of some 80 manuscript collections (including 20 landed estate archives), indexes to a number of key photographic collections and the NEWSPLAN database, listing library's newspaper holdings. In 2004, inaugural event in library's new exhibition area was the acclaimed James Joyce and *Ulysses* at the National Library of Ireland. It is succeeded by Yeats: The Life and Work of William Butler Yeats.

CONTACT
Aongus Ó hAonghusa, Director
Colette Byrne, Keeper (Administration)
Catherine Fahy, Keeper (Special Programmes)
Fergus Gillespie, Keeper (Genealogical Office) and Chief Herald
Gerard Lyne, Keeper (Manuscripts)
Brian McKenna, Keeper (Systems)
Dónall Ó Luanaigh, Keeper (Collections)

DESCRIPTION
The National Library is Ireland's major public research library, established 'to collect, preserve and make accessible materials on or relating to Ireland, whether published in Ireland or abroad, and a supporting reference collection'. To this end it seeks to build a comprehensive collection documenting the history and culture and life of Ireland. The Library's current collection of some 6,000,000 items constitutes the most outstanding collection of Irish documentary material in the world. In 1943, the library took responsibility on behalf of the state for matters relating to heraldry in Ireland. The Office of the Chief Herald of Ireland, formerly the Office of the Ulster King of Arms, has functioned as part of the library since that date. Since 1998, the library photographic collections have been housed in purpose built premises (*see* the NATIONAL PHOTOGRAPHIC ARCHIVE) in Dublin's Temple Bar. In 2004, a new exhibition facility was opened to the public together with a café, shop and seminar room. For the Office of the Chief Herald and the National Photographic Archive, *see* separate listings.

HOLDINGS
The library houses a collection of some 1,000,000 printed books, including pamphlets; approximately 17,000 linear feet of manuscripts; some 150,000 maps, either in print or manuscript form; about 2,500 current periodical titles; around 10,000 reels of microforms; 300 current newspaper titles, plus complete files of many non-current titles; about 600,000 photographs, which are held in the library's National Photographic Archive; and some 90,000 prints and drawings, including significant holdings of architectural records. Library collections concentrate on Irish history and society, including the Irish diaspora. Major collections are described in detail on the library's website. These include the Lawrence Collection, a collection of some 40,000 photographic plates documenting Ireland from the last decade of the nineteenth century until World War I; numerous literary manuscript collections, including the William Butler Yeats Collection, the James Joyce Collection, the

George Bernard Shaw Collection, the Patrick Kavanagh Collection and, most recently, the Sheehy Skeffington Papers and the Brian Friel Collection. The library continues to add to these outstanding collections. For example, in 2001 Michael and Gráinne Yeats added a further collection of some 100 notebooks, 130 files of loose papers and some 3,000 pages of automatic writing by W.B. Yeats and George Yeats to the family's earlier gifts of Yeats material to the National Library. In 2002, they donated the extensive personal library of William Butler Yeats. The Yeats collection is one of the largest literary collections in the National Library of Ireland and the largest collection of Yeats manuscripts in a single institution in the world. Also in 2001 the library purchased the manuscript draft of the 'Circe' episode of James Joyce's *Ulysses* for £1,384,953. The library's history holdings are second to none and include the papers of a number of family estates dating back as far as the sixteenth century. Among the more notable of these landed estate archives are: Castletown (County Laois), Clements (Counties Leitrim and Donegal), Clonbrock (County Galway), Coolattin (County Wicklow), De Vesci (County Laois), Doneraile (County Cork), Headford (County Meath), Inchiquin (County Clare), Lismore (County Waterford), Monteagle (County Limerick), O'Hara (County Sligo), Ormond (Counties Tipperary and Kilkenny), Powerscourt (County Wicklow), Prior-Wandesforde (County Kilkenny), Sarsfield (County Cork) and Wicklow (County Wicklow). Estate archives contain the records of the administration of estates by landlords and their agents and generally include leases, rentals, accounts, correspondence and maps.

Of special genealogical interest, the library holds microfilm copies of almost all Catholic parish registers from their respective start dates to 1880, microform copies of *Griffith's Valuation* and the tithe applotment books. The list of parish registers on microfilm can be consulted on the website in PDF format (requiring a copy if Adobe Acrobat Reader). The library does not provide copies of, or transcriptions from, registers. Original registers are generally in the custody of the parish priest. Also of interest to genealogists are the library's holdings of newspapers, trade and social directories and the many works of family and local history in the printed books collection. In the Department of Manuscripts, the records of the former landed estates (including rentals and mapped surveys) are valuable genealogical resources. The archives of the Office of the Ulster King of Arms, including a large collection of Irish heraldic and genealogical material, are held as a distinct collection – the Genealogical Office or G.O. Manuscripts – within the library. Other relevant material in the library's collections include the annual printed Army Lists, Royal Irish Constabulary publications, the 1796 Spinning Wheel Premium Entitlement List (on microfiche) and various other records of trades and professions. As research progresses, the appendices to nineteenth century parliamentary reports may prove useful.

The National Library's Genealogy Service is designed to assist those who wish to research their family history in Ireland and is available free of charge to all personal callers to the library. The service is operated by professional genealogists and experienced library staff who will advise on research methodology and sources. Free brochures, especially for the novice genealogist, are available. These include *Getting Started*, *Parish Registers in the National Library of Ireland* and *Valuation Records*.

LOCATION
Dublin city centre, adjacent to Leinster House (the seat of the Irish parliament) and to the National Museum of Ireland, close to Trinity College Dublin.

NATIONAL MUSEUM OF IRELAND

Museum of Country Life, Turlough Park
CASTLEBAR, COUNTY MAYO
Ireland

Museum of Decorative Arts and History, Collins Barracks, Benburb Street
DUBLIN 7

Museum of Archaeology and History, Kildare Street
DUBLIN 2

Museum of Natural History, Merrion Street
DUBLIN 2

Castlebar site
TELEPHONE: (094) 903 1755; FAX: (094) 903 1583
E-mail: tpark@museum.ie
Website: www.museum.ie

Dublin sites
TELEPHONE: (01) 677 7444; FAX: (01) 677 7450
E-mail: marketing@museum.ie
Website: www.museum.ie

HOURS:
Museums (all): Tu–Sa, 10.00am–5.00pm; Su, 2.00pm–5.00pm; closed Good Friday
and Christmas Day
Archives: by appointment

ACCESS AND SERVICES
Access to archives by appointment only. Contact Librarian. Events and activities for
people of all ages. Admission for self-guided visits free; public guided tours (2006),
€2 per person. Groups must book tours in advance. Rates for Dublin sites available
from the Education and Outreach Department. Bookings office: opening hours:
M–F, 10.00am–5.00pm. Castlebar site: telephone (094) 903 1751, fax (094) 903
1498, e-mail educationtph@museum.ie; Dublin sites: telephone (01) 677 7444, fax
(01) 679 1025, e-mail education@museum.ie. For information on current and
forthcoming temporary exhibitions, as well as for details of the range of exclusive
spaces for meetings and private events at Dublin sites, contact the Marketing
Department (details above). For Castlebar site, telephone (094) 903 1773; fax (094)
903 1583

CONTACT
Librarian for access to archives; marketing for all other enquiries

DESCRIPTION
The National Museum of Ireland houses the nation's artefacts dating back to 7000
BC. The museum is based in four sites as outlined below.
National Museum of Ireland – Decorative Arts and History
Collins Barracks could be said to be the National Museum of Ireland's largest Irish
artefact, having had a unique history all its own in another life. It now completes the
picture for the National Museum in Dublin and joins the two already famous
buildings in the museum's possession. On display are silver, ceramics, glassware,
weaponry, furniture, folklife, clothing, jewellery, coins and medals. All of these are

displayed with imagination in innovative and contemporary galleries, which entice the visitor to go further, look harder and examine more closely.

New approaches to exhibiting major collections in individual galleries include Irish Period Furniture, Irish Country Furniture, the Way We Wore and the recently opened Airgead – A Thousand Years of Irish Coins and Currency. While visiting Collins Barracks, visitors can see the work of one of the most influential designers and architects of the twentieth century, Irish born Eileen Gray. Visitors also have the chance to get behind the scenes and explore a working museum collection. Over 16,000 artefacts are on display in What's in Store? – a new visible storage area, which allows access to the reserve collections for the first time in the history of the National Museum.

National Museum of Ireland – Natural History
Opened in 1857 as the museum of the Royal Dublin Society, the Natural History Museum has developed as a cabinet style zoological museum with animals from all over the world. The history of collecting extends over two centuries and has resulted in a rich variety of animals, many of which are now endangered or extinct. Exhibitions in this museum have changed little in style for over a century, adding to the charm and rarity of this national treasure. The tradition of collecting and research continues and only a fraction of the two million specimens is on display.

National Museum of Ireland – Archaeology and History
This branch of the National Museum of Ireland houses a wonderful collection of artefacts dating from 7000 BC to the twentieth century, including the Ardagh Chalice, the Tara Brooch and the Derrynaflan Hoard. Special exhibitions include Ór – Ireland's Gold, a stunning collection of prehistoric gold ornaments, as well as Prehistoric Ireland and Viking Age Ireland. The Road to Independence tells the story of Ireland's history during the War of Independence (1919–21). In the recently opened Medieval Ireland 1150–1550, life in later medieval Ireland is explored through surviving artefacts divided into three galleries, entitled Power, Work and Prayer.

National Museum of Ireland – Country Life
This award winning museum, a branch of the National Museum of Ireland, is set in the spectacular grounds of Turlough Park and brings to life the traditions of rural life throughout Ireland from 1850 to 1950. Fascinating artefacts deal with domestic life, agriculture, fishing and hunting, clothing and textiles, furniture and fittings, trades and crafts, transport, sports and leisure and religion. The excellent hands-on public programmes which run throughout the year consist of art and craft workshops, demonstrations and performances. Groups can arrange a tailored programme for their visit.

HOLDINGS
The archives house the documentation, including correspondence, related to the museum's administrative, archaeological and historical work. Included among these collections are papers of some naturalists and archaeologists associated with the museum.

LOCATION
The National Museum of Ireland – Country Life is located eight kilometres east of Castlebar on the N5.
The National Museum of Ireland – Decorative Arts and History can be found three kilometres west of Dublin city centre along the north quays.
The National Museum of Ireland – Archaeology and History is in the city centre, near Leinster House (the seat of the Irish parliament).
The National Museum of Ireland – Natural History is located in Dublin city centre, parallel to Kildare Street.

NATIONAL PHOTOGRAPHIC ARCHIVE

Meeting House Square, Temple Bar
DUBLIN 2
Ireland

TELEPHONE: (01) 603 0371; FAX: (01) 677 7451
E-mail: photoarchive@nli.ie
Website: www.nli.ie

HOURS
Exhibitions and Reading Room: M–F, 10.00am–5.00pm
Exhibitions only: Sa, 10.00am–2.00pm

ACCESS AND SERVICES
Visitors welcome. Archive, which is part of National Library of Ireland, hosts regular programme of exhibitions, mainly based on materials in the collections held there. Reprographic services available for a fee, subject to copyright and other possible restrictions. Some 9,000 images have been digitised and can be viewed on National Library of Ireland website via Catalogue of Photographs. See also Sarah Rouse, *Into the Light: an Illustrated Guide to the Photographic Collections of the National Library of Ireland* (1998). A selection of images from the collection feature in Dr Noel Kissane, *Ex Camera 1869–1960*.

CONTACT
Sara Smyth, Assistant Keeper

DESCRIPTION
The National Photographic Archive houses the photographic collections of the National Library of Ireland. Opened in 1998, the archive building incorporates a substantial environmentally controlled storage area, together with darkrooms and a conservation area. The Reading Room, exhibition area and a small retail space combine to enhance access to the collections in the care of the archive.

HOLDINGS
There are some 610,000 photographs, the vast majority of which are Irish, in the various collections held by the National Photographic Archive. While most of the collections are historical, there is also some contemporary material. Subject matter ranges from topographical views to studio portraits, and from political events to early tourist photographs. The archive maintains an active collecting policy. The Independent Newspapers (Ireland) Collection (1912–97) is the largest collection at approximately 300,000 items. Work is currently underway to catalogue the

collections. Items from earlier years are available online. The other large collections are those created by the postcard and portrait studios that were in operation in many towns and cities of Ireland at the turn of the twentieth century. These include the Lawrence, Poole, Eason and Valentine Collections. The Clonbrock Collection of some 3,500 glass plate negatives from 1860 to 1930 provides an important record of life on a landed estate. The Keogh Collection, comprising 330 glass plate negatives, includes important images of the key political figures and events in Dublin during the period 1915–30. Other collections include the Morgan Collection (aerial photographs of Ireland during the mid-1950s), the Wiltshire Collection (Dublin 1951–70), the O'Dea Collection (Irish railways 1937–66) and the Clarke Collection (Dublin 1897–1904).

LOCATION
In the Temple Bar area of Dublin, close to the Irish Film Institute and the Gallery of Photography.

NATIONAL UNIVERSITY OF IRELAND, DUBLIN
See UNIVERSITY COLLEGE DUBLIN

Note: UCD is part of the National University of Ireland system, but it petitioned the Irish government successfully to keep its familiar name, i.e. UCD, so its full title is now University College Dublin, National University of Ireland.

OFFICE OF THE CHIEF HERALD/GENEALOGICAL OFFICE

2–3 Kildare Street
DUBLIN 2
Ireland

TELEPHONE: (01) 603 0311; FAX: (01) 662 1062
E-mail: herald@nli.ie
Website: www.nli.ie

HOURS
Heraldic Museum: M–W, 10.00am–8.30pm; Th–F, 10.00am–4.30pm; Sa, 10.00am–12.30pm. To consult manuscripts *see* opening hours of the National Library of Ireland Manuscripts Reading Room.

ACCESS AND SERVICES
Visitors welcome to the Heraldic Museum. In order to consult manuscripts, it is necessary to obtain National Library of Ireland manuscript reader's ticket. Main manuscript series listed in printed catalogue of manuscripts entitled *Manuscript Sources for the History of Irish Civilisation*, with three volume supplement. Manuscripts known as GO (Genealogical Office) Series. Summary catalogue of office's holdings appears in *A Guide to the Genealogical Office* (1998).

CONTACT
Chief Herald of Ireland, Fergus Gillespie

DESCRIPTION
Founded as the Office of the Ulster King of Arms in 1552, the Office of the Chief Herald is the oldest office of state in Ireland. The Chief Herald is the Heraldic

Authority for Ireland, responsible for the regulation of heraldic matters and the granting and confirming of coats of arms. The office has been a department of the National Library of Ireland since 1943.

HOLDINGS
Documents derived from the functions of the office include the registers of the Chief Herald, armorials and ordinaries of arms, funeral entries, lords' entries and records of knights dubbed. Roger O'Ferrall's *Linea Antiqua* is the most important source for ancient genealogies of Gaelic families and also contains exemplifications of arms. Other collections may be considered equally important to the researcher and certain information from now lost sources previously held in the Public Record Office of Ireland is of particular value. For example, the genealogical and historical information contained in the abstracts from the plea rolls of Henry III to Henry VI are a most important source for Norman genealogy. Extracts from the pipe rolls from Henry III to Edward III contain similar information. For a later period (1536–1810) tabulated pedigrees contained in the abstracts of wills proved at the prerogative court of the Archbishop of Armagh can be consulted. Other collections that, while not pedigrees, have been acquired as sources of genealogical information include Ecclesiastical Visitations, a list of high sheriffs of counties, a roll of freemen of the City of Dublin, lists of freeholders and a list of gentlemen attainted by King James. The Office of the Chief Herald does not undertake genealogical research or searches on behalf of members of the public. A list of researchers who have indicated a willingness to carry out research on a professional fee paying basis is available from the office. The National Library's Genealogy Service is freely available to all visitors who need advice on carrying out their own family history research in Ireland (*see* National Library of Ireland, Dublin).

LOCATION
Dublin city centre, near the National Library of Ireland and Leinster House (the seat of the Irish Parliament) and Trinity College Dublin.

ORDNANCE SURVEY OF IRELAND
Note: Archives transferred to NATIONAL ARCHIVES OF IRELAND, Dublin

PEARSE STREET LIBRARY
See CENTRE FOR DUBLIN AND IRISH STUDIES, Dublin

POETRY IRELAND/ÉIGSE ÉIREANN

2 Proud's Lane, off St Stephen's Green
DUBLIN 2
Ireland

TELEPHONE: (01) 478 9974; FAX: (01) 478 0205
E-mail: poetry@iol.ie
Website: www.poetryireland.ie

HOURS
By appointment

ACCESS AND SERVICES
Visitors welcome. Advance notice and ID required. No fees; laptops permitted.

CONTACT
Joseph Woods, Director

DESCRIPTION
Library sponsored by Poetry Ireland, a not for profit organisation founded to promote and support poets and poetry in Ireland.

HOLDINGS
Poetry Ireland has deposited on long term loan the Austin Clarke Collection of 6,000 volumes of poetry, prose, criticism and drama and the John Jordan Collection of 2,000 volumes of poetry, prose, criticism and fiction with University College Dublin Archives. Poetry Ireland plans to have both collections catalogued for its website and will refer enquiries to UCD. Poetry Ireland retains a small working library of poetry books, anthologies and journals that is available to the public for research and reading purposes by appointment.

LOCATION
City centre, off west side of St Stephen's Green, near Royal College of Surgeons.

THE QUAKER LIBRARY
See HISTORICAL LIBRARY, RELIGIOUS SOCIETY OF FRIENDS, Dublin

REGISTRY OF DEEDS

Henrietta Street
Dublin 1
Ireland

TELEPHONE: (01) 670 7500; FAX: (01) 804 8406
E-mail: david.hickey@landregistry.ie
Website: www.irlgov.ie/landreg

HOURS
M–F, 10.00am–4.30pm

ACCESS AND SERVICES
Visitors welcome. Registry provides variety of services for the public, including registration of deeds, search facilities (negative searches/common searches), copy facilities and genealogical services. Fees for service: search by members of the public in respect of each name, for each county, for each period of ten years or part thereof, €1.25; certified copy of memorial, €12; plain copy of microfilm of a memorial, 60c per page; any service for which no other fee is prescribed, €6; common search per name, per county, for each period of ten years or part thereof, €6; negative search per name, per county, for each period of ten years or part thereof, €12; general search, without limitation, each day by each member of the public against all indexes prior to 1970, €6.

CONTACT
Dave Hickey. E-mail: david.hickey@landregistry.ie

DESCRIPTION
The Registry of Deeds provides a system of voluntary registration of deeds and
conveyances affecting land. The system is based on a grantors' index, e.g. persons
who dispose of an interest in a property. In the case of property disposed after death,
the deceased's executor is the grantor and the executor's name and not the name of
the deceased person will appear in the names index. A deed and memorial (synopsis
of deed) is required for registration. Once registered, the deed is returned to the
lodging party and the memorial is retained by the Registry of Deeds.

HOLDINGS
Documents retained in the Registry of Deeds include: memorials (1708–present,
microfilmed 1930–present), transcripts (1708–1960, incomplete), abstracts
(1833–1969), names index or index of grantors and lands index (1708–1946). A
memorial is the synopsis of an original deed, with information on the names of all
parties to the deed, location of the property and details of the type of transaction. A
transcript is the handwritten/typed copy of the memorial. An abstract is the
summary of the memorial, containing the name of the grantor, grantee, description
of property and type of deed. The names index is the index of names of the persons
who have disposed of an interest in the property. The lands index is an index of all
transactions compiled in order of the names of the townland/street affected.

LOCATION
King's Inns, just off Bolton Street, almost directly opposite Dublin Institute of
Technology Bolton Street, on the north side of the Liffey, west of Parnell Square.
The registry can also be approached via Constitution Hill, opposite Broadstone Bus
Garage. The Luas red line stops at the Four Courts, approximately 600 metres away
via Church Street.

Note: See also Land Registry Offices:
Chancery Street, Dublin 7; telephone (01) 670 7500 (Counties Meath, Westmeath,
Cavan, Louth, Monaghan, Donegal, Leitrim, Longford)
Irish Life Centre, Lower Abbey Street, Dublin 1; telephone (01) 670 7500 (Counties
Kildare and Wicklow)
Nassau Building, Setanta Centre, Nassau Street, Dublin 2; telephone (01) 670 7500
(Counties Dublin, Galway, Mayo, Sligo, Clare, Roscommon)
Cork Road, Waterford; telephone (051) 30300 (Counties Cork, Kerry, Limerick,
Waterford,Tipperary, Laois, Offaly, Carlow, Kilkenny and Wexford)

REPRESENTATIVE CHURCH BODY LIBRARY

Braemor Park, Churchtown
DUBLIN 14
Ireland

TELEPHONE: (01) 492 3979; FAX: (01) 492 4770
E-mail: library@ireland.anglican.org
Website: www.ireland.anglican.org

HOURS
M–F, 9.30am–1.00pm, 2.00pm–5.00pm

ACCESS AND SERVICES

Visitors welcome, but advance notice preferred. No disabled access facilities. Laptops permitted; pencils only. Fees for photocopying. Of special genealogical and historical interest are a series of nine parish registers published by the library. These include: registers edited by Raymond Refaussé for the Parish of St Thomas, Dublin, 1750–91 and for Church of St Thomas, Lisnagarvey, County Antrim, 1637–46; by Colin Thomas for the Cathedral Church of St Columb, Derry, 1703–32 and 1732–75; by Susan Hood for the Holy Trinity Church, Cork, 1643–68; by James Mills for the Parish of St John the Evangelist, Dublin, 1619–99 (the oldest extant parish registers in Ireland); by Suzanne Pegley for the Parish of Leixlip, County Kildare, 1667–1778; by Herbert Wood for the Parish of St Catherine, Dublin, 1636–1715; and by Brigid Clesham for the Parish of St Nicholas, Galway, 1792–1840 (the library's most recent publication). Also of interest: Raymond Refaussé (ed.) *A Library on the Move: Twenty-Five Years of the Representative Church Body Library in Churchtown* (1995); *A Handlist of Church of Ireland Parish Registers in the Representative Church Body Library* (1996); and *A Handlist of Church of Ireland Vestry Minute Books in the Representative Church Body Library* (1996). In the Texts and Calendars series, published by Four Courts Press in association with the Representative Church Body Library, there are two titles currently available: Raymond Gillespie (ed.), *The Vestry Records of the Parish of St John the Evangelist, Dublin, 1595–1658*; and Raymond Gillespie (ed.), *The Vestry Records of the Parishes of St Catherine and St James, Dublin, 1657–1692*. For price and ordering information, contact Representative Church Body Library by mail, e-mail, phone or fax.

CONTACT

Raymond Refaussé, Librarian and Archivist

DESCRIPTION

The library was founded in 1931 and has been developed as the theological and reference library of the Church of Ireland and as the Church of Ireland's principal repository for its archives and manuscripts. It seeks to collect any printed, archival and manuscript material that is produced by or related to the Church of Ireland. The library is owned and funded by the Church of Ireland and is managed by the Library and Archives Committee of the Representative Church Body, which is the perpetual trustee for the real and movable property of the Church of Ireland.

HOLDINGS

The library houses some 40,000 volumes, focusing on theology and history, plus architectural records, archives and manuscripts, microforms, pamphlets, photographs and recordings. Major archival collections include: Church of Ireland archives chiefly for the Republic of Ireland, representing more than 900 parishes, mainly in Counties Carlow, Clare, Cork, Dublin, Galway, Kerry, Kildare, Kilkenny, Mayo, Meath, Westmeath and Wicklow; the records of 17 dioceses; the records of 15 cathedrals, especially Christ Church and St Patrick's in Dublin, St Canice's in Kilkenny and St Brigid's in Kildare. The archives also house medieval and early modern manuscripts, the records of the General Synod and the Representative Church Body, 1870–present, and the records of societies and organisations related to the Church of Ireland including schools, educational societies, missionary organisations and clerical groups from the eighteenth to the twentieth century. In addition, the collection includes miscellaneous ecclesiastical manuscripts, such as the papers of bishops, clergy and laity, correspondence, diaries, research notes and writings, scrapbooks, photographs and transcripts of non-extant Church of Ireland records from the seventeenth to the twentieth century. Also of interest are: the microfilms of church records in other custodies from the 17th to the 20th centuries; photographs of Church buildings, clergy, laity and church plate; and an oral history collection. *See also* the National Archives of Ireland, Dublin, and the Public Record Office of Northern Ireland, Belfast, for additional parish registers. Some original parish records are still in the custody of local clergy.

LOCATION
Adjacent to the Church of Ireland Theological College in Churchtown in the southern suburbs of Dublin. Take bus 14 from D'Olier Street (city centre) to Mount Carmel Hospital (Braemor Park). The library is opposite 33 Braemor Park.

ROYAL COLLEGE OF PHYSICIANS OF IRELAND

6 Kildare Street
DUBLIN 2
Ireland

TELEPHONE: (01) 661 6677; FAX: (01) 676 3989
E-mail: robertmills@rcpi.ie
Website: www.rcpi.ie

HOURS
M–F, 9.30am–1.00pm, 2.00pm–5.00pm

ACCESS AND SERVICES
Historic college building on Kildare Street recently underwent extensive, two-year refurbishment, reopening in October 2005. The refurbishment makes possible improved library facilities, including disabled access. Visitors welcome, but ID required and advance notice preferred. Library not actually open to the public, but willing to assist genuine researchers in medical history or genealogy. Fee schedule for the provision of genealogical information is being devised: this will most probably include direct access to index of names via library's website. Laptops permitted; pencils only. No fees for modest amount of photocopying, but fees exist for microform prints, e-mail, fax and scanning services. Advance notice for special service requests advisable. Library offers free college brochures. A copy of an article about the library and a history of the college available for purchase.

CONTACT
Robert Mills, Librarian

DESCRIPTION
The college was founded in 1654 and the library dates from 1713.

HOLDINGS
The library houses a collection of some 30,000 volumes of printed books, plus significant holdings of manuscripts, pamphlets, photographs and some 400 journal titles, though only about 15 are current. The library also holds architectural records relating to the RCPI building and a collection of portraits and sculpture that adorns the building. The collection focuses on medicine from earliest times to the nineteenth century, medical history and medicine in Ireland. Major collections include medical textbooks from the fifteenth century to the early twentieth, the

5,000 item Kirkpatrick Collection on Irish medical history, the 600 volume
Churchill Collection on the history of obstetrics and gynaecology, and the Travers
Collection of fine books on medicine, history, science and theology. Of special
interest to genealogists are the Kirkpatrick Archive, a collection of biographical
records (10,000 names) of Irish doctors from earliest times to the 1950s, the college
registers from 1692 to the present, and medical directories and registers published
from the 1840s to the present.

LOCATION
City centre, next door to the National Library of Ireland and a short walk from
Trinity College Dublin.

ROYAL DUBLIN SOCIETY

Ballsbridge
DUBLIN 4
Ireland

TELEPHONE: (01) 668 0866; FAX: (01) 660 4014
E-mail: library@rds.ie
Website: www.rds.ie

HOURS
Reading area and issue desk: Tu, F, 10.00am–5.00pm; W–Th, 10.00am–7.00pm; Sa,
11.00am–5.00pm
Reading area only: M, 10.00am–5.00pm
Closed public and bank holidays and Christmas–New Year period

ACCESS AND SERVICES
Primarily a facility for members of the society. Membership open to all, subject to
normal application and election procedures. Annual fee structure applies, with local,
regional and overseas rates. *Bona fide* researchers should furnish written application
from relevant faculty of their educational institution or from their organisation.
Charge applies according to nature of research or assistance required. Computer
catalogue used for general collection. Card catalogue exists for scientific publications.
Photocopying service operates through library desk. Laptops permitted.

CONTACT
Mary Kelleher, Librarian. Telephone: (01) 240 7288; e-mail: mary.kelleher@rds.ie
Gerard Whelan, Assistant Librarian/Library Administrator. Telephone: (01) 240
7256; e-mail: ger.whelan@rds.ie

DESCRIPTION
The Dublin Society was founded in 1731 (it became 'Royal' in 1820) for the
improvement of 'husbandry' (agriculture), 'manufactures' and other 'useful arts and
sciences'. One of the newly formed society's first acts was to establish a library. This
became one of the most significant collections in Ireland, going on to form the
nucleus of the National Library of Ireland collection when that body was established
in 1877. The society retained many of its scientific collections of books and journals,
which it continued to collect. The science collection developed through a
publication exchange programme with many institutions and like minded societies
across the world. Selected publications of some North American institutions can be

found in the holdings. In the nineteenth century, Dublin was to some degree regarded as the second city of the British Empire and the society's holdings reflect the diversity of learned inquiry of that age.

HOLDINGS
The general library contains over 200,000 volumes including over 4,000 relating to Ireland, many of them old and rare. There are 6,000 works and pamphlets on all branches of agricultural science including some 1,500 items of equestrian interest. These works form one of the most important collections on agriculture in the country. Of special research interest, the library contains the records of the Royal Dublin Society. These are in manuscript form dating from its foundation and in printed annual volumes since 1764. The diverse activities and interests the society pursued are recorded through the minutes of its meetings and a diversity of publications. The society acted as an intermediary for distributing funds that were awarded as premiums, provided by the Irish parliament prior to the Act of Union (1801) and afterwards from the British parliament. It was through the society's many endeavours that leading institutions of the state came into being, including the National Museum, the National Museum of Natural History, the Botanic Gardens, the National Veterinary College, the National Library and the National College of Art and Design.

LOCATION
In the main body of the Royal Dublin Society complex, with access through the members' entrance. The RDS is situated in Ballsbridge, approximately two miles south-east of Dublin city centre, on the Merrion Road. Visitors can travel on buses 7, 7A, 45, 46, 63 or 84. Two DART stations (Lansdowne Road and Sandymount) are within a ten to 15 minute walk of the RDS.

ROYAL IRISH ACADEMY

19 Dawson Street
DUBLIN 2
Ireland

TELEPHONE: (01) 676 2570/4222; FAX: (01) 676 2346
E-mail: library@ria.ie
Website: www.ria.ie

HOURS
M–Th, 10.00am–5.30pm; F, 10.00am–5.00pm; closed public and bank holidays, Easter Tuesday, Christmas–New Year period and two weeks in May/June for cleaning and checking of stock

ACCESS AND SERVICES
Visitors welcome; registration required. Registration forms available online at www.ria.ie/library%2bcatalogue/open or can be requested by telephone, fax, post or e-mail. Completed forms accompanied by a letter of introduction from an academy member or the faculty of a university together with valid ID, student card or passport should be presented. Reader's ticket issued for initial period of one year on payment of €12. Holders of a valid ALCID (Academic Libraries Cooperating in Ireland) card may gain automatic access to the library and are not required to pay a

fee. Laptops permitted; pencils only. Gloves issued for use of vellum manuscripts, drawings and rare items. Library offers ongoing exhibitions programme and participates in academy's celebrated publications and lecture programmes. Access to exhibitions free of charge. Entire collection catalogued: half on card catalogue; half online. Online catalogues accessible on website. Library currently managing retrospective cataloguing project which aims to have most catalogue records for printed works in the collections available on website in 2006. *Catalogue of Irish Manuscripts in the Royal Irish Academy* (28 fascicles, 1926–70) available for purchase from the Dublin Institute for Advanced Studies.

CONTACT
Siobhán Fitzpatrick, Librarian. E-mail: s.fitzpatrick@ria.ie
Bernadette Cunningham, Deputy Librarian. E-mail: b.cunningham@ria.ie

DESCRIPTION
The Royal Irish Academy was founded in 1785 as a society for 'promoting the study of science, polite literature and antiquities'. Anchored by its celebrated library, the academy promotes the sciences and the humanities through publications, lectures, conferences and cooperative programmes with other institutions. Currently, for example, it is working with the Department of Foreign Affairs on the multi-volume publication of a major series of historical documents charting the development of Irish diplomacy and foreign policy since 1919. The Royal Irish Academy also sponsors research on the *Irish Historic Towns Atlas*, the *Dictionary of Medieval Latin from Celtic Sources*, the *Dictionary of Irish Biography* and *Foclóir na Nua-Ghaeilge*.

HOLDINGS
The library houses an extraordinary manuscript and book collection, plus important holdings of artefacts, drawings, journals (approximately 7,000 titles), maps, pamphlets (50,000), photographs, antiquarian drawings, portraits and recordings. Its collection of over 2,000 manuscripts includes many of the oldest and most treasured original documents of Irish cultural history. These include the *Cathach*, or *Psalter of St Columba*, the oldest surviving Irish manuscript, written in Latin *c.* 560–630 AD; the *Stowe Missal*, the oldest extant mass book of the early Irish Church, *c.* 792–803 AD; the *Book of the Dun Cow*, the oldest extant literary manuscript in the Irish language, before 1106 AD; and the *Annals of the Four Masters*, written between 1632 and 1636 in Irish, chronicling Irish history from earliest times to 1616. Twenty-eight of the most important early Irish manuscripts are accessible online via the Irish Script On Screen website with which the academy library is cooperating on an ongoing basis (www.isos.dias.ie). The library houses the largest collection of Irish language manuscripts anywhere, plus important medieval and early modern manuscripts in Latin, French and English. It contains important modern manuscript material. Of special genealogical interest are the records of the nineteenth century Ordnance Survey and the papers of De La Ponce, Marquess MacSwiney and H.A.S. Upton. The library also houses the papers of individual members – including those of its founder, Lord Charlemont – and drawings of Irish antiquities. The Printed Book Collection of more than 100,000 volumes includes the 30,000 item Charles Haliday Pamphlet Collection, the library of composer and poet Thomas Moore, the Celtic Studies library of Osborn Bergin, Rev Richard Kirwan Collection of early scientific works, a collection of early Irish imprints and an Irish and international journal collection.

LOCATION

Nestled between St Ann's Church and the Mansion House (the Lord Mayor's residence) on Dawson Street, one block west of the National Library of Ireland, close to the north side of St Stephen's Green.

ROYAL SOCIETY OF ANTIQUARIES OF IRELAND

63 Merrion Square
DUBLIN 2
Ireland

TELEPHONE: (01) 676 1749; FAX: (01) 676 1749
E-mail: rsai@gofree.indigo.ie
Website: www.rsai.ie

HOURS

M, W–Th, 10.00am–12.00pm, 2.00pm–4.45pm; Tu, F, 2.00pm–4.45pm; closed August, Christmas–New Year period, Easter period and bank holidays

ACCESS AND SERVICES

Visitors welcome, but advance notice required. Staff happy to answer queries by post, fax or e-mail. No disabled access facilities. Laptops permitted; pencils only. Fee schedule applies: €5 per session for non-members. Special permission from council to view Du Noyer sketches. Photocopies cost 25–35c per sheet, post extra. The society publishes the *Journal of the Royal Society of Antiquaries of Ireland*, free to members, otherwise €33 annually.

CONTACT

Nicole Arnould, Librarian. E-mail: nicole@rsai.ie

DESCRIPTION

The society was founded in 1849 'to preserve, examine and illustrate all Ancient Monuments and Memorials of the Arts, Manners and Customs of the past, as connected with the Antiquities, Language, Literature and History of Ireland'. To this end, it sponsors lectures, talks and excursions and publishes a journal. It also maintains a research library, open to the public for a modest fee and free to members.

HOLDINGS

The library houses a collection of books and manuscripts focused primarily on pre-1800 Irish history. It also has a fine photographic collection, including a photographic survey done by members during the period 1870–1910, and a collection of glass slides called Darkest Dublin, made during a survey of the poor areas of Dublin in 1913. Other important collections are sketches by Georges Du Noyer and manuscript notes by Elrington Ball for his *History of County Dublin*. Journal articles and photographic collection of some genealogical interest.

LOCATION

Midway between Lower Baggot Street and Lower Mount Street, opposite Leinster House (seat of the Irish parliament), bordered on the west by Upper Merrion Street and on the east by Fitzwilliam Street East. The society is located nearer the Upper Merrion Street end.

ST PATRICK'S COLLEGE – CREEGAN LIBRARY

St Patrick's College, Drumcondra
DUBLIN 9
Ireland

TELEPHONE: (01) 884 2170
E-mail: info.library@spd.ie
Website: www.spd.dcu.ie/library

HOURS
Term time: M–Th, 10.00am–10.00pm; F, 10.00am–5.30pm; Sa, 10.00am–1.00pm
Vacation period: M–F, 10.00am–1.00pm, 2.00pm–5.00pm

ACCESS AND SERVICES
Members of the public wishing to read in library may do so on application at issue
desk. Borrowing privileges not available. General enquiries should be made to
information desk. St Patrick's College shares integrated online public access catalogue
(OPAC) with Dublin City University and The Mater Dei Institute of Education, the
first system in Ireland to provide full web search facilities in both English and Irish.
Catalogues provide single search point for over 350,000 book titles. Photocopy cards
of various values on sale in both library and resource centre and may be used in both
places. Reader/printer available for reading and copying microfilm and microfiche.
All special collections non-circulating and may be consulted only in library. Some
collections, e.g. Belvedere House Library, may be visited only by arrangement with
Librarian.

CONTACT
Evan J. Salholm, Librarian. E-mail: evan.salholm@spd.dcu.ie

DESCRIPTION
St Patrick's College was founded in 1875. In 1883 it was officially recognised as a
denominational teacher training college and in that year moved from 2 Drumcondra
Road to the historic Belvedere House, whose core dates to the seventeenth century.
The library building is mid-eighteenth century on its present campus. From its
beginnings until 1999, the college was administered by the Vincentian community, a
Roman Catholic religious order. It is now administered by a lay president, Dr Pauric
Travers. While St Patrick's College maintains an independent and separate identity, it
has been a college of Dublin City University since 1993 and all its courses are
accredited by DCU. The Roman Catholic identity of the college is fostered through
religious worship and campus ministry and all student teachers complete a course in
religious education. Current enrolment is approximately 2,500 students.

HOLDINGS
The college library contains over 150,000 books and 550 journals as well as
microfiche, microfilm and other materials. The collection is a balanced one for a
humanities college, with particular strengths in Celtic and Irish languages and
literature and in Irish history. Special collections include: Belvedere House Library,
the old Vincentian community library, which includes collections of publications by
former students and faculty members, some of whom are quite famous; the Dolmen
Press and Three Candles Press Collections; a collection of pre-1880 publications;
rare children's books, including Irish, e.g. Patricia Lynch; the Padraic Colum
Collection of printed material; the Gaelic League Collection, including letters

written to Henry Morris, a member of the Gaelic League and a graduate of the college; the P.W. Joyce Collection (in development); and a small collection of books from the library of Fr Donal Creegan CM, a distinguished historical scholar, a president of the college (1957–76) and a leading innovator in Irish education of his time. The collection is housed in Belvedere House Library and the library is named in his honour. The library also boasts the largest collection of Irish textbooks in the nation, arguably its most important special collection. More recently the library has begun actively collecting Abbey Theatre plays. Note: several of these special collections are currently uncatalogued.

LOCATION
On the N1, two miles north of the centre of Dublin City and nine miles south of Dublin Airport. The area is well serviced by public transport. Frequent buses from the city include 3, 11, 16 and 41. Drumcondra station is within walking distance. The college has good parking facilities.

TIERNAN MACBRIDE LIBRARY
See IRISH FILM ARCHIVE OF THE IRISH FILM INSTITUTE, Dublin

TRINITY COLLEGE LIBRARY

College Street
DUBLIN 2
Ireland

TELEPHONE: (01) 608 1657; FAX: (01) 608 3774
E-mail: consult staff directory on website
Website: www.tcd.ie/library

HOURS
Visitor areas (including Long Room and *Book of Kells* exhibition)
M–Sa, 9.30am–5.00pm; Su (May–September), 9.30am–4.30pm; Su (October–April) 12.00pm–4.30pm; bank holidays (October–April), 12.30pm–4.30pm
Reading Rooms
Department of Manuscripts
M–F, 10.00am–5.00pm; Sa, 10.00am–1.00pm
Department of Early Printed Books
Term time: M–F, 10.00am–10.00pm, Sa, 10.00am–1.00pm
Vacation period: as for Department of Manuscripts
Berkeley/Lecky/Ussher Library (Reading Rooms and collections for arts, humanities, social sciences, business, music and nursing) and Hamilton Science and Engineering Library
Term time: M–F, 9.00am–10.00pm; Sa, 9.30am–4.00pm
Vacation period: M–F, 9.30am–5.00pm; Sa, 9.30am–1.00pm
Map Library
Tu, Th, 2.00pm–4.45pm, W, 9.30am–1.00pm, or by appointment
John Stearne Medical Library (at St James's Hospital)
Term time: M–Th, 9.30am–9.45pm; F, 9.30am–8.30pm; Sa, 9.30am–1.00pm
Vacation period: M–F, 9.30am–5.00pm
Consult website for alterations

ACCESS AND SERVICES

Website gives details of holdings and services as well as access to online catalogue, the library shop and services available for visiting research workers and tourists. Online catalogue, available from website, indexes almost 80 per cent of holdings. Complete coverage expected by 2009. Library serves both heritage visitors and readers.

Heritage Visitors

Access to the Old Library exhibition area, Manuscripts Treasury and the Long Room is open to the public on payment of an admission fee. The main chamber of the Old Library, the Long Room, is nearly 65 metres in length and houses around 200,000 of the library's oldest books. In 1860 the roof was raised according to plans by architects Deane and Woodward, to allow construction of the present barrel vaulted ceiling and gallery bookcases. Marble busts are placed down either side. This collection began in 1743 when 14 busts were commissioned from the sculptor Peter Scheemakers. Other sculptors represented are Simon Vierpyl, Patrick Cunningham, John van Nost and Louis Francois Roubiliac, whose bust of the writer Jonathan Swift is one of the finest in the collection. The harp on exhibition, constructed from oak and willow with brass strings, is the oldest to survive from Ireland and probably dates from the fifteenth century. As an emblem of early bardic society, this is the harp that appears on Irish coins. The attribution to Brian Boru, High King of Ireland (d. 1014), is legendary. One of the dozen or so remaining copies of the 1916 Proclamation of the Irish Republic is on display.

Changing exhibitions of printed books and manuscripts from the library's collections are mounted in the Long Room. The *Book of Kells*, on display in the Treasury, was written around the year 800 AD and is one of the most beautifully illuminated manuscripts in the world. It contains the four gospels, preceded by prefaces, summaries and canon tables or concordances of gospel passages. It is written on vellum and contains a Latin text of the gospels in insular majuscule script accompanied by magnificent and intricate whole pages of decoration with smaller painted decorations appearing throughout the text. The manuscript has been on display in the Old Library since the nineteenth century. Accompanying the *Book of Kells* in the display are other manuscripts such as the *Book of Armagh*, the *Book of Durrow*, the *Book of Mulling* and the *Book of Dimma*.

The library shop offers a wide range of books, gifts and Trinity merchandise.

Reading Room

All members (staff and students) of the university are admitted to the Reading Rooms on production of their Trinity College identity card. Other readers will be admitted to use the library's collections (without borrowing rights) for study and research provided they satisfy the conditions of one of the variety of schemes or cross higher education institutional arrangements listed on the library's website or can demonstrate that Trinity is a library of last resort for their material. During busy periods access restrictions may apply. For instance, admissions may be confined to Saturdays only. Access to the Special Collections Department (manuscripts and maps) will normally only be permitted by prior arrangement with the heads of departments concerned. If intending researchers are unclear about procedures, it would be advisable to contact the library prior to visiting. *See* separate entries below for Trinity College Library – Department of Early Printed Books and Trinity College Library – Manuscripts Department.

CONTACT
Anne-Marie Diffley, Visitor Services. Telephone: (01) 608 2320; fax (01) 608 2690
Robin Adams, Librarian
Trevor Peare, Keeper (Readers' Services)

DESCRIPTION
Trinity College, the single constituent college of the University of Dublin, was
founded by Queen Elizabeth I in 1592 and so celebrated its first quatercentenary in
1992. It is the oldest university in Ireland and one of the older universities of
Western Europe. Based on the general pattern of the ancient colleges at Oxford and
Cambridge, Trinity has a main campus extending over 40 acres in a unique site in
the heart of the city.
    As a university library, the library serves the needs of the college's population of
15,000 undergraduate and postgraduate students and academic staff. As a research
library of international standing its rare and unique materials are consulted by
scholars from all parts of the world.
    Several of the library buildings are architecturally significant: six are located on
the college campus. The Old Library, completed in 1732, contains the Department
of Manuscripts, the Department of Early Printed Books and the Special Collections
Department, as well as the Long Room, the library shop, the exhibition gallery and
Manuscripts Treasury. The Berkeley/Lecky/Ussher complex (1967, 1974 and 2003)
consists of three units operating as a single library. The complex contains the main
administrative offices, the Reading Rooms and collections for arts, humanities, social
sciences, business and nursing as well as closed access stacks. The complex also
houses the Glucksman Map Library and Conservation Department.

HOLDINGS
The library is the largest library in Ireland, its collections of manuscripts and printed
books having been built up since the end of the sixteenth century. In addition to the
purchases and donations of four centuries, the library has since 1801 had the right
to claim all British and Irish publications under the terms of successive Copyright
Acts. The total book stock is now over four and a quarter million items and there are
also extensive collections of manuscripts, maps, printed music and electronic
resources.

LOCATION
City centre, entrance opposite the Bank of Ireland building, formerly the home of
the pre-1801 Irish parliament.

TRINITY COLLEGE LIBRARY – DEPARTMENT OF EARLY PRINTED BOOKS

College Street
DUBLIN 2
Ireland

TELEPHONE: (01) 608 1172; FAX: (01) 671 9003
E-mail: charles.benson@tcd.ie
Website: www.tcd.ie/library

HOURS

Term time: M–F, 10.00am–10.00pm; Sa, 10.00am–12.45pm
Vacation period: M–F, 10.00am–5.00pm; Sa, 10.00am–12.45pm

ACCESS AND SERVICES

See Trinity College Library, Dublin for general guidelines for library use.
Department's holdings may be read only in Early Printed Books Reading Room,
which is reserved for readers using this material. Special guidelines in force for
handling material in Reading Room, which includes use of pencils only. Books from
other reading rooms may only be transferred with special permission. There is a
printed catalogue known as the *Catalogus librorum impressorum qui in Bibliotheca
Collegii Sacrosanctae et Individuae Trinitatis ... juxta Dublin, adservantur.* Dublinii: E
Typographeo Academico, 1864–87. 9 vols (vol. 9 = supplement). It is available on
microfiche and is the collection's main working catalogue containing holdings of pre-
1850 books. There is also the *Guardbook Catalogue of Accessions 1873–1963.*
Material catalogued since 1963 is available online and contains a high level of detail,
such as entries for printers and publishers, illustrators, papermakers, binders and
provenance. There is also *Catalogus librorum in Bibliothecae Collegii Sanctae et
Individuae Trinitatis Reginae Elizabethae juxta Dublin.* Dublinii: typis et impensis
Johannis Hyde (*c.* 1715). Finally, the Department of Early Printed Books has started
on a project, supported by the Mellon Foundation, of recataloguing the older
collections, beginning with the accessions catalogue. This is being done by matching
books with existing electronic records. This effort will subsequently be enhanced by
adding provenance and copy specific information.

CONTACT

Charles Benson, Keeper of Early Printed Books. E-mail: charles.benson@tcd.ie

HOLDINGS

The Department of Early Printed Books houses some 300,000 pre-1900 volumes,
plus some modern collections. The early library collection reflected the academic
interests of the university in theology and religious controversy, classical literature, law,
mathematics and natural philosophy. Among the early collections of note acquired by
the library were those of Archbishop James Ussher (10,000 vols) in 1662, the Butler
family (1,400 vols) in the late eighteenth century and the Fergal family (20,000 vols)
in 1802. In 1801 the library became a legal deposit library for United Kingdom
publications. Until the late nineteenth century, accessioning policies were very
conservative, cataloguing only those items judged to be of academic merit or suitable
religious tenor. A consistent and active purchasing programme for antiquarian
materials did not begin until the 1960s, but made up for many of the earlier
deficiencies in the collection. While the department maintains a good representation
of very early printing from all over Continental Europe, the focus is on imprints from
North-West Europe, with considerable strengths in works printed in France and the
Low Countries from the sixteenth to the eighteenth centuries and, above all, in Irish
and English works. Political history is another area of strength, especially the
Netherlands, 1580–1780; the English Civil War; the Fronde; England 1680–90 and
the 1720s; England and Ireland, 1780–1820 (where the printed works are enhanced
by the Nicholas Robinson Collection of caricatures); the French Revolution,
1789–1800 (about 12,000 items); Ireland and England in the nineteenth century,
where the collections are being enhanced by the acquisition of English newspapers
(2,000 volumes), 1800–*c.* 1940, from the National Library on long term deposit.

One of the library's great strengths is in English language drama from 1660 to the present. Holdings of authors educated at Trinity College Dublin, such as Congreve, Farquhar and Goldsmith, are particularly good. French drama holdings are good but uneven, with particular strength in the seventeenth century. There are minor collections of Dutch, German and Spanish drama. Poetry in English is strong, especially for the period 1710–40, including much Swiftiana. Popular verse is represented in the J.D. White Ballads (900 items, c.1860–90). Eighteenth and nineteenth century English fiction, once an area of weakness, has been strengthened by recent purchases. There is some seventeenth and eighteenth century French fiction. Classical literature is present in quantity from the incunabula period on.

Not surprisingly, theology and religious controversy are among the strongest areas in the collection, with an especially strong collection of Bibles. There are about 1,200 Reformation tracts printed before 1545. Coverage of Anglican theology is excellent for the entire period and that of Roman Catholic theology is surprisingly good up to the end of the seventeenth century, reasonable for the eighteenth century and now improving for the nineteenth century. There is some Quaker and Presbyterian material.

The department also boasts significant holdings of pre-1830 maps, including most of the major atlases, the oldest being an edition of *Ptolemy's Cosmographia* of 1490. Ortelius, Mercator and Blaeu are well represented. In addition there are some 2,000 sheet maps printed before 1790. Ordnance Survey maps from the 1830s to the present can be found in the Map Library. There is a good collection of early mathematical books, including Euclid's *Opus elementorum* (1482), plus good holdings in geology, physics, chemistry, medicine, botany, engineering and architecture. There is a small amount of seventeenth century music and a fair collection of Handel's operas. The bulk of the early music, however, dates from the 1760s to the 1820s and came from Townley Hall in County Louth. There are about 1,600 items from this period, including recent purchases. Other early music collections are those of Ebenezer Prout (3,500 items) and the Strollers, an amateur *Singverin* (1,900 items). There is also music from the College Choral Society and College Chapel. Irish and English law is held in considerable quantity from the earliest editions and more recently editions of French customary law and *mémoires* are being collected.

For the post-1901 holdings there is a collection of recruiting posters issued in Ireland during World War I, the Samuels Collection of subversive ephemera taken up by the Royal Irish Constabulary (1914–21), the Cuala Press Archives, the personal library of James Stephens and Irish nationalist and radical newspapers, 1901–30.

LOCATION
East Pavilion of the Old Library building with access from the entrance hall of the Berkeley Library.

TRINITY COLLEGE LIBRARY – MANUSCRIPTS DEPARTMENT

College Street
DUBLIN 2
Ireland

TELEPHONE: (01) 698 1189; FAX: (01) 608 2690
E-mail: mscripts@tcd.ie
Website: www.tcd.ie/library

HOURS
M–F, 10.00am–5.00pm; Sa, 10.00am–1.00pm

ACCESS AND SERVICES
See Trinity College Library, Dublin for general guidelines for library use. Manuscript readers should first obtain reader's ticket from Berkeley Library and permission to consult manuscripts should be applied for in advance to Keeper of Manuscripts. The department offers photography and microfilming services. Guides include T.K. Abbott, *Catalogue of the Manuscripts in the Library of Trinity College, Dublin* (Dublin and London, 1900), a general catalogue of accessions to 1900, continued after that date in typescript form. Introductory leaflet available throughout the library. Sectional language catalogues have appeared in print, including T.K. Abbott and E.J. Gwynn, *Catalogue of the Irish Manuscripts in the Library of Trinity College, Dublin* (Dublin, 1921) and Marvin L. Colker, *A Descriptive Catalogue of the Mediaeval and Renaissance Latin Manuscripts in the Library of Trinity College Dublin* (Scholar Press for Trinity College Library, 1991). Peter Fox (ed.), *Treasures of the Library, Trinity College Dublin* (Dublin, 1986) discusses some of the library's major holdings. See also Bernard Meehan, 'Manuscript Accessions in Trinity College Library Dublin, 1982–2003, Part I', *Long Room* 48 (2003), 38–55.

CONTACT
Keeper of Manuscripts

HOLDINGS
Major collections include: corpus of medieval manuscripts, largely from the collection of James Ussher (d. 1656), but also including the library's greatest treasures: the *Book of Kells* (*c.* 800), *Book of Durrow* (*c.* 675), *Book of Armagh* (807), *Book of Dimma* (eighth century), *Book of Mulling* (eighth century), Matthew Paris's *Life of St Alban* (thirteenth century) and the *Fagel Missal* (fifteenth century). Also of great significance are: college muniments, sixteenth–twentieth century; Roman inquisitorial records, sixteenth–twentieth century; depositions of 1641; 1798 Rebellion papers; and the archives of the Royal Zoological Society of Ireland, 1836–*c.*1953. Family and private paper collections include those of: William King (1650–1729), Archbishop of Dublin; Thomas Parnell (1679–1718), poet; Earls of Donoughmore, sixteenth–twentieth century; Wynne family of Hazlewood, County Sligo and Glendalough, County Wicklow, eighteenth–twentieth century; Elvery family of Carrickmines and Foxrock, County Dublin, nineteenth–twentieth century; Sir William Rowan Hamilton (1805–65), mathematician and astronomer; Michael Davitt (1846–1906), author and politician; John Dillon (1851–1927), politician; Robert Erskine Childers (1870–1922), author and politician; Liam de Roiste (1882–1959); politician and author; John Millington Synge (1871–1909), poet and dramatist; Susan Mitchell (1866–1926), poet and editor; Thomas Bodkin

(1887–1961), art historian and gallery director; Thomas MacGreevy (1893–1967), poet and gallery director; Denis Johnston (1901–84), playwright and journalist; Frank Gallagher (1898–1962), journalist; Joseph Campbell (1879–1944), poet; James Stephens (1880–1950), author; Máirtín Ó Cadhain (1906–70), writer in Irish; George MacBeth (1932–93), poet and novelist; John Banville (1945–present), novelist; Samuel Beckett (1906–89), author; Herbert Butler (1900–91), essayist; Gerald Barry (1952–present), composer; John B. Keane (1928–2002), author; Tom Murphy (1935–present), playwright; Lilliput Press, Dublin archives 1984–2004; Gerard Victory (1921–95), composer and broadcaster; St John Ervine (1881–1971), writer, novelist, playwright (papers, manuscripts and correspondence); Risteárd Ó Glaisne (1927–2003), writer and Irish language activist (papers, manuscripts and correspondence); and James Wilson (1922–2005), composer (papers, scores and correspondence).

LOCATION
Old Library, with entry via the library shop and the Long Room.

UCD SCHOOL OF HISTORY AND ARCHIVES

Library Building, University College Dublin, Belfield
DUBLIN 4
Ireland

TELEPHONE: (01) 716 7555; FAX: (01) 716 1146
E-mail: seamus.helferty@ucd.ie
Website: www.ucd.ie/archives

HOURS
M–Th, 10.00am–5.00pm; F, 10.00am–4.00pm (subject to staffing)

ACCESS AND SERVICES
Visitors welcome, but by appointment only. Advance notice required. Disabled access facilities. Laptops permitted; pencils only. Collections not available unless catalogued. Fees for photocopying, microform print and digital imaging services. Website gives best current indication of holdings and is updated regularly.

CONTACT
Duty Archivist

DESCRIPTION
UCD School of History and Archives mainly houses the deposited private collections of papers of public figures, such as politicians and public servants; and the official papers of the university and its predecessors. Though it occupies space in the UCD library, UCD Archives is independent of the library.

HOLDINGS
The collections overwhelmingly date from the independence period (1921–present) and relate to the political, cultural and economic development of modern Ireland. Major collections include papers of Frank Aiken, Todd Andrews, Kevin Barry, Ernest Blythe, Colonel Dan Bryan, Michael Collins, John A. Costello, the Cumann na nGaedheal and Fine Gael parties, George Gavan Duffy, the Fianna Fáil party, Desmond FitzGerald, Michael Hayes, T.M. Healy, Sighle Humphreys, Hugh Kennedy, Tom Kettle, Sean Lester, Sean MacEntee, Sean Mac Eoin, Patrick

McGilligan, Eoin MacNeill, Mary MacSwiney, Terence MacSwiney, Michael MacWhite, Richard Mulcahy, Donnchadh Ó Briain, Daniel O'Connell, Kathleen O'Connell, Cearbhall Ó Dálaigh, Diarmuid Ó hEigeartaigh, Dan O'Herlihy, Ernie O'Malley, The O'Rahilly, Desmond Ryan, Dr James Ryan, Moss Twomey and Eamon de Valera.

Other collections include the records of predecessor institutions of the university, including the Catholic University of Ireland, 1854–1911; the Royal College of Science for Ireland, 1867–1926; the Museum of Irish Industry, 1846–7; Albert Agricultural College, 1838–1926; and the Royal Veterinary College of Ireland, 1900–60. The Franciscan 'A' Manuscript Collection, formerly housed in the Franciscan library, Killiney, County Dublin and still the property of the Franciscans, includes the *Martyrology of Tallaght* (fragment of the *Book of Leinster*), the *Annals of the Four Masters*, the *Psalter of St Caimin* and the *Liber Hymnoroum*. Family and estate paper collections dating from the seventeenth century include those of the: Bryans (Dublin); Caulfeilds (County Tyrone); de Cliffords (County Down); Delacherois (County Down); Fitzpatricks (County Laois); Hart-Synnots (Dublin); Herberts (County Kerry); Hutchinsons and Synge Hutchinsons (Dublin and County Wicklow); Potters (County Down); Rices of Mountrice (County Kildare); Uptons (Counties Westmeath and Louth); and Wandesfords (County Kilkenny). UCD Archives also include the trade union archives and labour related paper collections deposited through the Irish Labour History Society. These include archives of actors', bakers', coopers', municipal employees', plasterers', shoe and leather workers' and woodworkers' trade unions.

LOCATION
In the library building on the main university campus in Belfield, on the south-east side of Dublin, accessible by bus from city centre. *See* directions in following entry.

UNIVERSITY COLLEGE DUBLIN LIBRARY

University College Dublin, Belfield
DUBLIN 4
Ireland

TELEPHONE: (01) 716 7694; FAX: (01) 283 7667
E-mail: library@ucd.ie
Website: www.ucd.ie/library

HOURS
Term time: M–F, 8.30am–11.00pm; Sa–Su, 9.00am–9.00pm (Reading Room only on Sundays)
Vacation period: hours vary

ACCESS AND SERVICES
Visitors having genuine scholarly needs that can be met without detriment to students and staff of the college are welcome. One week's access given during term with a letter of introduction from reader's home library. Fee required for longer access. Readers should always have their own ID and must show it if requested. Full library collection catalogued online. Wireless internet available at selected posts throughout the James Joyce Library.

CONTACT:
James Joyce Library information desk. Telephone: (01) 716 7627; fax (01) 716 1148; e-mail: reader.services@ucd.ie

Branch libraries
Blackrock Library (Michael Smurfit Graduate School of Business) University College Dublin, Carysfort Avenue, Blackrock, County Dublin. Telephone: (01) 716 8069; fax: (01) 716 8011; e-mail: biclib@ucd.ie
Earlsfort Terrace Library, Earlsfort Terrace, Dublin 2. Telephone: (01) 716 7471; fax: (01) 475 4568; e-mail: libetgen@ucd.ie (This library will move to the Belfield Campus in December 2006)
Richview Library, University College Dublin, Clonskeagh Road, Dublin 6. Telephone: (01) 716 2741; e-mail: richview.library@ucd.ie
Veterinary Medicine Library, University College Dublin, Belfield, Dublin 4. Telephone: (01) 716 6208; e-mail: vetlib@ucd.ie

DESCRIPTION
UCD, which traces its origin to the Catholic University of Ireland, founded in 1854 with John Henry Newman as its first rector, has grown from modest beginnings to a five college institution with 35 schools. It has over 21,000 students. The James Joyce Library caters for humanities, social sciences, law and pure and applied sciences. The four branch libraries cater for business (Blackrock), medicine (Earlsfort Terrace), architecture and planning (Richview) and veterinary medicine. The Special Collections Department is housed in the James Joyce Library.

HOLDINGS
The library's holdings consist of over 1,000,000 volumes. Almost 80 per cent of the stock is on open access. An increasing number of electronic resources is being purchased. Approximately 15,000 purchased monographs and 2,550 donations are added to the stock each year. The library is a European Documentation Centre. The James Joyce Library houses good research collections in the areas of the humanities, social science, commerce, law and pure and applied sciences. Specific collections of note are Law and Official Collections and Development Studies. The Ordnance Survey maps of Ireland are housed in the Richview Library.
The collections incorporate the libraries of older institutions, such as the Royal College of Science of Ireland and the Museum of Irish Industry. They include the gifts and bequests of many former members of the college, those who made their careers as teachers and researchers in UCD and those who pursued careers elsewhere. The library has bought collections of value and pursues a vigorous acquisition policy.

LOCATION
UCD is mainly situated on a large, modern campus about 2.5 miles south of the centre of Dublin. It is served by a variety of public transport, including buses 3, 10 and 11B.

UNIVERSITY COLLEGE DUBLIN LIBRARY – SPECIAL COLLECTIONS

James Joyce Library, University College Dublin, Belfield
DUBLIN 4
Ireland

TELEPHONE: (01) 716 7149; FAX: (01) 716 1148
E-mail: special.collections@ucd.ie
Website:
www.ucd.ie/library/services_and_facilities/library_collections/special_collection/inde
x.html

HOURS
M–F, 10.00am–1.00pm, 2.00pm–5.00pm; closed Christmas period, Good Friday
and public holidays

ACCESS AND SERVICES
Visitors welcome by appointment. Letter of introduction may be required; students
should have letter from supervisor. Access charges: free for up to three working days.
Nominal charge negotiable through the Special Collections Department for up to
ten working days. For longer periods, users must purchase library admission card
from main information desk. All materials must be consulted in the Special
Collections Reading Room. Pencils only; laptops and digital photography (subject to
constraints of Irish copyright law) welcome; no photocopying permitted or
undertaken. Photography and scanning can be arranged for a fee. Most printed
material included in library's web catalogue; various finding aids available for
manuscript material and staff are happy to advise. See website for further
information.

CONTACT
Katherine McSharry, Librarian for Special Collections

DESCRIPTION
The Special Collections Department holds books, pamphlets and journal titles
printed before 1851 (in addition to some later titles of particular significance or
interest). All the library's manuscripts, as well as some maps, photographs, prints and
drawings and ephemera, are also located here, as are a number of important personal
collections of significant content or provenance.

Printed Collections
The foundation collections are drawn from the libraries of those bodies which
ultimately became part of University College Dublin, most notably the Catholic
University of Ireland. The strengths of the Catholic University library are primarily
in Catholic philosophy, theology and church history, but there is also significant
coverage of Irish literature and the Irish language, history, archaeology and classics.
Important individual collections from the Catholic University include those of
Archbishops Joseph Dixon (1806–66) and Daniel Murray (1768–1852).
Among the collections acquired since the establishment of University College
Dublin in 1909, three are particularly notable: the Ó Lochlainn, O'Kelley and
Sweeney Collections. The library of Colm Ó Lochlainn, bibliophile and owner of
the Three Candles Press, includes early printings, handsome bindings, broadside and
single ballads, songbooks and devotional literature. Francis J. O'Kelly's collection
encompasses Irish history, local history and especially Irish printing and printing

relating to Ireland from the seventeenth to the nineteenth century, with particular emphasis on pamphlets, many scarce. The bequest of John Lincoln Sweeney constitutes the major modern printed collection, including English, Anglo-Irish and American literature in fine and early editions, limited editions and signed copies. Other important printed collections include: the Heinrich Zimmer Library (Celtic studies); the Palles Collection (seventeenth and eighteenth century law books); the Curran Collection (literary first editions of James Joyce and of the Irish literary revival); the Tasso Collection deposited by David Nolan; John Manning's collection of children's books, mostly by English authors; the Quinn Collection (works by and about American poet Robert Frost); the Power Collection of rare sixteenth–nineteenth century editions concerning Catholic Ireland; a small collection of works from the controversial philosopher John Toland (1670–1722). In addition to this material, there are small sections on agriculture, engineering and science (including a notable group of nineteenth century palaeontology books). Irish publications for children and young adults are collected and kept as an archival collection. One copy of selected Anglo-Irish literary work is acquired and kept in its original condition. These items are available for research use only.

Manuscript Collections
The O'Curry, Morris, Ferriter and Ó Lochlainn Collections include manuscripts relating to Irish history, literature, religion and folklore. These are complemented by the series entitled Additional Irish Manuscripts, consisting of individual manuscripts in Irish; among these is Dubhaltach Mac Firbisigh's *Leabhar na nGenealach*, or *Book of Genealogies* and a transcription with translation of Brian Merriman's *Cúirt an Mheán-Oíche*.

Literary papers are well represented. Included are those of poet Patrick Kavanagh, writer Mary Lavin, novelist Maeve Binchy (an ongoing donation) and the deposited drafts and proofs of works by dramatist Frank McGuinness. In addition, the Constantine Curran Manuscript Collection includes over 400 letters from Irish writers and artists, among them James Joyce, while the Special Collections Department also houses the manuscript for Thomas Hardy's *Return of the Native*. In the Irish language, the collections include the valuable papers of writer Seán Ó Riordáin, ranging from diaries and correspondence to notebooks and copies of his published columns.

Other material: the Special Collections Department holds the library's first edition (produced between 1833 and 1846) of the Ordnance Survey of Ireland's six inch maps of Ireland, in addition to a selection of other historical Irish maps. There is also a small group of music scores by Sir Arnold Bax and 39 eighteenth century watercolours of Irish antiquities, done by or for Gabriel Beranger.

LOCATION
Level one of the James Joyce Library.

VALUATION OFFICE

Irish Life Centre, Lower Abbey Street
DUBLIN 1
Ireland

TELEPHONE: (01) 817 1000; FAX: (01) 817 1180
E-mail: info@valoff.ie
Website: www.valoff.ie

HOURS
M–F, 9.30am–4.30pm; closed religious and public holidays

ACCESS AND SERVICES
Visitors welcome. Customer service team provides inspection facilities for members of the public to view all current and archive rating records and maps, provides certified extracts from maps, current valuation certificates, historical valuation certificates from current to those of 1850s, known as backdated certificates, and provisional valuations, required for licensing applications. Team also deals with archival queries, commonly for genealogical research. Fees may apply. Daily research fee after one hour, €15.24, which is the maximum amount payable per day; 63c per sheet for monochrome photocopying; €1.27 per sheet for colour photocopying.

Search of current valuation list available through website at no cost. In addition, requests for research and certificates may be made through e-mail address above. A quotation of cost will be supplied and orders may be placed via website using credit cards.

CONTACT
Marion Richardson and/or Samantha McKeown

DESCRIPTION
The Valuation Office is the state property valuation agency. The core business of the office is the provision of accurate, up to date valuations of commercial and industrial properties to ratepayers and local authorities as laid down by statute. The office also provides a valuation consultancy service to other government departments, local authorities, health boards and the Revenue Commissioners.

HOLDINGS
The archive contains the original books of surveys carried out in the 1840s, books and maps of *Griffith's Valuation* from the 1850s, the original rating records and documentation showing revisions up to the current position. Of special interest to genealogists, the archive holds a list of occupiers of property for the 26 counties of the Republic of Ireland dating back to 1846. The following details are held in relation to each property: occupier name, townland, address, description of property, acreage of holding, rateable value and reference to its position on a valuation map. The archive is unique in that it can relate people to a particular property. The valuation maps are archived, so it may be possible to locate the exact position of a house or property of a particular family back to c. 1850.

The Valuation Office also holds valuations lists, valuation notebooks and files, maps, databases, manuals and publications. The valuation lists contain details of the current rateable valuation of commercial properties, hereditaments and tenements, and of the rateable valuation of commercial, domestic and land properties from 1852. (Rates on domestic property were abolished in 1978 and on agricultural land from 1984. Consequently, there has been no need to update these categories.) The valuation lists also contain information on those classes of property which have a rateable valuation but which have been identified by law and by legal decision as not required to pay rates. The lists are grouped geographically, corresponding to local authority areas, with administrative subdivisions in electoral district, townland or ward. Valuation notebooks and files contain a report of the inspection by the valuer of each property that has a rateable valuation placed upon it. Ordnance Survey maps show property boundaries for valuation purposes. Files contain papers, correspondence, briefings, submissions and reports produced in the performance of office functions. The databases – electronic, typed and manuscript – contain information associated with the establishment and revision of rateable valuations. Publications include *Guide to the Valuation Office Ireland*.

LOCATION
Diagonally opposite the Abbey Theatre, two blocks east of O'Connell Street in the city centre.

DÚN LAOGHAIRE LIBRARY – LOCAL HISTORY DEPARTMENT

Lower George's Street
DÚN LAOGHAIRE, COUNTY DUBLIN
Ireland

TELEPHONE: (01) 280 1147; FAX: (01) 284 6141
E-mail: localhistory@dlrcoco.ie
Website: www.dlrcoco.ie/library/lhistory.htm

HOURS
M, 10.00am–1.00pm, 2.00pm–5.00pm; Tu, Th, 1.15pm–8.00pm; W, F, 10.00am–5.00pm; Sa, 10.00am–1.00pm, 2.00pm–5.00pm; closed bank holiday weekends

ACCESS AND SERVICES
The Local History Department is based in the Dún Laoghaire Library, a branch of the Dún Laoghaire-Rathdown Public Library Service, headquartered at Duncairn House (first floor), 14 Carysfort Avenue, Blackrock, County Dublin (telephone (01) 278 1788; fax (01) 278 1792; e-mail libraries@dlrcoco.ie). Visitors welcome. Wheelchair access. Photocopying and microfilm services available for modest fee. Free internet access, available on five personal computers. Exhibitions mounted on a regular basis. Recent showings include: the Irish Civil War (1997), the 1848 Rebellion (1998), Dún Laoghaire Before the Railway (1998), Ships in the Bay (2000) and Ancient Places, Sacred Spaces (2001).

The Local History Department has been contributing for several years to a digitisation project called www.askaboutireland.ie, hosted by an Comhairle Leabharlanna, the Library Council. Contributions to date include Postcards of Dún Laoghaire-Rathdown; Selected Wild Flowers of Dún Laoghaire-Rathdown; The Big Houses of Dún Laoghaire-Rathdown; and Transport of Dún Laoghaire Port. A new digitisation project is in preparation, entitled, Then and Now, a look at how the landscape, monuments, archaeology, architecture and artefacts of the Dún Laoghaire-Rathdown area have changed over time. For further information on the history of the Dún Laoghaire-Rathdown area, contact the Dún Laoghaire Borough Historical Society, 7 Northumberland Park, Dún Laoghaire, County Dublin (telephone (01) 280 6213, after 6.00pm local time). Contact Colin Scudds, Honorable Secretary, Dún Laoghaire Borough Historical Society.

CONTACT
Any member of staff

DESCRIPTION

On 1 January 1994 Dublin County Council and the Corporation of Dún Laoghaire were dissolved and replaced by three new administrative counties, South Dublin, Dún Laoghaire-Rathdown and Fingal. It is the aim of the Local History Department to collect, preserve and make available for reference material on the history of the administrative county.

HOLDINGS

The collection includes directories dating from 1798, Council minutes from 1888, newspapers from 1819 and surveys and maps from 1730. The department also holds such genealogical resources as *Griffith's Valuation*, census returns, 1813–1911 and tithe applotment books. The photograph collection covers prints and drawings from the seventeenth century to the present. Highlights include copies of the Lawrence Collection, the Civil War (Ireland 1922–3) Series and the Dún Laoghaire Harbour Collection.

LOCATION

By rail, take DART to Dún Laoghaire station; the library is a ten minute walk from there. By bus, take bus 7, 7A, 8 or 46A from Dublin city centre; 59 from Killiney; 75 from Tallaght; or 111 from Loughlinstown. No parking available at the library.

DÚN LAOGHAIRE-RATHDOWN HERITAGE CENTRE

Listed under Dublin. The centre moved in April 2006 to Rathfarnham.

FRANCISCAN LIBRARY KILLINEY (FLK)

Dún Mhuire, Seafield Road
KILLINEY, COUNTY DUBLIN
Ireland

TELEPHONE: (01) 282 6760 (Friary), (01) 282 6091, extension 25 (Library); FAX: (01) 282 6993
E-mail: dmkilliney@eircom.net (Friary), ignatiusfen@eircom.net (Library)
Website: www.franciscans.ie (contains information about the provincial library in Killiney), www.isos.dcu.ie (website for Irish Script On Screen from Dublin City University – contains information on Irish manuscripts (MSS A))

HOURS

M–F, 10.00am–1.00pm, 2.30pm–4.30pm (subject to staffing)

ACCESS AND SERVICES

Visitors welcome, but by appointment only. Disabled access facilities. Fees for photocopying, carried out by Librarian. There is a printed catalogue of Irish manuscripts that are now in the care of UCD (*see* above). Some copies of the catalogue of MSS B (other than Irish) published in *Dun Mhuire Killiney 1945–95* still available from Librarian. The book is out of print. Collection catalogued on computer.

CONTACT

Fr Ignatius Fennessy, Information Officer. E-mail: ignatiusfen@eircom.net

DESCRIPTION
Private Franciscan library available to researchers by appointment.

HOLDINGS
The collection includes some 23,000 volumes, 1,000 pamphlets and 250 journal titles dealing primarily with Franciscan studies, the Irish language and Irish history, especially with respect to ecclesiastical and state history. Collections include: the papers of Eamon de Valera, Seán Mac Eoin, Muiris Ó Droighneáin and George Gavan Duffy, all four now in the care of University College Dublin Archives; the papers of Luke Wadding OFM; and a rare book collection that includes 26 incunabula (fifteenth century). The incunabula are also now in the care of UCD. The indexing of the papers of George Gavan Duffy, Seán Mac Eoin, Muiris Ó Droighneáin and Eamon de Valera is now complete.

LOCATION
From Dublin city centre take the DART to Killiney (30 minutes); walk for ten minutes up Station Road (a hill) and down the other side on Seafield Road, around corner at bottom of the hill. The entrance is on right hand side, with a green postbox on the wall and the name Dún Mhuire on an entrance pillar.

FINGAL GENEALOGY

Swords Historical Society Company Ltd, Carnegie Library, North Street
SWORDS, COUNTY DUBLIN
Ireland

TELEPHONE: (01) 840 0080; FAX: (01) 840 0080
E-mail: swordsheritage@eircom.net
Website: www.irish-roots.net/dublin-north-fingal.asp

HOURS
M–F, 1.00pm–4.30pm; or by appointment

ACCESS AND SERVICES
Fingal Genealogy is a fee based genealogical service centre that offers a complete range of genealogical research services, focusing on North County Dublin. Attached to museum reflecting aspects of local and national culture. A copy of the centre's initial search form can be printed from website. Initial fee €95.

Publications currently available from the Fingal Heritage Group (prices are in US$ and do not include postage) include: *In Fond Remembrance: Headstone Inscriptions from St Columba's Church of Ireland, Swords*, $2.50; *Swords Heritage Trail*, $1.50; *Working Life in Fingal: Recollections from North County Dublin*, $6.00; *Swords Voices*, parts 3, 5, 6, 7 and 8, $6; *Sewn by Candlelight: History of the Act of Union and Education in Swords*, $6; *A Great Benefit: Controversial History of Old Borough School, Swords*, $10; *A Hard Old Station: Musings on St Colmcille's Church*, $12.00.

CONTACT
Bernadette Marks, Coordinator

DESCRIPTION
Fingal Genealogy is a member of the Irish Family History Foundation, the coordinating body for a network of government approved genealogical research centres in the Republic of Ireland and in Northern Ireland that have computerised

tens of millions of Irish ancestral records of different types. Fingal Genealogy focuses on North County Dublin. Main towns in the area include: Balbriggan, Baldoyle, Balrothery, Balscaden, Blanchardstown, Clontarf, Donabate, Fingal, Lusk, Malahide, Naul, Portmarnock, Rush, Skerries and the 'county town', Swords.

HOLDINGS
Records include: Roman Catholic records, the earliest of which date from 1701; Church of Ireland records from 1705; and census records from as early as 1901. Fingal Genealogy also holds records of interment for all Church of Ireland cemeteries in its area, the earliest being Swords from 1705; vaccination records; school roll books; gravestone inscriptions for some local cemeteries; various trade directories; dog licence records; and 1916 volunteer records.

LOCATION
North of Dublin City, near Dublin Airport and close to several sites of interest, including Newbridge House, Skerries Windmill, Ardgillen Castle, Swords Castle and Malahide Castle.

COUNTY FERMANAGH

ENNISKILLEN LIBRARY

Hall's Lane
ENNISKILLEN, COUNTY FERMANAGH, BT74 7DR
Northern Ireland

TELEPHONE: (028) 6632 2886; FAX: (028) 6632 4685
E-mail: enniskillen.library@ni-libraries.net
Website: www.welbni.org/libraries/fermanagh_enniskillen.asp

HOURS
M, W, F, 9.15am–5.15pm; Tu, Th, 9.15am–7.30pm; Sa, 9.15am–1.00pm

ACCESS AND SERVICES
Visitors welcome. Borrowing privileges for visitors may be restricted. Disabled access. Fees for photocopying, microfilm prints, faxes and e-mail. Only five per cent of collection catalogued online. Printed finding aids available. Linked to emigration database of the Ulster American Folk Park.

CONTACT
Alex Hackett, Branch Library Manager
Margaret Kane, Assistant Librarian for Local Studies
Marianna Maguire, Senior Librarian Assistant, Local History

DESCRIPTION
Part of the Western Education and Library Board system, Enniskillen is the principal public library in County Fermanagh.

HOLDINGS
The library houses a general educational and recreational collection of some 21,000 books. Its Nawn Collection is one of the best and largest local studies collections at a public library in all of Ireland. This collection consists of some 30,000 books of Irish interest, plus prints, periodicals, paintings, photographs and an especially good collection of some 1,500 printed maps, including copies of County Fermanagh barony maps, a few county and Ulster maps from 1685, Ordnance Survey six inch maps for Fermanagh and Tyrone (1835, 1859, 1908) and Ordnance Survey grid maps. Other collections of note include: the W.B. Yeats Collection of some 400 volumes, including a considerable number of first editions; a collection on

Fermanagh author Shan Bullock; the extensive Local Newspaper Collection on microfilm from 1738 to the present; the Railway History Collection, which consists of some 200 books, journals and maps on the history and development of railways in Ireland from the mid-1800s to recent times; and the Military History Collection, focusing on Irish regiments, especially the Royal Inniskilling Dragoon Guards and the Royal Inniskilling Fusiliers.

The Genealogy and Heraldry Collection focuses on Irish interests but also covers English and Scottish interests. The collection includes a number of rarities. The man for whom the Nawn Collection is named, Frederick James Nawn, possessed an 'encyclopaedic knowledge of genealogy and family history', and the collection he built as divisional librarian reflects this interest.

Other material includes *Griffith's Valuation* of County Fermanagh, *c.* 1862, microfilm copies of all Board of Guardian minute books for Enniskillen, Irvinestown (Lowtherstown) and Lisnaskea Poor Law Union workhouses, *c.* 1840–94; hearth money rolls, 1660s, muster rolls, militia lists; electoral registers for County Fermanagh, 1978, 1982–6, 1988–9; a microfiche copy of the 1901 census of Ireland and name index for County Fermanagh, plus various other important genealogical sources, including directories, indexes and lists.

Periodicals include: *Familia*, 1987–present; *Irish Genealogical Research Society* (*Ireland Branch Newsletter*), 1986–present; *Irish Genealogist*, 1939–present; *Irish Heritage Links*, 1981–90/91; *Irish Links*, 1984–present; *North Irish Roots*, 1984–present; *Ulster Link*, 1987–8 (odd numbers only); and *Ulster Origins*, 1984–8 (5 vols).

The library also has a substantial collection of valuation revision lists for County Fermanagh. The earliest volumes cover the years 1864–5, 1869–70 and 1883–90. The larger section comprising approximately 110 volumes covers the years 1910–30. The lists are bound individually by Poor Law Union, Rural District and Electoral Division with a list of townlands inside each cover. Some volumes are in need of repair and could not be produced to the public.

There is a small collection of records of public elementary schools in County Fermanagh. These are mainly roll books for schools in the Clones area returned by the Public Record Office of Northern Ireland. For Lisroon there are roll books covering the period 1884–1954 (8 vols), Magheraveely, 1908–17 and Roslea, 1921–7. For the public elementary school of Letter in Templecarn parish there is a pupil register for the years 1951–7 bearing PRONI reference SCH 132/1/3. For that school PRONI will have retained the earlier volumes in the series starting in 1865 (SCH 3/1/1–2).

LOCATION
Town centre, at the corner of Hall's Lane and Queen Street, opposite the bridge over the north branch of the River Erne (route to Enniskillen Airport).

COUNTY GALWAY

GALWAY CITY LIBRARY

St Augustine Street
GALWAY
Ireland

TELEPHONE: (091) 561 666; FAX: (091) 565 039
E-mail: info@galwaylibrary.ie
Website: www.galwaylibrary.ie

HOURS
M, 2.00pm–5.00pm; Tu–Th, 11.00am–8.00pm; F, 11.00am–5.00pm; Sa,
11.00am–1.00pm, 2.00pm–5.00pm; Juvenile Library closes at 5.00pm each day.

ACCESS AND SERVICES
Visitors welcome. Memberships available for modest annual fee, allowing borrowing
privileges. ID required for application. Photocopying available for a fee; computers
provided for internet access subject to conditions.

CONTACT
Galway City Library Services: B. Kelly, Librarian with overall responsibility for
Galway City Library Services
Public Library: Josephine Vahey
Juvenile Library: Geraldine Mannion

DESCRIPTION
The largest of the 30 branch libraries in the Galway Library Service.

HOLDINGS
Galway City Library offers a good general collection of educational and recreational
material. The Local History Department and Archives have a separate entry below.

LOCATION
City centre, off Lower Abbeygate Street, one block south-west on William Street
from Eyre Square/Kennedy Park.

GALWAY CITY LIBRARY
– LOCAL HISTORY DEPARTMENT AND ARCHIVES

Galway Public Library (County Library Headquarters), Island House, Cathedral
Square
GALWAY
Ireland

TELEPHONE: (091) 562 471; FAX: (091) 565 039
E-mail: info@galwaylibrary.ie
Website: www.galwaylibrary.ie
HOURS
M–F, 9.30am–1.00pm, 2.00pm–5.00pm

ACCESS AND SERVICES
It is advisable to make an appointment through Local History Department by phone
or fax, as some material requires use of microform readers, which may have to be
reserved in advance.

CONTACT
Maureen Moran, Deputy County and City Librarian
Patria McWalter, Archivist

DESCRIPTION
The Galway Library Service was established in 1924 as an integral branch of the
Galway Local Authority Service. The service now has the following purpose built,
full time libraries: Galway City, Westside Library (city suburbs), telephone (091) 520
616; Ballinasloe, telephone (0905) 43464; Carraroe, telephone (091) 595 733;
Clifden, telephone (095) 21092; Oranmore, telephone (091) 792 117; Loughrea,
telephone (091) 847 220/224; Portumna, telephone (0509) 41261; and Tuam
(which holds microfilm copies of the 1901 and 1911 censuses), telephone (093)
24287. There are also the following sub-libraries: Athenry, telephone (091) 845 592;
Ballygar, telephone (090) 662 4919; Dunmore, telephone (093) 38923; Gort,
telephone (091) 631 224; Glenamaddy, telephone (0907) 59734; Headford,
telephone (093) 36406; Inishbofin, telephone (095) 45861; Inis Meain, telephone
(099) 73126; Inisheer, telephone (099) 75008; Killimor, telephone (0905) 76061;
Kilronan, Leenane, Letterfrack, telephone (091) 845 592; Moylough, Oughterard,
Roundstone, telephone (095) 35518; Spiddal, telephone (091) 504 028; Tiernea,
telephone (091) 551 611; and Woodford. A mobile library brings books to many
smaller towns and villages and a school bookmobile services over 200 primary
schools. The Headquarters Library houses the main local history collection and
archives.

HOLDINGS
This collection includes a comprehensive collection of old local newspapers, *Griffith's
Valuation*, local Board of Guardian minute books, local maps, local historical
photographs and the 1901 and 1911 censuses.
   There are virtually complete sets of Board of Guardian minutes, *c.*1840–1922,
for the Poor Law Unions of Clifden, Galway, Gort, Loughrea, Mount Bellew and
Tuam. There are substantial gaps in the series of Ballinasloe, and for Glenamaddy
minutes survive only for the years 1894–5 and 1914–15. There are indoor relief
registers for Gort 1914–20 and Tuam 1913–19.

Significant collections of records of administration are available for about a dozen estates, including: Blake Estate, near Tuam, 1666–1934 (including agent's correspondence and land surveys); that of Ffrench of Rahasane, near Loughrea, 1765–1897 (including agents' correspondence and inventory of auctioned items 1830s); that of St George Mansergh, Headford 1775–1853 (including volume of maps and a rent roll giving tenants' names and their holdings); that of O'Kelly of Castle Kelly, Aghrane, Killeroran, 1606–c.1880 (including wills and correspondence as well as marriage settlements).

The Newspaper Collection is of special interest because of its comprehensive coverage of the local area going back to 1823. Holdings (listed chronologically) include: *Galway Weekly Advertiser*, 1823–43; *Tuam Gazette*, 1824; *Western Argus*, 1828–33; *Galway Independent*, 1829–32; *Galway Free Press*, 1832–5; *Galway Patriot*, 1835–9; *Tuam Herald*, 1837–78; *Connacht Journal*, 1839–40; *Galway Vindicator*, 1841–99; *Galway Standard*, 1841–3; *Galway Mercury and Connacht Weekly Advertiser*, 1844–60; *Western Star*, 1845–69; *Galway Packet and Connacht Advocate*, 1852–4; *Galway Express*, 1853–1920; *Warden of Galway*, 1853; *Connacht Patriot and Tuam Advertiser*, 1859–69; *Galway Press*, 1860–1; *Galway American*, 1862–3; *Tuam News*, 1871–3; *Western News and Weekly Examiner*, 1878–92; *Tuam Herald*, 1883–1923; *Connacht People and Ballinasloe Independent*, 1884–6; *Western Advertiser*, 1884–96; *Western Star*, 1888–1902; *Galway Observer*, 1889–1923; *Western News and Galway Guardian*, 1899–1901; *Western News*, 1901–3; *Connacht Champion*, 1904–11; *Western News*, 1905–20; *Loughrea Nationalist*, 1905; *Galway Pilot*, 1905–18; *Connacht Tribune*, 1909–96; *East Galway Democrat*, 1913–21; *Western News and Galway Leader*, 1921–6; *Galway Observer*, 1925–66; *Connacht Sentinel*, 1927–45; *East Galway Democrat*, 1936–49; *Tuam Herald*, 1938–99; *Connacht Sentinel*, 1950–99; and *City Tribune*, 1984–99.

LOCATION
City centre, across the Salmon Weir Bridge, near the New Cathedral (the Cathedral of Our Lady Assumed into Heaven).

GALWAY FAMILY HISTORY SOCIETY WEST LTD

St Joseph's Community Centre, Ashe Road, Shantalla
GALWAY
Ireland

TELEPHONE: (091) 860 464; FAX: (091) 860 464
E-mail: galwayfshwest@eircom.net
Website: www.irishroots.net

HOURS
M–Th, 10.00am–4.00pm; F, 10.00am–1.00pm

ACCESS AND SERVICES
West Galway centre offers full range of fee based genealogical services to people interested in researching their Galway roots. Centre has access to over a million records for genealogical research. Initial enquiries and applications dealt with in rotation, with every effort made to deal with applications within four weeks of receipt. Initial assessment payment of €70 required with application, a copy of which can be downloaded from website or sent out from the centre on request. Cost

of commissioning a family history report will normally be in the range €190–€320, depending on amount of information located. Research consultations by appointment only, at a fee of €30 per half hour. In addition to providing full service for those who wish to have their family roots traced, the society offers publications for sale including: the journals *Galway Roots* 1–5; *Forthill Cemetery*; *Castlegar Graveyard Inscriptions*; *Inishbofin through Time and Tide*. Prices range from €10 to €15 plus postage. Write, phone or e-mail for exact quotation, including postage costs. Disabled access.

CONTACT
Mary Murray, Coordinator
Siobhan McGuinness, Researcher/Assistant Coordinator

DESCRIPTION
One of the Irish Family History Foundation's two designated family research centres for Galway, the other being East Galway Family History Society, Woodford. The main towns and villages in West Galway are: Galway City, Tuam, Clifden, Oughterard, Athenry and Kinvara. The Aran Islands and Inishbofin are also in this centre's catchment area. Parishes covered are: Abbeyknockmoy, Annaghadown, Aran Islands, Ardrahan, Athenry, Ballyconneely, Carraroe, Carna, Castlegar, Claregalway, Clarinbridge, Clifden, Clonbur, Cummer, Donaghpatrick, Dunmore, Galway City, Headford, Inishbofin, Kilconly/Kilbennan, Kilcummin/Oughterard, Kilannin, Killererin, Kinvara, Lackagh, Moycullen, Oranmore, Omey/Ballindoon, Rahoon, Rosmuc, Roundstone, Spiddal and Tuam.

HOLDINGS
The centre has access to the following records containing over 2,000,000 entries in the West Galway area: Roman Catholic, Church of Ireland, Methodist and Presbyterian Church records up to 1900; civil records of births, deaths and marriages from their inception in 1864 up until 1900; elector lists; gravestone inscriptions; indexed directories (*Slater's*, *Pigot's* and *Thom's*); parochial censuses (the oldest of which dates from 1821); newspaper obituaries; encumbered estates court rentals; workhouse census search forms for pension applications; tithe applotment books; *Griffith's Valuation* (1848–55); 1901 and 1911 censuses; Ordnance Survey maps showing townlands. The centre has also built up an extensive collection of local family history publications.

LOCATION
From Eyre Square take Eglington Street and follow St Francis Street to a set of traffic lights. Turn left and cross the Salmon Weir Bridge to the Roman Catholic Cathedral. Continue on University Road to a set of traffic lights in front of the University (Regional) Hospital. Turn left at the traffic lights onto Newcastle Road. Take the first right, which brings you onto Costello Road and Ashe Road. The centre is located in St Joseph's Community Centre, on the right hand side of the road.

NATIONAL UNIVERSITY OF IRELAND, GALWAY
– JAMES HARDIMAN LIBRARY

University Road
GALWAY
Ireland

TELEPHONE: (091) 524 411, extension 2540; FAX: (091) 522 394
E-mail: library@nuigalway.ie
Website: www.library.nuigalway.ie

HOURS
Term time: M–F, 9.00am–10.00pm; Sa, 9.00am–1.00pm. Extended opening hours apply during examinations, while shorter hours apply during vacation period. Hours differ for Special Collections Department (*see* separate entry below) and for Medical and Nursing Libraries located at University College Hospital.

ACCESS AND SERVICES
Visitors welcome, but advance notice preferred and ID required. External service fees apply for visitors seeking self service to library facilities and for those seeking borrowing privileges. The library also offers a customised information service tailored to the needs of businesses, industry professionals and individuals on a fee paying basis. Fees also apply for photocopying and microform prints. Disabled access. Website updated regularly and contains more detailed information. Free brochures available, including one entitled *Information Service for External Users*.

CONTACT
Marie Reddan, Librarian
Trish Finnan, Information Librarian, Commerce and External Liaison. Telephone extension: 3564; e-mail: trish.finnan@nuigalway.ie

DESCRIPTION
The James Hardiman Library supports the teaching and research interests of the National University of Ireland, Galway, originally founded in 1845 by Queen Victoria, along with universities in Cork and Belfast. NUI Galway, formerly University College Galway, is part of the National University of Ireland system, which includes campuses in Dublin, Cork, Limerick and Maynooth. The Galway campus has teaching and research interests in the sciences, engineering, law, commerce, medicine and humanities.

HOLDINGS
The library houses a collection of more than 270,000 volumes, 1,900 current periodicals, a range of electronic information products, a reference collection of Irish government publications, a European Documentation Centre, special collections (*see* separate entry below), newspapers, health and safety publications and an audiovisual collection.

LOCATION
Take N6 into Galway and follow signs for West Galway and Salthill. At junction of N6 and Newcastle Road, turn left. Take next left turn into campus.

NATIONAL UNIVERSITY OF IRELAND, GALWAY – JAMES HARDIMAN LIBRARY – DEPARTMENT OF SPECIAL COLLECTIONS AND ARCHIVES

University Road
GALWAY
Ireland

TELEPHONE: (091) 492 543, (091) 493 636; FAX: (091) 522 394
E-mail: marie.boran@nuigalway.ie, kieran.hoare@nuigalway.ie
Website: www.library.nuigalway.ie

HOURS
Term time: M, W–F, 9.00am–5.00pm; Tu, 9.00am–9.00pm
Vacation period: M–F, 9.00am–5.00pm

ACCESS AND SERVICES
Visitors welcome to consult material not available to them in their local repositories, but advance notice and ID required. Disabled access. Laptops and photography permitted; pencils only. External service fees for visitors seeking borrowing privileges. Fees for photocopying and microfilm prints, but photocopying of materials at staff discretion. Copying of archival material carried out by Archivist, at his discretion. Some 98 per cent of books in Department of Special Collections catalogued online. Printed and electronic finding aids available for archival holdings. Exhibitions of material from the collections held throughout the year. Free brochures available, including one entitled *Information Service for External Users*. Website updated regularly and contains more detailed information.

CONTACT
Marie Boran, Special Collections Librarian. E-mail: marie.boran@nuigalway.ie
Kieran Hoare, Archivist. E-mail: kieran.hoare@nuigalway.ie

DESCRIPTION
National University of Ireland, Galway – James Hardiman Library was founded in 1849 and has been developing special collections of both archival and printed material from its inception. Its areas of special interest include: Galway and West of Ireland studies; Irish literature in English; literature and publishing in the Irish language; and local history pertaining to all counties but particularly those in the province of Connacht and County Clare.

HOLDINGS
The Department of Special Collections houses some 40,000 volumes, plus significant holdings of journals, manuscripts, maps, microforms, newspapers, pamphlets, photographs and recordings. Major book collections include: the Bairéad Collection of Irish language material, particularly ephemera from the early days of the Gaelic revival movements; the Cairnes Collection of works on nineteenth century economy and society; the Coen Collection of local and Irish history, plus some religious and devotional material; the Déon Collection of modern French writing, including the publications of the donor, French author Michel Déon; the Delargy Collection of twentieth century Irish and European folklore; the Fanning Collection of Irish archaeology and history; the Freyer Collection of works by and about author Liam O'Flaherty (1896–1984); the Gregory Collection containing virtually all material published by and about Augusta, Lady Gregory (1852–1932), including associated works and biographies; the Hunt Collection of books on

twentieth century psychology and related subjects, especially from an American perspective; the Irish Women's Publishing Collection, with a focus on feminist publishers in Ireland since 1980; the Killanin Collection of some 3,500 volumes on twentieth century Irish literature, art and archaeology, plus world politics and horse racing; and the St Anthony's Collection of some 20,000 volumes from the library of St Anthony's College in Newcastle, Galway, with a concentration on devotional literature, theology, Irish and Church history.

Manuscript and Archive collections of special importance include: The De hÍde Collection of manuscripts gathered by Doughláis de hÍde (Douglas Hyde), founder of the Gaelic League, who collected folklore and music in the Irish language (a selection from the De hÍde manuscript collection now appears in digitised format in the Irish Script On Screen database (www.isos.dias.ie); the Bairéad Collection of papers and correspondence relating to the Gaelic League and related Irish language material; the LSB Manuscripts Collection of miscellaneous manuscripts on a variety of subjects, some in Irish; the Estate Papers Collection of material, such as rentals, marriage settlements, estate maps and household correspondence relating to landed estates, principally in the west of Ireland; the Revolutionary Ireland Collection of papers pertaining to the period 1914–22 in Ireland, especially County Galway; the County Galway Collection, which includes the records of the Galway Municipal Authority dating back to its foundation in 1484; the minute books for Galway Corporation, Galway Town Commissioners and the Galway Urban District Council; the Clifden Railway documents and the papers relating to LDF activity in Galway during World War II; the Academic Papers Collection containing the papers and books of distinguished faculty members, including John E. Cairnes, Mary Donovan O'Sullivan and Richard Doherty; the Theatre Archive containing the archives of Taibhdhearc na Gaillimhe, the Irish theatre founded in 1928, the Druid Theatre, founded in 1975, and the Galway Arts Festival, begun in 1977; the archives of the Lyric Players, Belfast; the Arthur Shields Archive; and the Photographic Archive, with special focus on Galway and UCG (University College Galway). Literary papers are also held, most notably those of John McGahern. Of special historical interest are two sets of papers relating to the Earls of Lucan. This County Mayo family goes back to the sixteenth century and this archive holds special importance for nineteenth and twentieth century Irish history, particularly in relations to land issues.

Though the library does not offer a family history enquiry service, the Department of Special Collections does house a variety of source materials for family history, including: the 1901 census for all the counties of Connacht and for County Clare (on microfilm); the 1911 census for County Galway only on microfiche; *Griffith's Valuation* for all the counties of Ireland (on microfiche and CD-ROM); parliamentary papers of the House of Commons relating to Ireland from 1801 to 1921 (on microfiche, with an index to the papers both in hard copy and on CD-ROM); Ordnance Survey maps; and an extensive range of reference books. There are also bound volumes of an index to surnames in *Griffith's Valuation* for the counties of Connacht (Galway, Leitrim, Mayo, Roscommon and Sligo), plus Counties Donegal, Clare, Longford and Offaly. Though no countrywide census was done before 1821, local surveys were sometimes undertaken. See John Grenham, *Tracing Your Irish Ancestors*, copies of which are available in the library, for a listing of the surveys published in journals.

LOCATION
Take N6 into Galway, follow signs for West Galway and Salthill. At junction of N6
and Newcastle Road, turn left. Take next left turn into campus. The Department of
Special Collections is located on the ground floor of the library.

DIOCESE OF CLONFERT ARCHIVE

St Brendan's, Coorheen
LOUGHREA, COUNTY GALWAY
Ireland

TELEPHONE: (091) 841 560; FAX: (091) 841 818
E-mail: clonfert@iol.ie
Website: homepage.eircom.net/~clonfert

HOURS
By appointment

ACCESS AND SERVICES
Visitors welcome but by appointment only. Advance notice and references required.
Pencils only. Photography not permitted. No disabled access facilities. No
photocopying or microfilm facilities available.

CONTACT
Bishop John Kirby

DESCRIPTION
Small diocesan archive, with few documents dating before 1900. There was no
permanent residence until 1907. Some bishops, on transfer, took their papers with
them to their new assignments. Clonfert is one of the smallest dioceses in Ireland,
with just 24 parishes.

HOLDINGS
Records and documents relating to the administration of the Roman Catholic
Diocese of Clonfert.

LOCATION
St Brendan's Cathedral is in Loughrea town centre, just off the N6, south-east of
Galway. Signposted.

EAST GALWAY FAMILY HISTORY SOCIETY

Woodford Heritage Centre
WOODFORD, COUNTY GALWAY
Ireland

TELEPHONE: (090) 974 9309; FAX: (090) 974 9309
E-mail: galwayroots@eircom.net
Website: www.galwayroots.com

HOURS
M–Th, 9.00am–4.30pm; F, 9.00am–1.00pm

ACCESS AND SERVICES
East Galway Family History Society offers a full range of fee based genealogical
services to people interested in researching their East Galway roots. Initial enquiries
answered promptly; family history report usually takes about four weeks. Cost of
conducting initial research is €65. Initial reports generally issued within 6–8 weeks
of receipt of completed form and fee. Fees based on time and expense involved in
carrying out a thorough assessment. The East Galway Family History Society offers a
range of publications relating to the area for sale. These include: *Lough Derg: the
Westside Story* (map); and *Woodford: a Guide to its Sights.*

CONTACT
Angela Canning

DESCRIPTION
One the Irish Family History Foundation's two designated family research centres for
County Galway, the other being Galway Family History Society West, Galway City.
Chief towns and villages of East Galway include: Ballinasloe, Loughrea, Gort,
Portumna, Glenamaddy and Mountbellew.

HOLDINGS
The earliest Roman Catholic parish records computerised at this centre start in
1799. Earliest Church of Ireland records date from 1747 for Loughrea. For the
parish of Ballinasloe only, the society has computerised Presbyterian records for the
period 1846–1900 and Wesleyan Methodist records for the period 1834–1900.
Altogether, the society has computerised about 1,000,000 pre-1901 records. Other
major sources include: civil records of births, deaths and marriages; the *Book of
Survey and Distribution*; some gravestone inscriptions for a small number of parishes;
and the *Woodford Parish Census*. Both the 1901 and the 1911 censuses are indexed.

LOCATION
14.5 miles south of Loughrea on the R351. Loughrea is 21.5 miles south-east of
Galway City on the N6.

COUNTY KERRY

KERRY GENEALOGICAL RESEARCH CENTRE
Note: Formerly the Killarney Genealogical Centre, the Kerry Genealogical Research Centre will not be in operation until January 2007. For information, please contact the Diocesan Secretary, Bishop's House, Killarney, County Kerry, Ireland.

KERRY ARCHAEOLOGICAL AND HISTORICAL SOCIETY
See KERRY LOCAL HISTORY AND ARCHIVES COLLECTION, Tralee

KILLARNEY GENEALOGICAL CENTRE
See KERRY GENEALOGICAL RESEARCH CENTRE

KERRY LOCAL HISTORY AND ARCHIVES COLLECTION

Kerry County Library, Moyderwell
TRALEE, COUNTY KERRY
Ireland

TELEPHONE: (066) 712 1200 (County Library), (066) 712 1200 (Local History and Archives Department); FAX: (066) 712 9202 (County Library), (066) 712 9202 (Local History and Archives Department)
E-mail: info@kerrycolib.ie, localhistory@kerrycolib.ie
Website: www.kerrycolib.ie

HOURS
County Library: M, W, F–Sa, 10.00am–5.00pm; Tu, Th, 10.00am–8.00pm
Local History and Archives Department: M–F, 10.00am–5.00pm; Sa, 10.00am–1.00pm, 2.00pm–5.00pm

ACCESS AND SERVICES
Visitors welcome. Membership available on application at no charge. ID required. Charges levied, however, on borrowing of books (30c per item borrowed; children up to and including second level students exempt from these charges). Online catalogue. The library is a focal point for cultural and educational activities in the community. Services include internet workstations, with free access for public use. Kerry Archaeological and Historical Society, established in 1967 for the collection, recording, study and preservation of material relating to the history and antiquities of County Kerry, also operates from the library.

CONTACT
Ann Ferguson, Information/Reference Services Librarian. E-mail:
aferguson@kerrycolib.ie
Eamon Browne, Local History Librarian. E-mail: ebrowne@kerrycolib.ie
Michael Lynch, County Archivist. E-mail: archivist@kerrycolib.ie

DESCRIPTION
The Kerry County Library is the flagship library in the nine library county system
that also includes the following branch libraries: Killarney (telephone (064) 32655,
fax (064) 36065); Ballybunion (telephone (068) 27615) Cahirciveen (telephone
(066) 947 2287); Castleisland (telephone (066) 714 1485); Dingle (telephone (066)
915 1499); Kenmare (telephone (064) 41416); Killorglin (telephone (066) 976
1272); and Listowel (telephone (068) 23044).

The new Local History and Archives Department at Kerry County Library
Headquarters, Tralee, was officially opened on 25 March 2002.

HOLDINGS
The library houses approximately 38,000 volumes of general educational and
recreational interest. It is also home to the Kerry Local History Collection. This
section aims to collect and make available as comprehensive as possible a collection
of material relating to the history of the county, including published books,
manuscripts, photographs, newspapers, video and sound recordings. The collection
includes: a comprehensive collection of local newspapers dating back to the 1820s; a
collection of books in Kerry and by Kerry authors; local maps (Ordnance Survey six
inch); Board of Guardian minute books, 1840s–1922; Rural District Council
minute books and financial records, 1899–1925; county and urban rates and
valuation records, 1900–86; county Grand Jury presentments, 1875–99; County
Board of Health minute books and administration files, 1923–42; County
Committee of Agriculture minute books, 1920–88; periodicals, e.g. *Journal of the
Royal Society of Antiquaries of Ireland, Journal of the Cork Historical and
Archaeological Society*; Irish Folklore Commission Schools Collection, 1937–8 (on
microfilm); tithe applotment books, 1820–35; *Griffith's Valuation* (*c.* 1850); 1901
and 1911 censuses (on microfilm); Tralee Gaol register, 1882–8; and specialised
collections of papers and family histories, including the Reidy family (literary
papers), Fr Ferris (topographical notes), papers relating to the Denny Estate, papers
relating to Antarctic explorer Tom Crean, Thomas Ashe papers and material on
Roger Casement. There are also two significant collections of solicitors' papers (M.J.
Byrne and Co., Listowel and Dr J.D. O'Connell, Tralee), which include substantial
estate and land material for the Listowel/North Kerry area and for the
Kenmare/Dromore/South Kerry area. Business archives include collections relating
to O'Brien Corkery General Merchants, Kenmare (1860s–1960s), William Lynn and
Sons, Tailors, Tralee (1916–70) and Dingle Harbour Commissioners (*c.* 1900–*c.*
1970).

Local newspaper holdings include: *Chute's Western Herald*, 1812–35; *Kerry
Advocate*, 1914–15; *Kerry Champion*, 1928–58; *Kerry Evening Post*, 1829–1917;
Kerry Evening Star, 1902–14; *Kerry Examiner*, 1840–56; *Kerry Independent*, 1880–4;
Kerry News, 1924–41; *Kerry People*, 1902–22; *Kerry Press*, 1914–16; *Kerry Reporter*,
1924–35; *Kerry Sentinel*, 1878–1917; *Kerry Star*, 1861–3; *Kerry Weekly Reporter and
Commercial Advertiser*, 1883–1920; *Killarney Echo and South Kerry Chronicle*,
1889–1920; *An Lóchrann*, 1913–20; *Munster Life*, 1897; *Raymond's Kerry Herald*,

teaching and research interests of students and faculty, with special interests in the areas of education, theology and the humanities. The John Paul II Library was opened in 1984, replacing the Russell Library as the university's main library.

HOLDINGS
The library houses a collection of more than 250,000 volumes, with significant collections built up by scholar professors from the mid-nineteenth century onwards. Particular strengths are in theology, religion and history. Early printed books, manuscripts and archives are housed in the Russell Library.

LOCATION
15 miles west of Dublin, off the M4. Served by buses 66, 66X and 67A from Dublin city centre and by trains from Dublin's Connolly station. The campus is located in the village centre. The John Paul II Library is located in the south (old) campus, across the footbridge *en route* to the north (new) campus.

ST PATRICK'S COLLEGE MAYNOOTH ARCHIVES

Russell Library
MAYNOOTH, COUNTY KILDARE
Ireland

TELEPHONE: (01) 628 5222; FAX: (01) 628 9063
E-mail: penny.woods@nuim.ie
Website: www.maynoothcollege.ie

HOURS
By appointment

ACCESS AND SERVICES
Visitors welcome, but advance notice and ID required. Wheelchair access. Laptops permitted; pencils only. Leaflets and pamphlets available. For access to College Archives permission must first be sought from the Archivist, Mgr Patrick J. Corish. Archival materials, including Salamanca Archives, may then be consulted in the Russell Library. Publications of interest include: Patrick J. Corish, *Maynooth College, 1795–1995* (Dublin, 1995); Patrick J. Hamell, *Maynooth Students and Ordinations, 1795–1984* (1982–4); and Patrick J. Corish, 'Maynooth College Archives', in *Catholic Archives* 13 (1993), 46–8.

CONTACT
Penelope Woods, Librarian, Russell Library

DESCRIPTION
St Patrick's College, Maynooth was founded in 1795 to educate and train Catholic clergy. In 1896 it was established as a pontifical university and in 1910 it also became a recognised college of the National University of Ireland. St Patrick's College is the National Seminary of Ireland and is administered separately from NUI Maynooth.

HOLDINGS
The archive houses the original records of the college plus the historical archive of the Irish College of Salamanca in Spain. Though more than 11,000 priests have been ordained at Maynooth, a fire in 1940 destroyed the matriculation register for the

period 1795–1940, removing an important family history record. This is a small domestic archive, of limited importance to genealogists. The Salamanca Archive of some 50,000 documents contains administration records not only of the Irish College in Salamanca, but also of the Irish Colleges of Alcala, Santiago and Seville. They cover a period of 350 years. The letters in the archive, which are kept in the library, have been listed on a database and in *The Salamanca Letters: a Catalogue of Correspondence (1619–1871)* (Maynooth, 1995).

LOCATION
In St Patrick's House, the Gothic quadrangle beyond St Joseph's Square, in the south cloister.

ST PATRICK'S COLLEGE MAYNOOTH – RUSSELL LIBRARY

MAYNOOTH, COUNTY KILDARE
Ireland

TELEPHONE: (01) 708 3890; FAX: (01) 628 6008
E-mail: penny.woods@nuim.ie
Website: www.nuim.ie/library

HOURS
M–Th, 10.00am–1.00pm, 2.00pm–5.00pm

ACCESS AND SERVICES
Researchers welcome, but advance notice and ID required. Visitors admitted at Librarian's discretion. Wheelchair access. Laptops permitted; pencils only. Leaflets and pamphlets available. Publications of interest include: Agnes Neligan (ed.), *Maynooth Library Treasures* (Dublin, 1995). Holdings are being added to the main NUIM online catalogue. Meanwhile, there are three card catalogues for books in Russell Library. These are also incorporated in John Paul II Library card catalogue. There is a published catalogue for Irish manuscripts: Paul Walsh, *Catalogue of Irish MSS in Maynooth College Library, Part 1* (Má Nuad, 1943); Pádraig Ó Fiannachta, *Clár Lámhscríbhinní Gaeilge Mhá Nuad*, fascicles 2–8 (Má Nuad, 1965–73); Pádraig Ó Fiannachta, *Clár Lámhscríbhinní Gaeilge: Leabhlarlanna na Cléire agus Mionchnuasaigh*, fascicles 1–2 (Baile Átha Cliath, 1978–80). Further additions to the Manuscript Collection are detailed in *Seanchas Ard Mhacha* VII, 2 (1974), *Léachtaí Cholm Cille* XI (1980), XVI (1986).

CONTACT
Penelope Woods, Librarian

DESCRIPTION
St Patrick's College, Maynooth was founded in 1795 to educate and train Catholic clergy. In 1896 it was established as a pontifical university and in 1910 it also became a recognised college of the National University of Ireland. St Patrick's College is the National Seminary of Ireland and is administered separately from NUI Maynooth. Lay students were first admitted to Maynooth in 1966 and today the National University of Ireland, Maynooth has an enrolment of more than 6,000 students. The library is administered by NUI Maynooth and serves both institutions. The library building, designed by A.W. Pugin (1812–52), was completed in 1861. In 1984 it was renamed for Charles Russell, President of Maynooth,

1857–80; it served as the main college library until the opening of the John Paul II Library in 1984.

HOLDINGS
Russell Library houses the university's collection of rare and early printed books and manuscripts. The collection totals more than 32,000 books, plus maps, architectural records, illuminated manuscripts and some 300 volumes of Irish manuscripts. The pre-1851 books collection focuses on theological works, many of which were printed on the continent, but also includes significant holdings in history, travel, classics, antiquities and science. Important holdings include: 59 incunabula, Maynoothiana, rare and interesting printings and bindings; 1,220 bound volumes of eighteenth and nineteenth century pamphlets, variously acquired, on diverse subjects; a Bible collection, including over 2,000 Bibles in almost 600 languages, from the sixteenth century to the 1960s, on permanent loan since 1986 from the National Bible Society of Ireland (formerly the Hibernian Bible Society, founded in 1806). The Map Collection includes a complete bound set of six inch Ordnance Survey maps, 1833–45, and a set of one inch Ordnance Survey maps (1903) with parish boundaries marked.

The Manuscript Collection is especially strong in Irish language materials. The Irish language manuscripts represent in particular the collections of three men: John Murphy (1772–1847), Bishop of Cork; Eugene O'Curry (1796–1862), Professor of Irish History and Archaeology at the Catholic University of Ireland; and Laurence Renehan (1797–1857), President of Maynooth College and of the Celtic Society. The Murphy Collection contains 114 bound volumes bequeathed to the college in 1848. The O'Curry Collection contains 115 volumes of material, all collected or transcribed by Eugene O'Curry. The Renehan Collection contains material collected for an ecclesiastical history of Ireland and, in addition to the Irish language material, includes 79 bound volumes of manuscripts in English, French and Latin. The Irish language manuscript collections are described and listed in a printed catalogue begun by Rev Paul Walsh in 1943 and completed by an tAthair Pádraig Ó Fiannachta. These have been microfilmed and may be consulted in the John Paul II Library.

LOCATION
In St Patrick's House, the Gothic quadrangle beyond St Joseph's Square, in the south cloister.

HISTORY AND FAMILY RESEARCH CENTRE

Riverbank, Main Street
NEWBRIDGE, COUNTY KILDARE
Ireland

Note: the History and Family Research Centre incorporates three related departments (Archives, Kildare Heritage and Genealogy Company Ltd and Local Studies Department) under one roof. See separate entries below. The facilities and premises have been redeveloped and the centre is now fully open to the public.

HISTORY AND FAMILY RESEARCH CENTRE – ARCHIVES

Riverbank, Main Street
NEWBRIDGE, COUNTY KILDARE
Ireland

E-mail: localhistory@kildarecoco.ie

ACCESS AND SERVICES
Limited access provided by the Local Studies Department, strictly by appointment.
Services in development.

DESCRIPTION
Kildare County Council is developing a county archive service based at the History
and Family Research Centre. In preparing for this, it was first necessary to identify
and preserve the public archive collections held in various locations throughout the
county. A specially adapted storage facility has now been assigned for the archives at
Newbridge.

HOLDINGS
Quality archive collections have survived for County Kildare, but these are currently
uncatalogued and are, therefore, not readily accessible.

LOCATION
Beside the public library in the History and Family Research Centre, Newbridge,
County Kildare. First turn on the left after the bridge.

HISTORY AND FAMILY RESEARCH CENTRE
– LOCAL STUDIES DEPARTMENT

Riverbank, Main Street
NEWBRIDGE, COUNTY KILDARE
Ireland

TELEPHONE: (087) 987 1046, (045) 432 690; FAX: (045) 449 721
E-mail localhistory@kildarecoco.ie
Website: www.kildare.ie/heritage

HOURS
Tu–F, 10.00am–1.00pm, 2.00pm–4.30pm; Sa, 10.00am–1.00pm, 2.00pm–4.30pm

ACCESS AND SERVICES
By appointment only.

CONTACT
Librarian

DESCRIPTION
The Local Studies Department forms an integral part of the Kildare County Library
Arts Service and ultimately, in partnership with Archives and the Kildare Heritage
and Genealogy Company Ltd, has become an integral part of the Riverbank
Cultural Campus. The Local Studies Collection is located in the History and Family
Research Centre. It is the focal point for local history research in County Kildare for
historians and enthusiasts alike. The new Reading Room and research facilities have
greatly enhanced the services on offer. The collection will be added to the

computerised catalogue on the county library's Horizon system, further enhancing the service and making it more accessible. Many important primary resources have also been added to the website to allow researchers even greater accessibility to the collection.

HOLDINGS

As well as containing an extensive collection of secondary source material the Local Studies Department includes many original sources. Among the most important items in the collection are the Ballitore Manuscripts, consisting of files of late nineteenth century correspondence, school notebooks, drawings etc of the Shackletons and other Quaker families from Ballitore, County Kildare. The Teresa Brayton Collection of books, newspaper cuttings and personal items forms another important part of the Local Studies Department's collection. Perhaps the most valuable source for the study of local history is the *Journal of the County Kildare Archaeological Society*, first published in 1891. In addition, the Local Studies Department holds *Griffith's Valuation*; tithe applotment books; six inch Ordnance Survey Maps, 1837, and other maps of the county from the eighteenth century; rentals from the Marquis of Drogheda and Verschoyle Estates; photographs from the Lawrence Collection etc. Microfilm holdings include the 1901 and 1911 censuses, Irish statutes, 1310–1761 and index; *Journal of the House of Lords*, 1634–98, 1703–25, 1727–52; and *Journal of the House of Commons*, 1613–1800. Newspaper holdings on microfilm below.

The Local Studies Department currently provides restricted access to the archives of Kildare County Council, which include important sources such as the minute books of the Naas Board of Guardians, 1839–c. 1922; and Kildare County Council minute books, c. 1899–1995.

The Kildare County Library has an extensive and impressive collection of local and national newspapers and periodicals.

Newspapers on Microfilm

Leinster Leader, 1881/2–1985, 1991–2004; *Kildare Observer*, 1880–1935; *Freeman's Journal*, 1763–1831; *Leinster Express*, 24 Sept 1831–84; *Irish Times*, March 1859–December 1895, 1904, 1905, 1914–23, January 1997–2003; *Dublin Penny Journal*, 1832–6

Newspapers in Hard Copy

Leinster Leader, 1983–present; *Kildare Nationalist*, 1983–present; *Weekly Nation*, 1898 (bound 1 vol.); *Weekly Nation*, 1899–present (bound 1 vol.); *The Nation*, December 1843–September 1844 (bound 1 vol.); *Dublin Penny Journal*, 1832–3, 1834–5; *Dublin Journal*, 1862; *Duffy's Hibernian Magazine* II (July–December 1862), III (January–June 1863); *Curragh News* (bound photocopy), February–September 1891; *Ballitore Magazine* (bound photocopy) 2nd series 1821; *Leixlip Life* (bound 4 vols), April 1973–March 1982; *Newbridge: New Link Magazine*, 1973–6; *Maynooth Newsletter*, 1975–present; *Lucan Times*, November–December 1989, 1990, January, March–May 1991.

Periodicals

Journal of the County Kildare Archaeological Society I–XIX (ii) (1891–2003); *Journal of the Royal Society of Antiquaries* 1–132 (1849–2002); *Irish Sword* 1–23 (1949–2004); *Quarterly Bulletin of the Irish Georgian Society* I–X (1958–67); *Collectanea Hibernica* 1–45 (1958–2003); *Analecta Hibernica* 1–29 (1930–80)

32–36 (1985–95); *Irish Historical Studies* 1–6, 9, 13, 18–22, 24, 27, 29, 31, 36–44, 81, 82 (incomplete); *Archivum Hibernicum* I–XXII (1910–74), XXXIV–XXXV (1977–81, 1988, 1990, 1993, 1995); *Studia Hibernica* 1–8, 10, 12–13, 15, 19 (incomplete); *Béaloideas*, 1927–2001 (incomplete); *Royal Geological Society of Ireland* III–IV (1844–50); X–XVIII (1862–89) (incomplete), index to vols I–XVIII; *Irish Ecclesiastical Record*, 1906–60 (incomplete); *Wolfe Tone Annual*, 1935, 1937–40, 1942–3, 1945–52, 1954–8, 1961–2 (incomplete); *Capuchin Annual*, 1930–71, 1973–7 (incomplete); *Irish Texts* I–XXV, XXVII–LV; *Catholic Bulletin*, 1914, 1917–18, 1920, 1925; *Studies* 1912–72 (incomplete); *Record of the Maynooth Union*, 1909–39 (incomplete); *Clongownian*, 1895–1974 plus index, 1975–80; *Association for the Preservation of the Memorials of the Dead*, 1895–1916 (incomplete), *Irish Family History* 2–20 (1986–2004); *Museum Ireland* 2–7, 9–13 (1992–2003) (incomplete).

LOCATION
Beside the public library in the History and Family Research Centre. First turn on the left after the bridge.

KILDARE HERITAGE AND GENEALOGY COMPANY LTD

History and Family Research Centre, Riverbank, Main Street
NEWBRIDGE, COUNTY KILDARE
Ireland

TELEPHONE: (045) 433 602
E-mail: kildaregenealogy@iol.ie
Website: www.kildare.ie/genealogy, www.irish-roots.net

HOURS
By appointment

ACCESS AND SERVICES
Visitors welcome. Approved family history research centre for those interested in tracing their family roots in County Kildare. Member of countrywide network of centres comprising Irish Family History Foundation. Consult website for fee schedule and application form.
   The company continues to computerise County Kildare's family history records as well as compiling a computerised index of the *Leinster Leader*, commencing in 1881.

CONTACT
Karel Kiely MA

DESCRIPTION
The Kildare Heritage and Genealogical Company is computerising the genealogical records of County Kildare including Roman Catholic and Church of Ireland registers; *Griffith's Valuation*, tithe applotment books, the 1901 and 1911 censuses, gravestone inscriptions, the *Leinster Leader* newspaper and birth, marriage and death notices from local papers. It has the largest database of County Kildare records in the world and is unique in its holdings of computerised indexes of parish records.

HOLDINGS
The company has indexed church records for both Roman Catholic and Church of Ireland parishes in County Kildare. Roman Catholic parish registers generally consist of baptism and marriage registers, although some confirmation burial registers also exist. Owing to the fact that the Roman Catholic Church was suppressed (by the Penal Laws) from the 1690s until 1829, the parish registers of different parishes have varying start dates. The earliest registers which still survive start from about 1740. Church of Ireland parish registers generally consist of baptism, marriage and burial registers. These start much earlier than the Roman Catholic ones, with some Kildare registers going back as far as the late 1600s. Lists of Catholic and Church of Ireland records can be found on the company's website.

LOCATION
Beside the public library in the History and Family Research Centre. First turn on the left after the bridge.

COUNTY KILKENNY

KILKENNY ARCHAEOLOGICAL SOCIETY

Rothe House, 16 Parliament Street
KILKENNY
Ireland

TELEPHONE: (056) 772 2893
E-mail: rothehouse@eircom.net
Website: www.kilkennyarchaeologicalsociety.ie

HOURS
M–Sa, 10.30am–5.00pm

ACCESS AND SERVICES
A fee based, not for profit organisation that offers genealogical research services to
persons interested in tracing their roots in County Kilkenny. It is a member of the
Irish Family History Foundation, the coordinating body for a network of
government approved genealogical research centres in the Republic of Ireland and in
Northern Ireland, which have computerised tens of millions of Irish ancestral records
of different types. Initial enquiries usually replied to within one week. Record
searches and partial searches usually take about one month and enquirers who
commission full reports can anticipate a delay of about three months. Initial
assessment costs €75 while a record search for one family unit over one generation
costs €40. Single record costs €15. Application form available through website.
Common surnames in Kilkenny City and County include: Murphy, Walsh,
Brennan, Maher, Butler, Phelan (and O'Phelan), Grace, Fitzpatrick, Comerford and
Ryan. The main towns and villages in this county in addition to Kilkenny City are:
Castlecomer, Callan, Freshford, Johnstown and Thomastown. Relevant publications
include: *Old Kilkenny Review*, 1978, 1980, 1986, 1988, 1990–94; *Kilkenny
Graveyard Inscriptions*, (Knocktoper No. 1 and St Patrick's No. 2); W. Nolan and K.
Whelan (eds) *Kilkenny: History and Society*; and *Kilkenny City and County: a
Photographic Record*. See website for a more comprehensive listing and prices.

CONTACT
Researcher

DESCRIPTION
Kilkenny Archaeological Society is the primary genealogical research service for
County Kilkenny, with some 2,000,000 genealogical records computerised.

HOLDINGS
Church records from 1754 to 1900 have been computerised. Kilkenny
Archaeological Society also holds copies of: Indexed *Pigot's* and *Slater's Directories*;
various estate rentals; a listing of some of the records of Kilkenny Corporation; and
files of the *Kilkenny Journal* newspaper and some of the *Moderator*, neither of which
is currently indexed, though indexing of the eighteenth century items has begun.

LOCATION
City centre, opposite the courthouse, a ten minute walk from Kilkenny Castle. The
nearest car park is on Parliament Street at the Market Cross Shopping Centre.

KILKENNY COUNTY ARCHIVES
See KILKENNY COUNTY LIBRARY, Kilkenny

KILKENNY COUNTY LIBRARY

NIB Building, 6 Rose Inn Street
KILKENNY
Ireland

TELEPHONE: (056) 779 4160; FAX: (056) 779 4168
E-mail: katlibs@iol.ie
Website: www.kilkennylibrary.ie

HOURS
M–F, 9.00am–1.00pm, 2.00pm–5.00pm; closed bank and public holidays

ACCESS AND SERVICES
Visitors welcome, but advance notice preferred. Advance booking of microform
reader/printers required. Internet access available. No disabled access facilities. Fees
for photocopying, microform prints and e-mail usage. Entire collection catalogued
online. There is a printed catalogue for the Local History Collection. Free brochures
available, and an in-house guide and directory of services available for consultation
in the Local Studies Department. The library's website has a section devoted to local
studies and provides a guide for researchers of genealogy in Kilkenny.

CONTACT
Declan McCauley, Assistant Librarian

DESCRIPTION
Headquarters library of the County Kilkenny library system. The library houses the
county's main local history collection.

HOLDINGS
The library system houses a collection of some 300,000 books, plus journals,
manuscripts, maps, microforms, newspapers, pamphlets, photographs and
recordings. The Local History Collection will be of special interest to visitors. It
consists of important holdings of local history items, a collection of material by
Kilkenny authors or pertaining to Kilkenny, local newspapers, genealogical historical

sources and Kilkenny files collected from assorted publications.

The library also oversees the Kilkenny County Archives, but most of these records are held offsite so advance booking is essential. The archives include Board of Guardian minute books for the Poor Law Unions of Castlecomer, Thomastown and Urlingford, *c.* 1850–*c.* 1900, and also Callan and Kilkenny, 1842–1922 (some gaps in all series). The minutes detail the management of the workhouses where the destitute poor were accommodated.

Grand Jury records include printed presentments for the Kilkenny City and County, 1839–56. Poll books for North Kilkenny 1897 and 1900 and registers of voters 1924–47 and 1964–present also survive. Local authority records include those of the Kilkenny County Council and Rural District Councils from 1899 and there are also deposits of records of local business firms including indentures of apprentices.

Genealogical resources are especially strong. These include virtually all the standard sources for Kilkenny, such as *Griffith's Valuation* (microfilm and hard copy); Ordnance Survey maps; 1901 and 1911 censuses; tithe applotment books; lists, directories and various surveys; and a very strong local newspaper collection going back to 1767. See website for details.

LOCATION
Kilkenny city centre. The Local Studies Department is still located at the NIB Building, 6 Rose Inn Street, Kilkenny.

COUNTY LAOIS

LAOIS AND OFFALY FAMILY HISTORY RESEARCH CENTRE
See IRISH MIDLANDS ANCESTRY, Tullamore

LAOIS COUNTY LIBRARY – LOCAL STUDIES COLLECTION

Laois County Library Headquarters, Aras an Chontae, J.F.L. Avenue
PORTLAOISE, COUNTY LAOIS
Ireland

TELEPHONE: (057) 867 4315 (HQ); Local Studies: (057) 867 4316 (HQ)
E-mail: library@laoiscoco.ie
Website: www.laois.ie/departments/libraries/local+studies

HOURS
Headquarters: M–F, 9.00am–1.00pm, 2.00pm–5.00pm
Portlaoise Branch Library: Tu, F, 10.00am–5.00pm; W–Th, 10.00am–7.00pm; Sa,
10.00am–1.00pm

ACCESS AND SERVICES
Visitors welcome. Modest membership fee required for borrowing privileges.
Photocopying services available.

CONTACT
Gerry Maher, County Librarian. E-mail: gmaher@laoiscoco.ie
P.F. Lynch, Local Studies Librarian. E-mail: pflynch@laoiscoco.ie

DESCRIPTION
Headquarters library for County Laois, with branch libraries in: Abbeyleix
(telephone (057) 873 0020, e-mail esutton@laoiscoco.ie); Clonaslee (telephone
(057) 864 8437, e-mail mcusack@laoiscoco.ie); Mountmellick (telephone (057) 862
4733, e-mail flynch@laoiscoco.ie); Mountrath (telephone (057) 875 6046, e-mail
jphelan@laoiscoco.ie); Portlaoise (telephone (057) 862 2333, fax (057) 866 3656, e-
mail library@laoiscoco.ie); Portarlington (telephone (057) 864 3751, e-mail
bdorris@laoiscoco.ie); Rathdowney (telephone (0505) 46852, e-mail
cafitzpatrick@laoiscoco.ie); Stradbally (telephone (057) 862 5005, e-mail
pnorton@laoiscoco.ie); and Timahoe (telephone (057) 862 7231, e-mail
mscully@laoiscoco.ie).

HOLDINGS
The Local Studies Collection, which is located at the headquarters library, consists of manuscripts, local newspapers, books, pamphlets, photographs, maps, estate papers and author materials relating to County Laois and Ireland. Estate papers include rentals for the Tipperary estate of the Countess of Milltown (1862–1969). The Poor Law Archive comprises minute books for the Poor Law Unions of Abbeyleix, Donamore and Mountmellick, *c.* 1844–*c.* 1920. The School Scheme Collection of folklore of 1937/8 is available on microfilm. Newspaper holdings include the *Leinster Express*, 1831, and the *Nationalist and Leinster Times*, 1883.
The library is building a collection of all published material on County Laois, including a complete set of journals of the Royal Society of Antiquities of Ireland. Survey works include tithe applotment books (1830s) and *Griffith's Valuation* (1850s).
The collection also has a complete set of the *Kildare Archaeological Journal*. There is a good collection of photographs of the area, including the Eason Collection, the Lawrence Collection, the Scully Collection and the Redmond Collection. Map holdings are highlighted by Sir William Petty's maps, 1685, Taylor and Skinner road maps, 1778, and the six inch Ordnance Survey maps of Queen's County (now County Laois), 1841.
The Laois County Council Archive includes rate books, 1934–57, microfilm copies of the tithe surveys for the county, 1823–38, the tenement valuation, *c.* 1853 and the 1901 census.

LOCATION
Town centre.

COUNTY LEITRIM

LEITRIM COUNTY LIBRARY (LEABHARLANN CHONTAE LIATROMA)

Main Street
BALLINAMORE, COUNTY LEITRIM
Ireland

TELEPHONE: (071) 964 5582 (Library), (071) 964 5567 (Local Studies); FAX: (071) 964 5572 (Library)
E-mail: ballinamorelibrary@leitrimcoco.ie, localstudies@leitrimcoco.ie
Website: www.leitrimlibrary.ie

HOURS
M, W, F, 10.00am–5.30pm; Tu, Th, 10.00am–8.00pm; Sa, 10.00am–5.00pm

ACCESS AND SERVICES
Visitors welcome. Disabled access; free internet access; photocopying and microform prints available for a modest fee. The entire collection is catalogued and can be consulted at the above website.

CONTACT
Reference staff

DESCRIPTION
The library is the central public library for County Leitrim.

HOLDINGS
The library houses the usual range of public library material. Of principal interest to visitors would be the Local History Collection, which includes Board of Guardian minutes and oral interviews with local people. Of special genealogical interest are holdings of *Griffith's Valuation*, tithe applotment books, the 1901 and 1911 censuses, Ordnance Survey maps, estate papers and a newspaper collection, all focusing on County Leitrim. There is also a collection of some 3,000 photographs, mostly dating from after 1970.

LOCATION
Main Street, Ballinamore.

LEITRIM GENEALOGY CENTRE (SINSEARLANN LIATROMA)

Main Street
BALLINAMORE, COUNTY LEITRIM
Ireland

TELEPHONE: (071) 964 4012; FAX: (071) 964 4425
E-mail: leitrimgenealogy@eircom.net
Website: www.irishroots.net/leitrim

HOURS
M–F, 10.00am–1.00pm, 2.00pm–5.00pm; closed bank holidays

ACCESS AND SERVICES
Visitors welcome. Disabled access. Service fees apply. Genealogical research service
for the County of Leitrim, based on fees set by the Irish Family History Foundation.
Local publications on sale.

CONTACT
Brid Sullivan

DESCRIPTION
Leitrim Genealogy Centre, established in 1986, is the Irish Family History
Foundation's designated genealogical research centre for County Leitrim. The centre
is one of the longest established IFHF centres. It provides full time professional
genealogy services for County Leitrim. Chief surnames found in County Leitrim
include: Reynolds, McGowan, Rooney, Flynn, Kelly, Gallagher, Moran, Dolan,
McLoughlin and McMorrow.

HOLDINGS
Main records include: Roman Catholic records, the earliest of which date from
1823; Church of Ireland records dating from 1783; Methodist records dating from
1840; and Presbyterian records dating from 1829. Records up to 1900 have been
computerised. The centre also holds copies of: *Griffith's Valuation*, tithe applotment
books, the 1901 and 1911 censuses, Ordnance Survey maps, gravestone inscriptions,
estate papers, newspapers and indexes to church and civil records, all focusing on
County Leitrim.

LOCATION
At rear of courthouse.

COUNTY LIMERICK

LIMERICK ANCESTRY

Note: Due to budgetary constraints, Limerick Ancestry closed in February 2004 and will remain so in the immediate future.

LIMERICK ARCHIVES

58 O'Connell Street
LIMERICK
Ireland

TELEPHONE: (061) 496 544
E-mail: archives@limerickcoco.ie
Website: www.limerickcoco.ie

HOURS
By appointment, Wednesday only

ACCESS AND SERVICES
Visitors welcome, but by appointment only. Advance notice, ID and registration required. Readers must agree to observe the regulations of the archives. See website for expanded access in 2007 as archives will move to a purpose built building on the outskirts of Limerick City.

CONTACT
City and County Archivist

DESCRIPTION
Limerick Archives is jointly funded by Limerick City Council and Limerick County Council and is the repository for local authority records. Limerick Archives also holds a large collection of records relating to predecessor bodies, private collections and actively accepts donations of material relating to Limerick City and County. Incarnated as Limerick Regional Archives in the late 1970s, Limerick Archives developed largely into a genealogy driven operation until 1998, when Limerick local authorities (Limerick City Council and Limerick County Council) took over the day to day administration of the service. The genealogy function was carried on as a separate but linked activity by Limerick Ancestry, which has since closed.

HOLDINGS

Holdings include administrative records for Limerick City (from 1841, with some older material related to St Michael's parish dating back to 1809) and County Limerick (from 1899, plus older Board of Guardian material and Grand Jury presentments).

There are almost complete collections of minute books for the Boards of Guardians of the Poor Law Unions of Kilmallock, Limerick and Newcastle West *c.* 1840–1922. There are minutes covering the period 1850–1922 for Croom Poor Law Union and the period 1870–91 for Glin. For Rathkeale only a single volume survived a fire at the workhouse; this covers the period January–November 1921. Kilmallock Poor Law Union also has rate books for the period 1842–73.

For St Michael's parish in the city of Limerick there is another series of rate books for the years 1810–46 (with gaps; microfilm copies available in PRONI). These are part of the archive of the Commissioners for the improvement of the parish.

There are also the following records with specific information about individuals: a register for St John's Fever and Lock Hospital, 1816; a microfilm copy of a census of Shanagolden and Foynes area of County Limerick 1846 giving names, occupations and numbers in each household, which carries several thousand names. This census was organised by Lord Monteagle and other local landlords. The original manuscript is held in the National Library of Ireland (MS 582). The manuscript runs to about 50 A3 size pages; estate papers: rent book for Lord Monteagle's estate, 1831–50; the archive of the old Limerick Corporation includes records of the Mayor's Tholsel or Small Debtors' Court, 1773–95 and 1811–13, a Court of Claims register, 1823–41, a register of admissions, 1832–41, and a register of paying orders, 1777–1801.

Among others, the archives also hold the private records of: solicitors (some 4,000 property deeds); the Encumbered Estates Court; the Monteagle Estate, 1800–1949; Limerick Chamber of Commerce; Limerick Harbour Commissioners; various companies; as well as microfilm collections of Limerick material held elsewhere. Property deeds have been fed to a local database, as have microfilm holdings. Handlists (short) of the various private collections also exist. Limerick Archives collects anything to do with the administrative, social, economic and cultural history of Limerick, and administrative collections for the city and county, e.g.: P14/Monteagle Estate Papers; PO1/Limerick Chamber of Commerce; PO2/Limerick Harbour Commissioners; PO9/Limerick Water Works Company; P10/Limerick County Militia Financial Records, 1803–29; P11/Geary's Biscuit Factory Papers; P12/Cannock and Company; P16/Limerick Custom House Papers; P21/Coote Family Papers; and P22/De Vere Papers.

LOCATION

The Reading Room is located on the second floor of the Library Headquarters building, on the city's main street.

LIMERICK CITY PUBLIC LIBRARY

The Granary, Michael Street
LIMERICK
Ireland

TELEPHONE: (061) 314 668, (061) 407 510; FAX: (061) 411 506
E-mail: citylib@limerickcity.ie
Website: www.limerickcity.ie

HOURS
M–Tu, 10.00am–5.30pm; W–F, 10.00am–8.00pm; Sa, 10.00am–1.00pm; closed
Saturdays of bank holiday weekends

ACCESS AND SERVICES
Visitors welcome. Modest fees for photocopying and microfilm prints. Borrowing
privileges may be restricted. Disabled access facilities. There is a searchable database
of the Limerick trade directories from 1769 to 1879 (work in progress) currently
only available in-house. Staff happy to run searches and produce reports from this
database.

CONTACT
Dolores Doyle, City Librarian. E-mail: ddoyle@limerickcity.ie
Michael Maguire, Reference and Local History Librarian. E-mail:
mmaguire@limerickcity.ie

DESCRIPTION
The Central Library at the Granary, along with one branch library at the Thomond
Shopping Centre, Roxboro, Limerick, is funded by Limerick City Council. It
provides a host of library services to the community, including the Local Studies
Collection.

HOLDINGS
The Local Studies Collection contains books, manuscripts, journals, newspapers,
photographs, articles, maps, reports and ephemera relating to Limerick City and
County past and present. Of special interest is the extensive collection of books
relating to the history, antiquities and society of Limerick, including the Kemmy
Collection of books relating to Irish history, religion and politics. Other collections
include the Seamus Ó Ceallaigh Collection containing the research files, journals
and books of the deceased *Limerick Leader* GAA columnist and renowned GAA
historian. The collection includes material dating to the early years of the GAA in
the Limerick area. The newspaper collection includes microfilm of: the *Limerick
Chronicle*, 1782–1975, 1982–present; *Limerick Leader*, 1893–1904, 1925–present;
General Advertiser or Limerick Gazette, 1806–20; *Munster Journal*, 1749–84 and
Limerick Evening Post, 1811–19. Other material includes: the *Journal of the
Association for the Preservation of the Memorials of the Dead in Ireland*, 1888–1931;
memorial records of Irish soldiers who died in World War I; business directories
from 1769; *Griffith's Valuation* for Counties Limerick and Clare; list of landowners
of one acre and more for the whole of Ireland, 1876; Seamus Pender's 1659 census
of Ireland; tithe applotment books for County Limerick; and registers of electors in
Limerick City, 1923, 1931–present.

LOCATION
Limerick city centre, in a landmark eighteenth century granary and bonded
warehouse which also houses Limerick Archives, close to the Hunt Museum.

LIMERICK COUNTY LIBRARY – LOCAL STUDIES COLLECTION

Limerick County Library Headquarters, 58 O'Connell Street
LIMERICK
Ireland

TELEPHONE: (061) 496 526; FAX: (061) 318 570
E-mail: libinfo@limerickcoco.ie, localstudies@limerickcoco.ie
Website: www.limerickcoco.ie/library

HOURS
Local Studies Department: M–F, 9.30am–1.00pm, 2.00pm–4.30pm
Dooradoyle Branch (main lending library): Tu–W, 10.00am–5.30pm; Th–F,
10.00am–8.30pm; Sa, 11.00am–5.30pm

ACCESS AND SERVICES
Visitors welcome. No membership fee. Photocopying and microfiche print services
available at cost of 20c per sheet. Books cannot be borrowed from Local Studies
Collection.

CONTACT
Damien Brady, County Librarian
Tony Storan, Limerick Studies
Margaret Franklin, Limerick Studies

DESCRIPTION
The Local Studies Collection (Limerick Studies) houses very strong holdings on local
history and is based in the headquarters of the Limerick County Library. The
headquarters library oversees a 25 branch county library system. Full time,
computerised branch libraries with internet access include: Abbeyfeale, Bridge Street,
Abbeyfeale (telephone (068) 32488, contact Michael McInerney, Senior Library
Assistant); Adare (telephone (061) 396 822, contact Margaret O'Reilly, Assistant
Librarian); Dooradoyle, Crescent Shopping Centre, Dooradoyle (telephone (061)
301 101, contact Noreen O'Neill, Executive Librarian); and Newcastle West,
Gortboy, Newcastle West (telephone (069) 62273, contact Aileen Dillane, Executive
Librarian). Please note that the headquarters library does not lend books. Its main
lending library is the Dooradoyle branch, located about two miles from headquarters
in a city suburb.

HOLDINGS
The library houses the standard collection of educational and recreational reading
material, including fiction, non-fiction, local history and children's stock. The bulk
of the local studies material is housed in the headquarters library, with a scattering of
local history materials deposited in most of the branch libraries. The Limerick
Studies Department houses a very wide collection of books, manuscripts, journals,
newspapers, photographs, maps, CD-ROMS, reports and archival resources of local
interest. Collecting focuses on works that document any aspect of Limerick, works
written by Limerick authors and works published in Limerick. Priority is given to

county history and antiquities, traditional areas of collecting interest. Sources of special genealogical interest include: *Griffith's Valuation*; Ordnance Survey letters; Civil Survey, 1654; the Béaloideas Collection for Schools, 1937–8; and *Baronies, Parishes and Townlands in Co. Limerick*, compiled by the Ballyhoura Architectural Survey. The collection also includes a large number of local newspapers and journals, mostly on microfilm, dating back to 1749. There are special collections on the Joyce brothers of Glenosheen and on local scholar Mainchin Seoighe.

LOCATION
Towards the Crescent end of O'Connell Street (not the city end) on the block before the Belltable Arts Centre, on the same side.

UNIVERSITY OF LIMERICK LIBRARY AND INFORMATION SERVICES

University of Limerick
LIMERICK
Ireland

TELEPHONE: (061) 202 166; FAX: (061) 213 090
E-mail: libinfo@ul.ie
Website: www.ul.ie/~library

HOURS
University Library
Term time: M–F, 8.30am–11.00pm; Sa, 9.00am–7.00pm; Su, 11.00am–6.00pm
Vacation period: M–F, 9.00am–5.00pm
Special Collections
M–W, F, 9.00am–5.00pm; Th, 9.00am–5.00pm

ACCESS AND SERVICES
Visitors welcome, but advance notice preferred and ID required. For access to Special Collections Department advance notice especially appreciated. Disabled access. Photocopying and microform prints available for a fee. Leaflets and booklets describing services (both print and electronic) and special collections are available.

CONTACT
Mary Dundon, Head, Reader Services. E-mail: mary.dundon@ul.ie
Patricia O'Donnell, Head, Information Services. E-mail: patricia.odonnell@ul.ie
Ken Bergin, Special Collections Librarian. E-mail: specoll@ul.ie

DESCRIPTION
The University of Limerick was established by the state in 1972 as The National Institute for Higher Education, Limerick. Full university status was granted by legislation enacted by the Irish parliament in 1989. It is the first new university established since the foundation of the state. The library supports the teaching and research interests of students and faculty, with special interests in the areas of engineering, science, business, computing, information sciences, education and the humanities.

HOLDINGS
The library houses some 260,000 volumes, plus significant holdings of journals, manuscripts, maps, newspapers, pamphlets, photographs and recordings. These represent general academic subjects, with special concentration on engineering,

business and computing/information services. Special collections include: the Regional Collection; the Dunraven Estate Papers; the Glin Estate Papers; the Eoin O'Kelly Collection of early nineteenth century Irish banknotes; and the Norton Collection. The last of these consists of more than 12,000 volumes mostly of an Irish interest, with a special focus on the Shannon River Valley. Highlights of the Norton Collection include collections on Charles Stewart Parnell, Daniel O'Connell, Oliver Goldsmith and Eamon de Valera; early Irish grammars and catechisms; nineteenth century reports, commissions and inquiries; Ordnance Survey letters and maps; photograph albums; and travel literature. One of the most significant recent acquisitions has been the papers of Kate O'Brien, who was born in Limerick in 1897. The latter collection is divided into six sections arranged thematically, addressing Kate O'Brien's personal life, literary life, media coverage, printed material, photographic material and death.

LOCATION
Two miles east of the ancient city of Limerick; easily accessible by taxi or bus. Ample parking available in designated areas.

GLENSTAL ABBEY LIBRARY

MURROE, COUNTY LIMERICK
Ireland

TELEPHONE: (061) 386 103; FAX: (061) 386 328
E-mail: librarian@glenstal.org
Website: www.glenstal.org/library

HOURS
By appointment: contact Librarian

ACCESS AND SERVICES
The Benedictine community has recently built a new library building to house its collection of books, manuscripts and archives, making these resources more readily available to the public. The new library is fully equipped with conference facilities and information resources. Visitors welcome by prior appointment.

CONTACT
Bro Patrick, Librarian

DESCRIPTION
Glenstal Abbey is a Benedictine monastery in County Limerick on the south-west coast of Ireland. A 500 acre estate with streams, lakes and woodland paths surrounds a castle built in the romantic Norman style. The abbey, which is dedicated to Saints Joseph and Columba, is home to a community of monks. Libraries have always been an important part of the Benedictine tradition since the order's founding in the sixth century.

HOLDINGS
The collection has grown steadily from its humble origins in 1927 and is now one of the most important private libraries in Ireland, holding approximately 58,000 volumes and nearly 100 journal runs. The focus of the library is primarily theological but it contains substantial holdings in the areas of Irish history, Irish literature, biography and art. It also has a collection of antiquarian books ranging in

date from the fifteenth to the nineteenth centuries and a restoration programme will shortly be undertaken to restore some of the more important of these.

LOCATION

12 miles outside Limerick City, accessible by car (off the R506 from either the N7 from Dublin or the N24 from Tipperary) or by bus (from the Limerick Rail Station once a day). The nearest airport is Shannon, about an hour's drive away.

COUNTY LONDONDERRY

COLERAINE LIBRARY

Queen Street
COLERAINE, COUNTY LONDONDERRY, BT52 1BE
Northern Ireland

TELEPHONE: (028) 7034 2561; FAX: (028) 7034 2561
E-mail: coleraine.library@ni-libraries.net
Website: www.neelb.org.uk/library-user/libraries

HOURS
M, Tu, F, 10.00am–8.00pm; W, Th, 10.00am–5.30pm; Sa, 10.00am–5.00pm

ACCESS AND SERVICES
Visitors welcome, but borrowing privileges may be restricted. Consult Librarian.
Disabled access. Fees for photocopying and fax services. Free internet access for all
Northern Ireland public library members. One membership card valid for all
libraries. Charge of £1.50 per half hour for non-members; ID required. Membership
of library open to anyone living, working or studying in the area.

CONTACT
Bernadette Kennedy, Branch Manager

DESCRIPTION
One of 28 member libraries in the North-Eastern Education and Library Board
Library Service network. Coleraine's Irish Collection offers material of great interest
to scholars.

HOLDINGS
Part of the collection previously held in the Irish Room at Coleraine is now held in
Coleraine Library. Coleraine holds a family history collection of approximately
1,649 books; and a good collection of maps, including Ordnance Survey maps for
County Londonderry (1830, sheets 1–50 (some missing); 1857, sheets 1–50 (some
missing)), map of County Londonderry townlands (1969); maps of parish
boundaries, Counties Antrim Londonderry, *Griffith's Valuation* maps for County
Londonderry (1862, sheets 1–50), plus other general maps of the surrounding area.
Newspapers include: the *Coleraine Chronicle* (1844–present), the *Northern
Constitution* (1877–present) and the *Ballymoney Free Press* (1870–present). Also of

interest are church records for Ballycastle, Ballymena, Ballymoney, Derry City, Coleraine, Limavady and Magherafelt, all on microfilm. Other works of interest include: *Griffith's Valuation* Books and *Griffith's Valuation* Year (1858–9); tithe applotment books (1826–8) in book form only; 1831 census (index only); 1901 census for County Antrim and County Londonderry (index). The Family History Collection includes manuscripts and notebooks of local historian Dr Hugh Mullin. The library is not yet able to house all of the Irish Room Collection owing to the size of the Coleraine library. A new library is planned, but not for the immediate future.

LOCATION
Town centre.

IRISH ROOM

County Hall, Castlerock Road
COLERAINE, COUNTY LONDONDERRY, BT1 3HP
Northern Ireland

Note: Closed; collection transferred to Coleraine Library. *See* above entry.

UNIVERSITY OF ULSTER LIBRARY, COLERAINE CAMPUS

Cromore Road
COLERAINE, COUNTY LONDONDERRY, BT52 1SA
Northern Ireland

TELEPHONE: (028) 7032 4345; FAX: (028) 7032 4928
E-mail: dj.mcclure@ulster.ac.uk
Website: www.ulster.ac.uk/library

HOURS
Term time: M–F, 8.45am–10.00pm; Sa, 1.00pm–5.00pm
Vacation period: M–Th, 9.00am–5.00pm; F, 9.00–4.00pm

ACCESS AND SERVICES
Visitors welcome but advance notice preferred. Borrowing privileges and database searching not usually extended to visitors. Application for access to Special Collections Department preferred. Disabled access. The entire University of Ulster shares a common catalogue database. Fees apply for photocopying and microform print services; advance notice preferred.

CONTACT
David McClure, Campus Library Manager

DESCRIPTION
The Coleraine campus is part of the four campus University of Ulster system, which also includes Belfast, Jordanstown (in Newtownabbey) and Magee (in Derry). Coleraine maintains two libraries: the Central Buildings Library, which houses material for the sciences and arts, and the South Buildings Library, which houses material for business and management, social sciences, informatics and health sciences.

HOLDINGS
The library houses a collection of some 280,000 bound volumes, plus significant holdings of journals (1,600 titles), manuscripts, microforms, newspapers, pamphlets and photographs. It boasts major collections in the areas of social sciences, health sciences, business and management, informatics, arts and education. It also houses a European Documentation Centre. The Special Collections Department, located in the Central Buildings Library, houses a number of important research collections, including the Henry Davis gift of early printed books and fine bindings, featuring 80 incunabula; the Irish Collection, including folklorist Henry Morris's collection of Irish material, the library of Belfast poet John Hewitt, the library and archive of writer Francis Stuart, the papers of playwright George Shiels and the Headlam-Morley Collection on World War I. The library also contains the natural history collections of A.W. Stelfox and E.N. Carrothers.

LOCATION
North coast of Northern Ireland, 34 miles south-east of Derry City.

CENTRAL LIBRARY

35 Foyle Street
DERRY, BT48 6AL
Northern Ireland

TELEPHONE: (028) 7127 2300; FAX: (028) 7126 1374
E-mail: jane.nicholas@ni-libraries.net
Website: www.welbni.org/libraries

HOURS
M, Th, 9.15am–8.00pm; Tu, W, F, 9.15am–5.30pm; Sa, 9.15am–5.00pm

ACCESS AND SERVICES
Visitors welcome, but ID required. Borrowing privileges for visitors may be restricted. Disabled access. General stacks open, but stacks in Special Collections Department closed. Entire collection catalogued online.

CONTACT
Maura Craig, Senior Librarian in charge of Local History Collection

DESCRIPTION
Opened in 1990, this handsome facility is the main branch library for the Derry City, located just outside the city walls. It has an important local studies department, with strong holdings of genealogical interest. The library has an electronic link to the emigration database of the ULSTER AMERICAN FOLK PARK, Omagh. It also has 21 public access computers. Members of any public library in Northern Ireland enjoy free access to the internet for one hour by showing their membership card. Charge of £1.50 per half hour for non-members. Students living in Derry are eligible to become members for the duration of their course.

HOLDINGS
The library houses more than 75,000 volumes, with access to a total stock of some 500,000 volumes in the Western Education and Library Board system. The Special Collections Department is one of the finest of its kind to be found in a branch library. The Irish and Local Studies Collections include more than 15,000 volumes,

2,500 photographs and 2,000 maps, with special emphasis on the west of County Londonderry, including Limavady and Dungiven. Of special genealogical interest are: holdings of local newspapers on microfilm dating back to 1829; *Griffith's Valuation*, 1860; Ordnance Survey maps, 1834, 1854, 1907 and *c.* 1948 series; 1901 census data; local history files; and an index to hearth money rolls for County Antrim (1669), County Londonderry (1663) and County Tyrone (1666).

LOCATION
On the west bank of the River Foyle, just south of the entrance to the city walls. City car park nearby.

COUNTY DERRY OR LONDONDERRY GENEALOGY CENTRE

10 Craft Village, Shipquay Street
DERRY, BT48 6AR
Northern Ireland

TELEPHONE: (028) 7126 9792; FAX: (028) 7136 0921
Website: www.irishroots.net/derry

HOURS
M–F, 9.00am–5.00pm

ACCESS AND SERVICES
Visitors welcome. Fee based genealogical research service for those interested in tracing their roots in County Londonderry and in the Inishowen Peninsula, County Donegal. The centre's database can now be searched online at www.irishgenealogy.ie, but this service does not provide full details. For example, it records child's name and year of birth in a birth search; and bride's and groom's names and year of marriage in a marriage search. The purpose of this signposting index is to give the client confidence in commissioning the centre for research. The centre receives no public funding and therefore depends on its search services for revenue. Application may be made by letter, telephone, fax, e-mail or in person. The centre publishes books of genealogical and local history interest. These include: *Irish Passenger Lists, 1803–1806*; *A New Genealogical Atlas of Ireland*; and *The Making of Derry: an Economic History*.

CONTACT
Brian Mitchell, Director

DESCRIPTION
The County Derry or Londonderry Genealogy Centre is the designated Irish Family History Foundation centre for County Londonderry. These centres aim to create a comprehensive database of genealogical sources that are known to exist, including church records of all denominations, civil records, land valuations, census records, gravestone inscriptions and various other local sources. The Derry centre offers a genealogical research centre for County Londonderry and the Inishowen Peninsula, County Donegal.

HOLDINGS
The centre collects copies of birth, marriage and death certificates, church registers, gravestone inscriptions, *Griffith's Valuation*, tithe applotment books and the 1901

census for County Londonderry in order to input them to the database. The Reference Collection also includes emigration books and some passenger lists.

LOCATION
City centre, within the walls, one block off the Diamond.

DERRY CITY COUNCIL ARCHIVES
See HERITAGE AND MUSEUM SERVICE, Derry

HARBOUR MUSEUM
See HERITAGE AND MUSEUM SERVICE, Derry

HERITAGE AND MUSEUM SERVICE

Harbour Square
DERRY, BT48 6AF
Northern Ireland

TELEPHONE: (028) 7137 7331; FAX: (028) 7137 7633
E-mail: museums@derrycity.gov.uk
Website: www.derrycity.gov.uk/museums

HOURS
M–F, 10.00am–4.30pm

ACCESS AND SERVICES
The Harbour Museum is housed in the former Londonderry Port and Harbour Commissioner's Office. Displays feature shipbuilding, emigration and port activities, plus an eclectic collection of artefacts gathered over the years. Items from the Civic Art Collection are also on display and are routinely changed. The museum serves as a research centre for the Archive Collection; material from the Archive Collection is regularly exhibited. First floor has no disabled access facilities. Appointment required to access Archive Collection. Photocopying and digital imaging services available on guidance from the Archivist.

CONTACT
Bernadette Walsh, City Archivist. E-mail: bernadette.walsh@derrycity.gov.uk

DESCRIPTION
The Harbour Museum is located in an 1880 building sympathetically converted for museum use in 1993. The Archive Collection includes materials documenting the local history Derry City and the surrounding region. The Archive Collection provides a rich and varied content for researchers, students and family historians. The Harbour Museum is the administrative headquarters for the Heritage and Museum Service of Derry City Council. Derry City Council also funds the development of the award winning Tower Museum and the Workhouse Museum. The Tower Museum includes two permanent exhibitions, The Story of Derry, a chronological look at the development of the city from early times, and The Armada Shipwreck: La Trinidad Valencera, containing a wide selection of artefacts excavated from Kinnagoe Bay during the 1970s from the wreck of La Trinidad Valencera. Visitors are welcome. There is no admission charge to the Harbour Museum or the Workhouse Museum, but an admission charge will apply for the Tower Museum.

HOLDINGS

Of special interest is the Derry City Council Archive Collection detailing the growth and development of the city from the late seventeenth century onwards. Private collections include the archives of various local businesses, including transportation companies; community organisations, such as the Northern Ireland Civil Rights Association (NICRA), and the papers of prominent Derry citizens. The collection also includes corporation records dating back to 1673, legal deeds, court records, architectural drawings, maps and a photographic collection. Recent donations have included a large collection of photographs and paper documents from members of the City of Derry Sub Aqua Club relating to the excavation of *La Trinidad Valencera* in Kinnagoe Bay.

The Archive Collections are available for consultation by appointment only. Unlisted collections will not be made available to the public.

LOCATION

City centre, alongside the Guildhall, close to the city walls.

TOWER MUSEUM

See HERITAGE AND MUSEUM SERVICE, Derry

WORKHOUSE MUSEUM

See HERITAGE AND MUSEUM SERVICE, Derry

UNIVERSITY OF ULSTER LIBRARY, MAGEE CAMPUS

Northland Road
DERRY, BT48 7JL
Northern Ireland

TELEPHONE: (028) 7137 5264; FAX: (028) 7137 5626
E-mail: sa.mcmullan@ulst.ac.uk
Website: www.ulster.ac.uk/library

HOURS

Term time: M–F, 8.45am–10.00pm; Sa–Su, 1.00pm–5.00pm
Vacation period: M–Th, 9.00am–5.00pm; F, 9.00am–4.00pm

ACCESS AND SERVICES

Visitors welcome but advance notice preferred. Borrowing privileges and database searching not usually extended to visitors. Application for access to Special Collections Department preferred. Disabled access. The entire University of Ulster shares a common catalogue database. About 90 per cent of Magee holdings are catalogued online. Fees apply for photocopying and microform print services; advance notice preferred.

CONTACT

Stephanie McMullan, Campus Library Manager

DESCRIPTION

The Magee campus is part of the four campus University of Ulster system, which also includes Belfast, Coleraine and Jordanstown (in Newtownabbey). Magee was founded in 1865 to prepare entrants for the Presbyterian ministry, and in 1984 Magee University College became part of the University of Ulster. The existing library was opened in 1990. The new Learning Resources Centre opened in September 2002.

HOLDINGS
The library houses a collection of some 63,000 bound volumes, plus significant holdings of journals (600 titles), microforms, newspapers, pamphlets and photographs. It specialises in the areas of informatics, art and design, business and management, social sciences, life sciences and engineering. It houses the important Irish Collection, consisting of some 6,000 volumes and 900 pamphlets, including a rare collection on the Siege of Derry in 1689. The Rare Book Collection has a particular strength in eighteenth century Irish printing. Other collections of interest include the Spalding Collection on eastern civilisations, a small collection of manuscripts on Irish Presbyterianism and a collection of some 3,000 photographic negatives of local interest. Journals in the collection include: *Derry Almanac*; *Journal of the Royal Society of Antiquaries of Ireland*, 1890–1992; and *Ulster Journal of Archaeology*, 1853–present.

LOCATION
From the south of the city approach by the Foyle Bridge and follow directions to the Magee Campus.

COUNTY LONGFORD

LONGFORD COUNTY LIBRARY – ARCHIVES AND LOCAL STUDIES

Library Headquarters, Town Centre
LONGFORD
Ireland

TELEPHONE: (043) 41124; FAX: (043) 48576
E-mail: info@longfordlibrary.ie
Website: www.longfordlibrary.ie/library

HOURS
M, W, 10.00am–8.30pm; Tu, Th, 10.00am–5.30pm; F, 10.00am–5.00pm; Sa, 10.00am–2.00pm

ACCESS AND SERVICES
Visitors welcome. Free internet access. Modest fees for photocopying and microfilm print services. Membership required for borrowing privileges. Disabled access facilities.

CONTACT
Mary Reynolds, County Librarian

DESCRIPTION
Archives and Local Studies are based in the Longford Branch Library, one of six libraries operated by Longford County Library headquarters. The others are: Ballymahon, Edgeworthstown, Granard, Drumlish and Lanesboro. The library system is funded by Longford County Council. The Longford Branch Library also offers a business information service.

HOLDINGS
Local Studies houses several collections of note, including collections on local writers Oliver Goldsmith, Padraic Colum and Maria Edgeworth. It also holds strong collections of estate maps of County Longford, tithe applotment books and local newspapers (microfilm and hard bound). It houses a substantial collection of archival and manuscript material of historical and genealogical interest. These include Poor Law Union archives; returns of Boards of Guardians, officers etc (Ballymahon, Drumlish, Granard and Longford); Rural District Council Archives; Longford County Council Archives; Urban District Council Archives; Petty Sessions material;

and Grand Jury presentments for County Longford (1817–95). Private material includes: the regulation and record book of the Longford militia (1793–1855); Maria Edgeworth Collection of letters (1815–94); and the Honorable L.H. King Harman Collection of estate records, account books and scrapbooks. For a detailed listing of the contents of each of these collections, consult website.

The Archives Service is at an early stage of development. A large proportion of its holdings is in storage and has yet to be processed (cleaned, arranged and listed). However, some important archives are available to the public and may be consulted in the Reading Room of library headquarters.

LOCATION
Town centre.

LONGFORD RESEARCH CENTRE

Longford Roots, 1 Church Street
LONGFORD

TELEPHONE: (043) 41235; FAX: (043) 41279
E-mail: longroot@iol.ie

HOURS
M–F, 10.30am–12.30pm

ACCESS AND SERVICES
Longford Research Centre offers a fee based genealogical research service for persons interested in tracing their roots in County Longford. Application form can be obtained from the centre's website, by e-mail or by contacting the centre directly. An initial search fee of €75 (or equivalent) required. The centre tries to keep fees to a minimum and the initial search fee charge is also the maximum amount charged. Success cannot be guaranteed in any search, however, and an unsuccessful search is usually more time consuming than a successful one. Please allow six to eight weeks for reply.

CONTACT
Mary Boland

DESCRIPTION
Longford Research Centre is the Irish Family History Foundation's designated research centre for County Longford. The IFHF is the coordinating body for a network of government approved genealogical research centres in the island of Ireland that have computerised tens of millions of Irish ancestral records of different types. Common County Longford surnames include: Farrell (or O'Farrell), Quinn, Kenny, Kiernan, Mulvey, Smith, Leavy, Kelly, Glennon, Keenan, Casey and Murphy.

HOLDINGS
The centre has computerised church records of baptisms, marriages and burials for the majority of Catholic parishes as early as 1779 and some Church of Ireland, Methodist and Presbyterian parishes. Also available to the centre are *Griffith's Valuation*, tithe applotment books, the 1901 census and civil records.

LOCATION
Town centre.

COUNTY LOUTH

LOUTH COUNTY ARCHIVES SERVICE

Old Gaol, Ardee Road
DUNDALK, COUNTY LOUTH
Ireland

TELEPHONE: (042) 933 9387; FAX: (042) 933 9304
E-mail: archive@louthcoco.ie
Website: www.louthcoco.ie

HOURS
By appointment, M–F, 9.00am–1.00pm, 2.00pm–5.00pm

ACCESS AND SERVICES
Appointment should be made beforehand, preferably one week in advance. Readers
required to complete application form on first visit and pay yearly subscription fee
(concessions for students, OAPs, unemployed and under 16s). Free internet access
for subscribers. Only processed/catalogued collections available. Material cannot be
borrowed. Reproduction fees apply. Research service available for long distance
researchers – queries catered for. Partial wheelchair access. Service is working towards
an online catalogue to be made available via its website.

CONTACT
Lorraine Buchanan, County Archivist. E-mail: lorraine.buchanan@louthcoco.ie

DESCRIPTION
Louth County Archives Service was founded in 2000 as a result of the passing of the
1994 Local Government Act. It is a repository for the public archives of County
Louth. This means that it currently holds or seeks the acquisition of archives of
Louth local authorities and their predecessor bodies. The mission statement of the
Archives Service is: 'the identification, preservation and availability of the valuable
public and private archives of County Louth'.

HOLDINGS
Holdings include almost complete series of minute books for the Boards of
Guardians of the Poor Law Unions of Ardee and Dundalk, c. 1841–1924, and also
Drogheda (with gaps). There are a few admission registers for Ardee workhouse, c.
1880–c. 1910.

Rate books survive for the Dundalk area, *c.* 1840–*c.* 1940, with a complementary set of manuscript valuation records, *c.* 1855–*c.* 1940 (these may be Grand Jury county cess records up to 1899). There is coverage for all of County Louth in the valuation series.

Fortunately for Louth, a county in the Pale region, exceptionally early records of town corporations survive, including Drogheda (1503–1970), Dunleer (1683–1773), Carlingford (1694–1835), Dundalk (1831–41), followed by Dundalk Town Commissioners (1840–99) and Dundalk Urban District Council (1899–1971). There are records for Ardee Town Commissioners and Louth County Council (*c.* 1650–*c.* 1850) and Rural District Council Records (1899–present). Grand Jury query books are available for the years 1815, 1823–99.

LOCATION
Entrance on Ardee Road, behind the Garda Station. Car parking facilities available adjacent to the building. Entrance to the car park is from St Malachy's Villas. Two minutes' walk from Dundalk train station.

LOUTH COUNTY LIBRARY
– REFERENCE AND LOCAL HISTORY LIBRARY

Dundalk Branch Library, Roden Place
DUNDALK, COUNTY LOUTH
Ireland

TELEPHONE: (042) 935 3190; FAX: (042) 933 7635
E-mail: library@louthcoco.ie
Website: www.louthcoco.ie

HOURS
Dundalk Branch Library: Tu, Th: 10.00am–5.00pm, 6.00pm–8.00pm; W, F–Sa, 10.00am–5.00pm; closed Saturdays of bank holiday weekends
Dundalk Reference and Local History Library: Tu–Sa, 10.00am–1.00pm, 2.00pm–5.00pm

ACCESS AND SERVICES
Visitors welcome, but borrowing privileges restricted. Disabled access facilities. Fees for photocopying and microfilm copy services. Approximately 85 per cent of collection catalogued online, including holdings of branch libraries. Free internet access for members, but visitors are also welcome to use this service within reason. No index to newspaper archives. The county has a separate archives service (*see* separate entry).

Located on the upper floor of the main Louth County Library building and houses the local history and genealogy sections, as well as an extensive collection of Irish history titles. The library offers a basic genealogical research service at a charge of €30. Waiting time approximately 2–3 weeks, depending on volume of requests. Photocopying service and study facilities.

CONTACT
Isabell Murphy. E-mail: isabell.murphy@louthcoco.ie

DESCRIPTION

The library is the flagship library in a five library county system. Louth County Council also operates branch libraries in: Drogheda (telephone (041) 983 6649); Ardee (telephone (041) 685 6080); Dunleer (telephone (041) 6861270); and Carlingford (telephone (042) 938 3020).

HOLDINGS

The holdings reflect the general educational and recreational reading interests of a public library, but there are several collections of interest to visitors, especially genealogists, including the Lawrence Collection of photographs of County Louth; *Louth Archaeological and Historical Journal* (1904–99); *Tempest Annual* (1863–1976), the local directory of Dundalk; local newspapers, including the *Dundalk Democrat* (1849–1996) and *Argus* (1973–present); and an extensive collection of local history books and books on Irish history.

Holdings of special genealogical interest include:

a database for Roman Catholic church records for County Louth that is not accessible to the public. This database covers the period from the mid-1700's up to 1900. These records cover 21 parishes, with a total of over 258,000 entries;

tithe applotment books (1820s) available on microfilm, showing names of occupiers of land, size of holdings and the sums to be paid in tithes for the purpose of maintaining the Church of Ireland;

lists of freeholders (1820s) – the names of occupiers and owners of land;

Griffith's Valuation (1854), showing the names of occupiers of land or buildings, the names of persons from whom these were leased and the amount and value of property held;

an index to surnames in the tithe applotment books and CD index to surnames in *Griffith's Valuation*;

local history books and directories, listing local people and businesses; and various histories on prominent local families;

1901 census records of County Louth, available on microfilm;

electoral lists of 1885 and 1915 for some County Louth parishes.

LOCATION

Town centre, next door to St Patrick's Cathedral. Car parking facilities (fees apply) available at the rear of the building. Entrance to the car park is from Ramparts Road.

COUNTY MAYO

BALLINA LIBRARY
See THE JACKIE CLARKE LIBRARY, Ballina

THE JACKIE CLARKE LIBRARY

Ballina Library, O'Rahilly Street
BALLINA, COUNTY MAYO

TELEPHONE: (094) 904 7557 (Castlebar number in use until formal opening of library)

HOURS
To be confirmed

ACCESS AND SERVICES
Non–lending collection: access restricted to academic scholars and *bona fide* researchers working on bibliographies or other studies of Irish material.

DESCRIPTION
The new library, which opened in Ballina in 2006, includes the library of the late Jackie Clarke, a local businessman and noted collector of books and antiquarian material. The collection represents the fruits of over 40 years of collecting and is regarded as one of the finest private libraries in the country.

CONTACT
Librarian

HOLDINGS
The Jackie Clarke Library includes extensive coverage of Irish history and politics with many rare and unique items and is particularly strong regarding the 1798 Rebellion, the 1916 Rising and the IRA campaigns from the 1940s to the 1960s. It comprises books, photographs, posters, legal papers, badges, newspapers, circulars, reports, letters, periodicals, memorial cards, minute books and articles from newspapers. The Irish revolutionary period from the Siege of Limerick to Wolfe Tone, the Young Irelanders, the Fenians, the Famine, the Land Wars, the War of Independence, the Civil War and the IRA campaigns from the 1940s to the 1990s are all represented in this collection. Mayo's involvement in all events is highlighted and many rare documents of local interest are included in the collection.

LOCATION
Town centre.

MAYO NORTH FAMILY HERITAGE CENTRE

Enniscoe, Castlehill
BALLINA, COUNTY MAYO
Ireland

TELEPHONE: (096) 31809; FAX: (096) 31885
E-mail: normayo@iol.ie
Website: www.mayo.irishroots.net

HOURS
M–F, 9.00am–4.00pm

ACCESS AND SERVICES
Mayo North Family Heritage Centre offers a fee based genealogical research service for persons interested in tracing their roots in North Mayo. Application form available on the centre's website; initial search fee of €95 (or equivalent) required. See website for sample report and explanation of terms and sources used in the reports. General enquiries answered immediately; otherwise response depends on type of research commissioned. Average cost of full report is €300. This centre and South Mayo Family Research Centre, Ballinrobe have worked closely together for nearly 15 years and share resources, including a website. There is a museum, gardens and shop at the centre. Seasonal operating hours: telephone for details. Disabled access.

CONTACT
Bridie Greavy, Supervisor

DESCRIPTION
Mayo North Family Heritage Centre is one of the Irish Family History Foundation's two designated research centres for County Mayo. The IFHF is the coordinating body for a network of government approved genealogical research centres in the Republic of Ireland and Northern Ireland that have computerised tens of millions of Irish ancestral records of different types. Common North Mayo surnames include: Gallagher, Durkan, McHale, Barrett, Kelly, Loftus, Gaughan and Lavelle.

HOLDINGS
The two Mayo centres have jointly compiled and input almost 2,000,000 genealogical records to a computer database, relying chiefly on church and civil records. These sources include: *Griffith's Valuation* (1856); parochial registers of baptism and marriage for Roman Catholic parishes including Kilconduff from 1808 and Church of Ireland parishes including Killala from 1704. For Methodist churches in the Castlebar circuit there are registers from 1829 and for the Presbyterian Church at Turlough the registers date from 1819. The earliest burial register is for Kilfian parish (probably Church of Ireland) from 1826. Other sources indexed include the civil registers of births, marriages and deaths beginning in 1864; the 1901 and 1911 censuses; all pre-1990 gravestone inscriptions; tithe applotment books (1825–42); some school roll books; some rent books; ads placed in the *Boston Pilot*, 1831–1900; and lists of Famine immigrants to the port of New York, 1847–51.

LOCATION
On the grounds of the Enniscoe Estate, 3.5 miles south of Crossmolina on the R315
route to Castlebar.

SOUTH MAYO FAMILY RESEARCH CENTRE

Main Street
BALLINROBE, COUNTY MAYO
Ireland

TELEPHONE: (094) 954 1214; FAX: (094) 954 1214
E-mail: soumayo@iol.ie
Website: mayo.irishroots.net/mayo

HOURS

M–F, 9.30am–12.00 pm, 1.30pm–4.00pm

ACCESS AND SERVICES
South Mayo Family Research Centre offers a fee based, genealogical research service
for persons interested in tracing their roots in South Mayo. Application form
available on the centre's website; initial search fee of €95 (or equivalent) required,
but discountable from cost of a comprehensive family history report. See website for
sample report and explanation of terms and sources used in the reports. General
enquiries answered immediately; otherwise response depends on type of research
commissioned. Average cost of full report is €300. Several other searches, e.g.
gravestone search, birth search, marriage search, location search, are available for
€15–€40 per search. These results are usually provided to visitors to the centre
within two hours.
    This centre and Mayo North Family Heritage Centre (Ballina) have worked
closely together for nearly 15 years and share resources, including a common
website.

CONTACT
Gerard M. Delaney, Manager

DESCRIPTION
South Mayo Family Research Centre is one of the Irish Family History Foundation's
two designated research centres for County Mayo. The IFHF is the coordinating
body for a network of government approved genealogical research centres in the
Republic of Ireland and in Northern Ireland that have computerised tens of millions
of Irish ancestral records of different types. Common South Mayo surnames include:
Walsh, Burke, Gibbons, Prendergast, Joyce, Murray, Gallagher, Lydon, Heneghan,
Murphy, O'Malley, Kelly, Moran, Duffy, O'Connor, Waldron and Farragher.

HOLDINGS
The two Mayo centres have jointly compiled and input over 2,500,000 genealogical
records onto an electronic database, relying chiefly on church and civil records.
These sources include: *Griffith's Valuation* (1855–7); all the parochial registers of
baptism and marriage for Roman Catholic parishes, the earliest of which is
Crossboyne and Tagheen with registers from 1791. For Church of Ireland parishes
the earliest registers are for Kilmaine and date from 1744. The earliest Presbyterian
registers surviving are for Aughavale and date from 1853.

Other sources indexed include the civil registers of births, marriages and deaths beginning in 1864; the 1901 and 1911 censuses of population; all pre-1950 gravestone inscriptions; and tithe applotment books (1825–42).

LOCATION
Town centre, in a refurbished schoolhouse on Main Street.

MAYO COUNTY LIBRARY – LOCAL STUDIES DEPARTMENT

Pavilion Road
CASTLEBAR, COUNTY MAYO
Ireland

TELEPHONE: (094) 9047 5557; FAX: (094) 902 4774
E-mail: ihamrock@mayococo.ie
Website: www.mayolibrary.ie

HOURS
Tu, W, 10.00am–8.00pm; Th, F, 10.00am–1.00pm, 2.00–5.00pm; Sa, 10.00am–4.00pm

ACCESS AND SERVICES
Visitors welcome. Free internet access. Photocopying and microfilm copies available for a modest fee. Membership required for borrowing privileges. Disabled access facilities.

CONTACT
Ivor Hamrock, Librarian
Austin Vaughan, County Librarian. E-mail: avaughan@mayococo.ie

DESCRIPTION
The Local Studies Department is located in Castlebar Library and is the central repository for a wealth of material on the history and heritage of County Mayo from earliest times to the present. Mayo County Library collects comprehensively material of local interest, including books, manuscripts, journals, newspapers, photographs, maps, CD-ROMs, microfilm and ephemera. It is part of the county library system, headquartered at Mountain View, Castlebar, County Mayo (telephone (094) 9047573). Mayo County Library Service operates 17 branch libraries. The Castlebar Library also offers a business information centre.

HOLDINGS
All the County Mayo branch libraries hold collections relating to the local history of their surrounding area. The Local Studies Department offers one of the strongest collections of its kind in all of Ireland. Special collections include: Michael Davitt (1846–1906) – complete works and related biographical and historical material; George Moore (1852–1933) – literary works, related biographical and critical material; George A. Birmingham (1865–1950) – collected literary works; and the 1798 Rebellion – events in Mayo. The department also maintains a collection of books, articles, maps and illustrations on County Mayo.

Archival materials include: Ballinrobe Poor Law Union records (1844–1926), including minute books, financial records, outdoor relief records and outgoing letter books. These records have been digitised and are now available in CD-ROM format at the Ballinrobe and Castlebar Libraries. The department also maintains a collection of all journals published locally, including: *Cathair na Mart* (journal of the Westport Historical Society), annually, 1982–present; *North Mayo Historical and Archaeological Society Journal*, annually, 1982–95; *Mayo Association Yearbook*, annually, 1984–present; *Castlebar Parish Magazine*, annually, 1971–present; *Journal of the South Mayo Family Research Centre*, annually, 1989–present; and *Muintir Acla*, quarterly, 1995–present.

Official publications of special local interest include: *Report of Her Majesty's Commissioners of Inquiry into the Working of the Landlord and Tenant (Ireland) Act* (Bessborough Commission, 1870); *British Parliamentary Papers, Famine Series*, vols 1–8 (1968–70); *Digest of Evidence Taken before Her Majesty's Commissioners of Inquiry into the State of the Law and Practice in Respect to the Occupation of Land in Ireland* (Devon Commission, HMSO 1847); Congested Districts Board for Ireland papers; and socio-economic reports on 21 districts in County Mayo (1892/9).

The Photographic Archive includes: the Wynne Collection, containing approximately 2,000 photographs taken by Thomas Wynne of Castlebar and his descendants, dating from 1870, that cover the west of Ireland, landscapes, architecture, streetscapes, studio portraits, historical events etc; selected views of Mayo subjects from the Lawrence Collection of the National Library; a collection of 28 glass photographic plates showing views of County Mayo, *c.* 1920s; postcards of County Mayo scenes, *c.* 1900; and a collection of postcards from the nineteenth century.

The Newspaper Collection includes extensive holdings of local and national papers dating from pre-Famine times to the present. See website for listing.

The Map Collection is also noteworthy and includes: a map of the Maritime County of Mayo in 25 sheets that was begun in 1809 and ended in 1817, by William Bald FRSE, printed in 1830 (scale two inches); Ordnance Survey six inch maps of County Mayo, 1839 and 1900; recorded monuments protected under Section 12 of the 1994 National Monuments (amendment) Act; and the County Mayo archaeological constraint maps, Office of Public Works, 1999.

Of special genealogical interest are the department's holdings of: tithe applotment books, *c.* 1830 (on microfilm); *Griffith's Valuation*, 1855–7; censuses of 1901 and 1911 for County Mayo (on microfilm); parish records for Oughaval, Burrishoole, Achill and Ballycroy; and gravestone inscriptions for Castlebar Old Cemetery, Meelick Old and Meelick New Cemeteries and Bushfield; and a manuscript of *Galway and Mayo Families* by Fr Munnelly. The department also boasts a strong collection of land surveys, drawn mostly from Ordnance Survey and Irish Manuscripts Commission publications. Finally, the department houses the impressive Folklore Collection, including microfilm copies of most of the material collected by schools in County Mayo for the Schools Scheme of 1937–1938 project, an 18 month effort by schoolchildren to document a wide range of Irish folk tradition, including folk tales and folk legends, riddles and proverbs, songs, customs and beliefs, games and pastimes and traditional work practices and crafts. *See also* Jackie Clarke Library, Ballina.

LOCATION
Town centre.

NATIONAL MUSEUM OF COUNTRY LIFE
See NATIONAL MUSEUM OF IRELAND, Dublin

MICHAEL DAVITT MUSEUM

Straide
FOXFORD, COUNTY MAYO
Ireland

TELEPHONE: (094) 31942/022
E-mail: davittmuseum@eircom.net
Website: museumsofmayo.com/davitt

HOURS
Su–Sa, 10.00am–6.00pm; closed Christmas Day, St Stephen's Day, New Year's Day
and Good Friday

ACCESS AND SERVICES
Visitors welcome. Disabled access. Admission fees apply. Pencils only in archives.
Internet access. Photocopying services for a modest fee. Pencils, books, postcards and
small souvenirs for sale. Museum also offers guided tours, a permanent exhibition
and an audiovisual presentation.

CONTACT
Curator

DESCRIPTION
The museum celebrates the life and work of the nineteenth century Irish nationalist
and radical land reformer Michael Davitt (1846–1906). It is housed in the restored
pre-Penal church in the village of Straide, County Mayo, where Michael Davitt was
baptised in 1846. Davitt is buried nearby in the grounds of the thirteenth century
Straide Abbey.

HOLDINGS
The museum contains an extensive collection of documents, photographs, Land
Acts, correspondence, postcards and other material connected with the life of
Michael Davitt.

These include: police reports, prison reports relating to Davitt and the Land
League; correspondence to and from Davitt; photographs of evictions, family
photos, Land League posters, personal items (i.e. rosary beads, walking stick, a dried
flower collected in the Holy Land and postcards from all parts of the world he sent
to his children); Land Acts from 1881; drums and flutes connected with the Land
League; cartoons and tributes and salutations paid to Davitt.

LOCATION
On the N58, between the towns of Castlebar and Ballina, north-west of Knock.

COUNTY MEATH

MEATH COUNTY LIBRARY HEADQUARTERS

Railway Street
NAVAN, COUNTY MEATH
Ireland

TELEPHONE: (046) 902 1451/134; FAX: (046) 909 7001
E-mail: colibrary@meathcoco.ie
Website: www.meath.ie/library, see also www.askaboutireland.ie (click on 'Places',
then 'County Meath')

HOURS
M, W, F–Sa, 10.00am–5.00pm; Tu, Th, 10.00am–8.30pm

ACCESS AND SERVICES
Visitors welcome. Wheelchair access. Photocopying at 20c per sheet and microfilm
printing at 60c for A4 and 80c for A3. Free membership and free internet access.

CONTACT
Frances Tallon, Local Studies Librarian. E-mail: ftallon@meathcoco.ie

DESCRIPTION
The library is the headquarters library for the county system, which includes 11
branch libraries.

HOLDINGS
In addition to the normal educational and recreational materials found in a county
library, Meath maintains a special collection on local history and genealogy.
Of special interest to family history researchers are Dr Beryl Moore's recordings of
gravestone inscriptions. Dr Moore was an indefatigable worker and she recorded all
the inscriptions in more than 35 graveyards in County Meath. She ranged all over
the county, except perhaps in the north-east part near the border with County
Monaghan. Her recordings are available in typescript. Some examples of her work
have been published in the *Journal of the Meath Archaeological and Historical Society*.
The inscriptions of several other graveyards have been recorded subsequently and
many others are currently being recorded.
   Meath is exceptionally fortunate to have available some 50 volumes of records of
the Meath County Infirmary including a (damaged) register of patients *c.* 1780–*c.* 1800

and also diet books listing the names of patients. With regard to the large landed estates in the county there are rentals of the Bligh Estate at Nobber, *c*. 1850, and rent books and letter books for the Mountainstown Estate near Navan, *c*. 1850. Minute books for the Boards of Guardians of the Poor Law Unions of Dunshaughlin, Kells, Navan and Trim survive for the period *c*. 1840–*c*. 1920 and there is also an incomplete series for Oldcastle. The Poor Law Archive includes some rate books for the period *c*. 1925–*c*. 1940.

The records of Meath County Council between the years 1899–1970 are arranged and listed. For the towns of Kells and Navan there are records of Town Commissioners from *c*. 1830 and Urban District Council records from 1899. For Trim some Corporation records for the seventeenth and eighteenth centuries survive. There are Town Commission records from *c*. 1880 to *c*. 1929 and Urban District Council records from *c*. 1920. A quantity of Trim records was destroyed during an occupation of the Town Hall in September 1920.

Other items of interest include newspapers, including the *Meath Herald*, 1845–96; *Meath Chronicle*, 1904–present (microfilm and hard copy); *Meath People*, August 1857–1863 (on microfilm); the *Irish Peasant*, February 1904 (one issue), 1903–6 (on microfilm); and the *Drogheda Independent*, 1924–48 (on microfilm).

The 1901 census for County Meath is available on microfilm, as are the 1911 census returns; there are also the surviving fragments of the 1821 census for 19 parishes in the baronies of Upper and Lower Navan and a register of persons planting trees in the county, 1814.

LOCATION
Town centre, opposite the bus stop. Public car parks on Circular Road, Fair Green and at the adjacent County Hall.

MEATH HERITAGE AND GENEALOGY CENTRE

Town Hall, Castle Street
TRIM, COUNTY MEATH
Ireland

TELEPHONE: (046) 943 6633; FAX: (046) 943 7502
E-mail: meathhc@iol.ie
Website: www.meathroots.com

HOURS
M–Th, 9.00am–5.00pm; F, 9.00am–2.00pm

ACCESS AND SERVICES
The Meath Heritage and Genealogy Centre offers a fee based record search service for those interested in tracing their family roots in County Meath. Enquirers to this centre can expect a reply within about two weeks. A copy of the centre's application form can be found on website. €30 euro (or equivalent) fee required for initial search. Common surnames in Meath include: Reilly, Smith, Lynch, Brady, Farrell, Farrelly, Kelly, O'Brien, Daly and Maguire. Chief towns include: Navan, Trim, Kells, Slane and Dunshaughlin. The centre offers a range of publications, including: *Trace your Meath Ancestors*; *The Boyne*; *The Battle of the Boyne*; *Trim*; and *Wellington*.

CONTACT
Noel E. French

DESCRIPTION
Meath Heritage and Genealogy Centre is the IFHF's designated research centre for
the County of Meath. The IFHF is the coordinating body for a network of
government approved genealogical research centres in the Republic of Ireland and in
Northern Ireland that have computerised tens of millions of Irish ancestral records of
different types.

HOLDINGS
The centre has computerised over 400,000 records to date. Church records
computerised include: Roman Catholic records from 1742, Church of Ireland
records from 1698 and Presbyterian records for Kells from 1873. Census returns
have also been computerised.

LOCATION
Town centre, beside Trim Castle.

COUNTY MONAGHAN

MONAGHAN COUNTY LIBRARY

The Diamond
CLONES, COUNTY MONAGHAN
Ireland

TELEPHONE: (047) 51143; FAX: (047) 51863
E-mail: moncolib@monaghancoco.ie
Website: www.monaghan.ie/library

HOURS
M, 2.00pm–5.00pm, 6.00pm–8.00pm; Tu–W, F, 11.00am–1.00pm,
2.00pm–5.00pm; Th, 2.00–5.00pm

ACCESS AND SERVICES
Visitors welcome, but ID required. Borrowing privileges for visitors available.
Consult Librarian. The library provides a genealogical reference service. Free internet
access for all members, 45 minutes per day. Annual membership fee, €3.

CONTACT
Joe McElvaney, County Librarian. E-mail: jmcelvaney@monaghancoco.ie
For local history queries, e-mail: clennon@monaghancoco.ie

DESCRIPTION
Headquarters library in Clones, with the building of a new headquarters
commencing in 2006. There are five branch libraries: the others are Ballybay,
Carrickmacross, Castleblayney and Monaghan Town.

HOLDINGS
Good local history collection, supported by a general collection of Irish interest, with
strong genealogical resources. Sources include: 1901 and 1911 censuses for County
Monaghan (on microfilm); *Griffith's Valuation*; tithe applotment books; gravestone
inscriptions recorded in printed sources for Catholic, Church of Ireland and
Presbyterian cemeteries throughout much of the county; street directories for
County Monaghan, including *Pigot's Directory* (1824), *Ulster Counties Directory*
(1895), *Gillespies County Monaghan Directory* (1897), *Monaghan County Alphabetical
List* (1900), *Monaghan County Yearbook* (1913), *Northern Standard Centenary
Supplement Directory* (1939), *MacDonalds Irish Directory* (1952) and *Members of the*

Established Church in Clones (1823); rentals, including Anketell Estate, 1784–1876 and Newbliss Estate, 1840–3 and 1852–3; parish histories; GAA club histories; and family histories.

Newspaper holdings include: *Northern Standard,* 1839–present; *People's Advocate,* 1876–1906; *Farney Leader,* 1908–9; *Clones Weekly Chronicle,* July 1883–November 1883; *Monaghan People,* 1906–8; *Anglo Celt,* 1885–1928; and *Dundalk Democrat,* 1849–1950.

LOCATION
Town centre. Clones is the most ancient of the towns in County Monaghan, built around the site of a sixth century monastery founded by St Tiarnach.

THE HERITAGE CENTRE

St Louis Convent
MONAGHAN
Ireland

TELEPHONE: (047) 83529; FAX: (047) 84907

HOURS
M–Tu, Th–F, 10.00am–12.00pm, 2.00pm–4.00pm; Sa–Su, 2.00–4.00pm

ACCESS AND SERVICES
Privately funded heritage centre open to the public for a modest admission fee. Disabled access facilities. The centre offers a permanent exhibition, which features documents, books, artefacts, crafts, newspapers, paintings, tapestries and photographs tracing the history of the St Louis women and their work. The sisters have been an integral part of County Monaghan and surrounding areas for almost 150 years and this exhibition documents not only their lives but also the life of this broader community, especially its social, educational and religious heritage. The exhibition also features documents and photographs of the order's overseas missions, including its schools in California, Brazil, Ghana and Nigeria.

CONTACT
Sr Mona Lally, Director

DESCRIPTION
The Heritage Centre is dedicated to the conservation and preservation of the historical, artistic and cultural heritage of the St Louis sisters, a Roman Catholic religious order of women founded in France in 1842. The origins of the community date back to the end of the French Revolution. The sisters formerly operated an industrial school and a boarding school for girls, and continue to operate a junior school and a large secondary day school.

HOLDINGS
The centre maintains a special collection that includes documents; liturgical and devotional items; crafts, including nineteenth century Belleek china and some magnificent Carrickmacross lace; antiques; and archival material, including records of members of the religious community, students and industrial school children. Records may be restricted. Consult Director.

LOCATION
On the grounds of the Monaghan convent, founded in 1859 by Mother Genevieve
Beale (1820–78), near the town centre.

MONAGHAN ANCESTRY

Clogher Historical Society, St Macartan's College
MONAGHAN
Ireland

TELEPHONE: (087) 631 0360 (for appointment only)
E-mail: admin@clogherhistoricalsoc.com
Website: www.irishroots.net/monaghan

HOURS
By appointment

ACCESS AND SERVICES
Visitors welcome by appointment, but postal enquiries preferred. Monaghan
Ancestry offers a fee based genealogical research service for those interested in tracing
their Monaghan roots. Estimates of costs made based on availability of records,
estimated time involved in preparing a report and format in which information is
required. Monaghan Ancestry publishes the annual *Clogher Record*, the journal of the
Clogher Historical Society. Clogher Diocese covers County Monaghan, County
Fermanagh, South County Tyrone and a small portion of County Donegal around
Bundoran and Ballyshannon. The journal, issued worldwide, is devoted to the
religious, social, economic, genealogical, archaeological and political history of the
diocese. Other publications include: *Old Monaghan 1785–1995*; Denis Carolan
Rushe, *History of Monaghan for Two Hundred Years, 1660–1860* (reissue); and James
Murnane and Peadar Murnane, *History of Ballybay*. Works currently in progress
include a new book on Clones parish and a book on the civil parishes of County
Monaghan.

CONTACT
Theo McMahon

DESCRIPTION
Monaghan Ancestry is the designated Irish Family History Foundation research
centre for County Monaghan. The IFHF is the coordinating body for a network of
government approved genealogical research centres in the Republic of Ireland and in
Northern Ireland that have computerised tens of millions of Irish ancestral records of
different types.

HOLDINGS
Monaghan Ancestry has computerised all Roman Catholic baptism and marriage
records, from their commencement up to and including 1880. Other sources include
tithe applotment books for 22 of the 23 civil parishes. Only one parish, Tydavnet,
does not have a detailed return in this series. Other records include: *Griffith's
Valuation*, 1858–61; the 1901 census for Counties Monaghan, Fermanagh and
Tyrone; gravestone inscriptions; international genealogical index, 1988 and 1992;
Royal Irish Constabulary records, 1816–1921; civil records (non-Roman Catholic)
of marriages for most parishes, 1845–1900; old age pension claims, some with

abstracts from the 1841 and 1851 censuses; rentals of the Rose Estate, Tydavnet, 1839–47 (these compensate to some extent for the loss of the Tithe Applotment Book for certain townlands in this parish); Templeton Estate rentals (mostly in Muckno parish) for 1805; Forster Estate rentals for certain townlands, 1802–8; Murray Ker Estate rentals (Kileevan/Newbliss), 1881–1911 and 1937; Kane Estate rentals, 1764; Famine Relief Books for Donagh and Errigal Truagh parishes by townland, January–May 1847; Dunaghmoyne vaccination register, 1869–84; index to Clogher wills, 1659–1857; Lennard Barrett Estate records and rentals for Clones, 1682–1845. In addition, the centre maintains a reference library, which includes all publications of the Clogher Historical Society, 1953–present.

LOCATION
Near town centre, in a private residence.

MONAGHAN COUNTY MUSEUM

1–2 Hill Street
MONAGHAN
Ireland

TELEPHONE: (047) 82928; FAX: (047) 71189
E-mail: comuseum@monaghancoco.ie
Website: www.monaghan.ie

HOURS
M–F, 11.00am–5.00pm; Sa, 12.00pm–5.00pm

ACCESS AND SERVICES
Visitors welcome. Free admission. Limited disabled access facilities. Access to archives by appointment only. Photocopying services available for a modest fee. The museum offers an award winning exhibitions programme, featuring material dating from c. 5000 BC to the present. Of special interest is Cross of Clogher, a fourteenth century oak cross decorated with bronze and semi-precious metals. Museum also houses a fine collection of early medieval crannog (lake dwelling) artefacts.

CONTACT
Liam Bradley, Curator

DESCRIPTION
Monaghan County Museum was established in 1974 by Monaghan County Council. It moved into its present quarters in 1986. It was the first local authority county museum in the Irish Republic and gained distinction in 1980 and 1993 by winning two European and Irish museum awards. The Monaghan County Museum received the Irish Museum of the Year Award for Best Collections Care, 2004. The museum collects the material heritage of County Monaghan, has a mainly Irish art collection and keeps some limited archive material that may be consulted by prior appointment.

HOLDINGS
In addition to artefacts and paintings, the museum has a small archive focusing on County Monaghan records. These include estate papers, some of which extend beyond the boundaries of Monaghan; Monaghan County Council minutes, rate books and ledgers, 1899–1959; Monaghan Urban District Council records; and

personal papers, including those of Charles Gavan Duffy (1816–1903). *See also* Franciscan Library Killiney for more information about Duffy records (specifically those of George Gavan Duffy, son of Charles), in the care of University College Dublin – Archives Department. The museum recently acquired a book of maps dating to 1791 of the Clermont Estate, which later became the Rossmore Estate covering the extended area around Monaghan Town. The book contains 90 maps of the estate's holdings, with detailed records of each tenant.

LOCATION
Town centre. Located on a hillside, across from Market House. Public car parks nearby.

COUNTY OFFALY

IRISH MIDLANDS ANCESTRY
(LAOIS AND OFFALY FAMILY HISTORY RESEARCH CENTRE)

Bury Quay
TULLAMORE, COUNTY OFFALY
Ireland

TELEPHONE: (0506) 21421
E-mail: info@offalyhistory.com; info@irishmidlandsancestry.com
Website: www.irishmidlandsancestry

HOURS
M–F, 9.00am–4.00pm

ACCESS AND SERVICES
The centre offers a fee based, full range genealogical research service. Appointments preferred for consultations at €25 per hour (deductible from further fees). Reports range from €149 to €300 plus postage. Initial enquiries are answered promptly; research usually takes from four to six weeks. The centre has indexed some 750,000 records in its database. Application form is available on the centre's website. Main surnames associated with Counties Laois and Offaly include: Kelly, Dunne, Molloy, Carroll, Egan, Dempsey, O'Connor, Daly, Fitzpatrick and Lalor. Principal towns include: (Offaly) Tullamore, Birr, Clara, Edenderry; (Laois) Portarlington, Portlaoise, Mountmellick and Mountrath. Publications offered by the centre include: *The Long Ridge* (Killeigh); *Quakers of Mount Mellick*; *Falling into Wretchedness: Ferbane, County Offaly in the Famine Times*; *Clara Parish: Burials from the Earliest Times*; and *Durrow in History*. Prices are exclusive of shipping and handling. See publications list at: www.offalyhistory.com/content/reading_resources/sale_publications/esker_press.

CONTACT
John Kearney, Coordinator

DESCRIPTION
Irish Midlands Ancestry, under the aegis of Offaly Historical and Archaeological Society, is the Irish Family History Foundation's designated research centre for the counties of Laois (formerly Queen's County) and Offaly (formerly King's County). The IFHF is the coordinating body for a network of government approved

genealogical research centres in the Republic of Ireland and in Northern Ireland that have computerised tens of millions of Irish ancestral records of different types.

HOLDINGS
The centre has indexed all available church records in the Laois and Offaly area. The earliest Roman Catholic parish records date from 1763. The earliest Church of Ireland records date from 1699 and the latest from 1876. Methodist records begin in 1830. Other material indexed includes: civil records for Laois and Offaly, 1864–1900; the Birr Workhouse register; births, marriages and deaths recorded in the *King's County Chronicle* newspaper (1845–65) and the *Leinster Express* (1831–51); entries in trade directories for the period 1788–1908; and the Geashill Estate rental for 1883.

LOCATION
Town centre, next to Tullamore Dew Heritage Centre.

OFFALY COUNTY LIBRARY – LOCAL STUDIES AND ARCHIVES SERVICE

O'Connor Square
TULLAMORE, COUNTY OFFALY
Ireland

TELEPHONE: (057) 934 6834; FAX: (057) 935 2769
E-mail: libraryhq@offalycoco.ie
Website: www.offaly.ie, librarysearch.offaly.ie (catalogue)

ACCESS AND SERVICES
Appointment is necessary to consult any item in Reading Room. Photocopying service available subject to copyright law. Restrictions may also apply in cases where material is sensitive or fragile. Microfilm reader/printer service provided.

CONTACT
Executive Librarian, County Library Headquarters

DESCRIPTION
The Local Studies and Archives Department holds a rich collection of material relating to Offaly's past.

HOLDINGS
The collection includes extant local government archives, private papers, local newspapers from the mid-nineteenth century to the present day, photographs and other images, maps and plans, local folk songs, printed books, journals and other media relating to the history and heritage of the county.

For general information on the collections, visitors should consult the staff of the Reading Room. Staff will take telephone enquiries, although more complex enquiries should be made by letter or e-mail. It is the library's policy to assist and facilitate visitors in their research but not to undertake research.

Researchers can consult the online library database for printed and other local sources and also the following publications by Offaly County Council, County Library Service: Murphy, Coughlan and Doran, *Grand Jury Rooms to Áras an Chontae: Local Government in Offaly* (Tullamore, 2003); Murphy, *Edenderry: a Leinster Town* (Tullamore, 2004); Fitzpatrick, *School, Community and Nation: the Papers of R.H. Moore, 1899–1956* (Tullamore, 2005)

LOCATION
Town centre.

OFFALY HISTORICAL AND ARCHAEOLOGICAL SOCIETY
See IRISH MIDLANDS ANCESTRY, Tullamore

COUNTY ROSCOMMON

GENERAL REGISTER OFFICE

Government Offices, Convent Road
ROSCOMMON
Ireland

Note: While the GRO has moved to Roscommon Town, the Research Room continues to be located at Joyce House, 8–11 Lombard Street East, Dublin. *See* note at General Register Office, Dublin.

TELEPHONE: (090) 663 2900; FAX: (090) 663 2999
E-mail: use responder form on website
Website: www.groireland.ie

HOURS
M–F, 9.30am–4.30pm; closed bank holidays

ACCESS AND SERVICES
Visitors welcome in Research Room on first come, first served basis. For €2, researchers can do a five year search of a given type of index book (births, marriages or deaths); for €20 they can gain access to all index volumes for up to six successive hours. Index books contain references to microfilm records of actual register entries, copies of which are then available from staff at a cost of €4 each. Copies may not always be available on the day ordered; limit of five copies per person per day. Additional copies posted out within two weeks. Details of type and extent of records held by the GRO can be found on its website. Birth certificate contains the date and place of birth, forename, father's name, place of residence and occupation, mother's name and maiden surname, and the name and address of the person who registered the birth. Death certificate contains name and address of the deceased person, date and place of death, marital status, occupation, age at last birthday, cause of death, and the name and address of the person who registered the death. A pre-1957 marriage certificate contains the date and place of marriage, the age, name and marital status, occupation and pre-marriage address, father's name and occupation of both spouses. A post-1957 marriage certificate contains the date and place of marriage, the age, name, marital status, occupation, pre-marriage address, parents' names of both spouses and the couple's future intended place of residence. Requests for certificates should be made in writing, including as many details as

possible of the event(s) in question. Mastercard and Visa credit cards accepted in person, by post or by fax. See website for details. GRO accepts personal cheques/bank drafts, international money orders and Irish postal orders denominated in euro. Note: euro denominated personal cheques, bank drafts or international money orders must be drawn on a branch of a bank located in the Republic of Ireland and be acceptable for clearance through the Irish cheque clearing system. Cash should be sent by registered post. There is ordinarily a five to six week backlog, though requests may be processed more expeditiously for good cause. The GRO does not provide research assistance.

CONTACT
Research staff

DESCRIPTION
The GRO is solely concerned with the administration of the civil registration system in Ireland. It provides photocopies or certified copies of entries in its birth, death or marriage registers on receipt of a postal application accompanied by the appropriate fee. The records and index are in a manual format, arranged chronologically, so specific details, especially dates, are needed for a search. Other details, such as the location of the event, the parents' names and the mother's maiden name of the ancestor in question, are helpful.

Fee Schedule (2006)
Please check website, as fees are subject to change.
Certificates (including particular search fees): birth, death, marriage, short birth, €10; additional copies, €8.
Authentication of an existing certificate, €10; additional copies, €10.
Search and photocopy of an entry in the register, €6; additional copies, €4.

HOLDINGS
The GRO holds index books for birth, death and marriage records after 1864 and microfilm records of the actual register entries. Note: for baptisms, marriages and burials prior to 1864, the only source for registration (except for non-Roman Catholic marriages, which have been civilly registered since 1845) is parish registers. To use these resources effectively, it is necessary to know the religious affiliation and often even the place of baptism, marriage or burial of the ancestor. Roman Catholic parish registers are still held by the parish priest, but most dating up until 1880 are available on microfilm in the National Library of Ireland. Access may require the written permission of the parish priest. Church of Ireland parish registers dating up until 1870 are public records. Most are still held in the local parishes, while some are held at the National Library of Ireland, Dublin, the Representative Church Body Library, Dublin, or the Public Record Office of Northern Ireland, Belfast. Presbyterian records are arranged by congregation and enquiries should be directed to the Presbyterian Historical Society, Belfast.

LOCATION
Town centre, close to the N63 and N61, near Abbey Street and the Roscommon County Library.

ROSCOMMON COUNTY LIBRARY

Abbey Street
ROSCOMMON, Ireland

TELEPHONE: (090) 663 7271; FAX: (090) 663 7101
E-mail: roslib@iol.ie
Website: www.iol.ie/~roslib

HOURS
Tu, Th, 1.00pm–8.00pm; W, 1.00pm–5.00pm; F–Sa, 10.00am–1.00pm,
2.00–5.00pm

ACCESS AND SERVICES
Visitors welcome, but borrowing privileges may be restricted. Photocopying services
available.

CONTACT
Richard Farrell, County Librarian

DESCRIPTION
Headquarters library for the county system, which also includes branches in
Castlerea, Boyle, Elphin, Strokestown, Ballaghaderreen and Ballyforan.

HOLDINGS
In addition to the usual collection of educational and recreational material, the
library houses a very fine local history and genealogy collection and archive. Archival
material includes: Board of Guardian minutes for Boyle, Castlerea, Roscommon and
Strokestown; Rural District Council minutes for Athlone No. 2, Boyle, Carrick-on-
Shannon, Castlerea, Roscommon and Strokestown; minutes of the Boyle Dispensary
District, Roscommon Board of Health (including acting for Athlone Rural District
Council), Roscommon County Council, Roscommon Pension Committee and
Roscommon Town Commissioners; Strokestown Rural District Council Labourers'
Acts (acting as Rural Sanitary Authority); and Roscommon Grand Jury records.
Newspapers on microfilm include: *Boyle Gazette and Roscommon Reporter*, 1891;
Dublin Penny Journal, 1832–6; *Irishman*, 1819–25; *The Nation*, 1842–52;
Roscommon Constitutionalist, 1889–91; *Roscommon Herald*, 1882–present;
Roscommon Journal and Western Impartial Reporter, 1828–1927; *Roscommon Weekly
Messenger and Roscommon Messenger*, 1848–1935; *Western Nationalist* (later
continued as the *Roscommon Champion*), 1907–20; and *Strokestown Democrat*,
1913–48. Several of the newspapers are available in hardbound copies. The library
also houses microfilm copies of other material of local interest, including *History of
Roscommon* (one reel); *Irish Topographical Prints and Original Drawings* (three reels);
Monasteries of Roscommon (one reel); Moran Manuscripts, 1548–50 (two reels); Rev
John Keogh's *Statistical Account of Co. Roscommon* (originally drawn up for Sir
William Petty's Down Survey, 1683); and the Irish Folklore Commission Schools
Collection (1937/8) for Roscommon (14 reels).

LOCATION
Town centre.

COUNTY ROSCOMMON HERITAGE AND GENEALOGY COMPANY

Church Street
STROKESTOWN, COUNTY ROSCOMMON
Ireland

TELEPHONE: (0719) 633 380; FAX: (0719) 633 398
E-mail: info@roscommonroots.com
Website: www.irishroots.net/roscmmn, www.roscommonroots.com

HOURS
M–F, 2.30pm–4.30pm

ACCESS AND SERVICES
The County Roscommon Heritage and Genealogy Company offers fee based, full
range genealogical research service to persons interested in tracing their family roots
in County Roscommon. Enquiries usually answered in about four to six weeks, but
during the summer season it may take slightly longer. Application form available
through website, where details of service provided and charges also listed. Common
surnames in County Roscommon are: Hanley, Beirne, Kelly, Brennan, Connor,
Flynn, Cox, McDermott, Brady and Farrell. Chief towns and villages in County
Roscommon include: Roscommon, Strokestown, Boyle, Elphin, Loughlynn,
Ballaghadereen, Castlerea and Knockcroghery.

CONTACT
Mary Skelly

DESCRIPTION
The County Roscommon Heritage and Genealogy Company is the designated Irish
Family History Foundation centre serving County Roscommon. The IFHF is the
coordinating body for a network of government approved genealogical research
centres in the Republic of Ireland and in Northern Ireland that have computerised
tens of millions of Irish ancestral records of different types.

HOLDINGS
The company has access to over 1,000,000 genealogical records relating to the
county. Main records include: Roman Catholic records starting between 1789 and
1865 depending on the parish; Church of Ireland records starting between 1796 and
1877 depending on the parish; Presbyterian records starting between 1857 and
1861; and Methodist records starting in the early 1840s. The company has also
computerised *Griffith's Valuation*; tithe applotment books; a list of '40 shilling
freeholders' for 1876; Pakenham-Mahon eviction lists from 1847; and Royal Irish
Constabulary records. The earliest census available that covers a large part of County
Roscommon dates from 1749. The company also holds civil records of birth,
marriage and deaths for the county from 1864 to 1900.

LOCATION
Town centre.

COUNTY SLIGO

COUNTY SLIGO HERITAGE AND GENEALOGY SOCIETY

Aras Reddan, Temple Street
SLIGO
Ireland

TELEPHONE: (071) 43728
E-mail: heritagesligo@eircom.net
Website: www.sligoroots.com

HOURS
M–F, 9.00am–5.00pm

ACCESS AND SERVICES
Visitors welcome. Full research enquiries might take up to two months to complete, but initial enquiries answered as soon as possible. See website for application form. Initial search fee €75 required for full search. The centre also provides a single record search facility which may meet requirements for a fee of €25 or its equivalent in other currencies (approximately US$30/£20 sterling). The centre can e-mail this record on receipt of appropriate fee. Payment may be made in the form of personal cheque, postal order or money order made payable to Sligo Heritage and Genealogy Centre. Payment by credit card (Visa or Mastercard) also acceptable. Please telephone or e-mail with details. However, please be advised that the centre's e-mail or website is not secure for sending credit card information.

The centre offers for sale a large selection of books of genealogical and local history interest.

CONTACT
Adrian Regan, Manager

DESCRIPTION
The society is the designated Irish Family History Foundation centre for County Sligo. IFHF centres aim to create a comprehensive database of genealogical sources that are known to exist, including church records of all denominations, civil records, land valuations, census records, gravestone inscriptions and various other local sources. The Sligo centre offers a genealogical research service for County Sligo. Common surnames in County Sligo include: Gallagher, Brennan, MacGowan, Kelly,

Gilmartin, Healy, Walsh, Hart, Feeney and MacDonagh. Towns in County Sligo include Sligo Town, Ballymote, Tobercurry and Collooney.

HOLDINGS
The society has collected more than 400,000 records relating to County Sligo. These have been computerised and are available on the database at the centre. These records include church records (Roman Catholic dating back to 1796, Church of Ireland dating back to 1762, Presbyterian dating back to 1806 and Methodist dating back to 1819); the 1901 census; *Griffith's Valuation*, 1858; tithe applotment books, 1823–37; the Elphin diocesan census of 1749; gravestone inscriptions; and various other genealogical sources.

LOCATION
In the North-West Tourism Complex, Sligo town centre.

SLIGO COUNTY LIBRARY

Westward Town Centre Complex, Bridge Street
SLIGO
Ireland

TLEPHONE: (071) 914 7190, (071) 915 5060; FAX: (071) 914 6798
E-mail: sligolib@sligococo.ie
Website: www.sligococo.ie/asp/services/services.asp (Click on 'County Library')

HOURS
M–F: 10.00am–12.45pm, 2.00pm–4.45pm

ACCESS AND SERVICES
Visitors welcome. No admission fees. Disabled access. Collection catalogued online in 2002. Printed catalogue and finding aids available. Publications include: John C. McTernan (ed.), *Sligo: Sources of Local History: a Catalogue of the Local History Collection, with an Introduction and Guide to Sources*, new edition (Sligo, 1994); D. Tinney (ed.), *Jack B. Yeats at the Niland Gallery Sligo*; and Hilary Pyle, *The Sligo–Leitrim World of Kate Cullen*.

CONTACT
See e-mail

DESCRIPTION
The main library for Sligo Town and County Sligo, with four additional service points.

HOLDINGS
In addition to the standard general collection, the library offers a good local history collection focusing on Sligo, the Yeats family, Countess Markievicz and the Gore-Booth family and the archaeology of Sligo. There is also a collection of newspapers published in Sligo from 1822 to the present. Special collections include those on: W.B. Yeats, Jack B. Yeats, Countess Markievicz, autographs and local authors.

Genealogical holdings for County Sligo include recordings of all gravestone inscriptions in some 150 graveyards in the county.

The Sligo Corporation Archive includes rate books, *c.* 1842–1977.

For landed estates there are some 90 volumes in the archive of an estate agent named Robinson who managed many estates in the county. This includes rentals for various estates from *c.* 1850.

There are also parish records (not complete), directories and details of World War I dead. There are microfilm copies of the 1901 census for County Sligo, tithe survey 1823–38, and also a set of the printed *Griffith's Valuation* for the county, *c.* 1855.

LOCATION
Ground floor section of the Westward Town Centre Complex, Sligo town centre.

COUNTY TIPPERARY

BRÚ BORÚ HERITAGE CENTRE

Rock of Cashel
CASHEL, COUNTY TIPPERARY
Ireland

TELEPHONE: (062) 61122; FAX: (062) 62700
E-mail: bruboru@comhaltas.com
Website: www.irishroots.net/stipp, www.comhaltas.com

HOURS
May–September: M–F, 9.00am–5.00pm
October–April: M–W, 9.30am–4.30pm

ACCESS AND SERVICES
The Brú Ború Heritage Centre offers a fee based full genealogical service to enquirers, with access to church, civil, land and census records for South Tipperary. Initial enquiries usually receive a reply within one month. Application form is available on the centre's website. The initial search fee, to accompany the form, is €75. Fees vary.

CONTACT
Deirdre Walsh

DESCRIPTION
Brú Ború Heritage Centre is the designated Irish Family History Foundation centre serving South Tipperary. The IFHF is the coordinating body for a network of government approved genealogical research centres in the Republic of Ireland and in Northern Ireland that have computerised tens of millions of Irish ancestral records of different types. Brú Ború, which means the Palace of Ború, is a cultural and interpretative village designed around a village green dedicated to the study and celebration of Irish music, song, dance, storytelling, theatre and Celtic studies. Common surnames in South Tipperary include: Ryan, Dwyer, Maher, O'Brien, Hayes, Quirke, Treacy, O'Meara, Macken, Maloney, Lonergan and Kearney. Main towns in South Tipperary include: Cashel, Cahir, Tipperary, Clonmel and Carrick-on-Suir.

HOLDINGS

The centre currently has computerised about 600,000 genealogical records. Main records include: Roman Catholic records, the earliest of which date from 1792; Church of Ireland records, some of which date from 1755; Methodist records dating from 1834; Tithe Applotment and *Griffith's Valuation* lists; civil birth, death and marriage records, 1864–1911; gravestone inscriptions for all of North Tipperary; and the 1901 census. Note: church and civil records terminate in 1900 or 1911. In addition to the main sources, the centre has also computerised Civil Survey and hearth money rolls (seventeenth century); street directories (nineteenth and twentieth century); encumbered estates records for Nenagh, 1854; Vestry Book for Borrisokane (nineteenth century); Poor Law rate books for Nenagh and Thurles Poor Law Unions, 1840s; and births, deaths and marriages in the *Nenagh Guardian*, 1838–66.

LOCATION

In the former residence of the County Gaol Governor (1842–86), which has been a convent, a secondary school and, since 1984, a heritage centre.

CASHEL AND EMLY ARCHDIOCESAN ARCHIVES (ROMAN CATHOLIC)

Archbishop's House
THURLES, COUNTY TIPPERARY
Ireland

TELEPHONE: (0504) 21512; FAX: (0504) 22680
E-mail: office@cashel-emly.ie
Website: homepage.eircom.net/~cashelemly/genealog

HOURS

Closed to visitors

ACCESS AND SERVICES

Parish records available through Tipperary Family History Research Centre (*see* separate entry). Originals made available only in exceptional circumstances.

CONTACT

Tipperary Family History Research Centre, Excel Centre, Mitchell Street, Tipperary. Telephone: (062) 80555; fax: (062) 80552; e-mail: research@tfhr.org; website: www.tfhr.org

HOLDINGS

Archives houses archdiocesan records, including parish records of marriages and baptisms, for the Roman Catholic Archdiocese of Cashel and Emly. This includes parishes in parts of North and South Tipperary and South-East Limerick. There are 46 parishes in all, with some records dating back to the late 1700s.

LOCATION

Archbishop's House, Thurles.

TIPPERARY LIBRARIES – TIPPERARY STUDIES

Thurles Regional Arts Centre and Library (from mid-2006)
THURLES, COUNTY TIPPERARY
Ireland

TELEPHONE: (0504) 21555; FAX: (0504) 23442
E-mail: studies@tipperarylibraries.ie
Website: www.tipperarylibraries.ie

HOURS
To be confirmed

ACCESS AND SERVICES
Visitors welcome. Disabled access facilities. Laptops permitted. Small fee charged for photocopies and microfilm copies. It is advisable to book microfilm equipment in advance. Certain archival material may not be copied. Internet and e-mail services also available.

It is planned to publish a guide to the sources available through Tipperary Studies in the Autumn 2006 entitled *Finding Tipperary*. Consult website for further details.

CONTACT
Mary Guinan-Darmody
John O'Gorman

DESCRIPTION
Tipperary libraries is the main public library for County Tipperary. It also serves as the headquarters for the County Tipperary Historical Society. Information regarding the society may be accessed through the Tipperary libraries website.

HOLDINGS
Tipperary Studies houses a large collection of published titles relating to all aspects of County Tipperary or written by Tipperary authors, as well as a comprehensive collection of newspapers from the county both in hard copy and on microfilm. Some titles such as the *Tipperary Star*, *Nationalist* and the *Guardian* are still being published, however. Much of the microfilm collection includes nineteenth century papers from all the major towns in County Tipperary. Maps of the county, including the first edition Ordnance Survey maps and *Griffith's Valuation* maps, are available on a database for consultation. Recent acquisitions include a historical postcards collection and a small photographic collection.

Genealogical sources include the 1901 and 1911 census returns; *Griffith's Valuation*; tithe applotment books; Board of Guardian material for almost all the Poor Law Unions in the county; the Religious Census, 1766; hearth money records, 1665–7; the Grand Jury presentments, *c.* 1840–1910, for North Tipperary; and some landed estate records. The Carrick-on-Suir Poor Law Union material is held by Kilkenny County Library.

LOCATION
Town centre.

TIPPERARY FAMILY HISTORY RESEARCH CENTRE

Excel Heritage Centre, Mitchell Street
TIPPERARY
Ireland

TELEPHONE: (062) 80555; FAX: (062) 80552
E-mail: research@tfhr.org
Website: www.tfhr.org

HOURS
M–F, 9.30am–4.30pm; closed bank holidays

ACCESS AND SERVICES
Visitors welcome. Free consultation provided. Fees for research services. Internet access available for a small fee.

CONTACT
Charlotte Crowe

DESCRIPTION
Tipperary Family History Research Centre, established in April 2001 as successor to Tipperary Heritage Unit, conducts research within the records of the Cashel and Emly Archdiocesan Archives (Roman Catholic), Thurles, County Tipperary.

HOLDINGS
Over 600,000 marriage and baptismal records, representing all 46 parishes that make up the Archdiocese of Cashel and Emly, have been indexed to date. The archdiocese includes parishes in parts of North and South Tipperary and South-East Limerick. Some records date back to the late 1700s, but the vast majority date from the 1800s.

LOCATION
Excel Heritage Centre, town centre. From Main Street turn onto St Michael's Street and take first left onto Mitchell Street.

COUNTY TYRONE

IRISH WORLD FAMILY HISTORY CENTRE

Family History Suite, 51 Dungannon Road
COALISLAND, COUNTY TYRONE, BT71 4HP
Northern Ireland

TELEPHONE: (028) 8774 6065
E-mail: info@irish-world.com
Website: www.irish-world.com

HOURS
M–F, 10.00am–4.00pm; appointment preferred

ACCESS AND SERVICES
Visitors welcome. In addition to providing full fee based genealogy research service, Irish World offers a range of heritage related products such as full colour coats of arms and publications on local history. The centre also has an online index to nearly half a million gravestone inscriptions from some 700 graveyards across historic Ulster.

CONTACT
Willie O'Kane, Research Consultant

DESCRIPTION
Irish World is the designated Irish Family History Foundation centre for Counties Tyrone and Fermanagh.

HOLDINGS
Irish World holds computerised baptism, marriage and death records for 22 Roman Catholic parishes, most dating up until the year 1900. Starting dates vary significantly, the earliest being 1783. Computerised records for five pre-1901 Church of Ireland parishes also vary, the oldest dating to 1801. The computerised records for Presbyterian parishes reflect only baptisms and marriages, with the earliest dating to 1821. See website for specific parishes and inclusive dates. Other sources include: civil records of births and deaths, 1864–1921, for Counties Fermanagh and Tyrone; civil records of marriages, 1845–1921, for Counties Fermanagh and Tyrone; 1901 census for Counties Fermanagh and Tyrone; *Griffith's Valuation* for all of Ireland; tithe applotment books for Counties Antrim, Armagh,

Londonderry, Down, Fermanagh, Tyrone, Monaghan, Cavan and Donegal; gravestone inscriptions for over 900 cemeteries in Counties Antrim, Armagh, Derry, Down, Fermanagh and Tyrone; list of flax growers for all of Ireland, 1796; crime and punishment records for all of Ireland, 1799–1800; transportation registers for all Ireland, 1839–57; and index to RIC records for all of Ireland, 1816–1921.

LOCATION
Town centre.

CENTRE FOR MIGRATION STUDIES

Ulster American Folk Park, 2 Mellon Road, Castletown
OMAGH, COUNTY TYRONE, BT78 5QY
Northern Ireland

TELEPHONE: (028) 8225 6315; FAX: (028) 8224 2241
E-mail: centremigstudies@ni-libraries.net
Website: www.qub.ac.uk/cms

HOURS
M–F, 10.30am–5.00pm; closed public holidays

ACCESS AND SERVICES
Visitors welcome at no charge. Reference only library collection. Disabled access. Collection catalogued on cards. New stock currently being added to the Northern Ireland online catalogue at www.ni-libraries.net. Internet access available. Charge of £1.50 for anyone who is not a registered member of the Northern Ireland Library Service.

The centre offers a master's programme on Irish migration studies through Queen's University Belfast, plus courses for visiting groups tailored to individual needs. It also hosts conferences, seminars and programmes on migration related topics. Staff respond to enquiries and offer advice on family history research involving migration records. Fees for photocopying and microform prints. Publications include: the autobiography of Thomas Mellon, whose family home is the nucleus of the Ulster American Folk Park, entitled *Thomas Mellon and His Times* (1994); E. Margaret Crawford (ed.) *The Hungry Stream: Essays on Emigration and Famine* (1997); and Patrick Fitzgerald and Steve Ickringill (eds), *Atlantic Crossroads: Historical Connections between Scotland, Ulster and North America* (2001). Booklets about The Ulster American Folk Park, Omagh, and the Mellon house are also available. The park offers a restaurant.

CONTACT
Christine McIvor, Senior Librarian

DESCRIPTION
The Centre for Migration Studies aims to serve the community as a leading international institution for the study of human migration, focusing on the peoples of Ireland worldwide. Migration studies is about advancing the understanding of the movement and settlement of people (including immigration, internal migration, seasonal migration and emigration) through multidisciplinary approaches (including history, politics, economics, language, literature, art and religion). The centre is a project of the Scotch-Irish Trust of Ulster, which supports the work of the Ulster

American Folk Park through partnership with the Department of Culture, Arts and Leisure, the five Education and Library Boards of Northern Ireland, Queen's University Belfast, the University of Ulster and Enterprise Ulster. CMS is a member of the Association of European Migration Institutions (www.aemi.dk) and has close links with Irish migration studies at University College Cork (migration.ucc.ie).

HOLDINGS
The CMS library contains some 11,500 volumes, 1,340 maps, plus significant holdings of journals, microforms and recordings. The focus of the collection is on Ireland and North America in the eighteenth and nineteenth centuries, and the links between the two. The collection was organised originally to support the activities of the Ulster American Folk Park and to this end the library developed strengths in the fields of agriculture, architecture, crafts and industry, social customs, biography, politics and religion. More recently the collection has expanded to cover the seventeenth and twentieth centuries and all aspects of Irish migration worldwide. Special collections of note include the CMS Irish Emigration Database, which contains some 32,500 primary source documents on all aspects of Irish emigration to North America, including Canada, from the early 1700s to the 1900s. Begun in 1988, new documents are being added to this database on a regular basis. Types of documents include ship passenger lists, emigrant letters, family papers and diaries of emigrants, shipping advertisements, newspaper reports, death and marriage notices of former emigrants, birth notices of children of Irish parentage, government reports and statistics of Irish emigration to North America. Another collection of special note is entitled The Art of European Migration, and is an image database designed to promote comparative study of the migration themes of departure, arrival and return.

The Irish Emigration Database is accessible in all Northern Ireland public libraries through the public access terminals. It is password protected so the assistance of library staff will be necessary. It is also available in PRONI under the same arrangement.

LOCATION
Ulster American Folk Park, five miles outside Omagh, on the A5 from Omagh to Strabane.

OMAGH LIBRARY

Spillars Place
OMAGH, COUNTY TYRONE, BT78 1HL
Northern Ireland

TELEPHONE: (028) 8224 4821; FAX: (028) 8224 6716
E-mail: omaghlibrary@ni-libraries.net
Website: www.ni-libraries.net

HOURS
M, W, F, 9.15am–5.30pm; Tu, Th, 9.15am–8.00pm; Sa, 9.15am–1.00pm, 2.00pm–5.00pm

ACCESS AND SERVICES
Visitors welcome, but advance notice preferred. Borrowing privileges for visitors may be restricted. Disabled access facilities. Fees for photocopying and microform prints.

Internet access available. Charge of £1.50 for anyone who is not a registered member of the Northern Ireland library service. Free leaflets and brochures available. The library is electronically linked to the emigration database of the Ulster American Folk Park, Omagh.

CONTACT
Patrick Brogan, Local History Librarian. E-mail: patrick.brogan@ni-libraries.net

DESCRIPTION
Part of the Western Education and Library Board system, Omagh is the branch library for the largest town in County Tyrone. Located in an attractive building, the Irish and Local Studies Department is especially strong.

HOLDINGS
The library houses a general educational and recreational collection, with access to some 500,000 volumes in the WELB system. The Irish and Local Studies Collection includes more than 5,000 volumes, with strong holdings of maps, microforms, journals and newspapers focusing on County Tyrone. It has all the standard genealogical reference sources for the area, including: microform copies of the 1901 census; the printed *Griffith's Valuation*, 1860; Board of Guardian minutes for Castlederg, Clogher, Omagh and Strabane, *c.* 1840–1900.

It is not generally known that the Omagh Library also holds significant collections of school records and duplicates of valuation records that have been returned from PRONI. The local valuation records now held in the Omagh Library cover the Rural District Council areas of Omagh, Castlederg, Clogher and Strabane. These volumes cover the years 1920–30, 1934–5 and 1957.

Records have also been transferred for at least six national schools in West Tyrone, including Calkill in Cappagh parish, for which there are roll books (1903–83), daily report books (1909–81), boys' and girls' registers (1931–52) and a register (1944–84). There are also roll books for this school for special subjects such as domestic economy and horticulture, a minute book and inspector's reports.

Other schools for which records are available are Beltany, Deverney (Recarson townland) and Edenderry in Cappagh parish, Carnkenny and Erganagh in Ardstraw and Tattykeeran in Clogherny parish.

LOCATION
Town centre, between Dublin Road and the Drumragh River.

ULSTER AMERICAN FOLK PARK

2 Mellon Road, Castletown
OMAGH, COUNTY TYRONE, BT78 5QY
Northern Ireland

TELEPHONE: (028) 8224 3292; FAX: (028) 8224 2241
E-mail: uafp.info@magni.org.uk
Website: www.folkpark.com

HOURS
April–September: M–Sa, 10.30am–4.30pm, (museum: 10.30am–6.00pm); Sundays and public holidays, 11.00am–5.00pm (museum: 11.00am–6.30pm)
October–March: M–F, 10.30am–3.30pm (museum: 10.30am–5.00pm; closed public holidays and Christmas–New Year period

ACCESS AND SERVICES
Visitors welcome. Admission fees apply: adults, £4.50; children (5–16 years), seniors and persons with disabilities, £2.50; families, £11.50; reduced rates available for groups. Children under five years free of charge. Educational visits must be booked in advance. Disabled access facilities. Free parking. Craft and gift shop, restaurant.

CONTACT
Evelyn Cardwell, Education Officer
Phil Mowat, Curator

DESCRIPTION
Large and sophisticated outdoor museum and indoor galleries devoted to Ireland and the New World in the eighteenth and nineteenth centuries. Restored and replicated structures, including a full scale emigrant ship, offer the visitor an opportunity to visit Ireland in the eighteenth and nineteenth centuries, board an emigrant ship and emerge in the New World. Exhibitions trace the history of the times, with special attention to agriculture, crafts, transportation and society. The original homesteads of the Mellon, Campbell, Devine, Hupp, Hughes and Fulton families are on display. The park is a wonderful place to entertain and educate children and adults. It is part of National Museums Northern Ireland, which also includes the Ulster Folk and Transport Museum, Holywood; the Ulster Museum, Belfast; and the Armagh County Museum, Armagh.

HOLDINGS
See Centre for Migration Studies, Omagh. The museum itself features exhibitions focusing on emigration, folklife of Ireland and America, agriculture, crafts, education, religion, shops and shipping, all with relevance to the eighteenth and nineteenth centuries.

LOCATION
Five miles outside Omagh, on the A5 from Omagh to Strabane.

ULSTER HISTORY PARK

Note: The Ulster History Park (150 Glenpark Road, Cullion, Lislap, Omagh, County Tyrone, BT79 7SU, Northern Ireland) closed in 2004 and the facility is in the process of being sold by Omagh District Council. It is being purchased by a consortium in the private sector, with plans to open the park again as a tourist facility in 2006. It is not known at this time if a library is planned.
From the 2002 edition: 'The Ulster History Park is a 35 acre outdoor museum that traces the history of settlement in Ireland from the arrival of the first Stone Age hunters and gatherers up to the Plantation period of the early 17th century. Full scale replicas of homes and monuments through the ages include megalithic tombs, a church and a round tower of the early Christian period, timber houses of the Stone Age farmers and reconstructions of a "rath" and crannog, homes of farmers in the first millennium AD. An indoor exhibition develops the theme of settlement and an audiovisual presentation explores the legacy of the past still visible in the landscape.'
Situated seven miles north of Omagh, on the B48 Omagh to Gortin Road.

COUNTY WATERFORD

WATERFORD COUNTY ARCHIVES SERVICE

Dungarvan Library, Davitt's Quay
DUNGARVAN, COUNTY WATERFORD
Ireland

TELEPHONE: (058) 23673; (058) 41231; FAX: (058) 42911
E-mail: archivist@waterfordcoco.ie
Website: www.waterfordcoco.ie

HOURS
Tu, 10.00am–2.00pm; F, 1.00pm–5.00pm; or by appointment

ACCESS AND SERVICES
Visitors welcome. For detailed description of services visit website. Archives Service located in library building; while no parking available immediately outside the library, parking available nearby.

CONTACT
Archivist

DESCRIPTION
The Archives Service is housed in Dungarvan Library and holds records of local authorities in County Waterford, past and present, plus private collections relating to Waterford.

A genealogist in residence was appointed for 2005 under the Celtic Trí project financed by the EU Interreg IIIA Fund to identify and make available sources for family history in the County Archives. This funding has also allowed for updates on the records available in the archive to be posted on the website and for the publication of a book entitled *Sources for Family History in Waterford County*.

HOLDINGS
The County Archives hold: Grand Jury records; Board of Guardian records; Rural District Council records (from 1899); Waterford County Council records; Dungarvan Town Council records; and private papers.

There are virtually complete sets of minute books of the Boards of Guardians for the Poor Law Unions of Dungarvan, Kilmacthomas, Lismore and Waterford, *c.* 1843–1923. There is also an unusual set of valuation books recording payments of

Grand Jury cess from 1869. Those dating up to 1875 are in annual volumes but a single large volume covers the period *c*. 1876–*c*. 1900. Since these volumes record the names of taxpayers annually, a search can show the probable year of death of a person when the name disappears. These records are arranged by barony, townland and parish.

On some estates payment of county cess was the responsibility of the landlord, in which case the names of occupiers of holdings are not given. These books thus contain fewer names of occupiers than surviving Poor Law rate books or the valuation revision books held in the Valuation Office, Middle Abbey Street, Dublin.

There is also a collection of Grand Jury records dating up until 1899 including presentments from 1865 and contract books for the period 1829–67.

Private papers include the Chearnley Papers (1671–1915), relating to lands predominantly in West Waterford; and the Hugh Ryan Papers, containing an important collection of political pamphlets relating to Irish nationalism and records relating to a survey carried out by Ryan of the gravestones of Mothel and Rathgormack. The Villiers-Stuart Papers are available on microfilm, as are papers from the Lismore (Devonshire) Estate, held in the National Library of Ireland. The County Archives hold the nineteenth century records for the Lismore Estate including rentals, tenants' application books and agents' correspondence, but these are not yet available to researchers as they are still being cleaned, sorted and listed. Also on microfilm are the tithe applotment books for County Waterford and the census records for 1901 and 1911.

LOCATION
Dungarvan Library building, town centre. Dungarvan lies between Cork City and Waterford City on the N25. There is a frequent bus service between Cork City and Dungarvan and between Waterford City and Dungarvan.

WATERFORD COUNTY LIBRARY HEADQUARTERS

Ballyanchor Road
LISMORE, COUNTY WATERFORD
Ireland

TELEPHONE: (058) 21370
E-mail: libraryhq@waterfordcoco.ie
Website: www.waterfordcountylibrary.ie

HOURS
M–F, 9.00am–5.00pm

ACCESS AND SERVICES
Visitors welcome. Disabled access facilities. Laptops permitted. Fee charged for photocopies. Free internet access.

CONTACT
Donald Brady, County Librarian

DESCRIPTION
Library headquarters mainly deals with administrative issues pertaining to the eight libraries in the county system: Cappoquin, Dungarvan, Dunmore, Kilmacthomas, Lismore, Portlaw, Tallow and Tramore. The Waterford Municipal Library, Waterford

City, is administered separately. Each library in the system offers the usual educational and recreational collections, plus access to the library system's online database and free internet access.

HOLDINGS
The library holds an impressive local studies and family history collection, of which core resources are all accessible online. Of special genealogical interest are: civil records for County Waterford, including all deaths registered from 1 January 1864 to 31 December 1901; *Griffith's Valuation*, 1848–64; gravestone inscriptions; historical trade directories, 1824–1910; war memorials; and Ordnance Survey maps and photographs. In addition, major texts, including the *Waterford and South East of Ireland Archaeological Journal* are now available on the website.

LOCATION
At the western end of Lismore, on main Killarney road.

WATERFORD CITY ARCHIVES

Waterford City Council, City Hall, The Mall
WATERFORD
Ireland

TELEPHONE: (051) 843 123; FAX: (051) 879 124
E-mail: archives@waterfordcity.ie
Website: www.waterfordcity.ie/archives

HOURS
By appointment, M–F, 9.00am–5.00pm

ACCESS AND SERVICES
Visitors welcome, but by appointment only. Readers required to complete an application form on their first visit and issued with a reader's ticket valid until the end of the calendar year. Photocopying facilities available at Archivist's discretion and depending on copyright restrictions as well as nature and condition of material in question. Much of the material has been listed and searchable databases for some categories of records are being prepared on an ongoing basis. In general Waterford City Archives cannot undertake detailed genealogical and historical searches, although it does contain material of genealogical interest. Each query will be dealt with on an individual basis, however, and where the City Archivist can help, he will do so.

CONTACT
Donal Moore, City Archivist

DESCRIPTION
Waterford City Council was the first local authority to appoint an archivist under the terms of Section 65 of the 1994 Local Government Act encouraging the establishment of local archives. A building in the centre of the medieval city was provided as a home for the City Archives and has been converted on a phased basis to provide work areas, secure storage spaces and a reading room.

HOLDINGS
The core of the archives' collections comprises material originating within Waterford
City Council (formerly Waterford Corporation) dating back to the seventeenth
century. Nevertheless, a conscious decision was made that the new facility would be
city archives and not just a repository for Waterford City Council's own records. The
archives have been given or lent a substantial number of items and collections by
groups, individuals, companies and institutions in the city and there is an active
acquisitions policy. At present the transfer or purchase of several significant
collections of archival material created in the city is being negotiated. The objective
exists also to 'repatriate' at least some of the material that left the city over the years
and is now housed in repositories outside the city. Principal holdings include:
Waterford Corporation minute books, 1654–1990s (59 volumes); Waterford
Corporation committee records, 1778–1940s (19 committees); Town Clerk's Office
records, 1700–1990s; Finance Office records, 1796–1980s; City Engineer's Office
records, 1700–1990s, including over 2,500 maps and plans (drawings) for the city
and its environs from the eighteenth century to the present, plus many reports and
photographs of completed and proposed works; estate records, 1670s–1970s,
including searchable database of expired leases of Waterford Corporation property,
1670s–1970s (over 1,100 entries); motor registration files from 1923; over 2,500
photographic prints of buildings, streets, events and people in the city,
1870s–present; school records (Mount Sion, St Patrick's, Manor (St John's) and
Presentation Primary Schools, 1880–1990s); and over 90 small, private and
institutional collections.
   Waterford City Archives also hold the records of Waterford Chamber of
Commerce (1797–1998) and Waterford Harbour Board (1816–1970s). In 2005 the
archives purchased the Annie Brophy Photographic Collection, a significant
collection of over 60,000 photographic negatives spanning the period from the
1920s to the 1970s.

LOCATION
Occupies a prominent position on High Street in the centre of the medieval city.
Part of the building dates back at least as far as the seventeenth century.

WATERFORD CITY COUNCIL CENTRAL LIBRARY

Lady Lane
WATERFORD
Ireland

TELEPHONE: (051) 849 975; FAX: (051) 850 031
E-mail: citylibrary@waterfordcity.ie
Website: www.waterfordcity.ie/library

HOURS
M–Tu, Th, Sa, 10.00am–5.30pm; W, F, 10.00am–8.00pm

ACCESS AND SERVICES
This is the main library in a three branch library system operated by the Waterford City
Council. The other branches are: Ardkeen (telephone (051) 849 755; fax (051) 874
100; hours: M, W, F, Sa, 10.00am–5.30pm, Tu, Th, 10.00am–8.00pm); Brown's Road
(telephone (051) 849 845; hours: Tu, W, F, 10.00am–1.00pm, 2.00pm–6.00pm).

All three branches have full disabled access with lifts, platform lifts, braille signs and a hearing loop in the Central Library. Catalogue available online with access to holdings and renewals for members. Service provides 50 personal computers with free internet access to members. In 2005 users logged 68,825 hourly sessions. Other services available include audio listening, television facilities, plasma information screen, optical scanning facilities and photocopying. Meeting, exhibition and lecture spaces are also available.

CONTACT
Jane Cantwell, City Librarian. E-mail: jcantwell@waterfordcity.ie

DESCRIPTION
Waterford City Council Central Library reopened in January 2004 after extensive renovation and expansion to over 2,000 square metres. It now extends to three public floors and an administrative floor at the upper level. The library has received an OPUS Building Award, an RIAI Award and the 2005 CILIP Award as winner of the Library as Heart of the Community category. The Ardkeen branch, based in a busy shopping centre, was also a winner of the 2003 CILIP Award.

HOLDINGS
The library houses 159,728 volumes. In addition to its educational and recreational holdings, the library has a solid local history and genealogical collection that includes most of the standard reference sources, such as Waterford newspapers with indices to a certain point, *Griffith's Valuation* in hard copy and on microfilm, Ordnance Survey maps for Kilkenny and Waterford City and County, the 1901 and 1911 censuses, city maps and infirmary records.

LOCATION
Central Library: city centre.
Ardkeen Library, Ardkeen Shopping Centre, Dunmore Road.
Brown's Road Library, Paddy Brown's Road.

WATERFORD HERITAGE SERVICES

St Patrick's Church, Jenkin's Lane
WATERFORD
Ireland

TELEPHONE: (051) 876 123; FAX: (051) 876 123
E-mail: mnoc@iol.ie
Website: www.waterford-heritage.ie; www.irishroots.net/waterfrd

HOURS
M–Th, 9.00am–5.00pm; F, 9.00am–2.00pm

ACCESS AND SERVICES
The Waterford Heritage and Genealogy Centre offers a fee based, full range genealogical research service for enquirers interested in tracing their roots in Waterford City and County. Application form can be found on the centre's website. The centre does commissioned work and does not have reading rooms available for the public. Chief surnames of County Waterford include: Power, Walsh, O'Brien, Murphy, Ryan, McGrath, Foley, Flynn, Morrissey, Kelly, Phelan and Sullivan. Main towns include: Waterford, Dungarvan, Lismore, Cappoquin, Clonmel and Carrick-

on-Suir (Clonmel and Carrick-on-Suir straddle the Tipperary–Waterford border). Publications include (prices quoted are in US$, inclusive of postage and handling): *The Connerys: Making of a Waterford Legend* , $16; *Waterford History and Society*, price on application; Eamon McEneaney, *Discover Waterford*, $20; J. Walsh (ed.), *Sliabh Rua: a History of its People and Places*, $40; and Frank O'Brien, *The O'Briens of Déise*, $25.

CONTACT
Carmel Meehan

DESCRIPTION
The Waterford Heritage and Genealogy Centre is the designated Irish Family History Foundation centre serving Waterford City and County. The IFHF is the coordinating body for a network of government approved genealogical research centres in the Republic of Ireland and in Northern Ireland that have computerised tens of millions of Irish ancestral records of different types.

HOLDINGS
Church records form the major source of electronic data. Roman Catholic records in County Waterford start in the year 1706; the latest parish to begin keeping records did so in 1852. Church of Ireland records in Waterford have various starting dates, depending on the parish, between 1655 and 1870. The earliest surviving and complete census for Waterford is that of 1901. Some census extracts for the period 1766 to 1851 also survive. Other genealogical sources available include: polling lists from 1755 and 1775; the Civil Survey of Ireland, compiled in the years 1654–6; subsidy rolls for County Waterford, 1662; householders of Waterford City, 1663; freemen of Waterford list, 1542; street and trade directories from 1788; gravestone inscriptions; local newspapers, 1771–present; biographical entries in local newspapers, 1770s–1820s; and a local history collection.

LOCATION
Town centre, in the former eighteenth century priest's residence next to St Patrick's Church.

COUNTY WESTMEATH

AIDAN HEAVEY PUBLIC LIBRARY ATHLONE

Athlone Civic Centre, Church Street,
ATHLONE, COUNTY WESTMEATH
Ireland

TELEPHONE: (090) 644 2157/58/59; FAX: (090) 649 4900
E-mail: gobrien@westmeathcoco.ie
Website: see www.athlone.ie/genealogy, www.westmeathcoco.ie/library

HOURS
M, 10.00am–5.30pm; Tu, Th, 10.00am–8.00pm; W, 11.00am–5.30pm; F,
10.00am–5.00pm; Sa, 10.00am–1.30pm

ACCESS AND SERVICES
Visitors welcome. Membership required for borrowing privileges. Disabled access.
Fifteen public access computer terminals with internet access. Special restrictions;
e.g. pencils only, apply with regard to use of the Aidan Heavey Collection.

CONTACT
Gearoid O'Brien, Executive Librarian

DESCRIPTION
Large municipal library, the flagship branch of Westmeath County Library Service,
with strong Irish, local studies and genealogy holdings. Staff will help with advice
and information where possible. For best results write or e-mail with details of needs
before visit. Specialises in material relating to South Westmeath. For North
Westmeath research purposes, *see* Westmeath County Library Headquarters – Local
Studies Collection.
The library recently acquired an outstanding collection of rare books and special
materials, the Aidan Heavey Collection, that qualifies it as a major research library.
The collection has been described by Patrick F. Wallace, Director of the National
Museum of Ireland, as 'an unparalleled gift with attaching obligations and
responsibilities. Personally I feel it's reason enough to permanently move to Athlone!'

HOLDINGS
In addition to main lending collection, Athlone Library holds a reference collection
with a number of relevant genealogical sources.

In 2006, the Athlone Library opened The Aidan Heavey Collection to the public. Aidan Heavey assembled one of the finest private libraries in Ireland, known especially for the very fine condition of its materials, and he and his wife Maureen donated the collection to his home town of Athlone. The collection includes several thousand volumes focusing on Irish history, topography and literature. In addition, the collection includes periodicals, journals, papers, manuscripts, photographs, documents, prints, drawings and a large collection of related ephemera. The collection totals more than 16,000 items. Highlights of the collection include strong material on Oliver Goldsmith; an extensive collection of Douglas Hyde material, including manuscripts; rare Bibles and prayer books in Irish, including Bedel's *Irish Bible* of 1685; and an extensive collection of sixteenth and seventeenth century rarities, including books, pamphlets and atlases – all in very fine condition.

The Aidan Heavey Collection also includes one of the finest collections of tours of Ireland in the eighteenth and nineteenth centuries; a comprehensive collection of Cuala Press, Dun Emer and Dolmen Press publications; a substantial collection of 1916 material, including original letters of Pearse, MacDonagh and Casement; and a very fine collection of twentieth century Irish literature, including many signed and limited editions by Yeats, Gogarty, Beckett, Kinsella, Heaney, Kennelly, Montague, O'Connor, O'Faoláin and O'Flaherty.

LOCATION
Town centre, in Athlone Civic Centre.

DÚN NA SÍ HERITAGE CENTRE

Knockdomney
MOATE, COUNTY WESTMEATH
Ireland

TELEPHONE: (090) 648 1183; FAX: (090) 648 1661
E-mail: dunnasimoate@eircom.net
Website: www.irishroots.net/wstmeath

HOURS
M–Th, 10.00am–4.00pm; F, 10.00am–3.00pm; Sa, 10.00am–4.00pm (April–October only). Guided tour by appointment (minimum 10 people).

ACCESS AND SERVICES
Dún na Sí Heritage Centre offers a fee based partial genealogical service to enquirers and has access to church, civil, land and census records for County Westmeath. Enquirers may expect a delay of up to two months before receiving a reply from the centre. There is an assessment fee of €95. Application form available on website.

CONTACT
Teresa Finnerty

DESCRIPTION
Dún na Sí Heritage Centre is the Irish Family History Foundation's designated research centre for County Westmeath. The IFHF is the coordinating body for a network of government approved genealogical research centres in the Republic of Ireland and in Northern Ireland that have computerised tens of millions of Irish ancestral records of different types. Chief surnames in County Westmeath include:

(Mc)Geoghegan, O'Growney, Brennan, O'Coffey, O'Mulleady, O'Malone, O'Daly, McAuley and McCormack. Main towns and villages include: Mullingar, Athlone, Castlepollard, Moate and Kilbeggan.

HOLDINGS
The centre has access to approximately 750,000 records. Main records include the following: Roman Catholic records for County Westmeath, starting in 1737; Church of Ireland records dating from 1710 (some available); Presbyterian records dating from 1800 (some available). Other sources include: *Griffith's Valuation*; *Pigot's Directory*; *Slater's Directory*; estate lists; voter lists; and the 1911 census.

LOCATION
Mount Temple Road, 0.6 miles from the Gap House pub.

WESTMEATH COUNTY LIBRARY HEADQUARTERS – LOCAL STUDIES COLLECTION

Dublin Road
MULLINGAR, COUNTY WESTMEATH
Ireland

TELEPHONE: (044) 40781/2/3; FAX: (044) 41322
E-mail: mfarrell@westmeathcoco.ie
Website: www.westmeathcoco.ie/services/library

HOURS
M–F, 10.00am–1.00pm, 2.00pm–5.00pm

ACCESS AND SERVICES
Visitors welcome. Reference only. Fees for photocopying.

CONTACT
Mary Farrell, County Librarian
Martin Morris, Archivist

DESCRIPTION
The Local Studies Collection is part of the County Westmeath library system and is located in Westmeath County Library Headquarters, Mullingar.

HOLDINGS
The Local Studies Collection contains a wealth of books, maps, journals, newspapers, photographs and ephemera relating to every aspect of life in County Westmeath, past and present. All books in the collection have a connection to Westmeath, in terms of authorship or subject matter. Authors represented in the library collections include: John Broderick, Leo Daly, Alice Dease, J.P. Donleavy, Desmond Egan, Lawrence Ginnell, Josephine Hart, Marian Keaney, Thomas Pakenham, Brinsley MacNamara, T.P. O'Connor, Padraic O'Farrell, A.J. Stanley, Michael Walsh, Fr Paul Walsh, Oliver Goldsmith and Christopher Nolan. The collection also includes directories, almanacs, topographical dictionaries, parish histories, GAA histories and unpublished works such as thesis and project material. There are some 3,500 items in this collection.

The Irish Collection is also housed at Westmeath County Library Headquarters and comprises 12,000 volumes on all aspects of Irish society. The library houses a number of special collections, from local newspapers to author collections. Newspaper holdings include: *Westmeath Journal*, 1813, 1823–34; *Midland Chronicle and Westmeath Independent*, 1827; *Athlone Independent*, 1833–6; *Athlone Sentinel*, 1834–61; *Westmeath Guardian*, 1835–96; *Athlone Conservative Advocate*, 1837; *Athlone Mirror*, 1841–2; *Westmeath Herald*, 1859–61; *Westmeath Independent*, 1860–82; *Westmeath Examiner*, 1882–1920, 1989–95; *Westmeath Examiner*, 1882–1995, excluding the years 1986, 1987 and 1988 (on microfilm); *Athlone Times*, 1889–1902; and *Midland Reporter and Westmeath Nationalist*, 1891–1939. The Photographic Collection contains some 2,500 prints of Westmeath including copies of the Lawrence Collection, 1870–1914. Maps include: Petty maps for County Westmeath; revised Ordnance Survey maps (1837) and their accompanying letters and name books, compiled under the direction of John O'Donovan; Geological Survey of Ireland, Westmeath (1860, one inch; 1913, six inch); Mullingar (1911, revised 1953, scale 1:2,500); *Irish Historical Towns Atlas No. 5, Mullingar* (Royal Irish Academy); and *Irish Historical Town Atlas No. 6, Athlone* (Royal Irish Academy).

Local government records include the following: Grand Jury presentments outlining the construction of roads in the county, 1802–87; Board of Guardian minute books, which detail the operation of the Poor Law system in the nineteenth and early twentieth centuries for Athlone (1849–1920) and Mullingar (1857–1921); Rural District Council minute books for Athlone (1899–1925), Ballymore (1900–25), Delvin (1919–23), Kilbeggan (1914–17) and Mullingar (1899–1925); valuation lists (1878–1972); Board of Health and Public Assistance minute books (1922–42); Westmeath County Council minute books (1899–1986); and Mullingar Commissioners' Books (1923–57).

Other records of special genealogical interest include: census records for the nineteenth century in addition to Pender's Census, 1659; and 1901 and 1911 census manuscript forms, providing detailed information on each resident of the county are available on microfilm. Gravestone inscriptions are available for the following parishes: Athlone Abbey Graveyard; Mount Temple Churchyard; Templecross Cemetery, Tisternagh Ballynacargy; All Saints, Mullingar; Lynn Church, Mullingar; Kilbixby Graveyard, Ballinacargy; Quaker Graveyard, Moate; St Mary's Church of Ireland, Moate, Kilcleigh and Killomenaghan.

The Kirby Collection contains approximately 250 different editions of *The Vicar of Wakefield* by Oliver Goldsmith (1728–74), a native of Westmeath. All the editions are illustrated and represent the work of the main Irish, British and continental illustrators of the day. The collection contains a number of fine bindings. The Howard Bury Collection, on permanent loan to the library, ranges from personal accounts of the diaries and tours at the beginning of the nineteenth century to details of local politics and electioneering in the mid-nineteenth century. It also includes prisoner of war diaries and accounts of the geographical and mountaineering expeditions of Colonel Howard Bury, and papers relating to the Belvedere Estate. The collection is named after Colonel Howard Bury, the former owner of Belvedere House. The Burgess Collection was assembled by Dr John B. Burgess (1885–1960) of Athlone. It contains: Athlone directories; wills and deeds; registers of Kiltoom Parish Church, St Mary's Parish Church and several other churches in the Athlone area; Athlone newspapers; a dictionary of Athlone biography; and vestry minutes of the Franciscan Abbey, Athlone. The John Broderick Collection contains an extensive collection of books, reviews, typescripts, etc by John Broderick (1927–89), the Athlone born novelist and critic.

Private papers include the following: the Fr Paul Walsh Papers, containing notes and unpublished material relating to this distinguished historian and scholar, born at Ballinea, Mullingar; and the Laurence Ginnell Papers, containing a selection of papers relating to this North Westmeath MP who was born in Delvin, County Westmeath.

LOCATION
Dublin Road, Mullingar.

COUNTY WEXFORD

WEXFORD COUNTY LIBRARY
– ARCHIVES SERVICE AND LOCAL STUDIES

Wexford Library Headquarters
ARDCAVAN, COUNTY WEXFORD
Ireland

TELEPHONE: (053) 912 4922/28; FAX: (053) 912 1097;
E-mail: archivist@wexfordcoco.ie, localstudies@wexfordcoco.ie
Website: www.wexford.ie/library/archive, www.wexford.ie/library/local%20studies

HOURS
By appointment

ACCESS AND SERVICES
The Archives Service is based in Wexford Library Headquarters, Ardcavan. This also
houses the core Local Studies Collection. However, most popular materials are
accessible from Wexford Town Library, off Redmond Square, Wexford (telephone
(053) 912 1637; fax (053) 912 1641). A biannual newsletter produced by Local
Studies, *Now and Then*, promotes recent developments in both the Local Studies and
Archives Services of Wexford County Council Public Libraries. The first issue was
published in September 2005.

CONTACT
Gráinne Doran, Archivist

DESCRIPTION
The Archives Service is responsible for identifying, collecting and making available
the archives, both public and private, of County Wexford, and for managing the
records of Wexford County Council.

HOLDINGS
Local Studies maintains collections in local and Irish history, genealogy, local
authors, local prints and photographs, archives, local newspapers (nineteenth
century) and maps, as well as the 1798 Collection. An increasing range of material is
carried on the online library, which is accessible via the library website.

LOCATION
Based in Wexford Library Headquarters, Ardcavan, approximately 1.5 miles from
Wexford town centre, on the R741 coast road.
Wexford Town Library is in the car park of McCauley's pharmacy on Redmond
Square, in the centre of Wexford Town.

WEXFORD COUNTY LIBRARY – LIBRARY MANAGEMENT SERVICES

Kent Building
ARDCAVAN, COUNTY WEXFORD
Ireland

TELEPHONE: (053) 9124922; FAX: (053) 912 1097
E-mail: libraryhq@wexfordcoco.ie
Website: www.wexford.ie/library

HOURS
See website

ACCESS AND SERVICES
Visitors welcome, but advance notice essential and preferably in writing for special
services. Disabled access facilities. Fee for photocopying, microfilm prints and fax
services.

CONTACT
See e-mail

DESCRIPTION
This is the management headquarters for County Wexford, which operates branch
libraries in Bunclody, Enniscorthy, Gorey, New Ross and Wexford Town. *See*
separate entry for Archives Services.

HOLDINGS
In addition to its general educational and recreational collection of more than
200,000 volumes, the library system maintains collections in local and Irish history,
genealogy, local authors, local prints and photographs, archives, local newspapers
(nineteenth century) and maps, as well as the 1798 Collection. For the bicentenary
of the 1798 Rebellion, the service compiled a brochure entitled *Mightier than the
Sword* (1998), which lists various introductory sources held by the libraries
documenting the history and culture of Wexford. These resources include all the
standard genealogical reference sources. The Photographic Collection and full text
articles from three of County Wexford's local history journals are accessible via the
library catalogue: this resource is in development.

LOCATION
Ardcavan, approximately 1.5 miles from Wexford town centre, on the R741 coast
road.

COUNTY WEXFORD HERITAGE AND GENEALOGY SOCIETY

Yola Farmstead Folk Park, Tagoat
ROSSLARE, COUNTY WEXFORD
Ireland

TELEPHONE: (053) 32611; FAX: (053) 32612
E-mail: wexgen@eircom.net
Website: homepage.eircom.net/~yolawexford/genealogy

HOURS
M–F, 10.00am–4.00pm

ACCESS AND SERVICES
County Wexford Heritage and Genealogy Centre offers a fee based, partial
genealogical service to those interested in tracing their roots in County Wexford.
Service to enquirers and the indexation of genealogical records continues. €95 initial
search fee. Application form available on website. Please note that genealogical
centres offer different services to clients. Please contact centre to ascertain current
prices and types of search available. The centre is based at the Yola Farmstead, a folk
and theme park. It documents the history of the Yola people, descendants of the first
Norman settlers in the south-east of Ireland. These settlers intermarried with the
native Irish and developed their own unique farming methods, customs, style of
dress, hairstyle and language. In addition to providing enquirers with information on
their Wexford ancestors, the centre retails heraldic plaques, coasters and crystal
items.

DESCRIPTION
County Wexford Heritage and Genealogy Society is the Irish Family History
Foundation's designated research centre for County Wexford. The IFHF is the
coordinating body for a network of government approved genealogical research
centres in the Republic of Ireland and in Northern Ireland that have computerised
tens of millions of Irish ancestral records of different types. Common surnames in
County Wexford include: Murphy, Sinnott, Doyle, Furlong, Walsh, Rossiter, Scallan,
O'Brien, Brown, Stafford, Devereux and Kavanagh. Main towns include: Wexford,
Enniscorthy, Gorey and New Ross.

HOLDINGS
Records include: Roman Catholic Records for County Wexford starting in 1671 and
Church of Ireland records dating from 1779. Also computerised are: Cantwell's
tombstone inscriptions (in part); Royal Irish Constabulary records; *Griffith's
Valuation* (c. 1853); *Bassett's Directory* (1885); *Thom's Directory*; *Pigot's Directory*; and
the complete set of *Hore's History of Wexford*.

LOCATION
Yola Farmstead, a folk and theme park located 2.5 miles south of Rosslare on the
R736.

WEXFORD TOWN LIBRARY

See WEXFORD COUNTY LIBRARY – LIBRARY MANAGEMENT SERVICES,
Ardcavan

COUNTY WICKLOW

WICKLOW COUNTY ARCHIVES
See WICKLOW COUNTY LIBRARY – LOCAL HISTORY COLLECTION AND
ARCHIVES, Bray

WICKLOW COUNTY LIBRARY
– LOCAL HISTORY COLLECTION AND ARCHIVES
Wicklow County Council Library Service Headquarters, Boghall Road
BRAY, COUNTY WICKLOW

TELEPHONE: (01) 286 6566; FAX: (01) 286 5811
E-mail: library@wicklowcoco.ie
Website: www.wicklow.ie/libraries

HOURS
By appointment

ACCESS AND SERVICES
Visitors welcome. Membership required for borrowing privileges.

CONTACT
Brendan Martin, County Librarian

DESCRIPTION
The Local History Collection is housed in the Wicklow County Library
Headquarters in Bray. The County Library operates branch libraries in: Arklow
(telephone (0402) 39977); Baltinglass (telephone (059) 6482300); Blessington
(telephone (045) 897 170); Carnew (telephone (055) 26088); Dunlavin (telephone
(045) 401 100); Enniskerry (telephone (01) 286 4339); Greystones (telephone (01)
287 3548); Rathdrum (telephone (0404) 43232); Tinahely (telephone (0402)
38080); and Wicklow (telephone (0404) 67025).

HOLDINGS
The Local History Collection includes books, journals and files on topics pertaining
to County Wicklow, its people and places. There are several special collections, most
notably the J.M. Synge Collection, the Charles Stewart Parnell Collection and the
1798 Collection. Newspapers on microfilm include: *Wicklow Newsletter*, 1858–99
(incomplete); *Arklow Reporter*, August–December 1890 (incomplete), 1891, and

January–June 1893; *Wicklow Star*, October 1895–February 1900. Local History also houses the archives for Wicklow County. Important records include: Wicklow Borough and Town Commission minutes, 1663–1888; Grand Jury presentments (1819–98); Public Health Committee and Electric Light Committee, late 1880s–1930s; Poor Law election return of votes cast, 1886; Rural District Council minute books, 1899–1925; register of licences issued (Motor Car Act) from 1904; rate books from 1924 (Wicklow County Council); correspondence relating to the Council, the Harbour and Esplanade Committee and the General Purpose Committee; sanatorium benefit register, *c.* 1930; proceedings of the Township Commissioner's Court (nineteenth century); legal material, 1880s; miscellaneous hospital documents, from 1930s; motor tax files, from 1920s; labourer's cottage rentals, from 1920s; Wicklow County Council correspondence, from 1899; valuation lists, from late nineteenth century; agenda books, from 1890s; minute books and committee minute books of Bray Urban District Council, from 1857; Poor Law minute books for Rathdrum Union and Shillelagh Poor Law Unions; rate books ,from 1860 (Bray Urban District Council); indoor registers for Rathdrum Union, 1842–1921; press letter books, 1867–1917; indoor register for Shillelagh Poor Law Union, 1842–1910; workmen's account books, 1868–1960s; manuscript assizes payments books, 1856–93; collectors' rate books, from 1876 (Bray Urban District Council); and the Rathdrum Poor Law Union Burial Board minute book, 1875.

LOCATION
Boghall Road, Bray. Bray is easily reached from Dublin city centre using the DART.

WICKLOW FAMILY HISTORY CENTRE

Wicklow's Historic Gaol, Kilmantin Hill
WICKLOW
Ireland

TELEPHONE: (0404) 20126; FAX: (0404) 61612
E-mail: wfh@eircom.ie
Website: www.wicklow.ie

HOURS
M–F, 10.00am–5.00pm

ACCESS AND SERVICES
The centre offers a fee based genealogical research service to persons interested in tracing their roots in County Wicklow. Initial search fee of €95; please allow four to eight weeks for initial report. Application form can be found on website. Services offered include: assessment (stage 1), family history records pack or family history report (stage 2), single record search. Initial search fee covers assessment. Description of each of these services can be found on website. Cost of family history records pack is €350 while the family history report – an attractively bound, comprehensive and customised report – costs €450–€550.

CONTACT
Catherine Wright, Manager

DESCRIPTION
The Wicklow Family History Centre is a genealogy research service established in
1987 by Wicklow County Council.

HOLDINGS
Records computerised include Roman Catholic and Church of Ireland parish
records, baptisms and marriages in Presbyterian churches and baptisms within the
circuit of Methodist churches in the county. In all, the centre holds over 275,000
baptism, 50,600 marriage and 40,000 burial records. Roman Catholic records do
not normally include burial records. The earliest parish records for County Wicklow
are Church of Ireland records, dating from the seventeenth century. The records for
Roman Catholic parishes as a rule do not start until the early nineteenth century,
although Wicklow Town records commence in 1747 – a distinction shared by only a
few parishes in the whole of Ireland. Other sources held include: tithe applotment
books; *Griffith's Valuation* printed reports and the accompanying maps; graveyard
inscriptions; census returns of 1901; Ordnance Survey townland maps; parish maps,
place name histories; hearth money rolls of 1669; the Religious Census, 1766; poll
book, 1745–59; corn growers, carriers and traders list, 1788–90; material relating to
the 1798 Rebellion; Wicklow Gaol records; convict records; commercial directories;
electoral registers and lists of landowners.

LOCATION
At the southern end of Wicklow Town, beside the courthouse.

APPENDIX 1

TRACING YOUR
COUNTY KILDARE ANCESTORS

Karel Kiely

For those who wish to do their own family history research, sources are available in the following places:

- National Library of Ireland, Kildare Street, Dublin 2
- National Archives, Bishop Street, Dublin 8
- General Register Office, Joyce House, Lombard Street East, Dublin 2
- History and Family Research Centre, Local Studies Department, Newbridge, County Kildare
- Local parishes

NATIONAL LIBRARY

PARISH REGISTERS

For most family history researchers, parish registers provide the earliest *direct* source of family information. Unlike most early records, parish registers provide evidence of direct links between one generation and the next (via baptismal registers) and one family and another (via marriage registers). Because of their importance for family history research, in the 1950s and 1960s the National Library of Ireland carried out a programme of microfilming all the Catholic parish registers available for filming at that time. As a result, the National Library holds microfilm copies of the registers of most Catholic parishes in Ireland (including the counties of Northern Ireland).

The registers are handwritten and include records of baptisms and marriages, but only rarely include records of deaths. Their starting dates can vary from the 1740s/1750s in some city parishes in Dublin, Galway, Waterford, Cork, and Limerick to the 1780s/1790s in counties such as Kildare, Wexford, Waterford and Kilkenny. The year 1880 was taken as the cut off point for the microfilming of parish registers as, by that year, civil registration was well under way (it began in 1864). Post-1880 genealogical information should be available from the record in the General Register Office.

The *List of Parish Registers on Microfilm* includes a list of parishes (by diocese), the covering dates of the registers in each parish and the National Library *call number* (P.xxxx) of each film. This list is available from the History and Family Research Centre, Local Studies Department and Kildare Heritage and Genealogy Company Ltd.

ACCESS TO MICROFILMS

Microfilms of registers for the following dioceses are freely available for consultation (counties or parts thereof in each diocese are given in parentheses):

- **Dublin** (Dublin, Wicklow, Carlow, Kildare, Laois, Wexford)
- **Kildare and Leighlin** (Kildare, Offaly, Laois, Kilkenny, Carlow, Wicklow, Wexford).

The quality of the information may vary from parish to parish. In general, baptismal registers contain: date of baptism; child's name; father's name; mother's name and maiden name; names of godparents (place of residence is often included). Marriage registers contain the names of the bride and groom and their witnesses. In some cases place of residence is also recorded.

Church of Ireland records are held in a variety of locations, including the National Archives, the Representative Church Body Library and local parishes. Please consult *A Table of Church of Ireland Parish Records*, available from the History and Family Research Centre, Local Studies Department to establish where records are held.

NATIONAL ARCHIVES OF IRELAND

The National Archives holds some Church of Ireland parish registers; tithe applotment books; *Griffith's Valuation*; 1901 and 1911 censuses; wills and testamentary records.

GENERAL REGISTER OFFICE

Civil registration commenced in 1864. Births, deaths and marriages for County Kildare are available from that date.

HISTORY AND FAMILY RESEARCH CENTRE – LOCAL STUDIES DEPARTMENT

The following can be inspected (by appointment with the librarian only):

- Alphabetical index to townlands of County Kildare
- 1641 *Book of Survey and Distribution*
- 1654 Civil Survey
- 1659 Pender's Census
- Hearth money rolls, 1662
- Tithe applotment books (1820s–1830s)
- *Griffith's Valuation* (1850s)
- Index to surnames of *Griffith's Valuation* and tithes
- 1840 Castledermot Census
- 1901 census
- Graveyard inscriptions
- Directories

LOCAL PARISHES

Names and addresses of parish priests/rectors are given in the Catholic Directory and the Church of Ireland Directory, available in Newbridge library.

APPENDIX 2

TITHE AND VALUATION RECORDS *c*.1823

Brian Trainor

Farmers of most agricultural land in Ireland were liable to pay to the rector of the established Church of Ireland a tithe or tax of one tenth of the yearly produce of the land and stock. This tax was especially unpopular with Presbyterians and Roman Catholics. Agitation against the tax forced the Government to change the law and make the tithe charge a financial one (instead of crops etc.) and levied on the landlord rather than on the tenant. In order to determine the amount of money to be charged in lieu of tithe all agricultural land liable to tithe had to be surveyed and valued. This work was done by local surveyors and the detail given is variable; unfortunately there are no maps accompanying the survey showing the locations of farms. The surveys provide the names of lease-holding tenants in each townland and thus serve as a sort of a farm census for the whole country. The tithe surveys for parishes in Northern Ireland for the years 1823–38 are deposited in the Public Record Office of Northern Ireland (FIN/5A) and those for the Republic of Ireland are available in the National Archives, Dublin (OL4). In order to conserve the original documents only microfilm copies of these surveys are produced to the public.

The earliest full valuation of property in Ireland was carried out in the 1830s. This valuation was carried out in each townland and parish and the surveyor's manuscript field books of this 'townland valuation' for parishes in Northern Ireland are deposited in the Public Record Office of Northern Ireland (VAL/1B) and those for the Republic are in the National Archives (OL4). No detail is given of buildings unless these were valued at £3.00 or more and this lower limit was raised to £5.00 in 1838 thus excluding most rural houses. Most of Ulster was valued before the threshold was raised to £5.00. with the result that many buildings in the North around £2.00 valuation are included. In towns many houses were substantial enough to reach the valuation of £3.00 or £5.00 and in these cases detailed measurements of rooms and outbuildings are sometimes given as well as names of occupiers. For the town of Downpatrick the names of 330 occupiers are given in the field book for the parish of Down *c*.1838 (VAL/1B/378 and OL4.0459).

The National Archives, Dublin has another set of these valuation field books 1830s for most parishes in Northern Ireland except for Co Tyrone. The first detailed valuation of all properties in Ireland began in the province of Leinster during the Great Famine in 1846, and the valuation was completed in Northern Ireland 1858–64. The manuscript field books of this valuation for Northern Ireland with annotated maps showing the precise location of holdings are held in PRONI (VAL/2B) and also the annual revisions recording changes in occupancy, consolidation of farms and the upheavals resulting from the Land Acts from the 1880s up to *c*.1950 (VAL/12B). Similar records exist for all parishes in the Republic of Ireland but these are held in the Valuation Office, Middle Abbey Street, Dublin.

Sir Richard Griffith, the great Commissioner of Valuation who was responsible for these massive surveys by central government arranged that a summary version of the valuation of 1846–64 for the whole country be made available in print. Some 200 volumes were published as official papers, one for each Poor Law Union or part. This printed valuation popularly known as 'Griffith's Valuation' appeared in the period 1847–1865. It is doubtful if any country in the world has such ready access in printed form to records detailing the value and acreage of farms and buildings, usually with the names of landlords and the exact locations marked on official maps held in the Public Record Office of Northern Ireland and in the Valuation Office, Dublin. A microfiche copy of the printed version of the valuation is available in the National Archives, Dublin.

The following tables provide the exact references for each parish for the tithe and valuation records that are held in PRONI and the National Archives, Dublin. This will be of particular use to family and local historians researching in these institutions.

In the National Archives cataloguing work is proceeding with their valuation records of the 1830s. The present staff inherited difficulties in dealing with large counties such as Cork and Tipperary, since these had been subdivided into two or three sections for the cataloguing of their holdings of Tithe Applotment books 1823–1838. For County Cork over twenty parishes are divided between N[orth], S[outh] and E[ast], and since parishes can still be further divided between two or three baronies it will be appreciated that no exact positioning of particular records (census searches, house books, etc.) can be readily achieved. Tom Quinlan, Senior Archivist in the National Archives, has been my indispensable support as I toiled with catalogues. He saved me from many errors. I take responsibility for those that remain in this present text which can only be considered, in part, as a report on work in progress.

PARISH/TOWN/VILLAGE	TITHES 1823–38 FIN 5A/	VALUATION 1830s VAL 1B/ FIELD BOOK (NA) OL4.	TENEMENT VALUATION c.1861–2 VAL 2B/1/	VALUATION REVISIONS c.1860–c.1930 VAL 12B/
Aghagallon	3	165A-B, 0069	54	9/1A-E
Aghalee	4	166, 0070	58B	9/2 A-E
Ahoghill	10	15D, 176, 179, 0001, 0059, 0080, 0082	64 A-C	3/1 A-E, 3A-D, 4A, 5A-J, 9A-D, 14A-F, 18A-E, 19A-D
Antrim	13	16, 0083, 180	5A-C, 51, 69	1/1A- F, 2A-C, 3A-C, 11A, 12A 22A-E, 28A-E
Ardclinis	15	147A-B, 0050	38	7/1A-E
Armoy	21	130, 0032 141, 0044	23A-B 37	2/1A-E 4/1A-D
Ballinderry	26	167, 0071	55A-B, 58B	9/3A-C
Ballintoy	27	131, 0033	24A-B	2/2A-E, 6A-D, 8/1A-E, 8A-E, 9/3A-E, 9A-E, 10A-F, 17A-E
Ballycastle (Ramoan)		280	2B, 1/28C	2/4A, 5A-C
Ballyclare (B'linny & B'nure)			7B	5A-B, 6A-B
Ballyclug	30	11, 0002	1	3/2A-E, 4A, 5A-V
Ballycor	24	0007/8	6, 11	4A-E, 7/2A-D
Ballyeaston (B'cor & Rashee)	24			
Ballylinny	38 & 67	112, 0014	7A	1/4A-E, 7A-F
Ballymartin	39 & 67	113, 0015, 124, 0025	11	1/14A-F, 29A-F
Ballymoney	40	142A-D 154 0045	35A-F 50A	4/3A-G, 5A-E, 12A-E, 14A-F, 23A-F, 24A-D
Ballymena (Kirkinriola)			66A-F	3/5K-V
Ballynure	44	114, 0016	11, 12	1/4A-E, 7/3A-E
Ballyrashane	46	137, 0039 30/14A-D	30A 6/1A-C	4/4 A, 5A-E,
Ballyscullion	47	181, 0084	72B	3/4A, 6A-E
Ballyscullion Grange of	Nil	182, 0089		3/4A, 6A-E
Ballywillin	51	137, 0040	30A	4/4A; 6/1A-C, 2A-E
Belfast	36	see Shankill	18, 21A-D	43/
Billy	56	132, 0034 138, 0041	24B 25A-B 31	2/6A-D, 9A-E, 10A-F, 4/5A-E, 6A-C, 7A-E, 30/8A-D
Blaris	57	168, 0072	56A-B 3	8/9A-T, 10A-C, 11A, 12A-E, 20/6A-G, 16A-E
Broughshane (Racavan)			3C	3/7A-E
Bushmills (Billy)			26	4/6A-C; 30/8A-D
Camlin	63	169, 0073	52	1/16A-F

PARISH/TOWN/VILLAGE	TITHES 1823–38 FIN 5A/	VALUATION 1830S VAL 1B/ FIELD BOOK (NA) OL4.	TENEMENT VALUATION c.1861–2 VAL 2B/1/	VALUATION REVISIONS c.1860–c.1930 VAL 12B/
Carncastle	66	150, 0055	42	7/4A-E
Carnmoney	67	115A-B, 0017	13A-B	5/7A-G, 12A-K
Carrickfergus	70	187, 0031	22A-E,	7/5A-F, 6A-D, 7A-C
Connor	83	12, 0003	2A-B, 8A	1/13A-E, 3/4A, 18A-E
Craigs (Ahoghill)	10	155 176 178 A-B	45, 65A-B	3/3A-D, 4A, 13A-E, 14A-F, 19A-D 20A-D
Cranfield	85	183, 0085	70	1/15A-F
Crumlin (Camlin)			51	1/16A-F
Culfeightrin	87	133, 0035	27A-B	2/8A-D, 11A-F, 15A-D, 16A-D
Derryaghy	91B	125, 0026 170, 0074	19A-B 57	8/2A-G, 5A-E
Derrykeighan	93	134, 0042, 139A-B	32	4/5A-E, 10A-E
Dervock (Derrykeighan)			33	4/10A-E
Doagh, Grange of	102	17A-B, 0009	7A	1/4A-E
Doagh, Village		7B		
Donegore		18, 0010	8A-B	1/17A-E
Drumbeg	117	126	20	8/15A-J, 20/3A-E
Drummaul (Randalstown)	124	184, 0086	71A-D	1/10B-E, 3/9A-D, 11A-D, 22A-F; 23A, 24A, 27A-E, 28A-E
Drumtullagh, Grange of	Nil	25B	2/9A-C	2/9A-E
Dunaghy	128	156, 0060	46A-B	3/4A, 8A-D, 22A-D
Dundermot, Grange of	130	157, 0062	46B	3/4A, 12A-D
Duneane	132	185, 0087	71D 72A-B	3/4A, 25A-E 10A-E, 15A-F
Dunluce	134	140	34A-B	4/4A, 5A-E, 21A-C, 6/1A-C, 2A-E
Finvoy	142	158A-C 0061	47A-B	4/11A-E, 12A-E, 25A-E
Glenavy	147*	171, 0075	58A-B	8/4A-D; 9/3A-E
Glenarm (Tickmacrevan)			41B	7/9A-H, 10A-E
Glenwhirry	Nil	13, 0004	3A	3/4A, 17A-D
Glynn	149	116	14	7/11A-D
Gracehill (Ahoghill)			64D	
Inispollan, Grange of	Nil	0051	39	2/14A-E
Inver	158	117, 0019	14	7/14A-G, 15B-M
Island Magee	159	118, 0020	15	7/12A-G
Kilbride	162	19, 0011	8B	1/4A-E, 20A-F
Killagan	172	144, 159, 0047	48	4/15A-F
Killdollagh	169	0063, 0046		30/14A-D

PARISH/TOWN/VILLAGE	TITHES 1823–38 FIN 5A/	VALUATION 1830S VAL 1B/ FIELD BOOK (NA) OL4.	TENEMENT VALUATION c.1861–2 VAL 2B/1/	VALUATION REVISIONS c.1860–c.1930 VAL 12B/
Killead	174	164A-C 0068	53A-C	1/8A-F, 9A-F, 19A-E, 26A-E
Killyglen, Grange of	181	151, 0056	44A	7/4A-E
Kilraghts	188	145, 0048	36	4/18A-E
Kilroot	190	119, 0021	16	7/18A-E
Kilwaughter	192	152A-B, 0057	43	7/13A-F
Kirkinriola	194	177, 66B-F, 0081	66A*	3/4A, 5A-V, 14A-F, 19A-D
Lambeg	196	127, 0028 172, 0076	59	8/7A-D, 9L 20/10A-F
Larne	197	153, 0058	44A-C	7/14A-G, 15A-M, 16A
Layd	198	148A-D, 0053	40A-B, 19A-F	2/7A-E, 14A-F,
Layd, Grange of	Nil	0052	39	2/14A-D
Lisburn	(See Blaris)		61A-D	
Loughguile	208	146A-D, 0049 160, 0064	37 & 48	4/1A-D, 2A-D, 8A-E, 9A-D, 15A-F
Magheragall	217	174, 0077	55B 62A-B	8/6A-F, 13A-E
Magheramesk	221	175, 0078	62B	8/14A-D
Mallusk Grange of	259	0067		
Muckamore Grange of	Nil	163	52	1/1A-F, 2A-C, 3A-C
Newtown Crommelin	228	161, 0065	49, 21A	3/22A-D
Nilteen Grange of	110	9, 0012	17A-E	
Portglenone	232	178A-B	67A-C	3/1A-E, 4A, 20A-D, 23A-E
Portrush (Ballywillin)			30B	4/22A-D
Racavan	250	14A-B, 0005	3A-B	3/4A, 7A-E, 24A-D
Raloo	234	120, 0022	17A-B	7/17A-E
Ramoan (Ballycastle)	235	135, 0037	28A-B	2/3A-G, 16A-D, 17A-E
Randalstown (Drummaul)			71E	23A, 24A
Rasharkin	236	162, 0066	50A-B	3/4A, 13A-E, 15A-D, 4/16A-F, 17A-E
Rashee	24	111, 0013	10	1/25A-F
Rathlin Is	238	136, 0038	29	17A-E, 18A-D
Shankill	36 247	121A-B, 0023 128 A-B, 0028	18 21A-D	5/3A-F, 4A-D, 5A-E, 6A-E, 8A-F
Shilvodan Grange of	83	186, 0088	73	28A-E
Skerry	250	15A-C, 0006	4A-C	3/7A-E, 16A-D, 21A-D

PARISH/TOWN/VILLAGE	TITHES 1823–38 FIN 5A/	VALUATION 1830s VAL 1B/ FIELD BOOK (NA) OL4.	TENEMENT VALUATION c.1861–2 VAL 2B/1/	VALUATION REVISIONS c.1860–c.1930 VAL 12B/
Stranocum (Ballymoney)			33	
Templecorran	257	122	16	7/18A-F
Templepatrick	259	123A-B, 0024 129A-B, 0030	7B, 10, 11, 18, 21C	1/14A-F, 29A-F
Tickmacrevan (Glenarm)	263	149, 0054	41A,	7/9A-H, 10A-E
Tullyrusk	269 & 147		173A-B	63 8/16A-D
Whitehead				7/19A

* Includes mill book

PARISH/TOWN/VI LLAGE	TITHES 1823–38 FIN 5A/	VALUATION 1830S VAL 1B/ FIELD BOOK (NA) OL4.	TENEMENT VALUATION c.1864 VAL 2B/1/	VALUATION REVISIONS c.1860–c.1930 VAL 12B/
Acton			32D	
Armagh	20	21A & B, 224 234, 0090 0110	1A-G, 22	10/4A-H, 5A-C, 6A-C, 7A-C, 8A-C, 9A-E, 25A-E
Ballymore	41	214, 248 0120	32A-C, 32E	11/1A-C, 11/5A-G, 15/23A-D, 15/24A-D
Ballymyre	42	239, 0102	13	15/2A-D
Blackwatertown (Clonfeacle)		249	2B	
Camlough (Killevy)		178		
Charlemont (Loughgall)		249	2B	
Clonfeacle	79	22, 225A & B 234, 0111	2A, 23	10/12A-F, 23A-E, 30A-E, 38A-D,
Creggan	86	240A & B 0103	14A-G 7A-D, 13/1A-F	12/2A-E, 3A-4E, 5A-E, 6A-E,
Crossmaglen (Creggan)			14G	
Derrynoose	95	23, 235, 248 0091, 0131	3A-C, 40	10/11A-E, 17A-E, 19A-D, 26A-C, 28A, 39A-E
Drumcree	119	226A & B, 234, 0112	24A-H	14/2A-C, 6A-C, 12A-13B, 14A
Eglish	136	24, 236, 248 0092, 0132	4, 41	10/10A-D, 22A-E
Forkill	143	215, 247, 248 0121, 0126	32E, 35A-C	12/5A-C,15/13A-B, 18A-D, 24A-C
Grange	150	25, 227, 234 0093, 0113	5, 25	10/23A-E, 25A-E, 31A-E, 33A-E
Jonesborough	160	243, 248, 0127	36	15/15A-C
Keady	161	26A-D, 237 248-9, 0094 0133	6A-D, 3B-C, 42	10/3A-B, 17A-E, 19A-D, 26A-C, 27A-C, 28A-B
Kilclooney	225	210A & B 216, 248, 249 0098, 0122	9A-C	10/13A-D, 29A-D, 34A-E
Kildarton	20 etc			10/24A-D, 25A-E, 29A-C
Killevy	178	217, 244A & B 248, 0123 0128	32E, 34C, 37A-J	12B, 15/1A-D, 1F, 1H, 3A-E, 6A-J, 15A-C, 17A-C, 18A-D, 22A-24C
Killylea (Tynan)		249		
Killyman	183	228, 234, 0114	27	10/30A-C
Kilmore	186	218, 248 229A & B 0115, 0124	26A-D, 33	10/25A-E, 11/4A-F, 31A-E, 33A-E, 37A-F
Lisnadill	202	27, 211, 241 0095, 0099 0104	8A, 10A-B 12B, 15	10/3A-D, 9A-E, 11A-E, 29A-D, 32A-E

PARISH/TOWN/VI LLAGE	TITHES 1823–38 FIN 5A/	VALUATION 1830S VAL 1B/ FIELD BOOK (NA) OL4.	TENEMENT VALUATION c.1864 VAL 2B/1/	VALUATION REVISIONS c.1860–c.1930 VAL 12B/
Loughgall	206	28, 230, 234 249, 0096	7, 28A-C	10/2A-E, 10/25A-E, 31A-E, 33A-E, 38A-D
Loughgilly	207	212, 219 245A & B, 248 0100, 0125	11, 29, 34A-C, 38A-B	10/34A-C, 11/3A-D, 15/3A-E,19A D, 23A-D, 24A-D
Lurgan (Shankill)			20C-G	14/9A-H
Magheralin	219	220, 234, 0106	17	14/5A-C
Markethill (Mullaghbrack)			12C	
Middletown (Tynan)				43D
Montiaghs	223	221, 234, 0107	18	14/11A-C
Mountnorris (Loughgilly)				32D
Mullaghbrack	225	213, 231, 234 0101, 0117	12A-B, 29	10/24A-D, 34A-E, 11/3A-E
Newry	226	232, 234,	39A-C	10/33A-D, 15/1A-
	246A-E, 248		H, 22/16A-C	
		0118, 0130		17A-C, 18A-D
Newtownhamilton	229	242A & B	16A-D	12/1A-D, 5A-E,
		0105		6A-E, 8A-E
Poyntzpass (Ballymore)				32D
Portadown (Drumcree etc)			24E-H	14/13A-N
Richhill (Kilmore)			26E	
Seagoe	245	222, 234, 0108	19A-D	14/3A-C, 4A-C, 7A-C
Shankill	248	223A & B 234, 0109	20A-G	14/5A-C, 9H
Tandragee (Ballymore)			11	11/5A-G
Tartaraghan	255	233A & B 234, 0119	21A-C	10/2A-C, 30A-C, 14/15A-D
Tynan	270	29A & B 238, 248 0097, 0134	8A, B 43A-D	10/11A-E, 17A-E, 22A-E, 35A-E, 39A-E

PARISH/TOWN/ VILLAGE	TITHES 1823–38 FIN 5A/	VALUATION 1830s VAL 1B/ FIELD BOOKS OL4. (NATIONAL ARCHIVES)	TENEMENT VALUATION c.1861–4 VAL 2B/3/	VALUATION REVISIONS c.1861–c.1930 VAL 12B/
Aghaderg	1	337, 351, 0419	42, 55B-D	16/14A-D, 18A-E, 22A-D
Annaclone	11	352, 0438, 0439	56	16/1A-F
Annahilt	12	338A & B, 383, 0445	35	20/1A-E
Ardglass	16	368, 311B, 0451	70A-B	18/1A-F, 27A
Ardkeen	17	35, 0388	7A-B, 23, 27	28/2A-F, 23/19A-F
Ardquin	18	36, 0389	8	18/2A-F
Ballee	23	369, 311B, 0452	71	18/1A-F, 22A-E
Ballyculter	32	370, 311B, 0453	72	18/11A-E, 22A-E, 25A-F
Ballyhalbert (St Andrew's)	33	0312, 0395	7B, 9	23/1A-4F, 19A-F
Ballykinler	35	376A & B, 311B	76	18/5A-F
Ballynahinch			28B	
Ballyphilip Slanes & Witter (Portaferry)	45 & 49	37, 0390	10	18/20A-F, 23/27A-D
Ballytrustan	45 & 49	38, 0391	11	18/20A-D, 23/27A-D
Ballywalter	50	39, 0392	9	23/6A-F
Banbridge (Seapatrick)			64B, C	16/7A-C, 8B-D
Bangor	54	31, 315, 0384, 0398	1A-C, 7B	23/7A-K, 8A
Blaris	57	324, 339 0406, 0420,	24A, 43	9A-S, 20/6A-D, 16A-G
Bright	62	377, 311B, 0458	77	18/15A-E
Castleboy	exempt	310, 0393	12	18/2A-F
Castlewellan (Kilmegan)			63B	18/4G
Clonallan	75	353, 0440	57A-C, 60A	22/5A-D, 23A-G, 25A-C
Clonduff	77	354, 0432	49A-C	22/6A-D, 10A-D, 12A-D, 20A-B, 20D, 20F-H
Clough (Loughinisland)			66D	18/5A-E
Comber	82	316A-C, 0407	2, 16A & B 25A	18/5A-E, 11A-F, 20A-E, 20/11A E, 23/3A-F
Crossgar (Kilmore)			28B	16/9A-E, 18/6A-F, 27A
Donaghadee	104	32, 0385	3A-C	23/10A-C, 13A-E 15A-B
Donaghcloney	105	340, 0423	44A-B 46C	21/4A-F, 9A-F
Donaghmore	108	355, 0441	58A-B	22/9A-E, 11A-E
Down	111	378, 0459	78A-D	18/7A-K, 12A-E, 26A-E
Dromara & Magherahamlet	112	341, 356, 384, 0421, 0433, 0446	36, 37, 50A-B	16/2A-E, 9A-E, 20/9A-D
Dromore	113	342, 0422	38A-F	16/10A-F, 21A-E, 23A-E, 20/2A-D

PARISH/TOWN/ VILLAGE	TITHES 1823–38 FIN 5A/	VALUATION 1830S VAL 1B/ FIELD BOOKS OL4. (NATIONAL ARCHIVES)	TENEMENT VALUATION c.1861–2 VAL 2B/3/	VALUATION REVISIONS c.1861–c.1930 VAL 12B/
Drumballyroney	116	357A & B	59A-C	16/4A-E, 24A-E, 22/20A-B, 20D, 20F-H
Drumbeg	117	326, 0408	25B-C	20/3A-E, 10B-E
Drumbo	118	327, 0409	25A-C	20/3A-E, 7A-F, 11A-E
Drumgath	120	358 & A B	59C 20C,	22/10A-D, 20A, 20E-H
Drumgooland	122	359, 0434	51A-D 20A-E	16/5A-F, 15A-D,
Dundonald	131	317, 0399	17	17/8A-G, 23/5A-F
Dundrum (Kilmegan)			79	18/9A-E, 27A
Dunsfort	135	371, 311B, 0454, 2360	73	18/11A-11E
Garvaghy	146	343, 360	39, 52	16/3A-E, 12A-E
Gilford (Tullylish)		0424, 0435	48E-F	16/13A-B
Greyabbey	151	33, 0386	4	23/16A-F, 21A-E
Groomsport			5	
Hillsborough	152	344A & B	45A-C	20/5A-D, 14A-E
Holywood	exempt	318	18A-D	10A-G, 11A-E, 17/2A-J, 10A-D, 43L/1-2, 43N/1-2
Inch	154	372, 0456	74	18/13A-D
Inishargy	155	311A & B, 0394	13	23/4A-F, 19A-F
Kilbroney	163	361, 0442	61A-B, 65A	19/15A-E, 21A-F
Kilclief	164	373, 379, 311B,0460	70A	18/25A-F
Kilcoo	166	362, 0436	53A-B, 62	19/7A-F, 11A-E
Kilkeel	171	390A & B 0464	81A-H	19/4A-E, 13A-E, 14A-J, 18A-E, 19A-F
Killaney	Nil	328, 0410	26	20/15A-D
Killinchy	179	319, 329, 335 0400, 0411, 0417	19, 23, 27, 33	18/14A-E, 19A-E 23/3A-F, 18A-E, 28A-E
Killyleagh	182	331, 336 0412, 0418	34A-C 80B	18/6A-F, 16A-F 18/15A-E, 27A
Killough				
Kilmegan	184	363A & B 380, 311B 385,0447, 0461	63A, 66B-C 79	18/4A-G, 9A-E, 24A-E
Kilmood	185	320, 0401	20	23/18A-E
Kilmore	187	330, 386 0413, 0448	28A, 66A 68	18/6A-F, 18A-E, 19A-E, 23A-D
Kircubbin (Inishargy)			5	
Knockbreda	195	321, 332 0402, 0414	18D, 21, 29	17/3A-B, 6A-H 20/7A-D
Knockbreda (Belfast Co. Borough)			43A/5-10, 15-23, 43K/1	43A/28-34, 38-39
Knockbreda (Ballymacarrett ED)			43A/28-34, 38-39	43A/28-34, 38-39
Lambeg	196	333, 0415	30	20/10A-F

PARISH/TOWN/ VILLAGE	TITHES 1823–38 FIN 5A/	VALUATION 1830S VAL 1B/ FIELD BOOKS OL4. (NATIONAL ARCHIVES)	TENEMENT VALUATION c.1861–4 VAL 2B/3/	VALUATION REVISIONS c.1861–c.1930 VAL 12B/
Lisburn (Blaris)			24B	
Loughbrickland (Aghaderg)			55A	
Loughinisland	209	387, 0449	66A-C	18/5A-F, 23A-D, 24A-E
Maghera	211	364, 0437	54	19/17A-F
Magheradrool	215	388A & B 0450	67A-B 68	18/3A-G, 10A-E 20/13A-E
Magherahamlet	112		68	18/10A-E, 20/9A-D
Magheralin	219	346, 0425	46A-C, 47C	21/1A-E, 6A-F, 7A-E
Magherally	220	345, 0426	40	16/19A-E
Moira	222	347, 0427	47A-C	21/7A-E
Newcastle (Kilmegan)			53A	19/20A-D
Newry	Nil	365, 389 0465	69A-K	16/3A-E, 22/7A-F, 14A-L, 16A-C, 17A-C, 19A-F
Newtownards	227	34, 322 0387, 0403	6A-D, 22A-B	23/21A-E, 22A-E, 23A-C, 24A-F, 25A-N
Newtownbreda (Knockbreda)			31	
Portaferry (See Ballyphilip)			14 23/26A	18/20A-F, 27A,
Rathfriland (Drumballyroney)			60B-C	22/21A-B, 22A-B
Rosstrevor (Kilbroney)			61C	
Rathmullan	239	374, 381, 311B, 0395	72, 80A	18/11A-E, 15A-E, 26A-E
St Andrew's (Ballyhalbert)	241	312, 0462		
Saintfield	242	334	32A-C	18/19A-E, 20/18A-E
Saul	244	375, 311B, 0416, 0457	75	18/7A-K, 22A-E
Seaforde			66D	
Seapatrick	246	348A & B, 366, 0428/9	41, 64A 44A	16/6A-H, 8A-D, 19A-E
Shankill		349, 0430	46A, 47B	21/5A-D
Slanes	45	313, 0396	15	23/27A-D
Strangford			14	
Tullylish	266	350, 0431	44B, 48A-D	16/25A-H, 21/4A-F, 8A-F
Tullynakill	267	323, 0404/5	23	23/28A-E
Tyrella	271	382, 311B, 0463	80A	18/26A-E, 27A
Waringstown (Donaghcloney)			44C	
Warrenpoint	75	367, 0443/4	65A-B	23A-G, 25A-C
Witter (Ballyphilip)	45	314, 0397		

PARISH/TOWN/ VILLAGE	TITHES 1823–38 FIN 5A/	VALUATION 1830S VAL 1B/ FIELD BOOKS OL4. (NATIONAL ARCHIVES)	TENEMENT VALUATION c.1861–2 VAL 2B/4/	VALUATION REVISIONS c.1861–c.1930 VAL 12B/
Aghalurcher	6 also D998/ 22/1	428A-B, 0502-4	19A-E	28/5A-D, 6A-D, 7A-E, 10A-E, 11 A-E, 19A-E, 20A-E, 21A-E, 22A-F, 23A-F, 24A-E
Aghavea	8	429, 0505-7	20A-C	28/6A-E, 11A-E, 13A-E, 19A-E, 22A-F
Belleek	55	415A-B, 0490	10	24/1A-E, 2A-E, 7A-E
Boho	60	41, 422, 0466 0496	1 & 15	24/6A-E, 26/1A-E, 22A-E, 37A-D
Cleenish	72	42, 432, 430A & B, 432, 0467-9 0497, 0508-9 0511 430A-B	1, 2A-D 7E 21	24/6A-E; 26/7A-E, 10A-E, 19A-D, 20A-E, 23A-E, 24A-F, 30A-F, 31A-E, 32A-E, 37A-E
Clones*	MIC 442/10	46, 0474	5A-D 6	25/1A-D, 2A-E 3A-E, 5A-E, 7A-E, 8A-D, 10A-E
Currin*	MIC 442/10	47A-D, 49 0475	6	
Derrybrusk	92	431, 433 0510, 0512	22	26/4A-E, 26A-E, 28/5A-E
Derryvullen	96	419 0491 0498 434 0513	11A-B 21, 22, 23A-C	26/2A-E, 3A-F, 5A-F, , 10A-E, 17A-K, 31A-E 27/9A-E, 11A-E, 13A-E, 15A-E,
Devenish	101	424 A-D 0498	16A-D	24/4A-E, 8A-E, 26/12A-F, 16A-E, 17A-K, 33A-E, 35A-E, 36A-E, 37A-E
Drumkeeran	123	416 A-B 0492, 3819	12A-C	27/3A-E, 4A-E, 5A-E, 6A-E, 7A-F, 8A-E, 16A-E
Drummully Ederny (M'culmoney)	125	410A-C 0476-9	6, 7B 13D	25/2A-E, 4A-E
Enniskillen	137	425A-B 435A-B 0499, 0514 3820/1	20C, 23A & B 24A-H	26/3A-F, 4A-E, 5A-F, 6A-F, 17A-K, 18A-H, 25A-E, 28/11A-E, 31A-E, 38A-F
Galloon	145	48, 411, 412 0478-81	5B, 7A-E	25/3A-E, 4A-E, 6A-E, 7A-E, 8A-E, 9A-E, 28/3A-E, 7A-E, 8A, 14A-E
Inishmacsaint	156	426A-C 0500	17A-D	24/3A-E, 5A-E, 26/12A-F, 36A-E

PARISH/TOWN/ VILLAGE	TITHES 1823–38 FIN 5A/	VALUATION 1830S VAL 1B/ FIELD BOOKS OL4. (NATIONAL ARCHIVES)	TENEMENT VALUATION c.1861–2 VAL 2B/4/	VALUATION REVISIONS c.1861–c.1930 VAL 12B/
Kesh (M'culmoney)			13D	
Killesher	177	43 0472, 0482-6	3A-C	26/9A-E, 11A-E, 13A-F, 19A-F, 27A-E
Kinawley	Nil	44, 413	4A-B 8A-E	26/9A-E, 11A-E, 28A-F, 29A-E, 28/1A-E, 2A-E, 12A-E, 15A-E, 16A-E, 17A, 25A-E
Lack (M'culmoney)			13D	
Lisnaskea (Aghalurcher)			27	
Magheracross	213	417, 436 0515	25A-B	26/2A-E, 3A-F, 34A-F, 27/2A-E, 9A-F
Magheraculmoney	214	418 0493	13A-D	27/7A-F, 10A-E, 12A-E, 14A-E, 15A-E
Newtownbutler (Galloon)			7F	
Pettigoe (T'carn)			12D	
Rosslea (Clones)			5E	
Rossory	240	45, 427A-B 0473, 0501	18 & 24B	26/7A-E, 16A-E, 17A-K, 30A-F, 32A-E
Templecarn	MIC 442/9	421 A-B 0494	14	27/3A-E
Tempo (Enniskillen)			28	
Tomregan	MIC 442/2	414, 0487-9	9	28/2A-E
Trory	265	420 437A-B, 0495, 0516	23C, 26	26/2A-E, 27/11A-E

* For border parishes, original records, were retained in Dublin and are now in the National Archives; microfilm copies MIC 442 in PRONI. Parishes include Clones, Currin, Templecarn and Tomregan.

PARISH/TOWN/ VILLAGE	TITHES 1823–38 FIN 5A/	VALUATION 1830S VAL 1B/ FIELD BOOKS OL4. (NATIONAL ARCHIVES)	TENEMENT VALUATION c.1858–9 VAL 2B/5/	VALUATION REVISIONS c.1860–c.1930 VAL 12B/
Aghadowey	2	51	1A-C, 2	30/1A-E, 2A-E, 6A-F, 11A-E, 13A-F, 15A-E, 18A-E
Aghanloo	7	511, 520, 1071	17A-B	31/1A-E
Agivey	nil	52	2	30/2A-F, 34/2A-E
Arboe	14	522, 1079, 1079A	25, 43A	34/26A-F
Artrea	22	523	26A-C, 43A	34/4A-E, 9A-G, 16A-E, 20A-F, 24A-F, 26A-F
Ballinderry	25	525, 1081	27, 43A	9/3A-C
Ballyaghran (Agherton)	28	539A & B 546A	10, 15A-B	30/4A-F, 17A-H
Ballymoney	40	540, 546A	11, 15B	4/3A-G
Ballynascreen	43	524, 1082	28A-C,	34/5A-E, 8A-E, 43A & C, 12A-F, 25A-F
Ballyrashane	46	53, 546A & B, 1068	12, 15B	30/14A-F
Ballyscullion	47	526, 1083	29A-B, 43B	34/6A-G, 9A-G
Ballywillin	51	541A-C, 546A	13, 15B	13A-G, 19A-E, 30/4A-F
Balteagh	52	513A & B 516, 1072	18	31/13A-G, 19A-E, 21A-E
Banagher	53	512A-E 548A & B 1073, 1095	19, 44	31/11A-E, 12A-F, 21A-F
Bellaghy (B'scullion)			29C	
Bovevagh	61	514A-C, 516 1074	17B, 20A-B, 21C	31/6A-E, 14A-E, 23A-D
Camus (Macosquin)	64A			
Carrick*		515	17B, 24A	31/13A-G, 14A-E, 23A-E, 24A-E
Castledawson (Magherafelt)			37H	
Clondermot (Glendermot)	76	549A-D	45A-D, 50	32/1A-G, 12A-F, 14A-F, 33/4A-C
Coleraine	81	53, 542A-D, 546A & C, 1069	3B-F, 14, 15B	30/4A-G, 9A-D, 14A-D, 17A-H
Cumber Lower	88	552, 1096	46, 50	32/1A-G, 4A-F, 13A-F
Cumber Upper	89	554, 1097	47A-B 50	31/12A-F, 32/2A-F, 5A-F
Derry, Deanery of	91A			
Derryloran	94	527, 1084	30, 43A	34/19A-F
Desertlyn	98	528, 1085	31A-B,	34/2A-E, 7A-E, 43A & C, 20A-F
Desertmartin	99	529, 1086	32A-B, 42	34/2A-E, 7A-E, 43A, 11A-F, 14A-E
Desertoghill	100	54A-C	4A-B	29/1A-D, 30/6A-F, 12A-F, 19A-F

PARISH/TOWN/ VILLAGE	TITHES 1823–38 FIN 5A/	VALUATION 1830S VAL 1B/ FIELD BOOKS OL4. (NATIONAL ARCHIVES)	TENEMENT VALUATION c.1858–9 VAL 2B/5/	VALUATION REVISIONS c.1860–c.1930 VAL 12B/
Drumachose	115	517A-F	17B, 22A-C	31/13A-G, 16A-E, 18A-G
Draperstown (Ballynascreen)			42	
Dunboe	129	55A & B	5A-C	30/3A-G, 5A-F, 10A-F
Dungiven	133	518A-C, 1075	21A-D	31/9A-F, 14A-E, 15A-F
Errigal	140	56	5C, 6A	30/12A-F, 13A-F, 31/12A-F, 13A-F, 18A-E, 19A-F
Faughanvale	141	550A & B 1098	48A-B, 50	31/3A-G, 10A-E, 32/6A-F, 12A-F
Fermoyle**	129		7	30/3A-E, 10A-E, 15A-E
Garvagh (Errigal)			6B	
Kilcronaghan	167	530, 1087	33A, 43A	34/8A-E, 14A-E, 28A-E
Kildollagh	169	543, 546A	15A-B	30/14A-F
Killelagh	196	532A & B 1070	34, 37A & D 43B	34/27A-E, 29A-E
Killowen	180	57	8	30/5A-F, 9A-D
Kilrea	189	58, 544, 1088	35, 43B	29/3A-F; 30/21A-21D
Learmont***	53	551	49A-B, 50	32/2A-F, 3A-F
Limavady (Drumachose)			22B-C	
Lissan	203	533A & B 1089	36A-B 43A & C	34/15A-F, 19A-F,
Londonderry (Templemore)			16C-H	
Macosquin	64A	59	5C, 9A-B	30/5A-F, 11A-F, 15A-E, 20A-F
Maghera	212	534A & B 1090	37A-G, 43B & C	34/8A-E, 11A-F, 13A-E, 17A-G, 23A-F, 27A-E, 29A-E
Magherafelt	216	535 1091	38A-C, 43A	34/2A-E, 9A-G, 18A-F
Magilligan	252	519A-C, 520 1076	17B, 23	31/1A-E, 3A-G, 4A-D, 5A-E
Moneymore			31B	
Swatragh (Maghera)			37G	
Tamlaght	251	536, 1092	39, 43A	34/26A-F
Tamlaghtard (Magilligan)	252			31/1A-E, 3A-G, 4A-F, 5A-E
Tamlaght Finlagan	253	521A-C 1077	24A-C	31/3A-G, 18A-G, 20A-G, 24A-E
Tamlaght O'Crilly	254	510, 537 545, 1093	40A-C, 43B	29/1A-D, 2A-D, 30/21A-D, 34/10A-F

PARISH/TOWN/ VILLAGE	TITHES 1823–38 FIN 5A/	VALUATION 1830S VAL 1B/ FIELD BOOKS OL4. (NATIONAL ARCHIVES)	TENEMENT VALUATION c.1858–9 VAL 2B/5/	VALUATION REVISIONS c.1860–c.1930 VAL 12B/
Templemore	91A	547A-F, 553A-D 1078	16A-J	32/8A-G, 10A-G, 11A-ZD, 33/1A-B, 2A-F, 3A-C, 5A-C
Termoneeny	261	538A & B 1094	41, 43B-C	34/17A-G, 23A-F, 28A-E
Upperlands (Maghera)				34/30A

* This parish was created in 1846 from parts of Balteagh, Bovevagh and Tamlaght Finlagan.
** This parish was created in 1843 out of Dunboe.
*** This parish was created in 1831 from parts of Banagher and Cumber Upper and Lower.

PARISH/TOWN/VILLAGE	TITHES 1823–38 FIN 5A/	VALUATION 1830S VAL 1B/	TENEMENT VALUATION c.1860 VAL 2B/6/	VALUATION REVISIONS c.1860–c.1930 VAL 12B/
Aghaloo	5	66B	6A-C	36/3A-D, 4A-B 38/3A-F, 8A-F, 21A-F
Aghalurcher	6	61A & B	1	36/11A-F, 14A-F
Arboe	14	618	18A-E 27	37/1A-F, 4A-G, 10A- F, 13A-G
Ardstraw	19	633A-F	35	35/5A-F, 8A-F, 17A-F
		637A-F	40A 47C	19A-F, 39/10A-E 41/27A-F, 42/ 1A-F, 2A, 7A-F, 12A-F, 17A-F, 27A-H
Artrea	22	619	19	37/4A-G, 21A-F
Ballinderry	25	620A & B	20	37/13A-G
Ballyclog	29	621A & B	21	37/1A-F
Beragh (Clogherny)		626A		
Bodoney Lower	58	643	45A-B	39/1A-E, 2A-E, 4A-D, 6A-E, 13A-D
Bodoney Upper	59	644 A & B	46 A-C	30/3A-E, 5A-F, 7A-G, 9A-G, 11A-G
Camus	64B & C	638 A-C	41	42/10A-G, 31A-M
Cappagh	65	626B	28 645A & B	41/6A-F, 17A-F, 47A-C 19A-F, 24A-F, 26A-F, 31A-F, 32A-G
Carrickmore (T'maguirk)		626A		
Carnteel	68	68	6C, 7A-B	36/3A-D, 4A-B, 5A-B, 7A-F, 18A-F, 38/1A-F, 3A-F, 10A-F
Castlederg (Urney)		626A		35/1A, 6A-F
Coagh (Tamlaght)		66A		
Coalisland (D'henry)		66A		
Clogher	73	62A-K 647	2A-F	36/1A-F, 2A-F, 6A-F, 8A-F, 9A-F, 10A-F, 11A-F, 14A-F, 16A-G
Clogherney	74	627	29	41/4A-G, 6A-F, 14A-F, 35A-F, 39A-F
Clonfeacle	79	610	9A-D	38/4A-F, 5A-F, 6A-F, 14A-F, 22A-F
Clonoe	80	69	10A-B	38/20A-F, 23A-F

PARISH/TOWN/ VILLAGE	TITHES 1823–38 FIN 5A/	VALUATION 1830S VAL 1B/	TENEMENT VALUATION c.1860 VAL 2B/6/	VALUATION REVISIONS c.1860–c.1930 VAL 12B/
Cookstown (Derryloran)		66A		
Cumber Upper		641		37/7A-C
Derryloran	84	622A & B	22A -B	37/5A-K, 7A-C, 11A-F, 15A-F, 21A-F
Desertcreat	97	623	24A-D	37/16A-F, 17A-F, 18A-F, 21A-F
Donacavey	103	63A & B, 628	2B, 3A-B 30	41/8A-F, 13A-E, 15A-F, 22A-F, 23A-F, 39A-F, 42A-E
Donaghedy	Nil	639A & B	42A-D	39/8A-E, 12A-E, 42/6A-G, 18A-G, 19A-G, 22A-F, 26A-G
Donaghenry	107	611	11A-B 18E	37/20A-G, 21A-F, 38/25A-F
Donaghmore	109A	612	12A-C	38/2A-F, 9A-F, 11A-F, 13A-F, 14A-F, 15A-F, 17A-N
Dromore	114	626A, 629	31A-B 33B	40/4A-F, 5A-F, 41/5-F, 16A-F, 25A-F, 43A-F
Drumglass	121	613	13 17A-N	38/5A-F, 15A-F,
Drumquin (Longfield E &W)		626A		
Drumragh	126	630A & B	32A -B	41/6A-F, 10A-F, 29A-F, 34A-M, 36A-M, 39A-F
Dungannon Middle	617		38/17A-N	
Errigal Keerogue	139	64A & B	4A-B	36/7A-F, 12A-F, 13A-F, 15A-F, 38/1A-F
Errigal Trough	MIC 442/10	65A-C	5	
Gortalowry (Derryloran)		66A		
Irishtown		626A		
Kildress	170	624	24A 25A-C	37/2A-F, 9A-F, 14A-F, 15A-F
Killeeshil	175	67	6C, 8	38/1A-F, 10A-F
Killyman	183	614	15A-C	38/5A-F, 16A-F
Kilskeery	191	631A & B	33A-B	40/1A-E, 2A-F, 4A-E, 5A-F
Learmount*			42D	
Leckpatrick	201	640	43A-B	42/5A-G, 22A-F, 31A-M
Lissan	203	625	26	37/3A-F, 11A-F
Longfield East	204	633A-F	36	41/18A-F, 34A-F

PARISH/TOWN/ VILLAGE	TITHES 1823–38 FIN 5A/	VALUATION 1830S VAL 1B/	TENEMENT VALUATION c.1860 VAL 2B/6/	VALUATION REVISIONS c.1860–c.1930 VAL 12B/
Longfield West	205	633A-F	37A-B	35/4A-F, 9A-F, 11A-F, 21A-F
Loy (Derryloran)		66A		
Omagh (Drumragh)				41/37A-G
Magheracross	213		33B	40/1A-E, 42/27A-H
Newtownstewart (Ardstraw)			40B	
Pomeroy	231	66A, 615	16A-D	37/16A-F, 38/2A-F, 13A-F
Stewartstown (Donaghenry)		66A		
Strabane (Camus & Urney)				42/31E-M
Tamlaght	251		27	37/4A-G
Termon Rock (Carrickmore)		626A		
Termonamongan	260	633A-F	38A-C	35/10A-F, 13A-F, 14A-F, 16A-F, 20A-F
Termonmaguirk	262	632, 646	34A-C	41/2A-F, 7A-F, 12A-F, 28A-F, 35A-F, 40A-F
Trillick (Kilskeery)		626A		
Tullyniskan	268	616	17	38/25A-F
Urney	MIC 442/8B	633A-F 642	39, 44	35/6A-F, 13A-F, 16A-F, 42/1A-F, 20A-G, 31A-M

* One townland only in Co Tyrone parish created 1831 from parts of Banagher and Cumber Upper and Lower.

There are two volumes containing valuations of properties in towns and villages in Co. Tyrone.
Val 1B|66A includes Coagh, Coalisland, Cookstown (including the townlands of Gortalowry and Loy which are both partly within Cookstown), Pomeroy and Stewartstown.
Val 1B|626A includes Beragh, Castlederg, Dromore, Drumquin, Fivemiletown, Termon Rock (Carrickmore), Irishtown (an unofficial name probably for an area on the outskirts of Omagh), and Trillick.

PARISH	TITHES 1823–38 TAB 3/	FILM	VALUATION FIELD BOOK 1830s OL4./ HOUSE BOOK [OL5.]	TENEMENT VALUATION FICHE c.1852–3	1841/1851 CENSUS SEARCH Cen /s/3
Agha	32	1	0163, 2016	2.G.12.	23-26
Aghade	43	2	0147	3.F.10.	12
Ardoyne	23	1	0148/53, 0179, 2036	2.B.4., 3.F.13	13-15
Ardristan	25	1	0180, 2037	2.B.4.	48
Ballinacarrig	6	1	0135, 1994,	1.B.4.	
Ballon	42	2	0154	3.G.2.	
Ballycrogue	7	1	0136, 1995	1.B.7.	
Ballyellin	36	1	0155, 0164, 0194, 2017	3.A.6., 3. G.9., 4.C.8.	16-17, 72-73
Baltinglass	13	1	0181, 2038	2.B.6.	49
Barragh	45	2	2005, 0197, 2010, 2059	3.G.10.	82
Carlow	4	1	0137, 1996	1.B.8.	1-5
Clonmelsh	5	1	0138, 1997	1.D.13.	
Clonmore	22	1	0182, 2039	2.B.7.	50-51
Clonygoose	37	2	0165, 2018	3.A.10.	27-28
Cloydagh	26	1	0174, 0139, 1998, 2028	1.E.1., 1.F.8.	42-43
Crecrin	21	1	2040, 0183	2.C.1.	
Dunleckny	33	1	0166, 2019	3.B.6.	29-30
Fennagh	24	1	0184, 0167, 2020, 2041, 0156	2.C.2., 3.C.9., 4.A.12.	18, 31
Gilbertstown	40	2	0157	4.A.13.	
Grangeford	9	1	0140, 1999	1.E.1.	
Hacketstown	19	1	0185, 2042	2.C.8.	52-54
Haroldstown	18	1	0186, 2043	2.D.5.	55
Kellistown	8	1	0141, 00158, 2000	1.E.6., 4.B.2.	6
Killerrig	3	1	0142, 2001	1.E.8.	7-9
Killinane	30	1	2029, 0168, 0175, 2021	1.F.12., 3.D.5.	44
Kiltegan	15	1	0187, 2045	2.D.8.	
Kiltennell	38	2	0169, 2022	3.D.5.	32-34
Kineagh	12	1	0188, 2044	2.D.9.	
Lorum	35	1	2023	3.E.4.	35-39
Moyacomb	46	2	0198	2.G.3.	83-84
Myshall	44	?	0159, 0170, 2011	3.E.10., 4.B.4.	19-22
Nurney	31	1	0143, 0160, 0171, 2002, 2024	1.E.11., 3.E.11., 4.C.4.	10
Oldleighlin	28	1	0176, 2030	1.G.1.	45-47
Painestown	1	1	0144	1.E.12.	
Rahill	11	1	0189, 2046	2.D.12.	57
Rathmore	17	1	0190, 2047	2.D.14.	58
Rathvilly	14	1	0191, 2048	2.E.1.	59-63
Sliguff	34	1	0172	3.E.13.	40-41
St.Mullin's	47	2	0195, 2056	4.C.10.	74-77
Straboe	16	1	0192, 2049	2.E.12.	64
Templepeter	41	2	0161	4.C.4.	
Tullowcreen	27	1	0177, 2031	2.A.4.	
Tullowmagimma	10	1	0145, 0162, 2003	1.E.4., 4.C.6.	11
Tullowphelim	20	1	0193, 2050	2.E.13.	65-71
Ullard	39	2	0196, 0173, 2025	3.E.10.	78-81
Urglin	2	1	0146, 2004	1.F.3.	
Wells	29	1	0178, 2032	2.A.11.	

PARISH	TITHES 1823–38 TAB 4/	FILM	VALUATION FIELD BOOKS 1830s OL4./ HOUSE BOOKS [OL5.]	TENEMENT VALUATION FICHE C.1857	1841/1851 CENSUS SEARCH Cen /s/4
Annagelliff	13	5	0224, [0061], [3787]	5 G 6	516-540
Annagh	16	5	0219, 0220, 0233, [0060 0069/70]	5.A.6., 5.F.2. 7.C.8.	470-482, 782-803
Bailieborough	23	5A	0199, 0206, [3772/5, 3798/9]	1.D.6., 1.A.14.	162-195
Ballintemple	26	5B	0212, [0047]	4.B.8.	284-341, 469
Ballyconnell (Tomregan)			[3800/01]		
Ballyjamesduff (Castlerahan)			[3802]		
Ballymachugh	28	5B	0213, [0048/9]	4.C.14.	342-3
Belturbet (Annagh & Drumlane)			[2387]		
Castlekeeran (Loughan)			[3764]		
Castlerahan	32	5B	2028A, [3764], [0037]	10.B.2.	2-40
Castleterra	11	4	0225, [0062/3]	6.A.6.	541-581
Cavan (Urney)			[3803]		
Crosserlough	30	5B	0200, [0038], 0214, [0050/1], 0226, [0064], 2029A, [3764], [3788],	6.C.3., 4.D.10. 4.F.10., 10.C.11.	41-86, 344-359, 582-584
Denn	14	5	0201, [0039], 0215, [0052/3], 0227, [3770], 2030A, 2033A, [3789/90]	6.C.4. 10.G.12. 4.E.5., 5.A.4. 10.C.13.	87-91, 360-365, 412, 585-631
Drumgoon	19	5A	0207, [0071], 0234	7.D.4., 8.D.8.	196-214, 632, 804-824
Drumlane	6	4	0221	2.D.12., 5.C.4.	483-513
Drumlumman	27	5B	0216, [0054/5]	4.E.9., 9.D.4.	366-440
Drumreilly			0238, [0079], 0239	2.E.4.	932-935
Drung	17	5	0235, [0072/3]	7.F.3.	825-857
Enniskeen	24	5A	0208, [3776/8]	1.E.13.	215-229
Kilbride	29	5B	0217, [0056], [3786]	4.E.9., 10.F.14.	441-449
Kildallan	7	4	0245	3.C.8., 3.E.12.	119-1134
Kildrumsherdan	18	5	0236, [0074/6]	7.G.12.	858-885
Killashandra	8	4	0246, [3804]	3.D.10., 3.F.2.	1135-1210, 1212
Killinagh	1	3	0240, [0080]	8.G.12.	936-1007
Killinkere	31	5B	0202, [0040], 0228, [3766], 2034A, [3791/2]	6.D.6., 1.B.9. 10.D.2.	92-120, 635-645
Kilmore	12	4	0218,[0057/8], 0229, [0065], [3793]	6.D.8., 4.E.11.	450-468, 646-675
Kinawley	3	4	0241, [0081/2], 0242	2.E.6., 9.B.6.	1008-1032
Knockbride	21	5A	0209, [3779/81], [3813]	2.B.8., 8.E.11.	231-257
Larah	20	5A	0230, [0066], 0237, [0077/8], [3794/6]	6.E.12., 5.G.3., 8.C.4.	676-704 887-931
Lavey	15	5	0231, [0067], [3795/6] [0041], [3767], [3764]	6.F.7. 9.G.10. 10.D.3.	705-757, 886 121-123
Loughan or Castlekeeran					
Lurgan	33	5B	0203, [0042], [3768]	10.D.8.	124-136
Moybolgue	25	5A	0210, [3782/3]	1.G.13.	258-262
Mullagh			0204, [0043], 2031A, [3771], [3806]	1.A.14., 9.G.10., 10.F.2.	137-154

PARISH	TITHES 1823–38 TAB 4/	FILM	VALUATION FIELD BOOKS 1830s OL4./ HOUSE BOOKS [OL5.]	TENEMENT VALUATION FICHE C.1857	1841/1851 CENSUS SEARCH Cen /S/4
Munterconnaught			0205, [0044], 2032A, [3769]	10.F.4.	155-161
Scrabby	9	4	0247, 2037A	4.B.5., 9.F.2.	1211, 1213-1227
Shercock	22	5A	0211, [0045], [3784/5], [3897]	2.A.4.	263-283
Swanlinbar (Kinawley)			[3808]		
Templeport	2	3	0243, [0083/4]	2.F.8., 9.B.7.	1033-1105
Tomregan	5	4	0222, [0059] 0244, [0085/6]	3.B.10., 2.D.13., 5.E.13.	514-515, 1106, 118
Urney	10	4	0223, [0068] 0232, [3797]	5.E.14., 6.G.10.	758-781
Virginia (Lurgan)			[3806]		

TOWNS	VALUATION HOUSE BOOK 1830s [OL5.]
Belturbet	[2387]
Kingscourt	[3799] [3805]

The 1821 census is available in the National Archives for 16 parishes: Annagelliff, Ballymachugh, Castlerahan, Castleterra, Crosserlough, Denn, Drumlumman, Drung, Kilbride, Kilmore, Kinawley, Larah, Lavey, Lurgan, Mullagh, Munterconnaught.

PARISH	TITHES 1823–38 TAB 5/	FILM	VALUATION FIELD BOOK 1830s OL4./ HOUSE BOOK [OL5.]	TENEMENT VALUATION FICHE 1855	1841/1851 CENSUS SEARCH Cen /s/5
Abbey	3	6	0268, 3818	1.A.12.	96-100
Bunratty	76	11	0248	2.D.10.	1
Carran	10	6	0269	1.B.5., 1.F.6.	101-106
Clareabbey	45	9	0304	3.D.8., 6.E.2.	638-640
Clondagad	46	9	0305	6.C.14.	641-664, 689
Clonlea	49	10	0314, 3840	9.D.4., 11.C.14.	874-878
Clonloghan	71	11	0249	2.D.14.	2
Clooney	18	7	0286	1.F.8., 4.G.4.	30-38, 303-311
Clooney	30	8	0262 08, 3807/08, 3809	2.G.10., 11.A.12.	30-38, 303-311
Doora	31	8	0263 8, 3809/10	2.G.12.	39-40
Drumcliff	43	9	0306	3.F.13.	665-677
Drumcreehy	2	6	0270, 3819	1.B.11.	107-110
Drumline	72	11	0250	2.E.3.	3
Dysert	25	8	0297, 3834	1.F.14., 3.C.6.	554-560
Feakle	33	8	0322	10.D.11., 11.F.2	994-1042
Feenagh	73	11	0251	2.E.6., 11.C.8.	
Gleninagh	1	6	3820, 0271	1.C.7.	111-113
Inagh	24	7	0298	4.F.2.	561-594
Inchicronan	27	8	0264, 3811/2	3.A.6., 11.B.5.	41-71
Inishcaltra			0323	10.E.10.	
Kilballyowen	57	10	0309	7.D.6.	694-724
Kilchreest	63	11	0279, 3828	5.F.10.	146-155
Kilconry	75	11	0252	2.E.9.	4-5
Kilcorney	9	6	0272	1.C.9.	114
Kilfarboy	39	9	0294	4.C.12.	407-435
Kilfearagh	56	10	0310	8.F.5.	725-758
Kilfenora	16	6	0287, [2412]	1.F.9., 4.G.13.	312-318
Kilfintinan	77	11	0254	9.B.5.	6-12
Kilfiddane	62	10	0280, 3829	5.G.6., 6.F.4.	173-191
Kilfinaghta	74	11	0253	2.E.11., 9.A.12., 11.C.8.	
Kilkeedy	20	7	0299	1.F.14.	595-606
Killadysert	64	11	0281, 3831	6.A.6.	156-172
Killaloe	53	10	0315, [0087], [2420/22]	9.D.8., 10.B.12	879-880
Killard	41	9	0295	7.A.6.	436-496
Killaspuglonane	14	6	0288	5.A.9.	319-324
Killeany	8	6	0273, 3821/22	1.C.12.	115-116
Killeely	78	11	0255	9.C.1.	13-15
Killilagh	12	6	0289	5.A.13.	325-354
Killimer	65	11	0282, 3832	6.F.4.	192-216
Killinaboy	21	7	0300, 3836	2.A.1.	607-613
Killofin	66	11	0283, 3830	6.B.9.	291-302
Killokennedy	51	10	0316, 3841/42	9.D.10.	881-888
Killonaghan	5	6	0274, 3823	1.C.14.	117-129
Killone	44	9	0307	3.E.4.	692-693
Killuran	48	10	3845, 3846, 0317	9.E.8., 11.D.7.	
Kilmacduane	55	10	0311, 3833	7.B.9., 8.A.12.	759-800
Kilmacrehy	13	6	0290	5.B.12.	355-369
Kilmaleery	70	11	0256	2.F.2.	16-17
Kilmaley	42	9	0308	3.E.11., 6.E.2.	678-688
Kilmanaheen	17	7	0291	5.C.12.	370-389

PARISH	TITHES 1823–38 TAB 5/	FILM	VALUATION FIELD BOOK 1830s OL4./ HOUSE BOOK [OL5.]	TENEMENT VALUATION FICHE 1855	1841/1851 CENSUS SEARCH Cen /s/5
Kilmihil	60	10	0284	3.C.4., 6.F.12.	217-274
Kilmoon	6	6	0275, 3824	1.D.5., 5.E.10.	130-131
Kilmurry	61	10	0285	6.C.5., 6.G.12.	18-23, 275-290, 497-553, 690
Kilmurry	40	9	0296	4.E.10., 7.B.9.	18-23, 275-290, 497-553, 690
Kilmurry	69	11	0257	11.C.10.	
Kilnamona	26	8	0301, 3837	3.C.14.	
Kilnasoolagh	67	11	0258	2.F.5.	24-25
Kilnoe	37	9	0324	10.E.10., 11.E.10.	691-693, 1043-1044
Kilraghtis	29	8	0265, 3813/14	3.B.2.	72-74
Kilrush	59	10	0312	8.D.3.	801-815
Kilseily	50	10	0318, 3847, 3848	9.E.9.	889-898
Kilshanny	15	6	0292	5.E.2.	390-406
Kiltenanlea	54	10	0319, 3849	9.F.9.	899-926
Kiltoraght	19	7	0293	1.F.10., 5.E.8.	406
Moyarta	58	10	0313	8.C.2.	817-873
Moynoe	35	8	0325	10.F.6.	1045-1053
Noughaval	11	6	0276, 3825	1.D.7., 1.F.6.	132-134
O'Briensbridge	52	10	0320, 3850	9.G.8., 10.C.14.	927-938
Ogonnelloe	47	10	0321, 3851	10.C.14.	939-943
Oughtmama	4	6	0277, 3826	1.D.9.	135-144
Quin	32	8	0266, 3815	3.B.9., 11.B.11.	75-89
Rath	22	7	0302, 3838	2.B.4., 4.G.2.	
Rathborney	7	6	0278, 3827	1.E.1.	145
Ruan	23	7	0303	2.B.10.	629-637
St Munchin	79	11	0259	9.C.7.	
St Patrick's	80	11	0260	9.C.10.	
Templemaley	28	8	0267, 3816/17	1.F.4., 3.B.11.	90-95
Tomfinlough	68	11	0261	2.F.9.	26-29
Tomgraney	34	8	0326, [2439]	10.F.11.	1054-1064
Tulla	36	9	0327, [0088, 2440/42]	11.E.2.	1080-1084

TOWNS	VALUATION HOUSE BOOK 1830s [OL5.]	TOWNS	VALUATION HOUSE BOOK 1830s [OL5.]
Ballyvaghan (Corranroo)	[2388/89]	Kilkishen	[2416]
Broadford	[2391]	Killadysert	[2417]
Carrigaholt	[2392]	Kilrush	[2423/26]
Clare	[2393/94]	Labasheeda	[2427/29]
Cooraclare	[2395]	Lahinch	[2411, 2412, 2430]
Corofin	[2396/98]	Liscannon	[2412]
Crusheen	[2399/400]	Milltown Malbay	[2431/33]
Ennis	[2401/09]	Newmarket-	
Ennistymon	[2410, 2411, 2412]	on-Fergus	[2434/35]
Kilkee	[2413/15]	Scariff	[2436]
		Sixmilebridge	[2437/38]

PARISH	TITHES 1823–38 TAB/	FILM	VALUATION FIELD BOOK 1830s OL4./ HOUSE BOOK [OL5.]	TENEMENT VALUATION FICHE 1851/3	1841/1851 CENSUS SEARCH Cen /s/6
Abbeymahon	6S/66	25	2203, [0470/71]		
Abbeymahon	6S/66	25	2203, [0470/71]	21.C.10.	932-938
Abbeystrowry	6S/52	24	[0260/63]	10.A.6.	267-270
Aghabulloge	6N/48	19	[0682/83]	32.E.8.	1082-1096
Aghacross	6E/32a	13	2160, [0314/5]	13.C.2.	
Aghada	6E/105	16	[0506/8]	23.C.9.	956-958
Aghadown	6S/55	24	[0264/67]	10.B.12.	271-277
Aghern	6E/69	14	[0658/60]	27.D.2.	1058a-1059
Aghinagh	6N/50	19	[0684/87]	32.F.13.	1097-1102
Aglish	6N/56	20	[0688/89]	31.F.12., 32.G.9.	
Aglishdrinagh	6N/24	18	2254, [0757/58]	23.E.2.	
Ardagh	6E/87	15	[0509/10]	22.D.10.	959
Ardfield	6S/61	24	2204, [0472/73]	21.D.8.	939
Ardnageehy	6E/42	13	[0009/11]	2.D.4., 3.C.1.	32-39
Ardskeagh	6E/2	12	[0452/53]	19.C.10.	
Athnowen	6N/57	20	[0699]	31.F.13., 32.A.10.	1103
Ballinaboy	6S/25	23	2220, [0370/72, 0597/98, 0599, 0570/72, 0690/91]	14.G.8., 32.B.2., 25.F.4., 24.F.4., 24.F.10.	973-974, 1104-1105
Ballinadee	6N/46	19	[0181/3], [0720/21]	33.F.10., 8.C.2., 8.C.4.	
Ballinadee	6S/74	25	2104, 2244, [0181/3]	33.F.10., 8.C.2., 8.C.4.	
Ballintemple	6E/108	16	[0511]	23.D.6.	960
Ballyclogh	6N/34	18	2255, [0410], [0759/61] [2445]	18.C.2., 35.D.12., 35.E.6.	1271
Ballycurrany	6E/53	14	2045a/46a, [0112/13]	3.B.6.	40
Ballydeloher	6E/59	14	[0114/17]	2.D.6.	
Ballydeloughy	6E/12	12	[0435A], 0446]	19.C.12.	891
Ballyfeard	6S/29	23	2221, [0600/02]	25.E.14., 25.F.8.	1021
Ballyfoyle	6S/35	23	2222, [0603/05]	25.E.14., 25.F.12	1022
Ballyhay	6E/1	12	[0452/53]	19.D.2.	892
Ballyhay	6N.20	18	2256, [0762/63]	35.E.14.	
Ballyhooly	6E/27	13	[0436/37], [2448/49]	19.C.2., 19.D.4.	893
Ballymartle	6S/26	23	[0599, 0606, 0672, 0673]	25.F.1., 25.G.2., 27.G.2.	1023-1025
Ballymodan	6S/20	22	2105, 2233 [0184/5, 0638/40]	26.E.14., 8.C.2., 8.C.14.	234-236, 1037-1050
Ballymoney	6S/70	25	2106, [0186/7]	8.C.2., 8.D.12.	237
Ballynoe	6E/70	15	[0661/63]	27.D.6.	1060-1062
Ballyoughtera	6E/94	15	[0512/13]	23.D.10.	
Ballyspillane	6E/62	14	2047a/48a, [0118/19]	3.G.11.	
Ballyvourney	6N/38	19	2245, [0722/23]	33.F.10.	1135-1170
Barnahely	6S/41	23	[0573/75]	24.F.4, 24.G.2.	975-981
Bohillane	6E/99	16	[0514]	23.E.2.	
Bregoge	6N/31	18	2257, [0764/66]	35.F.4.	
Bridgetown	6E/25	12	[0440]	19.D.10.	894
Brigown	6E/33	13	2161/62, [0316/23],	13.C.4.	465-470
Brinny	6S/17	22	2107, 2223, 2234 [0188, 0644/45, 0607/08]	26.G.4., 25.F.1., 25.G.8., 8.E.12.	1051-1052

PARISH	TITHES 1823–38 TAB	FILM	VALUATION FIELD BOOK 1830s OL4./ HOUSE BOOK [OL5.]	TENEMENT VALUATION FICHE 1851/3	1841/1851 CENSUS SEARCH Cen /s/6
Britway	6E/50	14	2049a/51a, [0664/66, 0120/21]	3.C.13., 3.G.13., 27.D.13.	41-42
Buttevant	6N/32	18	2258, [0767/69], [2461]	35.D.12.	1272-1280
Caheragh	6S/46	24	[0268/73], 2139/43, 2157		278-288
Caherduggan	6E/87	12	[0438/39],	19.E.2.	
Caherlag	6E/60	14	2051a/52a, [0122/23]	2.D.10., 4.A.1.	43-44
Cannaway	6N/55	19	[0695/96]		1110
Carrigaline	6E/84	15	2189, [0373/74, 0609/12, 0576/78]	14.C.9., 25.G.10., 24.F.4., 24.G.10.	493-509, 982-998
Carrigaline	6S/38	23	[0373/74, 0609/12, 0576/78]	14.C.9., 25.G.10., 24.F.4., 24.G.10.	
Carrigdownane	6E/13	12	[0446/47]	19.E.8.	
Carrigleamleary	6E/15	12	[0441/42]	19.E.10.	
Carrigrohane	6E/77	15	[0375/76, 0697/98]	15.A.7., 32.B.4.	1106-1109
Carrigrohane	6N/64	20	[0375/76, 0697/98]	15.A.7., 32.B.4.	
Carrigrohanebeg	6N/58	20	[0699], [0700]	32.B.10.	
Carrigtohill	6E/61	14	2053a, [0124/26]	2.E.3., 4.A.2.	45-50
Castlehaven	6S/53	24	2144, [0274/77]	10.D.7.	289-330
Castlelyons	6E/44	14	2054a/55a, 2163/64 [0324/25, 0127/30] [2460]	13.E.4., 3.C.14.	51-54
Castlemagner	6N/10	18	[0411], [2462]	16.D.12.	
Castletownroche	6E/17	12	[0443], [2466/68],	19.C.2., 19.E.4.	895
Castleventry	6S/13	22	2205, [0189/91, 0474/75]	6.D.4., 21.E.4.	331, 940
Churchtown	6N/27	18	2259, [0412/13], [0770/71] [2472]	16.E.9., 35.D.13., 35.G.8.	1281
Clear Island	6S/58	24	[0278/80]	10.E.11.	332
Clenor			[0444/45]	19.F.10.	
Clondrohid	6N39	19	2246, [0724/27]	33.G.14.	1171-1190
Clondulane	6E/38a	13	[0326]	13.E.8.	471
Clonfert	6N/1	17	[0414, 0420, 0431]	16.E.10.	710-733
Clonmeen	6N/13	18	[0415]	17.B.10.	734-740
Clonmel	6E/66	14	2056a, 2058a, [0131/33]	2.E.3.	55-62
Clonmelsh	6E/66	14		2.E.3.	
Clonmult	6E/58	14	2059a, 2060a, [0515/16, 0664/66, 0134/35]	4.B.3., 27.D.13., 23.E.4.	
Clonpriest			[0517/18]	22.E.4.	
Clontead	6S/83, 84	26	[0672/73, 0679]	27.G.3.	1074
Cloyne	6E/98	16	[0519, 0530/31]	23.E.4.	961
Coole	6E/45	14	[0136/38]	3.D.13.	
Cooliney	6N/23	18	2260, [0772/73]	36.A.2.	
Corbally	6N/66	20	[0699], [0700]	32.B.12.	
Corcomohide	6N/18	18	2261, [0774/75]	36.A.4.	
Cork City Parishes	6E/80	15		30.F.4., 30.D.8., 29.A.12., 29.G.14., 28.F.4., 28.G.3.	
Corkbeg	6E/107	16	[0528/29]	23.F.12.	
Courtmasherry			[0476]		
Creagh	6S/56	24	[0281/84]	10.F.2.	333-336

PARISH	TITHES 1823–38 TAB	FILM	VALUATION FIELD BOOK 1830s OL4./ HOUSE BOOK [OL5.]	TENEMENT VALUATION FICHE 1851/3	1841/1851 CENSUS SEARCH Cen /s/6
Cullen	6N/11	18	[0416, 0599, 0613]	18.F.10., 25.G.12.	741-780, 1026
Cullen	6S/27	23	2224, [0416, 0599, 0613]	18.F.10., 25.G.12.	
Currykippane	6E/75	15	2190, [0377/78]	15.A.10.	
Dangandonovan	6E/88	15	[0526/27]	22.F.1., 23.G.3.	
Derryvillane			2165/66 [0327/29], [0446/47]	19.G.2., 13.F.2.	472, 896
Desert	6S/79	26	2108, 2206 [0192/3, 0477/78]	21.E.6., 8.E.14.	
Desertmore	6N/61	20	[0701/02]	31.F.14.	1111-1112
Desertserges	6S/71	25	2109, 2131, 2235 [0194/6, 0646/47]	26.G.8., 8.F.4.	238-241, 1053-1054
Donaghmore	6S/68	25	2207, [0479/80, 0092/94], [3807]	33.A.7., 1.G.8., 21.E.8.	
Donaghmore	6N/49	19	[0479/78, 0092/94] [0703/04], [3807]	33.A.7., 1.G.8., 21.E.8.	1113-1114
Doneraile	6E/5	12	[2595/97]	19.C.3., 19.G.4.	897-900
Drinagh	6S/51	24	[0197/8, 0285/87]	6.D.12., 7.F.8., 10.G.13.	337-339
Drishane	6N/36	19	2247, [0417/18], [0728/29] [2599]	18.G.12., 34.G.12	781, 1192-1236?
Dromdowney	6N/35	19	2262, [0776/77]	36.A.6.	
Dromdaleague	6S/50	24	[0288/91]	11.A.8.	340-341
Dromtarriff	6N/12	18	[0419]	17.D.3.	782-784
Dunbulloge	6E/41	13	2061a, 2191 [0139/40, 0379]	2.E.10., 15.A.14.	62-65
Dunderrow	6N/68	20	[0614/15, 0672, 0674] [0705/06]	25.F.1., 26.A.4., 27.G.11.	
Dunderrow	6S/24	23	2225, [0614/15, 0672, 0674]	25.F.1., 26.A.4., 27.G.11.	1075, 1115-1117
Dungourney	6E/57	14	2062/63a [0525, 0141/42]	4.B.6., 23.G.6.	
Dunisky	6N/44	19	2248, [0730/31]	34.B.10.	1236-1237
Dunmahon	6E/20	12	2167, [0449]	20.A.12., 13.F.4.	901
Durrus	6S/45	24	2038a, 2039a, 2145/46, [0292, 0089/90]	1.A.14., 12.F.14.	342-350
Fanlobbus	6S/9	22	2110, 2132, [0199/201]	7.A.4.	351-356
Farahy	6E/7	12	2168, [0330/32, 0450]	20.B.2., 13.F.6.	902
Fermoy	6E/38	13	2169, 2201/2, [0333/37]	13.F.8.	473-474
Garranekinnefeake	6E/97	16	[0524]	23.G.8.	972
Garrycloyne	6N/54	19	[0095/97, 0697/98]	32.C.2., 2.A.2.	1118-1123
Garryvoe	6E/100	16	[0523]	23.G.12.	
Glanworth	6E/18	12	2170/71, [0338/40, 0451]	19.C.3., 20.B.8., 14.A.6.	903-905
Glenor	6E/16	12			
Grenagh	6N/72	20	[0098/100, 0697/98] [3808]	32.C.9., 2.A.4.	22-27
Gortroe	6E/49	14	2064/65, [0143/44]	3.D.14.	66
Hackmys	6N/22	18	2263, [0778/79]	36.A.8.	
Ightermurragh	6E/95	15	[0520/22]		963

PARISH	TITHES 1823–38 TAB	FILM	VALUATION FIELD BOOK 1830s OL4./ HOUSE BOOK [OL5.]	TENEMENT VALUATION FICHE 1851/3	1841/1851 CENSUS SEARCH Cen /s/6
Inch	6E/103	16	[0539/40]	24.A.11.	
Inchigeelagh	6N/42	19	2249, [0732/37]	33.D.12., 34.B.11.	
Inchigeelagh	6S/6	21	[0202/4]	33.D.12., 34.B.11., 7.D.8.	1238-1246
Inchinabacky	6E/65	14	2065a, [0145]	4.B.13.	
Inishcarra	6N/52	19	[0707/08]	32.C.9.	1124
Inishkenny	6N/69	20	[0380/83], [0699], [0700]	15.A.14.	510
Inishkenny	6E/83	15	2192, [0380/83]	32.D.6., 15.A.4.	
Inishannon	6S/22	23	2111, 2226 [0205/6, 0616/18]	25.F.1., 26.A.8., 8.G.8.	242-243, 1027-1029
Imphrick	6E/41	12			906
Imphrick	6N/29	18	2264, [0452/53], [0780/81]	36.A.10., 20.C.6.	
Island	6S/62	24	2112, 2208 [0207/8, 0481/82]	21.E.10., 8.G.14.	
Kilbolane	6N/17	18	2265, [0782/83]	35.D.13., 36.A.12., 31.G.3.	1282-1288
Kilbonane	6N/60	20	[0709/10]		1127
Kilbrin	6N/7	17	[0421/22]	17.D.12.	788-791
Kilbrittain	6S/73	25	2113, [0209/10]	9.A.4.	
Kilbrogan	6S/19	22	2236, [0641/45, 0648/51]	26.G.12.	1055
Kilbroney	6N/30	18	2266, [0784/85]	36.B.12.	1289
Kilcaskan	6S/2	21	2090/93, [0175]	4.E.4.	90-129
Kilcatherine	6S/1	21	2094/96, [0176/77]	5.A.4.	130-188
Kilcoe	6S/48	24	2147, 2158/59, [0293]	11.G.10.	358-366
Kilcorcoran	6N/6	17	[0423/24]	17.E. 10.	
Kilcorney	6N/37	19	[0738/40]	35.C.1.	1247-1251
Kilcredan	6E/101	16	[0537/38]	24.B.2.	
Kilcrohane	6S/44	23	2148, [0294/95]	12.A.10.	357, 367-374
Kilcrumper	6E/21	12	2172/73, [0341/42]	19.C.3., 20.C.10., 14.A.10.	
Kilcully	6E/74	15	[0384/85]	15.B.5.	
Kilcummer			[0454/56]	20.C.14.	
Kildorrery	6E/30	13	2174/75, [0343/45, 0457/58]	20.D.4., 14.A.12.	
Kilfaughnabeg	6S/14	22	2114, 2133 [0211/13]	6.D.10., 7.F.11.	375-378
Kilgarriff	6S/75	25	2115, 2209 [0214, 0483/84]	9.A.12., 21.E.14., 8.C.3.	244
Kilgrogan	6N/28	18	2267, [0786/87]	36.C.2.	
Kilgullane	6E/34	13	2176, [0346/47, 0449]	20.D.6., 14.B.6.	479
Kilkerranmore	6S/59	24	2210, 2216 [0215/17, 0485/87]	6.D.12., 21.F.2.	941-942
Killaconenagh	6S/4	21	2097/100, [0178/79]	5.C.8.	218-233
Killanully	6S/39	23	[0386], [0579/81]	25.A.14., 15.B.6.	999
Killanully	6E/86	15	2193, [0386]	25.A.14., 15.B.6.	
Killaspugmullane	6E/51	14	2066, [0146/47]	2.F.14.	68-69

PARISH	TITHES 1823–38 TAB	FILM	VALUATION FIELD BOOK 1830s OL4./ HOUSE BOOK [OL5.]	TENEMENT VALUATION FICHE 1851/3	1841/1851 CENSUS SEARCH Cen /s/6
Killathy	6E/28	13	[0458a]	20.D.8.	
Killeagh	6E/90 & 91	15	[0532/36], [2615]	22.F.1., 24.B.4.	964-966
Killeenemer	6E/19	12	[0449]	20.D.12.	
Killowen	6S/18	22	2237, [0652/53]	27.B.2.	
Killowillan	6E/110	16		27.B.2.	
Kilmacabea	6S/11	22	2117, 2134 [0218/20, 0296/97]	7.G.7., 11.B.14.	380-384
Kilmacdonogh	6E/96	16	[0544/45]	22.F.11., 24.B.4.	
Kilmaclenine	6N/33	18	2268, [0788/89]	36.C.4.	1290
Kilmahon	6E/104	16	[0541/43]	24.B.5.	
Kilmaloda	6S/72	25	2119, [0221/3]	8.C.3., 9.C.8.	245-246
Kilmeen	6S/10	22	2120, 2135, [0224/27, 0488/89, 0425/26]	17.E.12, 19.A.9., 6.D.12, 7.D.11., 21.F.12.	
Kilmeen	6N/5	17	2211, [0224/27, 0488/89, 0425/26]	17.E.12, 19.A.9., 6.D.12, 7.D.11., 21.F.12	247-249, 785-787, 792-813, 943
Kilmichael	6N/45	19	2250, [0741/44]	33.E.9., 34.D.1., 7.E.4.	
Kilmichael	6S/7	21	2121, 2136, [0228/31]	33.E.9., 34.D.1., 7.E.4.	1252-1253
Kilmocomoge	6S/5	21	2042a, 2043a 2118, 2149, [0232/33, 0298/99, 0091]	1.B.3., 6.D.2., 12.A.6.	1-21, 379
Kilmoe	6S/49	24	2150/52, [0300/303]	12.G.10.	385-409
Kilmoney	6S/42	23	[0582/83]	25.B.2.	
Kilmonogue	6S/32	23	2227, [0091], [0619]	25.F.1., 26.B.2.	1030-1032
Kilmurry	6N/47	19	2251, [0718/19], [0745/47]	34.D.3., 31.G.9.	1254-1255
Kilnaglory	6N/63	20	[0387/88], [0699], [0700]	15.B.7., 32.D.10.	
Kilnaglory	6E/82	15	2194, [0387/88]	15.B.7., 32.D.10.	
Kilnagross	6S/77	26	2122, [0234]	9.D.6.	
Kilnamanagh	6S/3	23	2101/03, [0180]	5.F.5.	189-217
Kilnamartery	6N/40	19	2252 [0748/50]	34.D.13.	1256-1257
Kilpatrick	6S/31	23	[0620/22, 0584/85]	26.B.8., 25.B.6.	1000
Kilphelan	6E/35	12	2177/78, [0348/49]	14.B.10.	
Kilquane	6E/52	14	2067, 2069/70, [0452/3]		
Kilquane		12	2067, [0148]	2.G.6., 20.D.14.	
Kilroan	6S/82	26	[0404/05, 0672, 0674]	16.B.2., 27.G.14.	
Kilroe	6N/8	18	[0427]	17.G.10.	814
Kilsillagh	6S/69	25	2212, [0490/91]	21.F.14.	944
Kilshanahan	6E/48	14	2070/71, [0149/50]	3.E.9.	67
Kilshannig	6N/16	18	2200, [0428]	18.C.8.	815-843
Kilworth	6E/36	13	2179, [0350/51] [2616]	14.B.12.	475-478
Kinneigh	6S/8	22	2137, [0235/37]	6.C.6., 7.E.8.	250-253
Kinsale	6S/85	26	[0675/76, 0677]	28.A.1.	1077-1078, 1298
Kinure	6S/33	23	[0623/25]	25.F.1., 26.B.12.	1033
Knockavilly	6S21	23	[0626/27]	25.F.2., 26.C.2., 31.G.10.	

PARISH	TITHES 1823–38 TAB	FILM	VALUATION FIELD BOOK 1830s OL4./ HOUSE BOOK [OL5.]	TENEMENT VALUATION FICHE 1851/3	1841/1851 CENSUS SEARCH Cen /s/6
Knockavilly	6N/67	20	[0626/27], [0711/12]	25.F.2., 26.C.2., 31.G.10.	1126
Knockmourne	6E/68	14	2072, 2180 [0352, 0667/68, 0151]	14.C.10., 3.E.13., 27.D.14.	70, 480-482, 1063-1066
Knocktemple			[0429]	17.G.14, 18.E.13.	844-851
Lackeen	6N/26	18	2269, [0790/90a]	36.C.6.	
Leighmoney	6S/28	23	2228, [0628, 0629]	26.C.6.	1034
Leitrim	6E/39	13	2181/82, [0353/55]	14.C.12.	
Liscarroll	6N/25	18	2270, [0791/93], [2627]	35.D.13., 36.C.8.	1291-1293
Liscleary	6S/40	23	[0586/88]	25.B.8.	1001-1002
Lisgoold	6E/54	14	2073/75, 0152/53	4.C.1.	
Lislee	6S/67	25	2213, [0492/94]	21.G.2.	945-953
Lismore & Mocollop	6E/40	13	2185, [0356/57]	14.D.4.	483-485
Litter	6E/29	12	[0358/59, 0459/60]	20.E.2., 14.D.6.	907
Little Island	6E/60	14	2075/76, [0154/56]	2.G.9.	
Macloneigh	6N/43	19	[0751/52]	34.E.11.	1269-1270
Macroney	6E/37	13	2185, [0360/64]	14.D.10.	489-490
Macroom	6N/41	19	2253, [0753/56], [2628/30]	34.F.2.	1258-1268
Magourney	6N/59	19	[0713/15]	33.B.12.	1128-1129, 1134
Mallow	6N/15	18	[0461, 0430], [2631/37]	19.C.3., 20.E.6., 18.E.14.	908-923
Mallow	6E/14	12	[0461, 0430]	19.C.3., 20.E.6., 18.E.14.	
Marmullane	6S/36	23	[0589/91]	24.F.5., 25.B.15.	1003-1005
Marshalstown	6E/32	13	2186, [0365/67]	14.E.6.	486-488
Matehy	6N/53	19	[0716/17]	32.D.14.	1130-1133
Middleton	6E/93	15	[0546/50], [2638/39]	24.B.10.	
Mogeely	6E/71, 89	15	[0551/55, 0669/71]	27.E.7., 24.D.3.	967, 1067-1073
Mogeesha	6E/64	14	2077/78 [0556/57, 0157]	4.C.5., 24.D.13.	968
Monanimy	6E/24	12	[0462/63]	19.C.3., 20.G.6.	924-925
Monkstown	6S/37	23	[0592/94]	24.F.5., 25.C.8.	1006-1016
Mourneabbey	6E/22	12	[0464]	21.A.2., 2.B.2.	28-31
Mourneabbey	6N/71	20	[0464, 0101/04]	21.A.2., 2.B.2.	
Moviddy	6N/59	20	[0718/19]	31.G.13.	
Murragh	6S/15	22	2123, 2238/39, [0238/40, 0654/55]	6.C.13., 27.B.4.	1056-1057b
Myross	6S/54	24	[0304/8]	11.C.5.	410-441
Nohaval	6S/34	23	2229, [0630/32]	26.C.10.	
Nohavaldaly	6N/4	17	[0432]	18.A.5.	852-876
Rahan	6E/23	12	[0465/66]	19.C.4., 21.A.4.	926-929
Rathbarry	6S/60	24	2214, [0241/43 [0495/6]	6.E.4., 22.A.8.	954
Rathclarin	6S/78	26	2124, [0244/46]	8.C.3., 9.D.14.	254-256
Rathcooney	6E/73	15	2195, [0389/91]	15.B.8.	511-517

PARISH	TITHES 1823–38 TAB	FILM	VALUATION FIELD BOOK 1830s OL4./ HOUSE BOOK [OL5.]	TENEMENT VALUATION FICHE 1851/3	1841/1851 CENSUS SEARCH Cen /s/6
Rathcormack	6E/43	13	2079/80, [0158/60]	3.E.14.	71-79
Rathgoggan	6N/21	18	2271, [0794/97]	35.D.13., 36.D.2.	1294-1297
Ringcurran	6S/86	26	2230, [0629, 0633, 0672, 0674, 0677/80]	26.D.2.	1076, 1079-1081
Ringrone	6S/81	26	2125, [0247, 0406/07, 0672, 0674, 0680]	8.C.3., 9.E.12., 16.A.14., 16.B.6., 28.D.2.	257, 707
Ross	6S/12	22	2126, 2138, 2215 [0248, 0250/52, 0497/98]	6.E.5., 22.B.4.	258-264
Rosskeen	6N/14 6N/70	18 20	[04330]	18.A.8.	877
Rostellan	6E/102	16	[0556/59]	24.E.1.	969
Shandrum	6N/19	18	2272, [0798/99]	35.D.14.	
Skull	6S/47	24	2153/56, [0309]	12.B.14.	442-463
St Anne's (Shandon)	6E/77	15	[0392/94], [2497/515]	15.C.8.	518-520, 601-609, 610
St Finbar's	6E/79	15	[0395/96], [2516/27]	32.A.7., 15.D.3.	
St Finbar's	6N/62	20	[0395/96], [0699]	32.A.7., 15.D.3.	521-534, 611-649
St Mary's (Shandon)	6E/76	15	2196, [0397/98], [2428/47]	15.F.8.	535-539, 650-676
St Michael's	6E/46	14	2081, 2197, [0161/63, 0399]	2.G.12., 15.F.14.	
St Nathlash	6E/10	12	[0467]	21.B.12.	930
St Nicholas	6N/65	20	[0400/1], [0699], [0700]	32.E.7., 15.G.1.	
St Nicholas	6E/81	15	2198, [0400/01] [2548/64]	32.E.7., 15.G.1.	677
Subulter	6N/9	18	[0434], [3809]	18.A.10.	
Templebodan	6E/55	14	[0164], 2081	4.C.10.	80
Templebreedy	6S/43	23	[0595/96]	24.F.5., 25.D.8.	1017-1020
Templebryan	6S/76	26	2127, [0253/54	9.F.4.	
Templemartin	6S/16	22	2240, [0656/57]	27.B.12.	
Templemichael	6S/23	23	2231, [0634/35]	26.D.4.	
Templemolaga	6E/31	13	2187, [0368/69]	14.F.2.	
Templenacarriga	6E/56	14	2083/84, [0165]	4.D.2.	491-492
Templeomalus	6S/63	24	2216, [0499/500]	22.B.6.	
Templequinlan	6S/64	25	2128/2217, [0255/56, 0501/02]	22.B.12., 9.F.8.	
Templeroan	6E/6	12	[0468]	19.C.4., 21.B.6.	931
Templerobin	6E.67	14	2085/86, [0166/71]	3.G.14.	81-89
Templetrine	6S/80	26	2129, [0257/58, 0408/09]	8.C.3., 9.F.10., 16.A.14., 16.C.6.	708
Templeusque	6E/47	14	2087, [0172/73]		
Timoleague	6S/65	25	2130, 2218, [0259, 0503], [2657]	22.C.2., 9.G.2.	265-266, 955
Tisaxon			2241	28.D.7.	
Titeskin	6E/106	16	[0560/61]	24.E.4.	
Trabolgan	6E/109	16	[0562/63]	24.E.6.	
Tracton	6S/30	23	2232, [0636/37a]	25.F.2., 26.D.8.	1035-1036

PARISH	TITHES 1823–38 TAB	FILM	VALUATION FIELD BOOK 1830s OL4./ HOUSE BOOK [OL5.]	TENEMENT VALUATION FICHE 1851/3	1841/1851 CENSUS SEARCH Cen /s/6
Tullagh	6S/57	24	[0310/13]	11.D.1.	464
Tullylease	6N/2	17	2273 [0435] [0800/01]	18.A.11., 36.F.4.	878-890
Wallstown	6E/9	12	[0458a, 0469]	21.B.12.	
Whitechurch	6E/72	15	2199 [0105/08, 0174/74a, 0402/03]	2.B.14., 3.B.13., 15.G.10.	
Whitechurch	6N/73	20	[0105/08, 0174/74a, 0402/03]	2.B.14., 3.B.13., 15.G.10.	541
Youghal	6E/92	15	[0564/69], [2661/69]	22.G.9.	970-972

TOWNS & VILLAGES	VALUATION HOUSE BOOK 1830s [OL5.]	TOWNS & VILLAGES	VALUATION HOUSE BOOK 1830s [OL5.]
Aghern Village	[2482]	Glanmire	[2607]
Bandon	[2454/58] [0641/43]	Glanworth	[2608/09]
Bantry	[2459]	Holy Trinity	[2483/96]
Ballincollig	[2443/44] [0693/94]	Inishannon	[2610]
Ballycottin	[2446, 2447]	Kanturk	[2611/13]
Ballyclogh	[2627]	Killawillin	[2614]
Ballymagooly	[2450]	Killeagh	[2615]
Ballynacorra	[2451/52]	Kilworth	[2616]
Ballyneen	[2453]	Kingwilliamstown	[2469]
Ballynoe Village	[2482]	Kinsale	[2617/21, 2623/24]
Berehaven	[2465]	Lady's bridge	[2625/26]
Boherboy	[2469]	Millstreet	[2640]
Bridebridge	[2460]	Miscellaneous	[2579/94]
Castlemartyr	[2463/64] [0520/22]	Mitchelstown	[2641/42] [0322?]
Castletown (Berehaven)	[2465]	New Glanmire	[2643]
Castletownsend	[2658] [0304/8]	Newmarket	[2644]
Cecilstown	[2469]	Newmarket	[2469]
Charleville	[2470/71] [0794/92]	Passage West	[2645]
Churchtown	[2627]	Queenstown	[2646/49] [0166/71]
Clonakilty	[2473/78]	Riverstown	[2650]
Cloyne	[2479/80]	Rockmills	[2651]
Coachford	[2481] [0713/15]	Ross Carbery	[2652/53]
Cobh (See Queenstown)	[2481]	Scartlea	[2447]
Conna Village	[2482]	Shanagarry	[2447]
Carraglass Village	[2482]	Shanagarry	[2654]
Douglas	[2598]	Shanballymore	[2655]
Dunmanway	[2600/602]	Skibbereen	[2656]
Farsid	[2660]	St Paul's	[2565/69]
Fermoy	[2603/06]	St Peter's	[2570/78]
Freemount	[2469]	Union Hall	[2658] [0304/8]
		Watergrasshill	[2659]
		Whitegate	[2660]

PARISH	TITHES 1823–38 TAB 7/	FILM	VALUATION FIELD BOOKS 1830s OL4./ HOUSE BOOKS [OL5.]	TENEMENT VALUATION c. 1857 FICHE	1841–1851 CENSUS SEARCHES Cen /s/7
Aghanunshin	18	29	0353, 2316, [0818]	9.A.12.	671-680
Allsaints	29	30	0365, [0832]	9.G.6., 11.A.2.	1345-1357
Aughnish	16	29	0354, 2317, [0819/20]	9.B.4. 12.D.11.	681-696
Ballintra (Drumhome)			[2671]		
Ballyshannon (Kilbarron)			[2671]		
Bundoran (Inishmacsaint)			[2671] [3810]		
Burt	25	30	0346, 2310/11, [0816] 2306	10.C.10.	563-583
Carndonagh					
Clonca	1	27	0340, 2307	7.B.4.	487-502
Clondahorky	10	28	0355, 2318, [0821]	3.F.10.	697-747
Clondavaddog	7	27	0356, 2319, [0822]	13.B.4.	748-808, 1667
Clonleigh	35	31	0368, 2329/30, [0833]	14.C.5.	1358-1384, 1387-8, 1930
Clonmany	2	27	0341, 2308	7.C.13.	503-517 [T550/37 in PRONI]
Convoy	36	31	0366, [0834]	14.F.2.	1528-1558
Conwal	17	29	0357, 0367, 2320/21, 2331	9.D.1. 11.C.12. 15.F.10.	809-882 1559-1580
Culdaff	4	27	0342, 2309, [0812/3]	7.E.10.	518-526
Derry (Templemore)					
Desertegny	20	29	0347	8.E.8.	584-595
Donagh	3	27	0343	7.G.6.	527-539
Donaghmore	39	31	0369, 2332, [0835]	13.E.8. 14.G.12.	1581-1621 1645
Donegal	49	32	0378-79, [2671]	2.G.6.	1668-1715
Drumhome	49	32	0380, [0842]	1.A.12.	1716-1799, 1847
Fahan Lower	21	30	0348	8.F.1.	596-629
Fahan Upper	22	30	0349, 2312	10.D.8.	630-644
Gartan	14	29	0358, 2322, [0823]	4.A.7. 9.B.6.	883-905
Glencolumbkille	42	32	0328, [0802] 2275, 2284	4.G.8.	1-51
Inch	24	30	0350, 2313/14	10.E.5.	645-653
Inishkeel	28	30	0329, 0336, 2276, 2285, 2289/90, 2300/02, 2305, [0803/04]	5.G.2. 5.B.3.	52-85 316-372
Inishmacsaint	52	32	0381	1.E.8.	1800-1808 1814-1819, 1824
Inver	46	32	0330, [0805/06], 2277	2.B.2.	86-187, 714

PARISH	TITHES 1823–38 TAB 7/	FILM	VALUATION FIELD BOOKS 1830s OL4./ HOUSE BOOKS [OL5.]	TENEMENT VALUATION c. 1857 FICHE	1841–1851 CENSUS SEARCHES CEN S|7|
Kilbarron	51	32	0379 0382	1.B.14. 7.A.4.	1803, 1807-1813 1819-1885
Kilcar	42	32	0331, 2278	5.C.1.	188-222
Killaghtee	45	32	0332, 2279-80, 2287, [0807]	2.D.9. 5.D.9.	223-245
Killea	33	31	0370, [0836]	11.B.2.	1389-1393
Killybegs Lower	41	32	0333, 0337, 2281, 2285, 2292/3, [0808/09]	6.C.4. 5.D.12.	246-261, 351 373-377
Killybegs Upper			0334, 2282, 2286-7, [0810]	5.E.9.	262-284
Killygarvan	13	29	0359, 2323, [0824]	12.G.13.	562, 906-930, 786
Killymard	47	32	0335, 2283, 2288, [0811]	2.E.12.	278, 285-315, 714
Kilmacrenan	15	29	0360, 2324, [0825]	4.A.9., 9.C.7. 12.F.3.	802, 931-993
Kilteevoge	37	31	0371	15.C.2.	1384-6, 1622-1644
Laghy (Drumhome)			[2671]		
Leck	30	31	0372	9.G.6.	863, 1394-1409
Letterkenny (Conwal)			[3811]		
Lettermacaward	27	30	0338, 2294/95, 2303	6.C.7.	378-397
Malin (Clonca)			[3812]		
Mevagh	11	28	0361, 2325	11.C.14.	517, 994-1075
Mintiaghs (Barr of Inch)	19	29	0351	8.G.10.	650-653
Moville Lower	5	27	0344, [0814]	8.A.14.	540-550
Moville Upper	6	27	0345, [0815]	8.C.11.	551-562
Muff	13	30	0352, 2315, [0817]	10.E.8.	654-670
Raphoe	34	31	0373, 2333-5, [0837/8]	10.B.3. 13.G.6.	1410-1445 1532, 1547
Raymoghy	34	31	0374, [0839/40]	10.A.3. 11.B.6.	1357-1667 1446-1486
Raymunterdoney	9	28	0362, 2326, [0826]	14.A.13. 4.A.11.	1076-1094
Stranorlar	38	31	0375, 2336	15.D.8.	1645-1660
Taughboyne	32	31	0376, [0841]	11.B.9. 14.B.3.	506, 1487-1527 1373, 1470
Templecarn	50	32	0383	3.D.4.	1886-1929
Templecrone	26	30	0339, 2304, 2296/9	6.D.4.	398-486
Templemore	20	29	0364, [0827/9]		

PARISH	TITHES 1823–38 TAB 7/	FILM	VALUATION FIELD BOOKS 1830s OL4./ HOUSE BOOKS [OL5.]	TENEMENT VALUATION c. 1857 FICHE	1841–1851 CENSUS SEARCHES CEN S|7|
Tullaghobegley	8	28	0363, 2327, [0827/29]	4.B.8.	433, 1095-1319
Tullyfern	12	29	0364, 2328, [0830/31]	12.B.11.	768, 794, 1320-1344
Urney	40	32	0377, 2337	13.F.10.	1661-1667

TOWNS	VALUATION HOUSE BOOK 1830s [OL5.]
Ballyshannon	[2671]
Bundoran	[3810, 2671]
Letterkenny	[3811]
Lifford	[2670]
Malin	[3812]
Pettigoe	[2671]
Killybegs	X.056 valuation book 1857

PARISH	TITHES 1823–38 TAB 9/	FILM	VALUATION FIELD BOOKS 1830s OL4./ HOUSE BOOKS [OL5.]	TENEMENT VALUATION 1848–52 FICHE	1841–1851 CENSUS SEARCHES Cen /s/9
Aderrig	49	34		4.G.2., 5.B.13	
Artaine/Artane		34	[0864/65], [2711]	2.G.10	
Baldongan	5	33	[0843]	1.A.8., 1.G.7	
Baldoyle		34		2.G.12.	
Balgriffin	34	34	[0866/67], [2711]	3.A.3.	
Ballyboghil	14	33		2.A.3., 2.A.6.	
Ballyfermot	59	34	[0931]	7.A.14.,	
& Palmerstown				8.A.7.	
Ballymadun	10	33	[0856]	2.A.8., 2.C.10.	
Balrothery	2	33	[0844/45], [2673]	1.A.9., 1.G.7.	1-5
Balscaddan	1	33	[0846/47]	1.C.3.	
Booterstown	71	35	[2675], [0895]	3.G.6., 4.C.7., 5.C.14.	300-301
Castleknock	26	34	[3814]	2.D.6., 2.G.1.	26
Chapelizod	27	34		2.E.6., 2.G.1.	27-28
Cloghran	31	34	[0868/69], [2711]	2.E.9., 2.G.1.	
Clondalkin	58	34	[0931a/34]	4.G.2., 5.B.1., 7.B.1, 8.A.7.	334-339
Clonmethan	12	33	[0857]	2.A.10., 2.C.10	20
Clonsilla	25	33	[0862]	2.E.10., 2.G.10	
Clontarf	46	34	[0870/71]	3.A.8.	30-31
Clonturk		34	[0872/74]	3.B.3.	32
Clorhran		33			
Coolock	35	34		3.B.12.	33-34
Cruagh	66	35		7.B.13., 8.A.7.	340
Crumlin	62	34	[0935], [2676]	7.C.1., 8.A.8.	341
Dalkey	78	35	[0896], [2677]	5.D.12.	302-305
Donabate	17	34		4.C.14., 4.F.6.	277-278
Donnybrook (St. Mary's)	68	35	[0897], [0936], [2679/87]	7.C.6., 8.A.8., 3.G.7., 5.E.7.	41-52
Drimnagh	61	34		7.C.7.	
Dublin city (No parish)					54-77, 79-87, 89, 92-135, 137-165, 167, 169-188, 190-209, 211, 213-215, 217-242, 244-251, 255-270, 272-275, 349, 362-3, 374
Esker		34		4.G.2., 5.B.13., 7.C.8., 8.A.8.	288-290
Finglas	24	33	[2690]	4.D.2., 4.F.6., 2.E.13., 2.G.1.	
Garristown	7	33	[0858]	2.A.13., 2.C.10.	21-23
Glasnevin	37	34	[2691], [0875/76]	3.C.2.	
Grallagh	8	33		2.B.13., 2.C.10.	
Grangegorman	43	34	[0877]	3.C.8.	35, 58, 212, 216
Hollywood	9	33	[0859]	2.B.14., 2.C.11.	
Holmpatrick		33	[0848]	1.C.9., 1.G.7	6-11
Howth	42	34	[0878], [3818]	3.C.11.	
Kilbarrack	41	34	[0879/80]	3.D.5.	36

PARISH	TITHES 1823–38 TAB 9/	FILM	VALUATION FIELD BOOKS 1830s OL4./ HOUSE BOOKS [OL5.]	TENEMENT VALUATION 1848–52 FICHE	1841–1851 CENSUS SEARCHES Cen /s/9
Kilbride	53	34		4.B.6.	291
Kilgobbin	79	35	[0898/99]	5.E.9.	306
Kill	77	35	[0900]	5.E.13.	307-308
Killeek	20	33		4.D.3., 4.F.6.	
Killiney	80	35	[0901/02]	5.F.6.	309-310
Killossery	15	33		4.D.4., 4.F.6.	
Killester	45	34	[0881]		
Kilmactalway	51	34		4.G.6., 5.B.13.	292
Kilmacud	73	35		5.F.10.	
Kilmahuddrick	52	34		4.G.9., 5.B.13.	
Kilsallaghan	19	33		4.D.6., 4.F.6.	279
Kiltiernan	81	35	[0903]	5.F.11.	311
Kinsaley	32	32	[0882]	3.D.8.	37
Leixlip	47	34		4.G.9., 5.B.13.	293-294
Lucan		34	[2705]	4.G.11., 5.B.14.	295-296
Lusk	4	33	[0849/53], [2706]	1.D.11., 1.G.8.	12-19
Malahide	28	34	[0883/84]	3.D.12.	38-39
Monkstown	75	35	[0904/21], [2707]	4.B.8., 4.C.7., 5.F.14.	312-318
Naul	6	33	[0860]	2.C.4., 2.C.11.	24-25
Newcastle	54	34	[2708]	5.A.1., 5.B.14.	297-298
Old Connaught	83	35	[0922]	6.D.4.	319
Palmerston	59	34	[0937], [2709]	7.C.9., 8.A.8.	
Palmerstown	11	33	[0861]	2.C.7., 2.C.11.	342-344
Portmarnock	33	34	[0885]	3.E.4.	
Portraine	18	33		4.D.9., 4.F.7.	
Raheny	40	34	[0886/88], [2710/11]	3.E.7.	
Rathcoole	55	34	[2715]	5.A.8., 5.B.14.	299
Rathfarnham	69	35	[0863], [0923], [3815]	7.C.14., 8.A.8., 6.D.12.	320-325
Rathmichael	82	35	[0924]	6.E.13.	
Saggart	56	34	[2720]	5.B.3., 5.C.1.	
Santry	30	34	[0894], [2711]	3.F.5.	
St Brides's					271
St Brigid's					78
St Catherine's	63	34	[0938]	7.C.14., 8.A.8.	345-346
St George's	44	34	[0889/91]	3.E.11.	252
St James'	60	34	[0939/42]	2.F.12., 2.G.1.	29, 166, 347-348, 350
St John's					168
St Jude's					351
St Kevin's					88
St Margaret's		34	[0894]	3.F.2.	40
St Mark's		35		4.B.9., 4.C.7.	
St Michan's					136, 243
St Mary's	85	36			
St Nicholas Within					210
St Nicholas Without			[0943/44]		
St Paul's					254

PARISH	TITHES 1823–38 TAB 9/	FILM	VALUATION FIELD BOOKS 1830s OL4./ HOUSE BOOKS [OL5.]	TENEMENT VALUATION 1848–52 FICHE	1841–1851 CENSUS SEARCHES Cen /s/9
St Peter's		35	[0945/47]	7.D.14., 8.A.9., 4.B.9., 4.C.7.	352-361
St Patrick's	84	36			
St Thomas'					90
St Werburgh's					276
Stillorgan	77	35	[0925/26]	6.F.4.	326
Swords	16	33	[2724/25]	4.D.14., 4.F.7., 3.F.10.	280-287
Tallaght	65	35	[0948/51], [2726]	7.G.3., 8.A.9.	364-373
Taney	70	35	[0927/28]	4.C.6., 6.F.10.	53, 327-328
Tully	76	35		6.G.9.	329-330
Ward		33		2.F.13.	
Westpalstown	13	33		2.C.9., 2.C.11.	
Whitechurch	72	35	[0929/30]	6.G.12.	331-333
Williamstown			[3816/17]		

TOWNS	VALUATION HOUSE BOOK 1830s [OL5.]	TOWNS	VALUATION HOUSE BOOK 1830s [OL5.]
Artaine	[2711]	Haroldscross	[2694, 2696, 2697]
Balbriggan	[2672/73]	Haroldcross E	[2695]
Balgriffin	[2711]	Islandbridge	[2698]
Ballybough	[2711]	Killester S.	[2711]
Balrothery	[2673]	Kilmainham	[2699]
Blackrock	[2674], [0904/21]	Kingstown	[2700/03] [0904/21]
Booterstown	[2675]	Little Bray	[2704]
Clontarf E	[2711]	Lusk	[2706]
Coolock	[2711]	Portobello	[2694]
Crumlin	[2676]	Raheny	[2710/11]
Dalkey	[2677]	Rathmines W	[2696]
Dolphin's Barn	[2678]	Richmond	[2711]
Donnybrook	[2679/87]	Ranelagh N	[2712]
Drumcondra	[2688]	Ranelagh S	[2713/14]
Dundrum	[2689]	Rathmines E	[2716/17]
Finglas	[2690]	Rathmines W	[2717]
Glasnevin	[2691]	Rush	[2718/19] [0854]
Glasthule	[2692]	Skerries	[2721/23] [0855]
Goldenbridge	[2693]		

PARISH	TITHES 1823–38 TAB 11/	FILM	VALUATION FIELD BOOKS 1830s OL4./ HOUSE BOOKS [OL5.]	TENEMENT VALUATION 1855–6 FICHE	1841–1851 CENSUS SEARCHES Cen /s/11
Abbey	121	41			
Abbeygormacan	112	41	[1026], [3833]	11.A.2., 2.B.2., 10.G.14, 14.B4.	1624-1625, 1774-1794
Abbeyknockmoy	41	40	0540, 051 0542, [0964]	6.A.2., 15.C.2., 17.B.12.	2408-2427
Addergoole	10	37		16.C.4.	825-871
Ahascragh	78	40	[0996], [2727/28]	2.A.6., 11.G.2., 1.E.12, 11.E.12, 11.F.14.	655-673, 702, 1184-1200, 1274-1280
Annaghdown	36	38	0543 /44, [0965]	6.A .3., 15.C.2.	471-508
Ardrahan	66	39	0588, [1018], [1037]	8.G.2., 9.F.10., 7.G.10., 9.B.14., 10.C.14.	703-712, 1438-1443, 1917-1919
Athenry	69	39	0520, 0545 0546, 0547 [0966], [3825], [2729/30]	6.B.4., 5.E.4., 5.C.14., 9.D.12.	49-67, 509-510, 713
Athleague				11.G.4.	1281-1290
Augheart	123	41			
Aughrim	77	40	[0997/98], [2731/32]	1.F.1., 1.B.9.	674-675, 1201-1204
Ballinchalla	No Tab	37	[1044]	13.G.8.,	2292-2301
Ballindoon	4	37	0537, [0960], [3831]	2.E.12.	289-300
Ballinrobe	No Tab	37	[1045]	13.G.10.	2302-2317
Ballymacward	46	39	[0999/100]	2.A.12., 10.B.12., 12.C.14., 1.F.7., 11.F.1.	1205-1216, 2428-2452
Ballynacourty	56	39		5.E.6.	714-729
Ballynakill	19	38	0528 , [0952], [2739/40]	7.D.10.	79-117?, 1626-1718?
Ballynakill		39	0538	11.G.9.	301-347?
Ballynakill	105	41	[0961], [3834]	11.B.12., 14.F.10.	1291-1295?
Beagh	90	40	[1019]	8.A.1.	1444-1494
Belclare	30	38	0548, [0967]	15.C.7.	511-518
Boyounagh	18	38	0529, [0953], [1047a]	6.F.12., 6.D.12.	118-127, 2453
Bullaun	91	40	[1043]	10.D.1.	1920-1922
Cargin	31	38	0549, 0550, [0968]	15.C.7.	519-521
Claregalway	55	39	0551/52/53, [0969]	6.B.8., 5.F.1.	522-533, 728-735
Clonbern	22	38	0530	6.G.12., 17.D.8.	128-169
Clonfert	111	41		2.C.8., 14.B.4.	1795-1821
Clonkeen	45	39		10.B.13., 12.D.4.	2454-2463
Clonrush	107	41		17.G.12.	1719-1726
Clontuskert	81	40		1.B.10., 2.B.8.	676-682
Cong	8	37	[1046]	13.E.4.	2318-2351
Cummer	34	38	0554/55/56, [0970]	15.D.13.	534
Derrymacloughney	122	41			
Donaghpatrick	26	38	0557 /58, [0971]	15.D.13.	535-559
Dunamon	21	38	0532, [0955]	17.F.1.	177
Donanaghta	115	41	[1027/29]	14.B.5.	1822-1834

PARISH	TITHES 1823–38 TAB 11/	FILM	VALUATION FIELD BOOKS 1830s OL4./ HOUSE BOOKS [OL5.]	TENEMENT VALUATION 1855–6 FICHE	1841–1851 CENSUS SEARCHES Cen /s/11
Dunmore	11	37	0533, [0956/57], [2745]	16.D.2., 7.A.7., 17.D.11.,	178-211, 872-967
Drumatemple	17	38	0531, [0954]	7.A.5.	170-176
Drumacoo	61	39	0592	5.F.10., 8.G.9.	736-750
Duniry	103	41	[1030], [3834], [3840]	11.A.4., 14.G.13.	1727-1739
Fahy	114	41		14.B.11.	1835-1843
Fohanagh	71	39	[1001]	1.F.12., 11.F.4., 1.C.8.	1217-1236
Grange	74	40	[1002/03]	10.A.10., 10.D.3.	1237-1243
Inishcaltra	106	41	[3835]	18.A.7.	1740-1747
Inisheer	84	40	0517, [3822]	5.D.4.	1-7
Inishmaan	83	40	0518, [3823]	5.D.5.	8-21
Inishmore	82	40	0519, [3824]	5.D.7.	22-48
Isertkelly	93	40	[3843]	10.D.3.	1923-1924
Kilbarron		41		18.A.14.	
Kilbeacanty	89	40	[1020]	8.B.5.	1495-1526
Kilbegnet	20	38	[0958]	7.E.10., 17.F.2.	212-226
Kilbennan	13	37		16.F.1.	968-993
Kilchreest	95	40	0593, [0983], [3844]	9.F.12., 10.D.4.	1925-1927
Kilcloony	80	40		1.C.8.	683-691, 699
Kilcolgan	63	39	0594	8.G.13.	751-762
Kilconickny	68	39	0521, 0595, [0984], [3826]	9.F.14., 9.E.10., 10.D.6.	763, 1928-1930
Kilconierin	68	39	0522, 0596, [0985], [3827]	9.G.5., 9.E.11., 10.D.12.	68-69, 764
Kilconla	12	37	[0972]	16.F.11.	994-1032
Kilconnell	72	40	[1004], [2774]	1.F.13.	1244-1250
Kilcooly	100	40	[3836]	11.A.7.	1748-1750
Kilcoona	33	38	0559, 0560	15.E.7.	560-567
Kilcroan	16	38	[0959]	7.B.4.	227-241
Kilcummin	23	38	[3846]	5. B.4., 12.G.14.	1964-2065
Kilgerrill	79	40	[1005/06]	1.G.6., 1.E.3.	692-698
Killinny	86	40			
Kilkerrin	39	38	[1047b/47c]	6.E.2.	2464-2527
Kilkilvery	29	38	[0973/74]	15.E.12.	568-570
Killaan	75	40	[1007]	1.G.7., 10.B.7., 10.D.13.	1931, 1251-1254
Killallaghtan	76	40	0587, [1008]	1.G.11., 1.E.7.	1255-1259
Killannin	24	38	[3845]	4.G.14., 13.C.7.	2054-2241
Killeany	32	38	0562, 0563, [0975]	15.F.1.	571-579
Killeely	58	39		9.A.4.	765-773
Killeenadeema	96	40	[1038]	10.D.13.	1932-1936
Killeenavarra	65	39		9.A.12.	774-785
Killeeneen	59	39	[0986]	9.B.3., 9.G.9.	786-788
Killererin	35	38	0534, 0564, 0565, [0976]	16.G.5., 17.C.11 17.D.12., 15.F.6.,	242-243, 580-598, 1033-1035, 2487

PARISH	TITHES 1823–38 TAB 11/	FILM	VALUATION FIELD BOOKS 1830s OL4./ HOUSE BOOKS [OL5.]	TENEMENT VALUATION 1855–6 FICHE	1841–1851 CENSUS SEARCHES Cen /s/11
Killeroran	48	39	[1017]	11.G.12.	1296-1353
Killian	47	39	[1016]	12.B.2.	1354-1415
Killimorbologue	116	41	[1031/32]	14.B.14.	1844-1849
Killimordaly	73	40	0523/25, [3828],	10.C.5.,	70, 1260-1265,
			[1010/11]	9.E.12.,	2528
				10.A.13.	
Killinny			[1021]	8.C.2.	1527-1534
Killinan	94	40	[0987], [1039]	12.B.2.	1937-1939
Killogilleen	67	39	[0988], [1040]	9.G.11.,	789-791, 1940
				10.E.14.	
Killora	60	39	[0989]	9.G.14.	792-799
Killoran	109	41	[1017], [3837]	1.E.10.,	700-701, 1753
				11.A.9.,	1850-1863
				2.B.11.	
Killoscobe	42	40		12.D.4.	2529-2558
Killosolan	43	39	[1009]	12.D.13.,	1266-1273,
				11.F.8.	2559-2581
Killower	27	38	[0977]	15.G.3.	599-604
Killursa	28	38	[0978]	15.G.6.	605-629
Kilmacduagh	88	40	[1022]	8.C.7.	1535-1561
Kilmalinogue (Portumna)	120	41		14.C.12.	1864-1867
Kilmeen	99	40	[3838], [1043]	10.F.1., 11.A.9.	1751-1752, 1941
Kilmoylan	37	38	[0979]		630-631
Kilquain	113	41		14.D.2.	1868-1878
Kilreekill	98	40	[3839]	2.A.10.,	
				11.A.12.	
Kiltartan	87	40	[1023]	8.D.6.	1563-1584
Kilteskill	101	40	[1041], [3840]	10.F.1., 11.B.2.	
Kilthomas	97	40	[1042]	8.E.4., 10.B.10,	1585-1590
				9.C.1.	1942-1952
Kiltormer	110	41	[1033]	2.C.1.	1879-1887
Kiltullagh	70	39	0526, [1012/13],	9.E.13.,	71-78
			[3829]	10.B.5.	
Kinvarradoorus	85	40	[1025]	8.E.7.	1591-1623
Lackagh	38	38	[0980]	6.B.13., 16.B.4.	632-642
Leitrim	102	41	[3841]	11.B.4.	1754-1761
Lickerrig		39	[0990]	10.A.7., 9.F.9.	
Lickerrig	64	39	0527, [3830]	10.F.4.	800
Lickmolassy (Portumna)	119	41	[1034/35]	14.D.6.	1888-1905
Liskeevy	12/9	37		16.G.6.	1036-1082
Loughrea	92	40	[1043], [2778/81]	10.F.5.	1953-1963
Meelick	118	41		14.E.9.	1906-1911
Monivea	44	39	[0981], [1014/15], [1047d]	6.C.9., 5.G.14.	2582-2606
				10.C.6., 17.C.13.	
Moycullen	25	38	[3847]	5.B.6.	2242-2289
Moylough	40	39	[2782/83]	6.F.9., 12.E.10.,	1416-1422,
				17.D.7., 12.C.6.	2607-2655
Moyrus	3	37	[0962]	3.A.8., 3.F.6.	348-429
Omey	2	37	0539, [0963], [3832]	3.D.7.	430-470

PARISH	TITHES 1823–38 TAB 11/	FILM	VALUATION FIELD BOOKS 1830s OL4./ HOUSE BOOKS [OL5.]	TENEMENT VALUATION 1855–6 FICHE	1841–1851 CENSUS SEARCHES Cen /s/11
Oranmore	52	39	[2784/87]	4.F.4., 4.G.10., 3.G.8., 4.B.2., 5.F.10.	801-821, 1109-1111
Rahoon	53	39	[3848]	5.C.10., 4.F.8., 4.C.10.	1112-1141, 2290-2291
Ross	7	37	[1047]	13.F.2., 14.A.1.	2352-2407
St Nicholas & Islands	54	39		4.F.7., 3.G.11., 4.B.3., 4.F.1.	1142-1162
Stradbally	57	39		5.G.9., 9.B.12	822-824
Taghboy		39		12.C.10.	1423-1437
Templetogher	15	38	0535	7.B.11.	244-287
Tiranascragh	117	41		14.F.1.	1912-1913
Tuam	14	37	0536, [0982], [2792/6]	16.G.14., 17.D.12., 16.A.11	288, 643-654, 1083-1108
Tynagh	104	41	[1036], [3840], [3842]	11.B.10., 15.A.1., 14.F.4.	1762-1773, 1914-1916

TOWNS & VILLAGES	VALUATION HOUSE BOOK 1830s [OL5.]
Ballinasloe	[2733/36]
Ballygar	[2737/38]
Ballynakill (Woodford)	[2739/40]
Clarin Bridge	[2741]
Clifden	[2742/43]
Craughwell (Killora)	[2744]
Eyrecourt	[2746]
Portumna	[2746, 2788/89]
Killimor	[2746]
Galway City	[2747/67] [1163-1183]
Gort	[2768/70]
Headford	[2771/73]
Killimor	[2775]
Kinvarra	[2776/77]
Roundstone	[2790/91]

PARISH	TITHES 1823–38 TAB 12/	FILM	VALUATION FIELD BOOKS 1830s OL4./ HOUSE BOOKS [OL5.]	TENEMENT VALUATION 1855–6 FICHE	1841–1851 CENSUS SEARCHES Cen /s/12
Aghadoe			[1135/38]	5.D.10., 9.G.12.	
Aghavallen	2	42	[1111/12]	6.F.12.	487-528
Aglish	74	44	[1139/43]	10.A.14.	935-945
Annagh	53	43	2571/2604, [1056/57], [1185]	2.G.12., 11.E.14.	1068
Ardfert	25	42	2572/2573/2605, [1048]	1.B.2., 11.F.10.	1-15, 1069-1074
Ballincuslane	56	44	2576/77/ 2606	11.F.14.	1075-1114
Ballinvoher	40	43	[1058/59]	2.G.14.	151-173
Ballyconry	8	42		7.A.8.	
Ballyduff	28	42	[1060/61]	3.A.13.	174
Ballyheige	16	42		1.C.2.	16-21
Ballymacelligott	49	43	2578/2607	12.A.6.	1115-1121
Ballynacourty	39	43	[1062/63]	3.B.2.	175
Ballynahaglish	45	43	2579/2607a	12.B.8.	1122-11252
Ballyseedy	54	44	2580/81	12.B.14.	1126
Brosna	52	43	[1186]	12.C.6.	
Caher	65	44	2559, [1120/21]	8.C.8.	639-658, 660-672
Castleisland	51	43	2587, [2802/03]	12.D.4.	1173-1233
Cloghane	27	42	[1064/65]	3.B.9.	191-196
Clogherbrien	46	43	2588/2609	12.F.4.	1234
Currans	59	44	2589/2610, [1144/46]	12.F.10., 10.B.6.	1235-1241
Dingle	35	43	[1066/67], [2806/07]	3.C.3.	197-210
Drumod	70	44	2560, [1122/23]	8.E.7.	673-731
Duagh	15	42	[1113]	7.A.12., 1.D.8.	22-48, 529-530
Dunquin	41	43	[1068/69]	3.E.4.	211-217
Dunurlin	32	43	[1070/71]	3.E.10.	
Dysert	13	42	2590	7.B.2., 1.D.12.	49-52, 531-534, 1242-1249
Dysert	61	44		12.G.2.	
Fenit	44	43	2591	12.G.8.	1250-1252
Finuge	14	42	[1049]	1.F.2.	53-60
Galey	6	42		7.B.6.	535-545
Garfinny	36	43	[1072/73]	3.E.14.	218
Glanbehy	67	44	2561, [1124/25]	8.G.9.	732-771
Kenmare	84	45	2554, [2808]	5.G.14.	448-460
Kilbonane	74	44	[1147/49]	10.B.8.	946-953
Kilcaragh	19	42	[1050]	1.F.8.	61-68
Kilcaskan	87	45	2555	6.B.7.	
Kilcolman	62	44	2592/93, [1150/51]	12.G.10., 10.C.6.	954-961, 1253-1267
Kilconly	1	42		7.C.4.	546-554
Kilcredane	76	44	[1152/55]	10.C.10.	
Kilcrohane	82	45	[1096/102]	4.D.14.	303-444
Kilcummin	77	45	[1156/59]	10.C.14.	962-1013
Kildrum	43	43	[1074/76]	3.F.3.	219-220
Kilfeighny	20	42		1.F.12.	69-83
Kilflyn	24	42	[1051]	1.G.8.	84-85
Kilgarrylander	57	44	2611, [1187]	13.A.8.	1268-1273
Kilgarvan	85	45	2556	6.B.14.	461-468
Kilgobban	31	43	[1077/78]	3.F.9.	221-233
Killaha	81	45	2569/70, [1160/62]	10.F.14.	1014-1019
Killahan	17	42	[1052]	2.A.2.	123-124

PARISH	TITHES 1823–38 TAB 12/	FILM	VALUATION FIELD BOOKS 1830s OL4./ HOUSE BOOKS [OL5.]	TENEMENT VALUATION 1855–6 FICHE	1841–1851 CENSUS SEARCHES CEN S|12|
Killarney	80	45	[1163/66], [2809/14], [3850]	10.F.14.	1020-1027
Killeentierna	60	44	2594 /2612, [1167/70]	13.B.8., 11.B.12.	1037-1039, 1274-1292
Killehenny	4	42	[1114]	7.C.12.	572-574
Killemlagh	68	44	[1126/27] 2562	9.B.2.	772-812
Killinane	66	44	2563, [1128/29]	9.C.3.	813-834
Killiney	30	42	[1079/80]	3.G.1.	126-134, 234-245
Killorglin	63	44	2545/2546/2564, 2595/2613, [1130/31], [1171/73], [2815/16]	13.C.2., 9.D.6 5.D.11., 11.B.14.	248, 264-272, 1028-1036, 835-848, 1293-1332
Killury	11	42	[1053]	2.A.8.	125
Kilmalkedar	34	43	[1081/84]	4.A.4.	246-247
Kilmoyly	22	42		2.B.12.	86-104
Kilnanare	73	44	[1174/77]	11.C.3.	1040-1046
Kilnaughtin	3	42	[1115]	7.D.10.	555-571
Kilquane	26	42	[1083/84]	4.A.11.	
Kilshenane	21	42	2542/2543, [1054]	2.C.10.	105-119
Kiltallagh	58	44	2596/97	13.D.12.	1334-1335
Kiltomy	18	42		2.D.6.	120-122
Kinard	37	43	[1085/87]	4.B.2.	249-253
Knockane	71	44	2549/2551, [1103/06]	5.E.5., 5.B.1.	273-301
Knockanure	10	42		7.F.2.	575-583
Lisselton	5	42	[1117]	7.F.6.	584-591
Listowel	9	42	[1118/19], [2817/18]	7.F.14.	592-618
Marhin	33	43	[1088/89], [1116?]	4.B.7.	
Minard	38	43	[1090/91]	4.B.10.	254-258
Molahiffe	72	44	[1178/80]	11.C.10.	1047-1059
Murher	7	42		8.A.6.	619-637
Nohaval	55	44	2598/2614	13.E.8.	
Nohavaldaly	78	45	[1181/84]	11.D.6.	1060-1067, 1336-1340
O Brennan	50	43	2599	13.E.8.	1341-1344
O Dorney	23	42	[1055]	2.E.2.	135-143
Prior	69	44	2565, [1132], [3849]	9.D.12.	849-903
Ratass	48	43	2600/2615	13.E.14.	1345-1353
Rattoo	12	42		8.B.6., 2.E.12.	144-150, 638
Stradbally	29	42	[1092/93]	4.C.3.	259-261
Templnoe	83	45	2550/2552/2553, [1007/10]	5.G.2., 5.B.2.	302, 445-447
Tralee	47	43	2601/2616, [1188], [2823]	13.F.10+14 [2824/33]	1354-1361
Tuosist	86	45	2557/2558	6.D.1.	469-486
Valencia	64	44	2566/2567/8, [1133/34]	9.E.13.	
Ventry	42	43	[1094/95]	4.C.9.	262-263

TOWNS	VALUATION HOUSE BOOK 1830s [OL5.]
Ballylongford	[2796a]
Blennerville	[2797/99]
Cahersiveen	[2800/01]
Castlemaine	[2804]
Chapelstown	[2805]
Milltown	[2819/20]
Sneem	[2821/22]
Tarbert	[2823]

PARISH	TITHES 1823–38 TAB 13/	FILM	VALUATION FIELD BOOKS 1830s OL4./ HOUSE BOOKS [OL5.]	TENEMENT VALUATION 1851 FICHE	1841–1851 CENSUS SEARCH Cen /s/13
Ardkill	10	46	0703	4.B.7.	1
Ardree	104	49	0738, [3873]	1.F.8.	
(Tankardstown)					
Ballaghmoon	115	49	0739, [3874]	1.F.9.	
Ballybought	81	48	0763, [3887]	4.E.14.	77
Ballybrackan	86	48	0800	2.B.7.	
Ballymany	63	47	0784, [3902]	6.C.8.	
Ballymoreustace	77	48	0762, [3888]	4.F.1.	79
Ballynadrumny	1	46	0704, [3851]	4.B.11.	2
Ballynafagh	30	46	0714, [3855]	5.E.10	14-15
Ballysax	64	47	0785, [3903]	2.E.14., 6.D.5.	135
Ballyshannon	92	48	0786/0801, [3904]	2.E.14., 6.C.8., 2.B.13	
Balraheen	16	46	0728, [3866]	3.D.14.	59
Belan	107	49	0740	1.F.10.	
Bodenstown	36	47	0753, [3951]	6.A.2.	
Brannockstown	78	48	0764, [3889]	4.F.11.	80
Brideschurch	35	47	0715, [3856]	5.E.13.	17-18
Cadamstown	4	46	0705, [3852]	4.C.1.	3-5
Carbury	9	46	0706, [3853]	4.C.6.	6-8
Carn	65	47	0787, [3905]	2.E.14., 6.C.9.	136-137
Carnalway	75	48	0765, [3890]	4.F.12.	81-84
Carragh	34	47	0716	5.F.1.	19-27
Carrick	5	46	0707	4.C.8.	
Castledermot	111	49	0741, [3875], [2840/42]	1.F.11., 2.F.2.	67-74
Castledillon	46	47	0823, [3941]	3.C.6.	
Churchtown	96	48	0779, [3897]	1.B.2.	108-110
Clane	33	47	0717, [3857], [2845/46]	5.F.4.	16, 28
Clonaghlis	48	47	0824, [3942]	3.C.7.	
Cloncurry	12, 56	46, 47	0729/0788, [3867], [3906]	3.E.6.	60-61, 138-140
Clonshanbo	15	46	0730, [3868]	3.E.2.	
Coghlanstown	76	48	0766, [3891]	4.G.3.	
Confey	21	46	0813, [3919], [3920]	2.G.7.	
Davidstown	99	48	0772	1.D.12.	111-114
Donadea	18	46	0731, [3869]	3.E.12.	
Donaghcumper	44	47	0814/0825, [3921]	2.F.12., 3.C.8., 3.D.1.	
Donaghmore	22	46	0815, [3922/23]	3.A.2.	
Downings	31	46	0718, [3858]	5.G.1	29-31
Duneany	84	48	0802	2.C.1.	
Dunfierth	7	46	0708, [3854]	4.C.11.	
Dunmanoge or Monmahennock	110	49	0742, [3876]	1.G.7.	
Dunmurraghill	17	46	0732, [3869]	3.E.13.	
Dunmurry	58	47	0789, [3907]		
Feighcullen	68	47	0721/0790, [3861], [3908]	4.A .2., 5.A.4.	37-39
Fontstown	93	48	0773/0803	2.C.3., 1.E.2.	115-118
Forenaghts	52	47	0826, [3943]	5.D.13.	
Gilltown	79	48	0767, [3892]	4.G.4.	85-86
Graney	113	49	0743	1.G.10.	
Grangeclare	58	47	0791, [3909]	4.A.14., 6.C.13.	
Grangerosnolvan	106	49	0744, [3878]	1.G.14.	

PARISH	TITHES 1823–38 TAB 13/	FILM	VALUATION FIELD BOOKS 1830s OL4./ HOUSE BOOKS [OL5.]	TENEMENT VALUATION 1851 FICHE	1841–1851 CENSUS SEARCH Cen /s/13
Greatconnell	72	48	0722, [3862]	5.A.8.	40-49
Haynestown	53	47	0827, [3944]	5.D.13.	
Harristown	89	48	0804	2.C.6.	
Jago	80	48	0768, [3893]	4.G.7.	87
Johnstown	41	47	0754, [3952]	6.A.4.	
Kerdiffstown	39	47	0755, [3953]	6.A.5.	
Kilberry	95	48	[3898]	1.B.13.	
Kilcock	13	26	0733, [3870], [2847/49], [4255]	3.F.1.	
Kilcullen	94	48	0736, [2850/51]	5.D.1.	63-66
Kildangan	87	48	0805	2.C.11.	
Kildare & Bishopscourt	61	47	0723/0792, [3910], [2852], [2853], [2854]	4.B.3., 6.D.11., 5.A .14.	141
Kildrought	26	46	0816, [3925], [3926/27]		147
Kilkea	109	49	0745, [3879]	2.A.1.	
Kill	50	47	0769/0828, [3945], [3894]	5.D.13., 4.G.8.	
Killadoon	27	46	0817, [3928], [3929]	2.G.5.	
Killashee	73	48	0756 /0770, [3895]	6.A .6.	88-90
Killelan	108	49	0746, [3880]	2.A.3.	
Killybegs	32	46	0719, [3859]	5.G.6.	32-35
Kilmacredock	23	46	0818, [3930]	2.G.7.	
Kilmeage	66	47	0724/0793, [3911]	6.C.13.	50-51
Kilmore	8	46	0709	4.C.14.	
Kilpatrick	11	46	0710	4.D.2.	9-10
Kilrainy	2	46	0711	4.D.5.	
Kilrush	91	48	0806	2.C.11.	
Kilteel	51	47	[3946]	5.E.3.	148-149
Kineagh	112	49	0747, [3881]	2.A.9.	
Knavinstown	83	48	0807	2.C.14.	
Lackagh	82	48	0808, [3918]	2.D.1.	
Ladytown	71	48	0725, [3864]	5.B.14.	
Laraghbryan	20	46	0819, [3931/32]	3.A.2.	150
Leixlip	24	46	0820, [2855/56], [3933/4], [3859]	2.G.9.	151-153
Lullymore	54	47	[3912]	4.A.4.	
Lyons	47	47	0830, [3947]	3.C.12	154
Mainham	19	46	0734, [3871]	3.E.3.	61
Monasterevin	85	48	0809, [2853], [2861/62]	2.D.9.	142
Moone	103	49	0748/0774/0794, [3882], [3913]	6.C.14., 1.E.4., 2.A.11	
Morristownbiller	69	47	0726, [3865]	5.C.1.	52-55
Mylerstown	3	46	0712	4.D.7.	11-13
Narraghmore	101	48	0749/0775/0781, [3883], [3899]	1.C.7., 1.E.6.	75-76, 119-124
Naas	40	47	[3954], 0757, [2864]	6.A.6.	91-101
Nurney	6, 90	46, 48	0713, 0810	4.D.10., 2.E.8.	143
Oldconnell	70	48	[3863]	5.C.7.	56-58
Oughterard	49	47	0831, [3948]	5.E.7.	
Painestown	114	49	0750, [3884]	2.B.2.	
Pollardstown	62	47	0796, [3914]	6.D.10.	
Rathangan	55	47	0797/0811, [3915], [2853], [2868]	6.C.14., 4.A.5., 2.E.12.	144

PARISH	TITHES 1823–38 TAB 13/	FILM	VALUATION FIELD BOOKS 1830s OL4./ HOUSE BOOKS [OL5.]	TENEMENT VALUATION 1851 FICHE	1841–1851 CENSUS SEARCH Cen /s/13
Rathernan	67	47	0727	5.C.11.	
Rathmore	43	47	0758, [3955]	6.B.10.	102-105
Relictstown	116	49			
Scullogestown	14	46	0735, [3872]	3.E.14.	
Sherlockstown	38	47	0759, [3956]	6.C.2.	
St John's	98	48	0782, [3900]		77, 125
St Michael's	97	48	0751/0783, [3885], [3901]		126
Stacumny	45	47	0832, [3949/50]		155
Straffan	28	46	0821, [3935/36]	3.A.14	156
Taghadoe	25	46	0822, [3937/38]	3.B.3.	
Tankardstown Ardree	105	49	0752/0776, [3886]	1.E.13., 2.B.2.	
Thomastown	57	47	0798, [3916]	4.B.2.	
Timahoe	29	46	0720 [3860]	5.G.11.	36
Timolin	102	49	0777, [2870]	1.E.13.	127-128
Tipper	42	47	[3957]	6.C.2.	106-107
Tipperkevin	74	48	0771, [3896]	4.G.13.	
Tully	60	47	0737/0799, [3917]	2.E.14., 6.D.2., 2.F.1., 5.D.12.	145
Usk	100	48	0778	1.F.4., 6.E.11.	129-134
Walterstown	88	48	0812	2.E.12.,	
Whitechurch	37	47	0761, [3958]	6.C.5.	

TOWNS	VALUATION HOUSE BOOK 1830s [OL5.]
Athy	[2834/37]
Ballitore	[2837/38]
Ballymore Eustace	[2839, 2851]
Celbridge	[2843/44, 2860]
Johnstown	[2864, 2869]
Kildare	[2852, 2853, 2854]
Kill	[2864]
Kilmeage	[2865/67]
Leixlip	[2855/56]
Maynooth	[2857/59] [3961]
Newbridge	[2865/67]
Prosperous	[2846]
Robertstown	[2865/67]
Sallins	[2864, 2869]

PARISH	TITHES 1823–38 TAB 14/	FILM	VALUATION FIELD BOOKS 1830s OL4./ HOUSE BOOKS [OL5.]	TENEMENT VALUATION FICHE 1849–50	1841–1851 CENSUS SEARCH Cen /s/14
Abbeyleix	14	50	0854, [3978]	2.C.4.	14
Aghaviller	104	54	0959, [3982]	8.C.2.	196-200
Aglish	140	55	0935	6.G.10.	137-139, 138A
Aharney	10	50	0872	3.E.2.	67-69
Arderra	136	55	0936	6.G.12.	
Attanagh	13	50	0855, [3962]	2.C.5.	15-17
Balleen	7	50	0873	3.E.8.	70
Ballycallan	41	51	0836	1.D.9.	
Ballinamara	38	51	0835	1.D.6.	
Ballybur	52	52	0975	9.A.6.	
Ballygurrim	119	54	0919	5.F.12.	
Ballylarkin	32	51	0837	1.E.3.	3-4
Ballylinch	83	53	0884	4.B.8.	
Ballytarsney	135	55	0937	7.A.2.	140
Ballytobin	97	54	0949	7.E.14.	
Blackrath	66	52	0885	4.B.9.	82
Blanchvilleskill	74	53	0886	4.B.10.	83
Borrismore	6	50	0874	3.E.11.	
Burnchurch	56	52	0976	9.A.6.	
Callan	47	51	0833, [2875/77]	1.A.4.	1-2
Castlecomer	15	50	0856, [3963], [3878/9] [4000/01]	2.C.7., 2.D.9.	18-25
Castleinch	51	52	0977	9.A.10.	
Clara	70	53	0877	4.B.11.	
Clashacrow	36	51	0838	1.E.5.	
Clomantagh	28	50	0839	1.E.6.	5-8
Clonamery	112	54	0920	5.G.2.	
Clonmore	131	55	0938	7.A.3.	141
Columbkille	89	53	0888	4.B.14.	84-87
Coolaghmore	93	54	0950	7.F.3.	
Coolcashin	8	50	0875	3.E.12.	
Coolcraheen	22	50	0857, [3964]	3.B.8., 1.E.10.	
Danesfort	57	52	0979	9.A.12.	226
Derrynahinch	106	54	0960, [3983/84]	8.C.11.	201-206
Donaghmore	18/	50	0858	2.C.12.	26-45
Dunbell	73	53	0889	4.C.6.	
Dungarvan	81	53	0890		
Dunkitt	121	55	0921	5.G.8.	119-123
Dunmore	26	50	0859, [3965]	3.B.9., 3.B.14.	46
Dunnamaggan	98	54	0961	7.F.9., 8.D.5.	
Durrow	11	50		3.E.13.	
Dysart	21	50	0860, [3966]	2.G.6., 3.A.11., 3.B.1.	47-49
Dysartmoon	113	54	0922	6.A.6.	
Earlstown	59	52	0979	9.B.3.	
Ennisnag	60	52	0980, [3985]	9.B.5., 8.D.6.	
Erke	1	50	0877	3.E.13.	71-72
Famma	91	53	0891	4.C.14.	
Fertagh	4	50	0841	3.F.11., 1.E.10.	73-76
Fiddown	128	55	0963, [3986]	8.D.6., 7.A.7.	142-149
Freshford	33	51	0842, [2880], [4002]	1.E.11.	9-9a
Garranamanagh	29	50	0843	1.F.7.	

PARISH	TITHES 1823–38 TAB 14/	FILM	VALUATION FIELD BOOKS 1830s OL4./ HOUSE BOOKS [OL5.]	TENEMENT VALUATION FICHE 1849–50	1841–1851 CENSUS SEARCH Cen /s/14
Gaulskill	122	55	0923	6.A.14.	124-126
Glashare	2	50	0879, 2695	3.G.6.	
Gowran	71	53	0892, [2883]	4.C.14.	
Graiguenamanagh	86	53	0893, [2884/5]	4.D.13.	88-97
Grange	50	52	0981	9.B.7.	
Grangekilree	58	52	0982	9.B.9.	
Grangemaccomb	19	50	0861, [3967]	2.D.7., 3.A.3., 3.B.10., 3.C.6., 3.C.8.	50-51
Grangesilvia	76	53	0894, [2882]	4.F.3.	98-99
Inistiogue	92	53	0895, [2886]	4.F.10.	101-103
Jerpointabbey	88	53	0896, [3979]	4.G.9.	
Jerpointchurch	102	54	0964, [3987]	8.D.7	207
Jerpointwest	108	54	0965, [3988]	4.G.11., 8.D.13.	
Kells	95	54	0984, 2696	9.B.10., 7.F.14.	170-178
Kilbeacon	110	54	0966, [3989]	8.E.1.	208
Kilbride	117	54	0925	6.B.4.	
Kilcoan	118	54	0926	6.B.8.	
Kilcolumb	123	55	0927	6.B.12.	127, 136
Kilcooly	34	51	0844	1.F.8.	
Kilderry	67	52	0898	4.G.13.	
Kilfane	85	53	0899	5.A.1.	
Kilferagh	54	52	0985	9.B.11.	
Kilkeasy	105	54	0967, [3990]	8.E.9.	209-212
Kilkenny	43-46	51	2694, [2889-2914], [4003-4007]	9.D.14., 9.F.13. 9.G.11., 10.A.11. 10.B.2.	185-195
Kilkerril	141	55			
Kilkieran	63	52	0900	5.A.5.	
Killahy	35, 109	51, 54	[3991] 0845	1.F.8., 8.E.12.	
Killaloe	48	52	0986, 0834	1.F.9., 9.B.12.	
Killamery	96	54	0953	7.G.7.	
Killarney	79	53	0901	5.A.6.	
Kilmacahill	72	53	0902	5.A.6.	104
Kilmacar	20	50	[3968]	2.G.10., 3.A.6.	52-54
Kilmacow	138	55	0940	7.D.8.	150
Kilmademoge	27	50	0863, [3969]	3.C.2.	
Kilmadum	62	52	0903, [3970]	3.A.2., 3.C.4., 5.A.11.	
Kilmaganny	100	54	0954	7.G.14.	179-183
Kilmakevoge	124	55	0928	3.C.2.	128
Kilmanagh	40	51	0847	1.F.10.	
Kilmenan	17	50	0865, [3971]	2.D.8., 8.A.10	55-56
Kilree	99	54		8.A.10	184
Knocktopher	103	54	0969, [3992] [2872]	8.F.4.	213-220
Lismateige	107	54	0970, [3994]	8.F.13.	221-223
Listerlin	115	54	0929, [3981], [3993]	8.G.2.	129
Mallardstown	94	54	0956	8.A.13.	
Mayne	22	50	0866, [3972]	3.B.10.	
Mothell	24	50	0904	2.G.13., 3.A.13., 3.B.2., 5.A.14.	57-59

PARISH	TITHES 1823–38 TAB 14/	FILM	VALUATION FIELD BOOKS 1830s OL4./ HOUSE BOOKS [OL5.]	TENEMENT VALUATION FICHE 1849–50	1841–1851 CENSUS SEARCH Cen /s/14
Muckalee	25	50	0868, [3973], [3995]	2.G.14., 3.B.6.	60-61, 224
Muckalee	130	55	0972	8.G.3., 7.C.3.	60-61, 224
Odagh	39	51	0848, [3974]	3.B.12., 3.C.6.	10
Outrath	53	52	0987	9.C.2.	227
Owning	127	55	0942	7.C.3.	163
Pleberstown	90	53	0905	5.A.14.	
Pollrone	134	55	0943	7.C.8.	164-165
Portnascully	139	55	0944	7.D.2.	166
Powerstown	82	53	0906	5.B.1.	105-107
Rossinan	111	54	0973, [3996]	8.G.5., 6.E.10.	
Rathbeagh	30	50	0880, [3976]	3.G.9., 2.D.8.	62-65
Rathcoole	64	52	0907	5.B.8.	
Rathkieran	133	55	0930	7.D.7.	167
Rathlogan	5	50	0881	3.G.12.	
Rathpatrick	125	55	0930	6.D.8.	130
Rathaspick	16	50	0870, [3975]	2.G.12.	
Rosbercon	116	54	0931, [2917]	6.E.2.	131-133
Rosconnell	12	50	0871, [3977]	2.C.10.	66
Shanbogh	120	55	0933	6.E.12.	134
Shankill	68	52	0911, [3980]	5.C.9.	108-110
Sheffin	9	50	0849	3.G.13., 1.G.7.	77-78
St Canice's	42	51	0850	1.G.8., 9.C.7.	
St John's	43	51	0908	5.B.10.	
St Martin's	69	53	0909	5.C.6.	
St Mary's	44	51	[4003/05]	9.G.11.	
St Maul's	45	51	[4006]	5.C.8.	111-112
St Patrick's	46	51	0991, [4007]	9.C.9.	228
Stonecarthy	61	52	0988, [3997]	9.C.5.	225
The Rower	114	54	0934		135
Thomastown	84	53	0912, [2919/21]	5.D.2.	113-117
Tibberaghny	129	55	0945	7.D.12.	168
Tiscoffin	65	52	0913	5.D.13.	
Treadingstown	77	53	0914	9.D.1., 5.E.4.	
Tubbrid	132	55	0946	7.D.13.	
Tubbridbritain	31	51	0851	1.G.14.	11
Tullaghanbrogue	49	52	0852	2.A.5.	12
Tullaherin	80	53	0915	5.E.6.	
Tullahought	101	54	0958	8.B.2.	
Tullamaine	45	52	0993	9.D.4.	
Tullaroan	37	51	0853	2.A.6.	13
Ullard	87	53	0916	5.E.10.	118
Ullid	137	55	0947	7.E.1.	
Urlingford	3	50	0883, [2922]	4.A.1.	79-81
Wells	75	53	0917	5.F.1.	
Whitechurch	126	55	0948	7.E.3.	169
Woolengrange	78	53	0918	5.F.1.	

TOWNS	VALUATION HOUSE BOOKS 1830s [OL5]
Ballyhale	[2871/72] [3998/99]
Ballyragget	[2873]
Bennettsbridge	[2874]
Goresbridge	[2881/82]
Higginstown	[2872]
Johnstown	[2807/88]
Mullinvat	[2872] [2916]
St Canice	[2889/93, 2903/05]
St John's	[2894/96, 2906/08]
St Mary's	[2897/900, 2909/11]
St Maul's	[2901, 2912/13]
St Patrick's	[2902, 2914/15]
Stoneyford	[2872] [2918] [4008]

PARISH	TITHES 1823–38 TAB 24/	FILM	VALUATION FIELD BOOKS 1830s OL4./ HOUSE BOOKS [OL5.]	TENEMENT VALUATION FICHE 1850/51	1841–1851 CENSUS SEARCH Cen /s/24
Abbeyleix	41	85	1537, 1550, 1564, [2932/35]	3.F.10., 1.D.12., 3.B.2.	44-47
Aghaboe	23	85	1528, 2702	2.C.6., 1.E.2.	5-12, 29-32
Aghmacart	32	85	1538	1.F.2.	33
Aharney	36	85	1539	1.G.2.	
Ardea	5	84	1566, [2954/59]	5.A.6.	82-84
Attanagh	37	85	1540	1.G.4.	
Ballyadams	43	85	1575, [4010]	6.D.2., 1.A.8.	
Ballyroan	38	85	1551, [2939]	3.C.4.	
Bordwell	29	85	1529, 1541	2.D.4., 1.G.7.	34
Borris	10	84	1558, [2940]	4.D.6.	52-54
Castlebrack	1	84	1585	7.A.8.	
Clonenagh & Clonagheen	9	84	1552, 1559, 1565 [2952/53]	3.F.12., 4.F.1., 3.D.4.	55, 59-81
Cloydagh	53	86	1569	5.F.6.	
Coolbanagher	6	84	1567	5.B.12.	
Coolkerry	31	85	1530, 1542	2.D.6., 1.G.10.	
Curraclone	18	85	1576, [4011]	6.D.4.	
Donaghmore	25	85	1531, [2944]	2.D.8.	
Durrow	33	85	1543, [2945/47]	1.G.14.	35-39
Dysartenos	14	84	1560, 1577, [4012]	4.F.6., 6.D.10.	103
Dysartgallen	42	85	1553	3.D.5.	48
Erke	27	85	1532, 1544	2.E.2., 2.A.12.	13-15
Fossy or Timahoe	40	85	1554, 1578, [4013]	4.F.8., 6.E.2., 3.E.7.	49-51
Glashare	35	85	1545	2.B.2.	
Kilcolmanbane	13	84	1555, 1561	4.F.12., 3.E.14.	
Kilcolmanbrack	39	85	1556	3.F.1.	
Kildellig	28	85	1546	2.B.4.	
Killabban	49	86	1521, 1570, [2938, 4009]	5.F.10.	1, 88-93
Killenny	15	84	1579, [4015]	6.E.4.	
Killermogh	30	85	1547	2.B.6.	40-41
Killeshin	51	86	1571	6.A.8.	94-98
Kilmanman	2	84	1586, [2942/3]	7.B.4.	106-107
Kilteale	12	84	1562, 1580, [4014]	4.F.8., 6.E.6.	
Kyle	21	85	1533	2.E.6.	16-21
Lea	7	84	1568, [1189]	5.C.8.	85-87
Moyanna	16	84	1581, [4016]	6.E.10.	104
Mountrath			[2961/63]		
Monksgrange	48	86	1522	1.C.2.	2-3
Offerlane	8	84	1589	7.F.14.	111-135
Rahan			[1189A]		
Rathaspick	47	85	1523, 1572	1.C.4., 6.B.14.	4, 99-101
Rathdowney	24	85	1534, 1548, [2948, 2967/68]	2.E.14., 2.B.10	22-25
Rathsaran	26	85	1535	2.G.14.	26
Rearymore	3	84	1587	7.C.10.	
Rosconnell	34	85	1549, 1557	2.B.12., 3.F.2.	42-43
Rosenallis	4	84	1588, [2954/60]	7.D.8.	108-110
Shrule	50	86	1573	6.C.6.	102
Skirk	22	85	1536	3.A.4.	27-28
Sleaty	52	86	1574	6.C.8.	

PARISH	TITHES 1823–38 TAB 24/	FILM	VALUATION FIELD BOOKS 1830s OL4./ HOUSE BOOKS [OL5.]	TENEMENT VALUATION FICHE 1850/51	1841–1851 CENSUS SEARCH Cen /s/24
St John's	44	85	1524	1.C.10.	
Straboe	11	84	1563	4.G.1.	56-58
Stradbally	27/17	84	1582, [4017], [2969/72]	6.F.4.	105
Tankardstown	46	85	1525	1.C.12.	
Tecolm	45	85	1526	1.D.2.	
Timahoe/Fossy			[4018]		
Timogue	19	85	1583, [4018]	6.G.4.	
Tullomoy	20	85	1584, [4019]	6.G.6., 1.D.4.	

TOWNS	VALUATION HOUSE BOOK 1830s [OL5.]
Abbeyleix	[2932/35]
Arless	[2951]
Ballickmoyler	[2951]
Ballinakill	[2936/37]
Ballybrittas	[2960]
Ballylynan	[2938, 2951]
Ballyroan	[2939]
Castletown	[2941, 2947]
Clonaslee	[2942/43, 2960]
Erril	[2948]
Graigue	[2949/50, 2951]
Maryborough	[2952/53]
Mountmellick	[2954/59, 2960]
Portarlington	[2964/66]

PARISH	TITHES 1823–38 TAB 16/	FILM	VALUATION FIELD BOOKS 1830s OL4./ HOUSE BOOKS [OL5.]	TENEMENT VALUATION 1856 FICHE	1841–1851 CENSUS SEARCH Cen /s/16
Annaduff	13	61	1057, 1062	3.A.2., 6.D.4., 4.A.8., 6.E.10.	494-504, 675-680
Carrigallen	15	61	1047	1.E.14., 6.A.12.	1-39
Cloonclare	5	60	1051, 1065, 2699, [4257]	5.D.4., 4.B.8.	137-193, 752-769
Cloone	17	61	1048, 2698, [4256], [2924]	6.C.4., 6.F.5.	40-60, 681-722
Cloonlogher	4	60	1052	4.D.8.	194-202
Drumlease	3	60	1053 [4258]	4.D.12.	203-252
Drumreilly	9	60	1049, 1054, [4256], [4020], [4259]	2.F.2., 1.F.13	61-92, 253-311
Fenagh	12	61	1050, 1058, 1063	6.D.5., 2.A.14., 7.B.13.	93-94, 505-512, 723-727
Inishmagrath	8	60	2697, [4021], [4260]	4.E.14.	312-379
Killanummery	6	60	1055, [4261],	5.A.8.	380-426
Killarga	7	60	1056, [4022], [4262]	5.B.11.	427-493
Killasnet	2	59	1066, 2700	5.E.1.	770-808
Kiltubbrid	11	61	1060	3.F.1.	595-669
Kiltoghert	10	60	1059, [4023]	3.A.12.	513-594
Mohill	16	61	1061, 1064, [2931]	4.A.6., 6.E.5.	670-674, 728-751
Oughteragh	14	61	[4256]	2.A.14., 6.D.2.	95-136
Rossinver	1	59	1067, 2701	1.A.12., 5.F.14.	808-870

TOWNS	VALUATION HOUSE BOOK 1830s [OL5.]
Ballinamore	[2923]
Drumahaire	[2925]
Drumkeeran	[2926]
Drumsna	[2927]
Keshkerrigan	[2928]
Manorhamilton	[2929/30]

PARISH	TITHES 1823–38 TAB 17/	FILM	VALUATION FIELD BOOKS 1830s OL4./ HOUSE BOOKS [OL5.]	TENEMENT VALUATION FICHE 1850/52	1841–1851 CENSUS SEARCH Cen /s/17
Abbeyfeale	74	65	2749, [1252/54], [2973]	6.B.14.	318-352
Abington	61	64	2703-04, 2769-2771	1.A.14., 8.C.2.	532-537
Adare	89	66	2757-58-59, [1221/22], [1250], [2974/75]	7.E.8., 7.E.12., 11.G.5., 13.A.2.	268-272, 446-448
Aglishcormick	60	64	2705, [1237]	1.B.6., 3.E.2.	1-3
Anhid	93	66		13.B.1.	
Ardagh	11	62	2790, [1255/56]	10.F.12., 6.D.6.	353, 583-586
Ardcanny	27	62	2760	7.E.8., 7.F.4.	449-450
Ardpatrick	121	67	2728	4.D.6.	182-183
Askeaton	14	62	[1190/91], [1190/91] [2976/77]	2.E.10.	60-65
Athlacca	95	66		13.B.3.	273-276
Athneasy	131	67	2729, 2800, [1270]	9.E.14., 4.D.8.	184-185
Ballinacurra	131	67	[3040]		
Ballinard	109	66	2801, [1271/72]	9.F.4.	
Ballingaddy	122	67	2730	4.D.14.	186
Ballingarry	81	65	[1223/25], [1243/44]	11.G.6.	66-67, 93-108, 187-191
Ballingarry	125	67	2731-32, [4024], [2978/81]	4.E.6.	66-67, 93-108,187-191
Ballinlough	111	66	2802, [1271/72]	9.F.8.	663
Ballybrood	57	64	2706	1.B.8.	4
Ballycahane	38	63	2777, 2803, [1273/74]	8.F.8., 8.F.12., 9.F.12	542-544
Ballylanders	126	67	[1245], 4025/26	4.F.2.	192-211
Ballynamona	110	66	2804, [1275]	9.F.14.	
Ballynaclogh	66	64		3.E.4.	
Ballyscadden	119	66	2734		
Bruff	96	66	[2982/83]	13.B.8.	277-283
Bruree	84	65	[1226/28], [2983]		109-110, 284-285
Caheravally	50	63		1.B.12.	
Caherconlish	53	64	[2985]	1.C.4.	5-15
Cahercorney	106	65	2805, [1271/72]	9.G.2.	
Caherelly	55	64	2707	1.D.4.	
Cahernarry	51	63	2708	1.D.10.	
Cappagh	17	62	[1192/95], [1192/95]	2.F.10.	68-69
Carrigparson	49	63	2709	1.D.14.	
Castletown	64	64	[1238]	3.F.4.	
Chapelrussell	26	62	2761-62	7.E.8.	451
Clonagh	19	62	[1196], [1196a/97]	2.F.13.	70
Cloncagh	80	65	[1229]	12.C.8.	111-115
Cloncrew	85,86	65		12.C.14.	116
Clonelty	73	65	2750, [1257/58]	6.C.7.	355-357
Clonkeen	47	63		1.E.4.	
Clonshire	18	62	[1198/200]	2.G.1.	
Colmanswell	87	65		12.D.2.	117
Corcomohide	83	65	[1230/31]	12.D.5.	118-132
Crecora	35	63	2778	8.G.2.	545-546
Croagh	22	62	2721, [1201/02]	2.G.2.	71-74
Croom	91	66	2779, [1222], [1232], [2987/88]	8.G.8.	286-300
Darragh	129	67	2735 [1246]	4.G.2.	212-227

PARISH	TITHES 1823–38 TAB 17/	FILM	VALUATION FIELD BOOKS 1830s OL4./ HOUSE BOOKS [OL5.]	TENEMENT VALUATION FICHE 1850/52	1841–1851 CENSUS SEARCH Cen /s/17
Derrygalvin	46	63	2710	1.E.6.	
Donaghmore	48	63	2711	1.E.10.	
Doon	63	64	2772-73	8.E.2., 3.E.8., 3.F.6.	172-177, 538
Doondonnell	20	62	2722, [1203]	2.G.14.	75
Drehidtarsna	90	66	[1222]	12.E.9., 13.D.9.	
Dromcolliher			[2989/90]		133-143
Dromin	97	66		13.D.9.	301-304
Dromkeen	58	64	2712	1.E.14.	
Dunmoylan	7	62		10.G.7.	587-588
Dysert	92	66		13.D.14.	
Effin	102	66	2736, [4027/28]	13.E.1., 4.G.10.	228-230, 305-307
Emlygrennan	117	66	2737	4.G.14.	231
Fedamore	104	66	2713, [1276/77], [2993]	1.F.4., 9.E.8., 9.G.4.	664-674
Glenogra	105	66	2806, [1278/79]	10.A.4.	675
Galbally	120	67	2738, [4029], [2991]	5.A.6.	232-237
Grange	72	65	2751, [1259]	6.D.12.	358-359
Grean	65	64	2714, [1239]	1.F.6., 3.G.14.	
Hackmys	100	66		13.E.6.	308-310
Hospital	112	66	2807-08, [1280], [4032], [2994]	9.E.9., 10.A.10.	
Inch St Lawrence	56	64	2715	1.F.10.	
Iveruss	24	62	2763-64	7.E.9., 7.F.14.	76, 452-455
Kilbeheny	130	67	2739, [4030]	5.B.14.	238-247
Kilbolane	88	65		12.F.6.	
Kilbradran	9	62	2791, [1196], [1203]	10.G.12., 3.A.2.	
Kilbreedy	101	66	2740	13.E.8.	248-249
Kilbreedy Major	115	66	2809, [1247]	10.B.8., 5.D.6.	
Kilcolman	8	62	2792	11.A.2.	589
Kilcornan	25	62	2765-66	7.E.9., 7.G.8.	456-461
Kilcullane	108	66	2810, [1281]	9.E.9.	676-677
Kildimo	28	62	2767-68	7.E.9.	462-468
Kilfergus	2	62	2793	11.A.5.	590-611
Kilfinnane	124	67	2741, [1248], [4031], [2995]	5.D.12.	250-251
Kilfinny	79	65	[1222], [1233/34]	12.F.7.	144
Kilflyn	128	67	2742, [1249]	5.F.10.	253-258
Kilfrush	113	66	2811, [1282]	10.C.2.	
Kilkeedy	29	62	2780-81, 2789	8.F.8., 8.G.14.	547-552
Killagholehane	78	65	2752, [1260]	6.E.1.	360-366
Killeedy	77	65	2753, [1261]	6.E.7.	354, 367-412
Killeely	30	62	[3011], [3035]	14.B.2., 14.B.10., 13.G.8., 13.G.12	178
Killeenagarriff	43	63	2716	1.F.14.	31-32
Killeenoghty	37	63	2782	9.B.6., 13.E.10.	553
Killonahan	34	63	2783	8.F.8., 9.B.8., 13.E.11.	311-313
Kilmallock (Sts. Peter & Paul)			[2996/7]		

PARISH	TITHES 1823–38 TAB 17/	FILM	VALUATION FIELD BOOKS 1830s OL4./ HOUSE BOOKS [OL5.]	TENEMENT VALUATION FICHE 1850/52	1841–1851 CENSUS SEARCH Cen /s/17
Kilmeedy	82	65	[1235/36]	12.F.12.	145-171
Kilmoylan	6	62	2794	11.B.12.	612-619
Kilmurry	42	63	2717	1.G.10.	33-36
Kilpeacon	103	66	2784, 2812, [1283/84]	9.B.12., 10.C.4.	678
Kilquane	127	67	2743	5.G.8.	259-261
Kilscannell	23	62	2723, [1196a/97], [1204/05]	3.A.2.	77
Kilteely	69	64	2813, [1271/72]	3.E.9., 4.A.12.	178, 679
Knockainy	107	66	2814 ,[1285] [2994]	9.E.9., 10.C.6.	680-681
Knocklong	118	66	2744	5.G.12.	262-264
Knocknagaul	36	63	2785	9.B.14.	
Limerick city			[2998-3035]		474-531
Lismakeery	15	62	[1206/08]	3.A.6.	
Loghill	3	62	2795	11.C.12.	620-626
Ludden	52	64		2.A.2.	37-38
Mahoonagh	76	65	2754. [1262/63]	6.G.2.	413-416
Monagay	75	65	2755, [1264/67]	7.A.1.	417-443
Monasteranenagh	39	63	2786, 2815, [1286/87]	8.F.9., 9.C.4., 13.E.13.	682-685, 554-560
Morgans	12	62	2724, [1209/11]	3.A.9.	
Mungret	32	63	2787	8.F.9., 9.C.10.	561-577
Nantinan	16	62	2725, 2796, [1212/15]	11.D.6., 3.A.11.	78-80, 627-632
Newcastle	71	64	2756, [1266/69]	11.D.7., 7.C.1.	444-445
Oola	68	64	[1240]	3.E.9., 4.B.2.	179
Particles	123	67	2745-46-47	6.A.6.	265-267
Rathjordan	59	64		2.A.6.	
Rathkeale	21	62	2726, [1216/18, 3041/44]	3.B.5.	81-92
Rathronan	10	62	2797	11.D.8.	633-659
Robertstown	5	62	2798	11.E.8.	
Rochestown	54	64		2.A.10.	
Shanagolden	4	62	2799, [3045]	11.D.6.	660-662
St John's	1	62	[3007]	14.B.2., 14.C.3., 2.A.10.	
St Lawrence's	44	63	2718, [3012]	14.B.3., 14.E.7., 2.A.12.	
St Michael's	33	63	2788, [3006]	14.B.3., 14.F.10., 8.F.9., 9.D.10.	493-499, 530-531, 578-580
St Munchin's	31	63	2789, [3014], [3034], [3035]	14.B.5., 15.C.14., 13.G.8., 14.A.2.	500-508, 581-582
St Nicholas	45	63	2719, [3015], [3032], [3035]	15.D.5., 13.G.8., 14.A.6., 2.B.2.	39
St Patrick's	41	63	2720, [4034], [3033]	14.B.5., 15.D.10.	40-41, 509-529
St Peter's & St Paul's	114	66		7.D.6.	469-473
Stradbally	40	63		2.C.2.	42-59
Tankardstown	99	66		13.E.14.	
Templebredon	70	64	[1240/42]	4.B.14.	180-181
Tomdeely	13	62	2727, [1219/20]	3.D.9.	
Tullabracky	94	66	2816, [1251], [1288/89]	13.F.2.,	314-316

PARISH	TITHES 1823–38 TAB 17/	FILM	VALUATION FIELD BOOKS 1830s OL4./ HOUSE BOOKS [OL5.]	TENEMENT VALUATION FICHE 1850/52	1841–1851 CENSUS SEARCH Cen /s/17
Tuogh	62	64	2774-2776	8.C.2., 8.E.6.	539-541
Tuoghcluggin or Cluggin	67	64		4.C.4.	
Uregare	98	66	2817 [1290]	13.F5., 10.E.10.	317, 686-687

TOWNS	VALUATION HOUSE BOOK 1830s [OL5.]
Cappamore	[2986]
Castleconnel	[2985]
Glin	[2992]
Herbertstown	[2993]
Killeely	[3011, 3035]
Limerick No. 1 & 2	[2998]
Limerick No. 3	[2999]
Limerick No. 4	[3000]
Limerick No. 5	[3001]
Limerick No. 6	[3002]
Limerick No. 7	[3003]
Limerick No. 8	[3004]
Limerick No. 9	[3005]
Montpelier	[2985]
Moroe	[3036]
No. 1-14	[3016/29]
Pallas Green	[3037]
Pallaskenry	[3038]
Patrickswell	[3039/40]
St John's 11	[3007]
St John's 12	[3008]
St John's 13	[3009]
St John's 14	[3010]
St Lawrence	[3012]
St Mary's	[3013] [4033]
St Mary's	[3030/31]
St Michael's 10	[3006]
St Munchin's	[3014, 3034, 3035]
St Nicholas	[3015, 3032, 3035]
St Patrick's	[3033]

PARISH	TITHES 1823–38 TAB 18/	FILM	VALUATION FIELD BOOKS 1830s OL4./ HOUSE BOOKS [OL5.]	TENEMENT VALUATION 1854 FICHE	1841–1851 CENSUS SEARCH Cen /s/18
Abbeylara	7	68	1116-17, [1291]	2.D.8.	25-31
Abbeyshrule	23	69	1158-59, [1294]	1.F.12.	331-332
Agharra	24	69	1160-61	1.G.2.	
Ardagh	9	68	1099, 1134-35, 2818	4.A.4., 3.E.4.	1-3
Ballymacormick	14	69	1100-01, 1136-37	4.B.3., 3.E.7.	292
Cashel	19	69	1147-48	1.A.14., 3.G.4.	313-318
Clonbroney	5	68	1102-03, 1118-19, 2819, [1293]	2.B.12., 2.E.4.	32-65
Clongesh	3	68	1124-25	4.D.6.	161-165
Columbkille	4	68	1120-21	2.F.7., 5.C.8.	66-111
Forgney	25	69	1162-63, 1162-63	1.G.4.	333-337
Granard	6	68	1104-05, 2819/20, [1292], [3062/65]	2.B.12., 3.A.1.	112-133
Kilcommock	20	69	1138, 1149-50, 1164	1.D.12., 1.C.4., 1.G.11.	292-299, 319-322
Kilglass	16	69	1106-07, 1139-40, 1165	1.F.4., 4.B.9., 1.E.3., 1.G.12.	300, 339-341
Killashee	13	69	1126-27, 1141-42	4.F.3., 1.E.7., 3.F.1.	301-304
Killoe	1	68	1122-23, 1128-29	3.C.8., 5.C.8., 2.D.6., 4.F.7.	134-160, 166-282
Mohill	2	68	1130-31	4.E.12.	283-286
Mostrim	10	68	1108-09	2.B.13.	4-14
Moydow	15	69	1143-44	1.E.7., 3.F.12.	305-309
Noughaval	26	69	1151-52, 1166-67	1.C.12., 1.G.14.	
Rathcline	18	69	1153-54	1.C.12., 3.G.4.	323-329
Rathreagh	12	68	1110-11	1.F.6.	15-16
Shrule	21	69	1155, 2821	1.C.12.	330
Street	11	68	1112-13	2.D.1.	17
Taghsheenod	17	69	1145-46, 1168-69	1.E.10., 2.A.5.	310-312
Taghshinny	22	69	1156-57, 1170-71	1.D.10., 2.A.6.	338, 342
Templemichael	8	68	1114-15, 1132-33	4.B.10., 5.B.11.	18-24, 287-291

TOWNS	VALUATION HOUSE BOOK 1830s [OL5.]
Ballymahon	[3056, 3057]
Drumlish	[3058/59]
Edgeworthstown	[3058, 3060/61]
Longford	[3058]
Newtownforbes	[3058, 3061]
Keenagh	[3066]
Lanesboro[ugh]	[3067]
Longford	[3068/69]

PARISH/TOWN	TITHES 1823–38 TAB 20/	FILM	VALUATION FIELD BOOKS 1830s OL4./ HOUSE BOOKS [OL5.]	TENEMENT VALUATION 1854 FICHE	1841–1851 CENSUS SEARCH Cen /s/20
Ardee	29	71	1172, 2822, [3071/2]	1.A.14.	1-9
Ballybarrack	14	70	1199, [4049-50]	5.A.13.	189
Ballyboys	3	70	1195, [4045]	6.A.9.	110-111
Ballymakenny	62	72	1193 & 3a, 1214, 2848, [4035-36]	2.E.14., 2.D.12.	280
Ballymascanlan	1	70	1196, 1200, 2843, 2844, [4046, 4051]	6.A.12., 5.A.14.	112-154, 190-92
Barronstown	10	70	1201	5.B.1.	193
Beaulieu	61	72	1215, 2849, [1300]	2.F.2.	281
Cappoge	38	71	1173, 2823	1.C.10.	10
Carlingford	2	70	1197, 2845, [4047]	6.C.13.	155-188
Carrickbaggot	51	71	1216, 2850	2.F.4.	
Castlebellingham (Gernonstown)			[3073]		
Castletown	11	70	1198, 1202 ,[4052-53, 1295]	6.G.13., 5.B.5.	194
Charlestown	27	71	1174, 2824	1.C.12.	11-12
Clogher	57	72	1217, 2851, [3074]	2.F.6.	
Clonkeehan	21	71	1236, 2866, [4070]	2.C.8.	336
Clonkeen	26	71	1175, 1176, 2825	1.D.2.	13-17
Clonmore	46	71	1218	2.F.13.	282
Collon	48	71	1219, 2842, [3075]	2.A.12.	282-297
Creggan	6	70	1203, [4054]	5.B.8.	195-198
Darver	20	71	1237, 2867, [4071]	4.F.2.	
Drogheda			[3076/90, 3100, 4037-4043]		79-109
Dromin	37	71	1177, 2826	1.D.9.	
Dromiskin	19	71	1238, 2868, [4072]	4.F.4.	337-344
Drumcar	35	71	1178	1.D.13.	18-21
Drumshallon	55	72	1220, 2853, [1296]	2.G.2.	298-301
Dunany	43	71	1221, 2854, 2855	2.B.9.	302-303
Dunbin	13	70	1204, [4055-56]	5.B.13.	199-211
Dundalk	12	70	1205, 2846, [3101/9, 4044, 4057-58]	5.C.4., 5.F.2.	213-241
Dunleer	44	71	1222, 2856, [1297, 3110]	2.B.12.	304
Dysart	45	71	1223, 2857	2.G.8.	305
Faughart	5	70	1206, 2847, [4059]	5.D.5.	242-257
Gernonstown	32	71	1179, 2828	1.E.6.	22-25
Haggardstown	15	70	1207, 2847, [4060-61]	5.D.13.	258-265
Haynestown	16	70	1208, 2847, [4062-63]	5.E.2.	
Inishkeen	9	70	1209, 1239, 2847	5.D.2., 4.F.13.	266-268
Kane	8	70	1210, 2847	5.E.3.	269
Kildemock	40	71	1180, 2829	1.E.11.	26-28
Killanny	23	71	1181, 2830	4.E.6.	29-35
Killincoole	18	71	1240, 2869, [4073]	4.F.13.	
Kilsaran	31	71	1182, 2831	1.F.2.	36-47
Louth	17	70	1183, 1211, 1241, 2832, 2870, [4065-66, 4074]	5.E.5., 2.C.8., 4.G.2., 4.E .11.	270-272 345-354
Manfieldstown	22	71	1242, [4075]	2.C.10.	
Mapastown	28	71	1184, 2833	1.F.7.	48-49
Marlestown	50	71	1224, 2858	2.G.11.	306
Mayne	56	72	1225, 2859	2.G.12.	
Monasterboice	54	72	1226, 2860, [1298]	2.G.14.	307-309

PARISH	TITHES 1823–38 TAB 20/	FILM	VALUATION FIELD BOOKS 1830s OL4./ HOUSE BOOKS [OL5.]	TENEMENT VALUATION 1854 FICHE	1841–1851 CENSUS SEARCH Cen /s/20
Mosstown	41	71	1185, 2834	1.F.9.	50-51
Mullary	49	71	1227, 2861, [1299]	3.A .5.	310-315
Parsonstown	53	71	1228	3.A.10.	
Philipstown	7	70	1212	5.E.9.	52-56, 273
Philipstown	24	71	1186, 2835 [4067]	1.G.1.	
Philipstown	59	72	1229, 2862 [1301]	3.A.10.	
Port	47	71	1230	3.A.11.	
Rathdrumin	52	71	1231, 2863	3.B.1.	316
Richardstown	34	71	1187, 2836	1.G.8.	
Roche	4	70	1213, 2847 [4068]	5.E.10.	274-279
Salterstown	42	71	1232	2.C.6.	
Shanlis	36	71	1188, 2837	1.G.10.	
Smarmore	39	71	1189, 2838	1.G.12.	
Stabannan					58-62
St Mary's (Drogheda)	64	72	[4040, 4069]	3.E.10.	66-70
St Peter's	63	72	1194, 1233, 2842 [4041]	2.D.13., 3.G.2.	71-78
Stickillin	33	71	1191, 2840	2.A.7.	
Tallanstown	25	71	1192, 2841	2.A.8.	63-65
Termonfeckin	60	72	1234, 2864 [3111]	3.B.4.	317-320
Tullyallen	58	72	1235, 2865	3.C.6.	321-335

PARISH	TITHES 1823–38 TAB 21/	FILM	VALUATION FIELD BOOKS 1830s OL4./ HOUSE BOOKS [OL5.]	TENEMENT VALUATION FICHE 1855–57	1841–1851 CENSUS SEARCH Cen /s/21
Achill	19	74	1243, [4077]	11.A.2.	1-142
Addergoole	16	74	1298, [4167]	1.A.14., 7.A.14.	2586-2628
Aghagower	48	75	1244, 1294, 2904	14.C.12., 14.G.8.	143-161, 2421-2446
Aghamore	70	76	1268, [4127]	8.G.8., 12.A.12.	640-817
Aglish	24	74	1249, 2872, [4089-90]	5.D.14.	313-337
Annagh	73	76	1269, [4128]	8.G.12.	818-930
Ardagh	14	74	1299, [4168]	1.A.14.	2629-2641
Attymass	36	75	1277, 2889	2.B.10.	1655-1704
Balla	59	75	2884	6.F.14.	469-475
Ballinchalla	52	75	1287, [4150]	2.G.10.	2255-2263
Ballinrobe	50	75	1288, [4151-52, 3119/23]	3.A.4.	2264-2288
Ballintober	30	74	1245, 1250, 2873, [4078, 4091-92]	14.D.10., 2.E.10., 5.G.1.	162, 338-345
Ballynahaglish	18	74	1300, [4169-71]	1.B.7.	2641-2669
Ballyhean	27	74	1251, 2875, [4093-94]	6.A.1.	346-356
Ballyovey	34	75	1252, 2874, [4096]	2.E.11.	357-380
Ballysakeery	12	73	1301, [4172]	1.C.8.	2670-2689
Bekan	72	76	1270, [4131]	9.B.14.	931-975
Bohola	43	75	1278, 2890	6.G.10., 13.A.4.	1705-1766
Breaghwy	26	74	1253, 2876, [4099-4102]	6.A.13.	381-382
Burriscarra	31	74	1254, 2877, [4103]	2.F.10., 6.B.6.	383-387
Burrishoole	20	74	1246, [4079-80]	11.C.12.	163-240
Castlemore	69	76	1271, [4135]	7.E.4.	976-1009
Cong	55	75	1289, [4153-55, 3135]	3.C.7.	1441-1596, 2289, 2290-2310
Crossboyne	63	76	1262	8.A.12.	476-511
Crossmolina	13	73	1302, [4175-76, 4191]	1.D.6.	2690-2737
Doonfeeny	3	73	1303, [4177]	10.A.12.	2738-2762
Drum	29	74	1255, 2878, [4106]	6.B.8.	388-390
Inishbofin (Island)	46	75	1295, 2902	9.G.4.	2447-2454
Islandeady	23	74	1247, 1256, 2879 [4081, 4109]	14.D.11.	241-252, 391-409
Kilbeagh	66	76	1272, [4138]	7.F.1., 12.C.10.	1010-1117
Kilbelfad	17	74	1304, [4181]	1.F.14.	2763-2779
Kilbride	4	73	1305, [4179]	10.B.14.	2780-2794
Kilcolman	61	76	1263, 1273, [4141]	8.C.7., 7.F.3.	512-577, 1118-1176
Kilcommon	2	73	2885-2887	4.D.4., 11.F.12.	1441-1596 2289, 2311-2361
Kilcommon	51	75	2898, [4156]	3.D.14., 9.E.12.	
Kilconduff	41	75	1279, 2891, [4146]	13.B.2.	1767-1862
Kilcummin	5	73	1306, [4180]	10.C.6.	2795-2824
Kildacommoge	42	75	1257, 1280, [4112, 4147]	6.D.2., 6.G.10	410-418, 1863-1876
Kilfian	7	73	1307	1.G.11., 10.D.1.	2825-2859
Kilgarvan	35	75	1281, 2892	2.C.9.	1877-1966
Kilgeever	47	75	1296, 2903, 2905	15.D.6.	2445-2501
Killala	10	73	1308, [4182, 3138/39]	10.E.1.	2860-2865

PARISH	TITHES 1823–38 TAB 21/	FILM	VALUATION FIELD BOOKS 1830s OL4./ HOUSE BOOKS [OL5.]	TENEMENT VALUATION FICHE 1855–57	1841–1851 CENSUS SEARCH Cen /s/21
Killasser	38	75	1282, 2893	13.D.4.	1967-2028
Killedan	44	75	1283, 2894, [4148]	13.E.14.	2029-2160
Kilmaclasser	22	74	1248, [4082]	14.E.7.	253-270, 311-312
Kilmainebeg	56	75			2362-2369
Kilmainemore	54	75	1291, [4159]	3.F.10.	2370-2392
Kilmeena	21	74	2871, [4083]	11.F.7., 14.E.14.	271-310, 311-312
Kilmolara	53	75	2899	3.G.11.	2393-2394
Kilmore	1	73	2888	4.G.13.	1597-1654
Kilmoremoy	15	74	1309, [4185]	2.A.1.	2866-2902
Kilmovee	68	76	1274, [4143]	12.F.5.	1177-1371
Kilturra	65	76	1275, [4144]	12.G.14.	1372-1379
Kilvine	64	76	1264, [4085]	8.E.7.	578-609
Knock	71	76	1265, 1276, [4086, 4145]	8.F.1., 9.D.13.	610-627, 1380-1440
Lackan	6	73	1310	10.E.11.	2903-2925
Manulla	28	74	1258, 2880 [4115]	6.D.7.	419-425
Mayo	60	76	1266, 1292 [4087, 4162]	4.A.3., 2.G.8., 6.G.7., 8.F.3.	628-631, 2395
Meelick	40	75	1284, 2895	13.G.11.	2161-2198
Moorgagagh	57	75	2900	4.A.6.	
Moygawnagh	11	73	1311, [4187]	10.F.5.	2926-2937
Oughaval	45	75	1297, 2906, [4166]	15.A.8.	2502-2585
Rathreagh	8	73	1312, [4188]	10.F.12.	2938-2941
Robeen	49	75	1293, [4163]	4.A.7.	2396-2409
Rosslee	32	75	1259, 2881, [4118]	2.G.1., 6.E.1.	426-427
Shrule	58	75	2901, [4164, 3144/45]	4.B.5.	2410-2420
Tagheen	62	76	1267, [4088]	8.F.11.	632-639
Templemore	39	75	1285, 2896	7.A.3.	2199-2232
Templemurry	9	73	1313, [4190]	10.G.2.	2942-2954
Toomore	37	75	1286, 2897, [4149]	14.A.11.	2233-2254
Touaghty	33	75	1260, 2882, [4121]	2.G.3.	428-429
Turlough	25	74	1261, 2883, [4124]	6.E.3.	430-468

TOWNS	VALUATION HOUSE BOOKS 1830s [OL5.]
Ballaghadereen	[3112,3113]
Ballyhaunis	[3113, 3124/35]
Ballina	[3114/17]
Ballindine	[3118]
Ballyharris	[3124/25]
Belmullet	[3126/27]
Castlebar	[3128/31]
Clare	[3132/33]
Claremorris	[3134]
Foxford	[3136/37]
Kiltamagh	[3140]
Louisburgh	[3141]
Newport	[3142/43]
Swineford	[3146]
Westport	[3147/49
Westport Quay	[3150/51]

PARISH	TITHES 1823–38 TAB 22/	FILM	VALUATION FIELD BOOKS 1830s OL4./ HOUSE BOOKS [OL5.]	TENEMENT VALUATION FICHE 1855–57	1841–1851 CENSUS SEARCH Cen /s/22
Agher	138	80	1314, 1323, 2907	9.A.4., 9.A.12.	4
Ardagh	17	77	1386 (Part Missing), 2960, [4206]	5.C.12., 5.C.6.	
Ardbraccan	50	78	1404	7.E.10.	197-202
Ardcath	102	79	1344, 2922	2.G.14.	47-49
Ardmulchan	79	79	1434	7.C.6.	263
Ardsallagh	57	78	1405	7.F.6.	203-207
Assey	116	79	1315	7.D.14.	
Athboy	70	78	1381, [3152]	9.F.12.	134-139
Athlumney	80	79	1435	7.C.9.	264-271
Balfeaghan	141	80	2909, 2915	4.F.6.	
Ballyboggan	110	79	1399	4.G.10.	
Ballygarth	100	79	1345, 2923-24	3.A.7.	
Ballymagarvey	68	78	1331, 2917	7.B.6.	12
Ballymaglassan	135	80	1422	4.B.7.	
Balrathboyne	36	77	1372, 1406, [4197]	6.A.8., 6.A.2.	107-109, 208
Balsoon	117	79	1316, [1302]	7.E.1., 9.A.4.	
Bective		79	1415	7.E.2.	
Brownstown	84	79	1436	7.C.14.	272
Burry	35	77	1373, [4198]	6.A.11.	
Castlejordan	111	79	1400	4.G.14.	187-189
Castlerickard	108	79	1382, 1401	10.A.1., 9.E.12.	
Castletown	11	77	1387	5.C.14., 6.F.4.	144-145
Churchtown	55	78	1407	7.F.7.	209
Clonalvy	106	79	1346, 2925	3.A.8.	18-19
Clonard	109	79	1402	5.A.8., 9.F.1.	190-196
Clongill	15	77	1388	6.F.7.	
Clonmacduff	73	79	1416	8.F.12.	
Collon		78	1460	2.E.12.	294-297
Colp	61	78	1332, 2918	3.C.1.	13-17
Cookstown	129	80	1423	4.B.9.	
Crickstown	128	80	1424, 2956	4.B.10.	
Cruicetown	5	77	1362	5.D.14.	72-75
Culmullin	137	80	1324, 1425, 2908	4.B.11., 3.G.7.	5-8
Cushinstown		79	1437	4.D.11.	273-274
Danestown	88	79	1333, 1438, 2919	7.B.7., 7.D.1.	
Derrypatrick	123	80	1317	3.F.12.	1-3
Diamor	29	77	1356	8.B.10.	
Donaghmore	52	78	1408	4.B.11.	?
Donaghmore	133	80	1426	7.E.9.	210-216
Donaghpatrick	38	78	1374, 1409, [4199]	6.A.14., 7.E.6., 7.F.14.	110-111
Donore		78	1334, 2920	3.C.11.	20-25
Dowdstown	85	79	1439	7.D.2.	275
Dowth	48	78	1461	2.G.8.	298-299
Drakestown	12	77	1389	6.F.8.	
Drumcondra	18	77	1455, [4207]	2.C.13., 5.C.11.	282-287
Drumlargan	139	80	1325, 2910	9.A .13.	
Dulane	33	77	1375, [4200]	6.A 14.	112
Duleek	64	78	1335, 1347, 2926-27	3.D.2., 3.A.11.	26-41, 50-55
Duleek Abbey		79	1348, 2928-29	3.B.3.	
Dunboyne	145	80	1354, 2939, [4194-95, 3154]	4.A.6.	

PARISH	TITHES 1823–38 TAB 22/	FILM	VALUATION FIELD BOOKS 1830s OL4./ HOUSE BOOKS [OL5.]	TENEMENT VALUATION FICHE 1855–57	1841–1851 CENSUS SEARCH Cen /s/22
Dunmoe	53	78	1410	7.G.1.	
Dunsany	95	79	1440	4.D.12.	
Dunshaughlin	126	80	1427, 2948, 2949, [4212, 1307]	4.B.13.	257-260
Emlagh	7	77	1363	5.E.1.	76
Ennisken	9	77	1364, 1390	5.E.1., 5.C.14.	
Fennor	58	78	1336, 2921	7.B.7.	
Follistown	82	79	1441	7.D.3.	276
Gallow	140	80	1326, 2911	9.A.13.	
Galtrim	121	79		9.A.6.	
Gernonstown	41	78	1462	6.G.8.	300-302
Girley	39	78	1376, 2941 [4201]	6.B.4.	113-114
Grangegeeth		78	1463	2.E.14.	303-305
Greenoge	134	80	1428	4.C.7.	
Inishmot	20	77	1456, [4208]	2.D.8.	
Julianstown	66	78	1337, 1349, 2930-31 [4192]	3.E.4., 3.B.3.	
Kells		77	1377, [4213, 3155/57]	6.B.7.	115-117
Kentstown	67	78	1338	7.B.8	
Kilbeg	4	77	1365, [4196]	5.E.5.	77-84
Kilberry	16	77	1391	6.F.10.	146-151
Kilbrew	125	80	1429, 2950	4.C.8.	261
Kilbride	24	77	1357	4.B.4.	?
Kilbride		80	1355	8.B.12.	56-57
Kilcarn	81	79	1442	7.D.4.	277
Kilclone	143	80	1327, 2911	3.G.10.	
Kilcooly	78	79	1417	8.F.14.	256
Kildalkey	71	79	1383	10.A.1.	140
Killaconnigan	72	79	1384	10.A.11.	141-142
Killallon	30	77	1358	8.B.13.	58
Killary	23	77	1457, 2961, [4209]	2.D.9.	288-290
Killeen	94	79	1443	4.D.13.	
Killegland	130	80	1430, [4205]	4.C.10.	
Killeagh	26	77	1359	8.C.6.	59-61
Killyon	107	79	1403	5.B.6., 9.F.7.	
Kilmainham	2	77	1366	5.E.11.	85-93
Kilmessan	120	79	1318	3.F.13.	
Kilmoon	98	79	1444	4.E.1.	
Kilmore	136	80	1328, 2913	3.G.12.	9-10
Kilsharvan	65	78	1339, 1350, 2932-33	3.E.7., 3.B.4.	
Kilshine	14	77	1392	6.G.3.	
Kilskeer	31	77	1378, [4202-03]	6.C.12., 8.E.8.	118-120
Kiltale	122	80	1319	3.G.2.	
Knock	13	77	1393	6.G.5.	152
Knockcommon	63	78	1340	7.B.10.	42-43
Knockmark	124	80	1320	3.G.4.	
Laracor	113	79	1395, 2942, [1303]	9.B.4.	157-160
Liscartan	51	78	1411	7.G.1.	
Lismullin		79	1145	7.D.6.	
Loughan (Castlekeeran)	32	77	1379	6.D.8.	121-129
Loughbrackan	19	77	2962	2.E.2.	291
Loughcrew		77	1360	8.C.12.	62

PARISH	TITHES 1823–38 TAB 22/	FILM	VALUATION FIELD BOOKS 1830s OL4./ HOUSE BOOKS [OL5.]	TENEMENT VALUATION FICHE 1855–57	1841–1851 CENSUS SEARCH Cen /s/22
Macetown	97	79	1446	4.E.4.	
Martry	49	78	1412	6.A.3.	217-219
Mitchelstown	21	77	1458, 2962a, [4210]	2.E.5.	292
Monknewtown		78	1464	2.G.10.	306-312
Monktown		79	1447	7.D.7.	278-279
Moorechurch	101	79	1351, 2934-35	3.B.5.	
Moybolgue	1	77	1367	5.F.2.	94
Moyglare	144	80	1329, 2916	4.A.2., 4.F.7.	
Moylagh	27	77	2940	8.D.2.	63-68
Moymet	75	79	1418	8.G.1.	
Moynalty	3	77	1368	5.F.8.	95-103
Navan	54	78	1413, [4214, 3160]	7.G.3.	220-251
Newtown	6	77	1369	5.G.11.	
Newtownclonbun	77	79	1419	8.G.4.	
Nobber	10	77	1370, 1394	5.G.12., 5.D.5.	153-156
Oldcastle	25	77	1361, [3161]	8.D.9.	69-71
Painestown	62	78	1341	7.B.14.	46
Piercetown	105	79	1342, 1352, 2936	7.C.4., 4.A.3.	
Rataine	56	78	1414	8.A.12.	253-254
Rathbeggan	132	80	1431, 2951, 2957	4.C.11.	
Rathcore	115	79	1330, 1396, 2914, 2943, [1304]	9.B.14., 9.B.2.	11, 161-171
Rathfeigh	92	79	1448	4.E.6.	
Rathkenny	40	78	1465	6.G.11.	313-341
Rathmore	69	78	1385	10.B.5.	143
Rathmolyon	114	79	1397, 2944-47, [1305, 3162]	9.C.11.	172-182
Rathregan	131	80	1432, 2952	4.C.13.	
Ratoath	127	80	1433, 2953-54, 2958-59 [3163]	4.C.14.	262
Rodanstown	142	80		4.F.9.	
Scurlockstown	119	79	1321	9.A.9.	
Siddan	22	77	1459, [4211]	2.E.6.	293
Skreen	91	79	1449	4.E.7.	280
Slane	44	78	1466	7.A.5.	342-347
St Marys	60	78	1343	3.E.9.	44-45
Stackallan	46	78	1467	7.B.1.	348-349
Staffordstown	83	79	1450	7.D.9.	
Staholmog	8	77	1371	5.G.13.	104-106
Stamullin	104	79	1353, 2937-38	3.B..9	
Tara	89	79	1451	7.D.9.	
Teltown	20/37	78	1380, [4204]	6.D.14.	130-133
Templekeeran	86	79	1452	7.D.11.	
Timoole	93	79	1453	4.E.12.	
Trevet	96	79	1454, 2955	4.E.12., 4.D.10.	281
Trim	112	79	1398, 1420, [1306, 3167/70]	8.G.5., 9.D.8.	183-186, 255
Trubley	118	79	1322	9.A.11.	
Tullaghanoge	74	79	1421	9.A.2.	
Tullyallen	45	78	1468	2.G.13.	

TOWNS	VALUATION HOUSE BOOK 1830s [OL5.]
Clonee	[3153]
Dunboyne	[3154]
Kells	
Longwood	[3158]
Mornington	[3159]
Robinstown	[3164]
Summerhill	[3165/66]

PARISH/TOWN	TITHES 1823–38 TAB 23/	FILM	VALUATION FIELD BOOKS 1830s OL4./ HOUSE BOOK [OL5.]	TENEMENT VALUATION c.1858–61 FICHE	1841/1851 CENSUS SEARCH Cen /s/3
Aghabog	12	82	1481/2, 2967/8	4.D.10., 5.E.12., 8.G.12.	241-291
Aghnamullen	18	82	1469/70, 2963/4	2.C.8., 3.E.2., 5.D.6.	1-87
Ballybay	17	82	1471/2, 1502/3, [3171]	4.A.4., 3.A.B.	88-121
Carrickmacross			[3173/74]		
Castleblayney			[3175]	2.G.11.	
Clones	9	81	1483/4, 1504/5, 2969-76, [1309/10], [3172]	4.D.14., 7.C.10., 9.A.2.	292-323 647-663
Clontibret	15	82	1473/4, 2965, [1308]	3.B.6., 8.E.12.	122-213
Currin	13	82	1485/6, 2977-8	4.G.9., 5.F.12.	324-345
Donagh	2	81	1518, 3012, [1313]	6.C.8.	797-812
Donaghmoyne	20	83	1492/3, 2990	1.A.14., 3.G.6.	411-520
Drummully	11	82	1487	5.A.6.	346-348
Drumsnat	5	81	1506-7, 3003	7.D.8.	664-666
Ematris	14	82	1488-9, 2981	5.G.8.	349-367
Emyvale (Donagh)			[3177]		
Errigal Trough	1	81	1519, 4437	4.B.8., 6.F.5.	813-866
Glaslough (Donagh)			[3176]		
Inishkeen	21	83	1494, 3002	9.B.13.	521-542
Killanny	23	83	1496/7, 2993/4	1.D.14.	543-554
Killeevan	10	82	1490/1, 2982/5	5.A.13., 9.A.4.	368-410
Kilmore	6	81	1508/9, 3004	7.E.8.	667-677
Magheracloone	22	83	1498/9, 2994/6	2.A.8.	555-569
Magheross	19	83	1500/1, 3001/2, [3173/4]	1.E.11.	570-646
Monaghan	7	81	1510/11, 3005/6, [1311], [3178/80],	8.B.3.	678-717
Newbliss (Killeevan)			[3181]		
Smithborough (Clones)			[3182/3]		
Muckno	16	82	1475/6, [3175]	2.E.2.	214-238
Tedavnet	3	81	1512/3, 3010	6.G.10.	718-765
Tehallan	4	81	1514/5, 3011, [1312]	8.A.2., 8.G.7.	239-240, 766-770
Tullycorbet	8	81	1516/7	7.F.14., 8 .G.3.	771-796

PARISH	TITHES 1823–38 TAB 15/	FILM	VALUATION FIELD BOOKS 1830s OL4./ HOUSE BOOKS [OL5.]	TENEMENT VALUATION 1854 FICHE	1841–1851 CENSUS SEARCH Cen /s/15
Aghancon	38	58	1005, 3018, 3036 [1319, 1349]	7.C.6., 6.D.1.	12-15, 79-80
Ardnurcher (Horseleap)	3	56	1031, 3069, [1389]	4.G.9.	
Ballyboy	27	57	3014, [1314/16, 3184]	2.B.7.	1-7
Ballyburly	6	56	3084, [1394/95, 1409/10]	1.E.7., 1.D.10.	334- 336, 352-354
Ballycommon	21	57	1036, 3075, [1396/97]	4.C.14.	
Ballykean	29	57	1040, 3068, [1384, 1403/05]	6.A.2., 4.E.12.	337-340
Ballymacwilliam	7	56	1044, 3085, [1411/12]	1.E.11	355
Ballynakill	24	57	1018, 3032	1.A.12.	127-130
Birr	34	58	0994, 3019, [1320/21]	2.E.10., 3.A.1.	16-36
Borrisnafarney	51	58	1006 [1350]	6.D.12.	81
Castlejordan	5	56	1019, 1045, 1046, [1362, 1413/14]	1.F.1.	131, 356-359
Castletownely	48	58	1007, 3038, [1351]	6.D.14.	
Castropetie (Monasteroris)	23	57			
Clonyhurk	30	57	1041, 3079, [1406]	7.F.8.	341
Clonmacnoise	8	56	1023, 3060, [1369]	3.B.9.	151-179
Clonsast	25	57	3034, [1363/64]	1.B.3.	132-137
Corbally	40	58	0995, 1008, 3039 [1322, 1352]	7.C.12., 6.E.2.	
Croghan	19	57	1037, [1398]	1.D.13.	341
Cullenwaine	50	58	3040, [1353]	6.E.4.	82-84
Drumcullen	32	57	1021, 3058, [1366/67]	1.G.10.	148-149
Dunkerrin	46	58	1010, 3041, [1354]	6.E.12.	
Durrow	15	56	1001, [1338/40]	5.C.1.	54-55
Eglish	31	57	1022, 3059, [1368]	2.A.8.	150
Ettagh	43	58	0996, 3021, [1323, 1355]	7.C.14., 6.F 8.	85-95
Finglas	49	58	1012, 3034, [1356]	6.F.14.	
Gallen	12	56	1024, 3061, [1370/71]	3.A.3.	180-199
Geashill	28	57	1030, 3080, 3081, [1385/87, 1407/08]	7.G.10., 6.A.2., 1.E.4., 4.E.12.	284-305, 343-346
Kilbride	4	56	1032, 1002, 3070, 3031, [1390/91]	4.G.13.	56-62, 306-326
Kilbride (Tullamore)	17	57	[1341/42]	5.C.9.	
Kilclonfert	20	57	1038, 3077, [1399/400]	4.D.5.	347-348
Kilcolman	41	58	1013, 3023, 3044, 3055, [1324/25, 1356a]	2.C.13., 6.G.2.	37-40, 96-102
Kilcomin	45	58	3046, [1357]	6.G.6.	
Kilcumreragh	1	56	1033, 3072, [1392]	5.B.2.	
Killaderry	22	57	1039, 3078, [1401/02]	4.D.13.	349-351
Killagally (Wheery)	11	56	[1381/83]	4.A.6.	274-283, 349-351
Kilmurryely	42	58	1014, [1358]	6.C.12.	104-107
Killoughy	26	57	3015-3016, [1317/18]	4.F.5.	8-11
Kilmanaghan	2	56	1034, 3073, [1393]	5.B.6.	327-333
Kinnitty	36	58	0997, 3024, [1326/27, 3198/99]	2.D.2.	41
Lemanaghan	9	56	1025, 3062-3063, [1372]	3.F.5., 5.B.14.	200-242
Letterluna	33	58	0998, 3025, [1328/29]	2.D.10.	42-46

PARISH	TITHES 1823–38 TAB 15/	FILM	VALUATION FIELD BOOKS 1830s OL4./ HOUSE BOOKS [OL5.]	TENEMENT VALUATION 1854 FICHE	1841–1851 CENSUS SEARCH Cen /s/15
Lusmagh	14	56	3065, [1373/75]	3.D.3.	243-250
Lynally	18	57	1003, [1343/45]	5.F.1.	63-67
Monasteroris (Edenderry)	23	57	3035, [1365]		138-147
Rahan	16	56	1004, [1346/48]	5.F.10.	68-78
Reynagh	13	56	1026, 3066, [1376/78]	3.E.1.	251-267
Roscomroe	37	58	3028, [1330/32]	2.E.2.	47-48
Roscrea	39	58	1015, 3026, [1333/34, 1359]	7.D.4., 7.A.4.	49-50, 108-110
Seirkieran	35	58	1000, 3029, [1335/37]	2.E.4., 7.D.8.,	51-53
Shinrone	44	58	1016, 3049, [1360, 3212/13]	7.A.8.	111-123
Templeharry	47	58	1017, 3050, [1361]	7.B.4.	124-126
Tisaran	10	56	1027, 3067, [1379/80]	3.G.12.	268-273
Wheery/Killagally				4.A.6.	274-283

TOWNS	VALUATION HOUSE BOOK 1830s [OL5.]
Ballycumber	[3185]
Banagher	[3186/87]
Birr (See Parsonstown)	
Crinkell	[3188/89]
Clara	[3190/91]
Edenderry	[3192/94]
Frankford	[3195]
Ferbane	[3196/97]
Moneygall	[3200/01]
Parsonstown	[3202/06]
Philipstown	[3207/08]
Portarlington	[3209/10]
Shannon Bridge	[3211]
Tullamore	[3214/17]

PARISH	TITHES 1823–38 TAB 25/	FILM	VALUATION FIELD BOOKS 1830s OL4./ HOUSE BOOKS [OL5.]	TENEMENT VALUATION 1857–8 FICHE	1841–1851 CENSUS SEARCH Cen /s/25
Ardcarn	4	87	1617	2.G.6., 4.D.12.	378-414
Athleague	44	89	[3218]	5.A.12.	1-13
Aughrim	19	88	1636	4.G.4.	888-892
Ballintober	18	88	1625	8.E.2.	523-534
Ballynakill	35	88	1612	6.D.12.	349
Baslick	16	88	1626	8.E.8.	535-549
Boyle	2	87	1613, [3222/25]	3.B.2.	415-446
Bumlin	26	88	1637	7.C.4.	893-921
Cam	51	89	1590	1.E.7.	14-31
Castlemore	98	87	1630	9.D.12.	638-647
Clooncraff	21	88	1638	4.G.14., 7.C.14.	922-935
Cloonfinlough	28	88	1639	6.E 10., 7.D.8.	936-942
Cloontuskert	40	89	1606-07	5.F.8.	273-293
Cloonygormican	34	88	1613	6.D.13., 8.D.6.	350-365
Creagh	57	90	1634	2.D.4.	862-864
Creeve	13	87	1631, 1640	4.F.12., 7.E.5.	648-653
Drum	56	90	1591	1.A.14.	32-42
Drumatemple	33	88	1614	8.D.10.	366-371
Dunamon	37	88	1615	6.E.1.	
Dysart	53	89	1592	1.F.5.	43-50
Elphin	22	88	1641, [3227]	7.E.6.	943-985
Estersnow	6	87	1619	3.D.10.	447-461
Fuerty	43	89	1593	5.B.11.	52-77
Kilbride	38	88	1608, 1642	7.F.11., 5.G.4.	294-316, 956
Kilbryan	3	87	1620	3.E.4.	462-463
Kilcolagh	11	87	1632	3.G.14., 3.G.4.	654-668
Kilcolman	9a	87	3088	9.E.1.	669-677
Kilcooley	25	88	1643	7.F.12.	987-989
Kilcorkey	14	88	1627	8.F.4.	550-554, 697-698
Kilgefin	39	89	1609	6.A.5.	317-332
Kilglass	31	88	1603, 1644	7.G.4., 6.F.12.	185-217
Kilkeevin	15	88	1628	8.F.13.	571-601
Killinvoy	46-?	89	1594	2.A.1., 5.C.14.	78-84
Killukin	7	87	1621	3.E.9., 4.E.1.	464-468, 990-995
Killukin	27	88	1645	7.G.4.	
Killummod	8	87	1623	3.E.11., 4.E.8.	469-477
Kilmacumsy	12	87	1633	4.A.8.	678-688
Kilmeane	45	89	1595	5.D.9.	85-90
Kilmore	45	88	1604	4.C.10.	218-226
Kilnamanagh	9	87		4.B.1., 9.E.2.	689-696
Kilronan	1	87	1623	3.E.12.	478-501
Kilteevan	42	89	1610	6.B.3.	333-337
Kiltoom	52	89	1596	1.F.12.	91-100
Kiltrustan	23	88	1646	7.G.12.	996-1001
Kiltullagh	17	88	1629	9.B.5.	603-637
Lissonuffy	29	88	1647	8.A.9.	1002-1034
Moore	58	90	1635	2.E.1.	865-887
Ogulla	24	88	1648	8.B.8.	1035-1047
Oran	36	88	1616	6.E.3.	372-377
Rahara	48	89	1597	2.B.10.	101-106
Roscommon	41	89	1611, 3087, [3231/33]	6.C.1.	338-347

PARISH	TITHES 1823–38 TAB 25/	FILM	VALUATION FIELD BOOKS 1830s OL4./ HOUSE BOOKS [OL5.]	TENEMENT VALUATION 1857–8 FICHE	1841–1851 CENSUS SEARCH Cen /s/25
Shankill	20	88	3090	4.B.8., 8.B.13., 10.B.12.	1048-1052
St John's	49	89	1598	2.A.12., 5.E.9.	107-117
St Peter's	55	90	1599	1.C.11.	118-139
Taghboy	50	89	1600	2.A.2., 5.E.9.	140-153
Taghmaconnell	54	89	1601	1.C.2., 2.C.10.	51, 154-171
Termonbarry	32	88	1605	7.A.8.	227-264, 348
Tibohine	10	87	3089	9.E.6., 10.C.14.	699-861
Tisrara	47	89	1602	5.E.9.	172-184
Tumna	5	87	1624	3.G.10., 4.E.13.	502-505, 522

TOWNS	VALUATION HOUSE BOOK 1830s [OL5.]
Athlone (Part)	[3219]
Ballyfarnham	[3220]
Bellanagare	[3221]
Castlereagh	[3226]
Frenchpark	[3230]
Keadew	[3220]
Knockcroghery	[3228]
Lanesborough	[3229]
Loughglynn	[3230]
Roosky	[3231]
Strokestown	[3234]

PARISH/TOWN	TITHES 1823–38 TAB 26/	FILM	VALUATION FIELD BOOKS 1830s OL4./ HOUSE BOOKS [OL5.]	TENEMENT VALUATION 1858 FICHE	1841–1851 CENSUS SEARCH Cen /s/26
Achonry	19	93	1675	6.G.10.	375-491
Aghanagh	38	94	1683	1.F.4.	776-803
Ahamlish	1	91	1649, 1650	3.F.10.	1-24
Ballymote			1667, [3238]		
Ballynakill	31	93	1684	6.A.10.	804-828
Ballysadare	16	93	1676, 1685, [3239]	5.E.4., 5.F.2., 6.G.8.	492-498, 829-839
Ballysumaghan	30	93	1686	6.A.4.	840-850
Calry	4	91	1651, 1652, 3091	4.E.2.	25-34
Castleconor	14	92	3092	2.C.4., 3.A.1.	580-593
Cloonoghil	23	93	1668	6.F.6.	239-245
Dromard	13	92	1679	3.D.11.	594-605
Drumcliff	3	91	1653-54	4.B.5.	35-74
Drumcolumb	32	93	1687	1.G.3.	851-858
Drumrat	27	93	1669	1.D.6.	246-260
Easky	9	92	1680	2.E.10.	606-642
Emlaghfad	21	93	1670	1.D.13., 6.D.1., 6.G.2.	261-297
Kilcolman	40	94	1664	1.A.12.	121-150
Kilfree	39	94	1665	1.B.5.	151-214
Kilglass	8	92	1681	2.F.14.	643-660
Killadoon	35	94	1688	1.G.3.	859-870
Killaraght	41	94	1666	1.C.9.	215-238
Killaspugbrone	5	91	1655-56	4.F.9.	75-78
Killerry	28	93	1689	5.G.6.	871-887
Killoran	17	93		5.E.4., 7.D.8.	499-525
Kilmacallan	34	93	1690	1.G.9., 6.B.6.	888-899
Kilmacowen	7	91	1657-58	4.G.7.	79-82
Kilmacshalgan	10	92	1682	3.A.13.	661-691
Kilmacteige	20	93	1677	7.E.12.	526-555
Kilmactranny	37	94	1691	1.G.11.	900-935
Kilmoremoy	15	92	3093	2.C.6.	692-732
Kilmorgan	22	93	1671	6.C.8.	298-309
Kilross	29	93	1692	5.G.1.	936-941
Kilshalvy	26	93	1672	1.E.1., 6.G.4.	310-331
Kilturra	25	93	1673	6.G.4.	332-339
Kilvarnet	18	93	1678	7.E.6.	556-561
Rossinver	2	91	1659-60	4.A.12.	83-91
Shancough	36	94	1693	2.A.12.	942-949
Skreen	12	92	3094	3.C.10.	733-747
St John's	6	91	1661-63	5.C.14., 5.A.14., 5.A.2., 5.B.4., 4.E.13.	92-120
Sligo Town			[3241/53]		562-579
Tawnagh	33	93	1694	6.C.4.	950-954
Templeboy	11	92	3095	3.B.12.	748-775
Toomour	24	93	1674	1.E.9., 6.E.2.	340-374

TOWNS	VALUATION HOUSE BOOK 1830s [OL5.]	TOWNS	VALUATION HOUSE BOOK 1830s [OL5.]
Aclare	[3235]	Collooney	[3239]
Ardnaree	[3236/37]	Riverstown	[3254]
Bellahy	[3240]	Tobercurry	[3254]

PARISH/TOWN	TITHES 1823–38 TAB	FILM	VALUATION FIELD BOOKS 1830s OL4./ HOUSE BOOKS [OL5.]	TENEMENT VALUATION 1848–51 FICHE	1841–1851 CENSUS SEARCH Cen /s/27
Abington	27N/28	96		17.F.8.	
Aghacrew	27S/4	98	3208, 3218-20	7.F.14.	134-136
Aghnameadle	27N38	96	3273, [1787/93	14.F.10.	251-255, 257-260
Aglishcloghane	27N/4	95	3250, [1727/28]	15.G.8.	184-186
Ardcrony	27N/13	95	3251, [1729/30]	16.A.2.	187-191
Ardfinnan	27S/94	100	3170, [1555/56, 3259]	5.A.4.	91-93
Ardmayle	27S/37	99	3235, [1632/34]	8.D.12.	152-153
Athnid	27N/71	97	3137, [1496]	12.A.14.	
Ballingarry	27N/10	95	3252, [1731/36, 3260]		192-196
Ballingarry	27S/77	100	3293, [1854/61, 3260]	16.A.8., 10.E.2.	339-349
Ballintemple	27S/77	98	3209, 3228, [1607]	7.F.4.	
Ballybacon	27S/97	101	3171-72, [1557]	5.A.8.	
Ballycahill	27N/68	97	3230, [1468/69]	6.E.12.,12.A.14.	
Ballyclerahan	27S/101	101	[1510, 3261]	3.D.12.	55
Ballygibbon	27N/29	96	3274, [1794/95]	14.G.6.	256, 261
Ballygriffin	27S/14	98	[1415/16]	1.A.14.	
Ballymackey	27N/31	96	[1796/99]	14.G.11.	262-263
Ballymurreen	27N/79	97	3138, [1470/71]	12.B.4.	
Ballynaclogh	27N/36	96	[1800/03]	15.A.8.	264-265
Ballysheehan	27S/38	99	3237, [1635/37]	8.E.6.	154
Baptistgrange	27S/68	99	3238, [1638/39]	8.F.2.	
Barnane-ely	27N/51	97	3190, [1581]	13.D.12.	
Barrettsgrange	27S/60	99	3238, [1640/41	8.F.6.	
Borrisokane	27N/8	95	3253, [1737/38, 4219, 3264/66]	16.A.14.	197-204
Bourney	27N/45	97	3192, 3204-05, [1584/87, 1599]	13.E.2.	121-122
Boytonrath	27S/56	99	3239, [1642]	8.F.10.	155
Brickendown	27S/43	99	3240, [1643, 1680]	8.F.12.	156
Bruis	27S/27	98	3097, [1417/18]	1.B.6.	1
Buolick	27S/72	99	3294, 3311, [1862/64]	10.F.10.	350-352
Burgesbeg	27N/22	96	3282-83, 3289, [1834]	17.F.14.	
Borrisnafarney	27N/47	97	3191, [1582/83]	13.D.14.	
Caher	27S/91	100	3147, [1558/59, 3270/73]	5.B.6., 3.D.2.	94-98
Carrick	27S/116	101	3148, [1514/16]	3.D.4.	56-59
Cashel (See St John Baptist)					
Castletownarra	27N/19	96	3284, [1835]	17.G.12.	301-304
Cloghprior	27N/12	95	3254	16.B.12.	205
Clonbeg	27S/33	98	3098, 3123, 3124, [1418]	1.B.10.	2-4
Clonbullogue	27S/32	98	3099, 3125, [1421]	1.C.12.	5
Cloneen	27S/54	99	3241, 3295-96, [1644/45, 1688/90, 1865/67]	8.F.14., 10.G.6.	
Clonmel St Mary's	27S/114	101	[1550/51, 3296/3309]	4.D.2.	75-88
Clonoulty	27S/3	98	3211, 3222, [1609]	7.G.8., 1.D.4.	137, 139-140
Clonpet	27S/28	98	3127, [1433]	1.D.6.	
Clogher	27S/1	98	3210, 3221, [1608]		138
Colman	27S/66	99	3238 ,[1646/48]	8.G.6.	
Cooleagh	27S/45	99	[1649/51]	8.G.8.	
Coolmundry	27S/63	99	3241, [1652]	8.G.12.	
Corbally	27N/43	97	3192, 3206, [1588/91, 1599]	13.F.4.	123-124
Cordangan	27S/29	98	3100, 3124, 3128, 3136 [1422/24]	1.D.10.	6

PARISH/TOWN	TITHES 1823–38 TAB	FILM	VALUATION FIELD BOOKS 1830s OL4./ HOUSE BOOKS [OL5.]	TENEMENT VALUATION 1848–51 FICHE	1841–1851 CENSUS SEARCH Cen /s/27
Corroge	27S/25	98	3136, [1425/26]	1.E.10.	
Crohane	27S/78	100	3297, 3313, [1868/69]	10.G.8.	353
Cullen	27S/17	98	3101, [1427/29, 3295]	1.E.14.	7-11
Cullenwaine	27N/46	97	3193, [1592/93]	13.G.2.	
Dangandargan	27S/49	99	[1430/31, 1653/54, 1663]	1.F.6., 8.G.14.	
Derrygarth	27S/92	100	3171-72, [1560/61]	5.D.6.	
Dogstown	27S/57	99	[1655/58]	9.A.2.	
Dolla	27N/35	96	[1804/05]	15.A.12.	265a-271
Donaghmore	27S/67	99	3149, 3238, [1659]	9.A.4., 3.F.6.	
Donohill	27S/2	98	3102, 3212-13, 3223-24, [1432, 1434, 1610/11]	8.A.10., 1.F.8.	
Doon	27N/57	97	[1622/23]	6.F.2.	143
Dorrha	27N/2	95	3255, [1743/45]	16.C.2.	206-209
Drangan	27S/48	99	[1660/62, 1664]	9.A.6.	157-159
Drom	27N/62	97	[1472/73]	12.B.6.	
Dromineer	27N/15	96	3256, [1746/48]	16.D.2.	
Emly	27S/22	98	3103, [1435/36, 3310]	1.G.2.	12
Erry	27S/39	99	[1665/67]	9.A.14.	160
Fennor	27S/71	99	3298, 3311, 3322, [1870/72]	11.A.2.	354
Fertiana	27N/74	97	[1474/75]	12.B.12.	
Fethard	27S/62	99	3238, [1668/70, 3311/15]	9.B.2.	161-164
Finnoe	27N/7	95	3257, [1749/52]	16.D.5.	210
Gaile	27S/36	99	3242, [1671, 1672/73]	9.C.6.	165-166
Galbooly	27N/75	97	[1476/77]	12.C.1.	
Garrangibbon	27S/106	101	3150, 3299, 3313, [1517/20, 1873/76]	11.A.10., 3.F.8.	
Glenbane	27S/23	98	3104, 3129, [1437]	2.A.4.	
Glenkeen	27N/54	97	[1624/25]	6.F.5.	144-147
Grangemockler	27S/84	100	3300, 3313, [1877/80, 1924/25]	11.A.14.	
Graystown	27N/74	100	3237, 3301, 3312, 3313, [1881/82]	9.C.8., 11.B.4.	355
Holycross	27S/73	97	3139, [1478]	9.C.10., 12.C.3.	42 [166a]
Holycross	27S/35	98	3242, [1672/73, 1674/75]		
Horeabbey	27S/41	99	[1675a/77]	9.C.12.	
Inch	27N/66	97	[1479/80]	12.C.11.	
Inishlounaght	27S/102	101	3151, [1521/23]	3.F.10.	
Isertkieran	27S/102	100	3302, 3313, [1883/85]	11.B.12.	
Kilbarron	27N/6	95	[1753/56]	16.D.12.	
Kilbragh	27S/59	99	[1678, 1679]	9.C.14.	
Kilcash	27S/107	101	3152, [1524/26]	3.G.8.	60-61
Kilclonagh	27N/67	97	3137, [1496]	12.D.3.	
Kilcomenty	27N/24	96	3285, [1836/37]	18.B.10.	305-306
Kilconnell	27S/51	99	3243, [1681/83, 1680]	9.D.2.	
Kilcooly	27N/77	97	[1481/82]	11.B.14., 12.D.3.	
Kilcooly	27S/73	99	3303, 3312, 3313, 3314, [1886/91]		356-359
Kilcornan	27S/16	98	3106, [1433/40]	2.A.6.	13-15
Kilfeakle	27S/20	98	3107, [1441/42]	2.A.10.	16
Kilfithmone	27N/61	97	[1483/84]	12.D.4.	
Kilgrant	27S/110	101	3153, [1527/29]	3.G.12.	62

PARISH/TOWN	TITHES 1823–38 TAB	FILM	VALUATION FIELD BOOKS 1830s OL4./ HOUSE BOOKS [OL5.]	TENEMENT VALUATION 1848–51 FICHE	1841–1851 CENSUS SEARCH Cen /S/27
Kilkeary	27N/37	96	3275, [1806/07, 1810]	15.B.4.	
Killaloan	27S/115	101	[1530]	4.A.4.	
Killardry	27S/31	98	3105, 3125, 3130, [1443/44]	2.B.2.	17-19
Killavinoge	27N/49	97	3195, 3202, [1594]	13.G.4.	125
Killea	27N/48	97	3196, [1595]	13.G.14.	126
Killeenasteena	27S/55	99	[1684, 1717]	9.D.6.	167
Killenaule	27S/75	100	3304, 3312, 3313, [1892/94, 3317/19]	11.C.14.	360
Killodiernan	27N/11	95	3258, [1757/60]	16.E.8.	223
Killoscully	27N/25	96	3286, [1838/39]	18.C.9.	307-312
Killoskehan	27N/50	97	3197, [1596]	14.A.6.	
Kilmastulla	27N/23	96	3287[1840]	18.D.9.	313
Kilmore	27N/34	96	3276, [1811/15]		272-283[A]
Kilmore (Oughterleague)	27S/7	98	3214, 3226, [1612]	8.B.10., 15.B.6.	141-142
Kilmucklin	27S/12	98	[1445, 1450]	2.B.12.	
Kilmurry	27S/112	101	3154, [1431/33]	4.A.6.	63
Kilnaneave	27N/39	96	3277, [1816/17]	15.G.12.	284-288
Kilnarath	27N/27	96	3288, [1841/43]	18.E.6.	314-319
Kilpatrick	27S/5	98	3215, 3227, [1613/15]	8.B.14.	
Kilruane	27N/30	96	3278, [1761/62, 1818/20]	16.E.12., 15.D.5	289-291
Kilshane	27S/30	98	3108, 3136, [1446/47]	2.B.14.	
Kilsheelan	27S/111	101	3155, [1534/36]	4.A.14.	64-67
Kiltegan	27S/109	101	3156, [1437/39]	4.B.6.	
Kiltinan	27S/69	99	3238, [1685/87, 1688/90]	9.D.8.	168
Kilvellane	27N/26	96	3284, [1844/45]	18.F.6.	320-334
Kilvemnon	27S/83	100	3305, 3312, 3313, 3315-16, [1895/902]	11.D.14.	361-363
Knigh	27N/16	96	3260, [1763/65]	16.E.14.	
Knockgraffon	27S/64	99	3244, [1691/92]	9.D.12.	169-170
Laginstown	27S/117	101			
Latteragh	27N/40	96	3279, [1821/23]	15.D.9.	292
Lattin	27S/26	98	3109, [1417, 1448]	2.C.7.	20-24
Lickfinn	27S/76	100	3306, 3313, 3317, [1903/05]	11.F.4.	
Lisbunny	27N/32	96	3279, [1824/26]	15.D.13.	
Lismalin	27S/80	100	3307, 3318, [1906/11]	11.F.6.	364
Lisronagh	27S/104	101	3157, [1540]	4.B.8.	68
Lorrha	27N/1	95	3261, [1769/71]	16.F.4.	211-216
Loughkeen	27N/5	95	3262, [1766/68]	16.G.4.	217-221
Loughmoe East	27N/64	97	3140-42, [1485/86]	12.D.5.	
Loughmoe West	27N/63	97	[1487/89]	12.D.14.	43
Magorban	27S/44	99	3245, [1693/95]	9.E.8.	
Magowry	27S/47	99	[1696/99]	9.E.12.	
Modeshil	27S/81	100	3308, 3313, 3323, [1912/14]	11.F.10.	
Modreeny	27N/14	96	3263, [1772/74]	17.A.2.	222, 224-234
Molough	27S/99	101	3173-74, [1564]	5.D.11.	99-101
Monsea	27N/17	96	3264, 3289, [1775/77, 1846/47]	17.B.7., 18.G.10.	
Mora	27S/65	99	3246, [1700/02]	9.F.2.	171-172
Mortlestown	27S/86	100	3175, [1562/63]	5.D.14.	

PARISH/TOWN	TITHES 1823–38 TAB	FILM	VALUATION FIELD BOOKS 1830s OL4./ HOUSE BOOKS [OL5.]	TENEMENT VALUATION 1848–51 FICHE	1841–1851 CENSUS SEARCH Cen /S/27
Mowney	27S/79	100	3319, [1915/17]	11.F.14.	365
Moyaliff	27N/59	97	[1626]	7.A.8.	148-150
Moycarky	27N/78	97	[1490/91]	12.E.6.	44-45
Moyne	27N/65	97	[1492]	12.E.11.	46
Neddans	27S/98	101	3176-77, 3186, [1565]	5.E.2.	
Nenagh	27N/18	96	3265, 3279, [1778/79, 1827/29, 3325/33]	17.B.12., 15.E.3.	235-248, 293
Newcastle	27S/100	101	3187, [1566/68]	5.E.5.	102-106
Newchapel	27S/102	101	3158, [1541/44]	4.B.10.	69-74
Newtownlennan	27S/113	101	3159, 3309, [1545/46, 1918]	11.G.2., 4.C.4.	
Oughterleague	27S/8	98	3110, 3131, 3216, 3228, [1431, 1449, 1616]	8.C.6., 2.C.8.	
Outeragh	27S/70	99	3246, [1703/05]	9.F.6.	173
Peppardstown	27S/53	99	3241, [1706/08]	9.F.8.	
Rahelty	27N/72	97	[1493/94]	12.F.4.	47-49
Railstown	27S/50	99	[1709, 1717]	9.F.12.	
Rathcool	27S/52	99	3241, [1710/11]	9.F.14.	
Rathkennan	27S/1a	98	3217, 3229	8.C.12.	
Rathlynin	27S/13	98	3111, [1450, 1451]	2.C.10.	25
Rathnaveoge	27N/44	97	3198, [1597/98, 1599]	14.A.8.	127
Rathronan	27S/108	101	3160, [1547/49]	4.C.10.	
Redcity	27S/61	99	3238, [1712]	9.G.6.	
Relickmurry and Athassel	27S/21	98	3132, 3096, 3236, [1452/56]	2.C.14., 9.G.8.	26-29
Rochestown	27S/93	100	[3568, 1569/70]	5.F.4.	
Roscrea	27N/42	97	3207, [1600/03, 3334/44]	14.A.14.	128-132
Shanrahan	27S/88	100	3179, [1571/72]	5.F.5.	108-112
Shronell	27S/24	98	3112, 3133, [1417, 1457]	2.E.7.	30
Shyane	27N/70	97	3137, [1495, 1496]	12.F.9.	
Solloghhodbeg	27S/11	98	3113, [1458/59]	2.E.10.	31
Solloghodmore	27S/10	98	3114, 3134, [1460/61]	2.E.14.	32-35
St John Baptist (Cashel)	27S/42	99	3247, 3310, 3312, 3320, [1713/16, 1717, 1919/21]	9.G.10., 11.G.4.	174-182
St Johnstown	27S/46	99	[1718/20]	10.B.8.	
St Patricksrock	27S/40	99	3248-49, [1721/22]	10.B.12.	
Temple	27S/34	98			
Temple-etney	27S/105	101	3162, [1552/54]	4.F.14.	89-90
Templeachally	27N/21	96	3290, [1848/51]	18.C.11.	335-337
Templebeg	27N/56	97	[1627/28]	7.B.8.	
Templebredon	27S/15	98	3117, [1462/64]	2.F.10.	
Templederry	27N/41	96	3280, [1830/32]	15.E.8.	294-297
Templedowney	27N/33	96	[1810, 1833]	15.F.2.	298-300
Templenoe	27S/19	98	3116, [1450, 1466]	2.G.12.	
Templemichael	27S/85	100	3311, 3321, [1922/23, 1924/25]	11.G.6.	366
Templemore	27N/60	97	3145, 3199, [1497/98, 1604, 3346/51]	14.D.2., 12.F.10.	50-51
Templeneiry					36-38
Templeree	27N/52	97	3200, [1605]	14.D.6.	133
Templetenny	27S/87	100	3179, 3188, [1573/75]	5.G.11.	113-118
Templetoughy	27N/53	97	3201, [1499, 1606]	14.D.12., 12.G.13.	

PARISH/TOWN	TITHES 1823–38 TAB/	FILM	VALUATION FIELD BOOKS 1830s OL4./ HOUSE BOOKS [OL5.]	TENEMENT VALUATION 1848–51 FICHE	1841–1851 CENSUS SEARCH Cen /s/27
Terryglass	27N/3	95	3265a, [1780/83]	17.D.10.	248-250
Thurles	27N/69	97	[1500/04, 3352/60]	12.G.13.	52-53
Tipperary	27S/18	98	3118, 3136, [4218, 3361/67]	3.A.4.	39-41
Toem	27N/58	97	[1629]		
Toem	27S/9	98	3119, 3135, [1469]	3.B.14., 7.B.14.	
Tubbrid	27S/89	100	[1576]	6.B.9.	119-120
Tullaghmelan	27S/95	100	3180-81, 3189, [1577]	6.C.7.	74
Tullaghorton	27S/96	100	3182-83, [1578]	6.C.11.	
Tullamain	27S/58	99	3246, [1679, 1723/26]	10.C.14.	
Twomileborris	27N/76	97	[1505/09]	13.C.3.	54
Upperchurch	27N/55	97	[1630/31]	7.D.2.	151
Uskane	27N/9	95	3266, [1784/86]	17.E.7.	
Whitechurch	27S/90	100	3184, [1579/80]	6.D.3.	
Youghalarra	27N/20	96	3291, [1852/53]	19.B.12.	338

TOWNS	VALUATION HOUSE BOOK 1830s [OL5.]
Abbey	[3255/58]
Ballyporeen	[3262]
Bansha	[3263]
Borrisoleigh	[3267/69]
Cappagh White	[3274/75]
Carrick-on-Suir	[3276/82]
Cashel	[3283/90]
Clogheen	[3291]
Cloghjordan	[3292/94]
Cullen	[3295]
Golden	[3316]
Killenaule	[3317/19]
Marlfield	[3320/21]
Mullinahone	[3322/24a]
Silvermines	[3345]
Toberaheena	[3368/69]
Toomevarra	[3370/72]

PARISH/TOWN	TITHES 1823–38 TAB 29/	FILM	VALUATION FIELD BOOKS 1830s OL4./ HOUSE BOOKS [OL5.]	TENEMENT VALUATION 1848–51 FICHE	1841–1851 CENSUS SEARCH Cen /s/29
Affane	19	102	3365-66, [1944/46]	4.A.4.	
Aglish	68	104		2.E.5., 2.E.12.	62-65
Ardmore	69	104	3356, 3357-59	2.E.5., 2.F.14.	66, 72
Ballygunner	58	103	3407, [1985/87]	6.D.6.	130
Ballylaneen	34	103	3367-72, [1947, 4220]	4.B.2.	73-76
Ballymacart	74	104		2.E.5., 3.B.10.	67
Ballynakill	51	103	3408. [1988/91]	6.D.9.	
Clashmore	71	104	3360, 3361	2.E.5., 3.B.14.	68
Clonagam	11	102	3465, 3479, 3495, [2118/19]	8.D.14.	244-250
Clonea	32	103	3373-75, [1948/50]	4.C.2.	
Colligan	27	102	3376, [1951/52]	3.G.8., 4.C.6.	77-78
Corbally	66	104	3409, [1992/95]	6.D.11.	131
Crooke	60	104	3410, [1996/99]	6.D.12.	132-136
Drumcannon	47	103	3436-37, [2000/03, 2073/82]	7.D.14., 6.E.2.	186-220
Dungarvan	30	103	3377, [1953/54], [3383]	3.G.8., 4.C.12.	79-87
Dunhill	44	103	3438-39, [2083/86]	7.F.8.	221-226
Dysert	6	102	3466, 3480, 3489, 6496, [2120/21, 4227]	8.E.13.	
Faithlegg	53	103	[2004/09]	6.E.2.	137-139
Fenoagh	8	102	3467, 3481, 3490, 3497, [2122/23]	8.F.4.	
Fews	25	102	3378, [1955, 4226]	4.G.8.	88
Guilcagh	12	102	3468, 3482, 3498, [2124/26, 4226]	8.F.9.	251
Inishlounaght	1	102	3426a-3428, [2067/68]	7.A.14.	178-179
Islandikane	48	103	3440-41, [2087/91]	7.G.4.	227-232
Kilbarry	54	103	3411, [2010/14]	6.E.6.	
Kilbarrymeadan	36	103	3379-80, [1956]	4.G.12.	89-91
Kilbride	46	103	3442-43, [2092, 2103]	7.G.10.	233-235
Kilburne	42	103	3444-45, [2093/95, 4223]	7.G.14.	236
Kilcaragh	57	103	[2015/18]	6.E.8.	
Kilcockan	17	102	3331, [1926/28]	1.A.14., 1.B.2.	1-2
Kilcop	59	104	3412, [2019/22]	6.E.9.	
Kilculliheen	13	102	3435, [2023/24, [2072]	7.C.14., 9.D.10., 9.D.14.	280
Kilgobnet	23	102	3381-82	5.A.10.	92-98
Kill St Lawrence	55	103	3419, [2025/28]	6.F.4.	
Kill St Nicholas	52	103	3414, [2029/31]	6.F.5.	
Killaloan	4	102	3469, 3483, 3499, [2127/28]	8.F.11.	
Killea	65	104	3413, [2032/36]	6.E.10.	140-154
Killoteran	38	103	3464, [2096/97]	8.A.4.	
Killure	56	103	[2037/40]	6.F.12.	155
Kilmacleague	62	104	3415, [2041/44]	6.F.12.	156-162
Kilmacomb	63	104	[2045/48]	6.G.3.	163
Kilmeadan	37	103	3449-50, 3470, 3484, 3491, 3500, [2098/100, 2129/30]	8.F.13., 8.A.8.	237-238
Kilmolash	28	103	3361, 3383-84, [1957/58]	5.B.14., 3.C.14.	69
Kilmoleran	7	102	3471, 3476, 3485, 3501, [2131/32]	8.G.1.	252
Kilrossanty	24	102	3385-86, [1959/60, 4221]	3.G.9., 5.C.4.	99-100

PARISH/TOWN	TITHES 1823–38 TAB 29/	FILM	VALUATION FIELD BOOKS OL4./ HOUSE BOOKS [OL5.]	TENEMENT VALUATION 1848—1 FICHE	1841–1851 CENSUS SEARCH CEN s|29|1
Kilronan	2	102	3430-33, [2069/71]	7.B.6.	180-185
Kilronan	43	103	3451-52, [2101/02, 2103]	8.B.4.	
Kilrush	31	103	3387-88, [1961/62]	5.D.8.	
Kilsheelan	5	102	3472, 3486, 3502, [2133/34]	8.G.12.	
Kilwatermoy	28/16	102	3332, [1930]	1.B.10.	3-4
Kinsalebeg	72	104	3362-63	2.E.6., 3.D.4.	
Leitrim	13a	102	3333, [1931/32]	1.C.6.	
Lickoran	21	102	3390-91, [1963]	5.E.2.	101-103
Lisgenan or Grange	73	104		3.E.4.	70, 104
Lismore and Mocollop	14	102	3334-35, 3350-54, [1933/38], [3387]	1.A.14., 1.C.8.	5-51
Lisnaskill	41	103	3453, 3464, [2104/07]	8.B.6.	239
Modelligo	20	102	3392-93, [1964/67]	3.G.9., 5.E.6.	105 [105a]
Monamintra	61	104	[2049/51]	6.G.6.	
Monksland	35	103	3394-95, [1968/71]	3.G.9., 5.F.4.	
Mothel	10	102	3473-74, 3487, 3492-93, 3503, [2135/36, 4228]	8.G.14.	253
Newcastle	40	103	3396-97, 3454-55, 3464, [1972/74a, 2108/11]	5.F.10., 8.B.10.	240
Newtownlennan	75	104			
Rathgormuck	9	102	3475, 3488, 3494, 3504, [2137, 4224]	9.A.11.	254-264
Rathmoylan	67	104	3420, [2052/56]	6.G.6.	164-172
Reisk	45	103	3456-57, 3464, [2112/15]	8.B.14.	241
Ringagonagh	70	104	3364	2.E.6., 3.E.14.	71
Rossduff	64	104	3421, [2057/60]	6.G.10.	173-174
Rossmire	26	102	3398-99, [1975/77, 2138/39]	9.B.5., 3.G.9., 5.F.12.	106-110
Seskinan	22	102	3400, [1978/79]	3.G.9., 5.G.8.	111-125
St John's [without]	50	103	3424, [2061/64, 3415/17]	9.D.10., 9.E.14.	278, 175-177, 273, 284
St Mary's Clonmel	3	102	3478, 3505-07, [2140, 4225]	9.B.5.	265-269
Stradbally	33	103	3389, 3401, [1980/82]	3.G.10., 6.A.10.	126-127
Tallow	15	102	3346, [1939/41, 3394]	1.A.14., 2.B.10.	52-56
Templemichael	18	102	3347, 3348, 3355, [1942/43]	1.A.14., 2.C.14.	57-61
Trinity without	39	103	3458-59, [2116/17, 3426/35]	8.C.6., 9.D.11., 10.B.8.	242-243
Waterford City Parishes	49	103	(see below)		270-294
Whitechurch	29	103	3402-03, [1983/84]	3.G.10., 6.B.10.	128-129

TOWNS	VALUATION HOUSE BOOK 1830s [OL5.]
No. 1 Kilculliheen	[3399]
No. 2 St John's Within	[3400] [3414]
No. 3 St John's Without	[3401] [3415/17]
No. 4 St Michael's	[3402] [3418]
No. 5 St Olave's	[3403] [3419]
No. 6 St Patrick's	[3404] [3420]
No. 7 St Peter's	[3405]
No 8 St Stephen's Within	[3406] [3421]
No. 9 St Stephen's Without	[3407] [3422/24]
No. 10 Trinity Within	[3408] [3425]
No. 11 Trinity Without	[3409] [3426/35]
No. 12 Trinity Without	[3410]
No. 13 Trinity Without	[3411]
No. 14 Trinity Without	[3412]
No. 12? Trinity Without	[3413]
Waterford (Town)	[3438]
Abbeyside	[3373]
Cappoquin	[3374/75]
Carrickbeg	[3376/78]
Carrick-on-Suir	[3379/81]
Clonmel	[3382]
Dunmore	[3384, 3389]
Kilmacthomas	[3385/86]
Passage	[3388/89]
Portlaw	[3390/93]
Tramore	[3395/98]

PARISH/TOWN	TITHES 1823–38 TAB 30/	FILM	VALUATION FIELD BOOKS 1830s OL4./ HOUSE BOOKS [OL5.]	TENEMENT VALUATION 1854 FICHE	1841–1851 CENSUS SEARCH Cen /s/30
Ardnurcher (Horseleap)	50	106	1747	5.D.10., 7.A.10.	164-167
Athlone			[3439/41]		1-12
Ballyloughloe	46	106	1695	1.E.3.	18-19
Ballymore	36	106	1761	1.G.14., 2.F.2.	214-218
Ballymorin	38	106	1762	4.G.8.	219
Bunown	30	105	1740	1.B.8.	123-127
Carrick	59	107	1722	5.G.2.	83
Castlelost	63	107	1723	5.G.4.	84-85
Castletowndelvin	27	105	3511-12, [3446/7]	3.A.4.	45-55
Castletownkindelan	51	107	1748, [2144, 3448]	5.E.2.	168-183
Churchtown	40	106	1763	4.G.10.	220-223
Clonarney	24	105	1710-11	3.B.9.	
Clonfad	62	107	1724	5.G.11.	86-88
Conry	39	106	1764, 3524	4.G.14.	
Delvin					56-68
Drumraney	32	105	1741, [2143]	1.D.4., 2.D.10.	128-136
Durrow	54	107	1749, 3522	7.A.13.	184-185
Dysart	43	106	1744, 1750-51, [4232]	5.A.2., 6.D.12., 5.F.5.	147, 186
Enniscoffey	58	107	1725	6.A.2.	
Faughalstown	7	105	1732	3.D.3., 4.A.2.	96-101
Foyran	1	105	1733, 3515	4.A.3.	102-106
Kilbeggan	52	107	1752-53, [2145, 3449]	7.C.6.	187-188
Kilbixy	13	105	3523, [3455]	4.E.6.	199-201
Kilbride	60	107	1726, 3516	6.A.5.	89-91
Kilcleagh	47	106	1696-97	1.F.5.	20-28
Kilcumny	23	105	1712-13, [2141]	3.B.12.	
Kilcumreragh	49	106	1698-99, 1754, [2146]	1.D.8., 1.A.14.	189-192
Kilkenny West	31	105	1742 [4230]	1.C.1., 2.E.5.	137-141
Killagh	28	105	1714-15	3.C.2.	
Killare	37	106	1765, 3525, [3444]	2.F.8.	224-225
Killua	25	105	1716-17	3.C.4.	
Killucan	44	106	1718-19, 3513, [4229]	3.C.12., 6.B.8., 3.F.11.	74-82
Killulagh	26	105	1720-21, [2142]	3.C.12.	69-73
Kilmacnevan	12	105	[3455]	4.F.2.	202-203
Kilmanaghan					29-30
Kilpatrick	8	105	1734	3.D.7.	
Lackan	15	105	1702	5.B.8.	31-33
Leny	17	105	1703	5.B.11.	34
Lickbla	2	105	1735, 3517	3.D.9., 4.A.10.	107-109
Lynn	56	107	1727	6.A.8.	
Mayne	3	105	1736	4.B.2.	110-112
Moylisker	57	107	1728	6.A.12.	92-93
Mullingar	42	106	1729, 1745, 3520, [3451/54, 4231]	6.E.13., 6.A.14.	148-158
Multyfarnham	16	105	1704, 3509, [3443]	5.C.3.	35
Newtown	53	107	1730, 1755-56	5.F.5., 6.B.1.	94-95, 193-198
Noughaval	29	105	1743	1.D.2., 2.E.6.	142-146
Pass of Kilbride	61	107	1731	6.B.4.	

PARISH/TOWN	TITHES 1823–38 TAB 30/	FILM	VALUATION FIELD BOOKS 1830s OL4./ HOUSE BOOKS [OL5.]	TENEMENT VALUATION 1854 FICHE	1841–1851 CENSUS SEARCH Cen /S/30
Piercetown	33	106	3526	2.F.13., 5.A.10.	226-228
Portloman	22	105	1705	5.C.8.	
Portnashangan	19	105	1706	5.C.12.	36
Rahugh	55	107	1757, [2147]	5.F.14., 7.C.1.	
Rathaspick	11	105	1758, [3455]	4.B.12., 4.F.9.	204-210
Rathconnell	41	106	1746	6.E.1.	159-163
Rathconrath	34	106	1766, 3521	2.G.2., 5.A.11.	229-231
Rathgarve	4	105	1737, 3518	3.D.9., 4.B.10.	113-116
Russagh	10	105		4.C.2.	211-212
St Feighin's	5	105	1738	3.E.8.	117-120
St Mary's (Athlone)	6	105	1739, 3519	2.A.4.	1-17, 121-122
St Mary's	45	106	3508	3.F.6.	
Stonehall	18	105	1707	5.C.14.	37-38
Street	9	105	1759	4.C.5., 4.G.1.	
Taghmon	21	105	1708	5.D.3.	39-43
Templeoran					213
Moygoish	14	105			
Templepatrick	35	106		2.G.3.	
Tyfarnham	20	105	1709, 3510	5.D.7.	44

TOWNS	VALUATION HOUSE BOOK 1830s [OL5.]
Ballinagore	[3442]
Ballinalack	[3443]
Ballymore	[3444]
Ballynacarrigy	[3445]
Castlepollard	[3443]
Clonmellan	[3447]
Collenstown	[3443]
Finnea	[3443]
Killucan	[3443]
Moate	[3450]
Rathowen	[3445]
Rochfordbridge	[3456]
Tyrrellspass	[3457/58]

PARISH/TOWN	TITHES 1823–38 TAB 31/	FILM	VALUATION FIELD BOOKS 1830s OL4./ HOUSE BOOKS [OL5.]	TENEMENT VALUATION 1853 FICHE	1841–1851 CENSUS SEARCH Cen /s/31
Adamstown	50	109	1792-93, 3542, [2169]	6.G.4.	44-47
Ambrosetown	102	111	1828, 3555, [2191]	10.C.11.	174-178
Ardamine	30	109	1767, [2148]	5.C.2.	1-3
Ardcandrisk	71	110	1918, [2282]	8.C.4.	
Ardcavan	85	110	1910, 3646, [2273a]	8.F.2.	449-453
Ardcolm	86	110	1911, 3647, [2274]	8.F.6.	454
Artramon	84	110	1912, 3648, [2275]	8.F.11.	455-458
Ballingly	80	110	1919, [2283]	8.C.6.	475
Ballyanne	46	109	1794, [2170]	6.G.11.	48-56
Ballybrazil	89	110	1897, 3620, [2261]	5.G.12.	402
Ballybrennan	136	111	1841, [2204]	9.A.4.	210-216
Ballycanew	24	109	1867, 3583, [2228/29]	4.A.14.	263-268
Ballycarney	6	108	3604, [2247]	1.E.3.	299-302
Ballyconnick	103	108	1829, 3556, [2192]	10.C.14.	
Ballyhoge	53	109	1795-96, 1920, 3543, [2171, 2284]	2.D.6., 1.B.4.	
Ballyhuskard*	58	110	1768, 3527, [2149]	3.D.8.	4, 21-25
Ballylannan	79	110	1921, [2285]	7.F.8.	476-479
Ballymitty	81	110	1922, [2286]	8.C.7.	480
Ballymore	129	111	1842, [2205]	9.A.6.	217-218
Ballynaslaney	64	110	1769, 1913, 3649 [2150, 2276]	3.C.13., 1.B.9.	
Ballyvaldon	62	110	1771, [2151]	3.C.4.	26
Ballyvaloo	68	110	1770, 3528	3.B.6.	
Bannow	105	111	1830, 3557, [2193]	10.D.2.	179-180
Carn	138	111	1843, [2206]	9.A.10.	219
Carnagh	54	109	1797-98, 3544, [2172]	7.A.4.	57-63
Carnew	3	108	1868, 1184, 3584, 3605 [2230, 2248]	5.A.13., 3.B.6., 4.B.7	303-310
Carrick	78	110	1923, [2287]	8.C.9.	481
Castle-Ellis	60	110	1772, 3529, [2152]	3.B.9.	27
Chapel	44	109	1799, [2173]	2.D.9.	64-66
Clone	11	108	1885, 3606, [2249]	1.E.10.	311-314
Clongeen	72	110	1924, [2288]	7.F.12.	
Clonleigh	42	109	1800, 3545, [2174]	7.A.6.	67-71
Clonmines	97	111	1898, 3621, [2262]	6.A.1.	
Clonmore	45	109	1801-02, 1925, [2175, 4234]	2.D.14., 1.B.6	72-73
Coolstuff	76	110	1926, [2289]	8.D.1.	
Crosspatrick	13	108	3585-75, [2231]	4.B.5.	
Donaghmore	31	109	1773, 1869, 3530, 3587 [2153/54, 2232]	4.B.7., 5.C.10.	5-7
Doonooney	51	109	1803, [2176]	11.A.13.	
Drinagh	120	111	1844, [2207]	9.B.12.	
Duncormick	106	111	1831, 3558, [2194]	10.C.12.	181-182
Edermine	63	110	1774	3.F.10.	28
Ferns	7	108	1870, 1886, 3588, 3607 [2233, 2250]	1.D.3., 5.B.5., 1.B.12.	315-316
Fethard	99	111	1899, 3623, [2263]	6.A.2.	403-418
Hook	100	111	1900, 3624, [2264]	6.B.1.	
Horetown	74	110	1927, [2290]	7.G.5.	482-483
Inch	16	108	1871, 3589, [2234]	7.G.11.	

PARISH/TOWN	TITHES 1823–38 TAB 31/	FILM	VALUATION FIELD BOOKS 1830s OL4./ HOUSE BOOKS [OL5.]	TENEMENT VALUATION 1853 FICHE	1841–1851 CENSUS SEARCH Cen /s/31
Inch	73	110	[1928, 2291]	4.B.7.	269, 484
Ishartmon	133	111	1845, [2208]	9.B.5.	
Kerloge	117	111	1846, [2209]	9.B.7.	
Kilbride	8	108	1887, 3608, [2251]	5.B.5., 1.D.1.	317-319
Kilbrideglynn	77	110	1929, [2292]	8.D.4.	485-486
Kilcavan	19	108	1872, 3590, [2235]	4.E.3., 5.D.5.	
Kilcavan	101	111	1775, 1832, 3531, 3559 [2155, 2195]	8.A.10., 10.E.8.	183-184, 270-271
Kilcomb	4	108	1888, 3609, [2252]	5.B.6.	320-322
Kilcormick	25	109	1776, 1873, 3532, 3591 [2156, 2236]	1.B.12., 3.A.5., 5.E.8.	8-9, 272-273
Kilcowan	107	111	1833, 3560, [2196]	10.E.11.	185-186
Kilcowanmore	52	109	1804-05, [2177]	2.E.7.	
Kildavin	118	111	1847, [2210]	9.B.8.	220-221
Kilgarvan	69	110	1930, [2293]		487-490
Kilgorman	17	108	1874, 3592, [2237]	4.F.10.	
Killag	109	111	1834, 3561, [2197]	10.F.1.	
Killann	36	109	1806-07, 3546, [2178]	2.E.1.	74-88
Killenagh	29	109	3534, 3548	5.D.6.	
Killesk	93	111	1901, [2265]	6.B.5.	419
Killiane	122	111	1848, [2211]	9.C.1.	
Killegney	43	109	1808-09, 3547, [2179]	2.F.10.	89-104
Killila	61	110	1777, 3533	3.G.3.	29
Killincooly	33	109	1778, 3535, [2157]	3.A.11.	10
Killinick	125	111	1849, [2212]	9.C.3.	
Killisk	59	110	1779, 3536, [2158]	3.E.7.	30-32, 419
Kilmacree	123	111	1850, [2213]	9.C.7.	222
Kilmakilloge	21	108	1780, 1875, 3593, [2159, 2238]	4.G.2., 5.E.5.	33-34, 274-277
Kilmallock	65	110	1781, 3537, [2160]	3.D.2.	35-38
Kilmannan	104	111	1835, 3562, [2198]	10.F.4.	
Kilmokea			1902		420
Kilmore	110	111	1836, 3563, [2199]	10.F.11.	187-189
Kilmuckridge	34	109	1782, 3538, [2161]	3.A.14., 5.E.9.	
Kilnahue	18	108	1876, 3594, [2239]	4.D.2.	278-281
Kilnamanagh	32	109	1783, [2162]	5.D.12.	11-14
Kilnenor	15	108	1877, 3595, [2240]	5.A.3.	282
Kilpatrick	83	110	1914, 3650, [2278]	1.B.10., 8.G.1.	459-462
Kilpipe	14	108	1878, 3597, [2241]	4.A.10.	283
Kilrane	131	111	1851, [2214]	9.C.9.	223-224
Kilrush	2	108	1889, 3610, [2253]	1.C.3.	323-335
Kilscanlan	55	109	1810, 3549, [2180]	9.A.9.	105-109
Kilscoran	130	111	1852, [2215]	9.C.12.	225-234
Kiltennell	28	109	1784, [2163]	5.D.14.	15
Kiltrisk	27	109	1785, 1879, 3539, 3598 [2242]	4.C.12., 5.D.14.	284
Kilturk	111	111	1837, 3564, [2200]	10.G.8.	
Lady's Island	136	111	1853, [2216]	9.D.3.	
Liskinfere	23	108	3599-3600, [2243]	4.C.1.	285
Maudlintown	116	111	1854 ,[2217, 3518/21]		235
Meelnagh	35	109	1786, [2164]	3.A.14., 5.E.14.	16-18

PARISH/TOWN	TITHES 1823–38 TAB 31/	FILM	VALUATION FIELD BOOKS 1830s OL4./ HOUSE BOOKS [OL5.]	TENEMENT VALUATION 1853 FICHE	1841–1851 CENSUS SEARCH Cen /s/31
Monamolin	26	109	1787, 1880, 3601, [2165, 2244]	4.F.1., 5.F.1.	19-20, 286-288
Monart	10	108	1890, 3611, [2254]	2.C.5.	336-350
Moyacomb	1	108	1891, 3612, [2255]	1.D.3, 3.B.9.	351-356
Maglass	124	111	1855, [2218]	9.D.5.	236
Mulrankin	108	111	1838, 3565, [2201]	10.G.12.	190-201
Newbawn	49	109	1811-12, 1932, [2181, 2294]	7.A.11., 8.A.5.	110-113, 491-494
Oldross	48	109	1813, 3550, [2182]	7.A.14.	114-126
Owenduff	91	111	1903, 3627, [2267]	6.B.14.	421-424
Rathaspick	119	111	1856, [2219]	9.D.12.	
Rathmacknee	121	111	1857, [2220]	9.E.3.	237
Rathroe	95	111	1904, 3628, [2268]	6.C.10.	425-428
Rossdroit	38	109	1814-15, [2183]	2.G.3.	127-130
Rosslare	128	111	1858, [2221]	9.E.7.	238-246
Rossminoge	20	108	1881, 3602, [2245]	4.C.6.	289-293
Skreen	67	110	1790, 1916, 3540, 3651, [2280, 3509]	11.B.10., 8.G.10.	39-40, 463-466
St Helen's	132	111	1859, [2222]	9.F.5.	247
St Bridget's			[3522/23]	10.C.9.	
St. Doologes			[3524/26]	10.C.7.	
St Iberius				10.B.9.	
St Iberius	135	111	1860, 3572-73, [2223, 3527/30]	9.F.6.	248-249
St James & Dunbrody	94	111	1905, [2269]	6.C.13.	429-440
St John's	40	109	1816-17, 3551, [2184, 3531/36]		
St John's	113	111	1861	9.G.2.	
St Margaret's	137	111	1862, [2166, 2224]	9.F.10., 8.G.6.	
St Margaret's	87	110	1788, 1915, 3652, [2279]	11.B.10.	250, 467-468
St Mary's	47	109	1818, 3574-75, [2185, 3537/39]	10.C.4.	131-145, 251, 357-364
St Mary's (Enniscorthy)	12	108	1892, 3613, [2256]		
St Mary's (N Barry)	5	108	1893, 3614, [2257]		357-364
St Michael's	127	111	1789, 1863-64, 3576, [2225, 3540/43, 3544]	9.F.11.	
St Michael's of Feagh			[3540/44]	10.A.7.	
St Mullin's	41	109	1819-20, [2186]	7.E.6.	
St Nicholas	66	110	[2167]	3.C.3.	41
St Patrick's			[3545/48]		
St Peter's	115	111	1865, 3579, [2226, 3544, 3549/52]	9.G.14.	
St Selskar's			[3553/55]	10.B.2.	
Tacumshin	134	111	1866, [2227]	9.E.13.	
Taghmon	75	110	1839, 1933, 3566, [2202, 4236] [3510/11]	8.A.9., 8.D.12	202-204, 495-502
Tellarought	90	110	1906, 3629, [2270]		441-442
Templescoby	39	109	1823-24, [2188]	3.A.2.	171
Templeshanbo	9	108	1894, [2258]	2.B.10.	365-395

PARISH/TOWN	TITHES 1823–38 TAB 31/	FILM	VALUATION FIELD BOOKS 1830s OL4./ HOUSE BOOKS [OL5.]	TENEMENT VALUATION 1853 FICHE	1841–1851 CENSUS SEARCH Cen /S/31
Templeshannon	57	109	1791, 1895, 3541, 3615-16, [2168, 2259]	1.E.2., 3.E.13.	41-43
Templetown	98	111	1907, 3630, [2271]	6.E.3.	443
Templeludigan	37	109	1821-22, 3552, [2187]	7.E.12.	146-170
Tikillin	82	110	1917, 3653, [2281]	8.G.11.	469-474
Tintern	96	111	1908, 3631, [2272]	6.E.13.	444-446
Tomhaggard	112	111	1840, 3567, [2203]	11.A.6.	205-209
Toome	22	108	1882, 1896, 3603, 3617, [2246, 2260]396-401	5.B.11., 4.F.7.	294-298, 396-401
Wexford Town	114	111			251-262
Whitechurch	88	110	1825, 1909, 3553, 3632, [2189, 2273] [3460]	7.F.7., 6.F.11.	447-448
Whitechurchglynn	56	109	1826-27, 1934, 3554, [2190]	11.A.14.	172-173

* Enniscorthy workhouse included.

TOWNS	VALUATION HOUSE BOOK 1830s [OL5.]
Arthurstown	[3459, 3460, 3464]
Ballaghkeen	[3461]
Ballycanew	[3490]
Ballygarret	[3463]
Ballyhack	[3464]
Blackwater	[3462]
Camolin	[3465/66]
Castlebridge	[3467]
Clohamon	[3468/69]
Clonroche	[3470]
Coolgreany	[3471, 3490]
Courtown	[3472]
Duncannon	[3460, 3464]
Duncannon	[3473]
Enniscorthy	[3474/84]
Ferns	[3485]
Ford	[3487]
Fethard	[3460, 3486]
Gorey	[3463, 3488/89, 3490]
Monamolin	[3491]
New Ross	[3492/506]
Newtownbarry	[3512/16]
Oilgate	[3507]
Riverchapel	[3508]
Saltmills	[3486]
Screen	[3509]
Watch House	[3517]

PARISH/TOWN	TITHES 1823–38 TAB 32/	FILM	VALUATION FIELD BOOKS 1830s OL4./ HOUSE BOOKS [OL5.]	TENEMENT VALUATION 1852–4 FICHE	1841–1851 CENSUS SEARCH Cen /s/32
Aghowle	55	114	1969, 3736-39, [2338]	6.B.6.	72-75
Ardoyne		114	1970, 3740-42, [2339]	6.B.14.	76
Arklow	50	114	1935, 3653a-3654, [2295, 3556/58]	4.A.8.	1-12
Ballinacarrig			1994		
Ballinacor	34	113	3691-93, [4237]	5.A.7.	38
Ballintemple	47	114	1936, 3655-56, [2297]	4.C.5.	
Ballymacsimon (Glenealy)			3715		39
Ballynure	15	112	1984, 3782-84, [2346]	5.A.13.	
Ballykine			3694-98, [4238]	5.A.13.	
Baltinglass	20	112	1986, 3785-87, [2347]	1.E.2., 1.D.10.	113-119
Blessington	2	112	1977, 3765-66, 3564/65, 4246]	2.C.6.	89-91
Boystown	4	112	1978, 3767-68, [4247]	1.B.5., 2.D.2.	92-98
Bray	12	112	3731, [2330/31, 3566/68]	2.F.2.	64
Burgage	3	112	1979, 3769, [4248]	2.D.11.	99
Calary	23	123	1948, 1959, 1965, 3677-79, 3716, [2310, 2314/ 16, 2332/33]	2.G.4., 5.B.12., 3.C.14.	24-25, 47, 65
Carnew	59	114	1971, 3743-46, [2340, 3569/71]	6.D.3.	77-83
Castlemacadam	44	114	1937, 3657-58, [2296]	4.C.10.	13-14
Crecrin	53	114	1972, 3747-48, [2341]	6.C.2.	
Crehelp	6	112	1980, 3770, [4249]	1.B.9.	
Crosspatrick	57	114	1951, 1973, 3749-51, [2342]	5.F.10., 6.C.2.	84-87
Delgany	13	112	1966, 3732-33, [2334/35]	2.G.8.	66
Derrylossary	24	113	1960, 3680-83, 3717, [2311, 2317/18]	5.C.2.	27-34
Donaghmore	19	112	1986, 3788-91, 3806, [2348]	1.G.5.	120-126
Donard	9	112	1981, 3771-72, [3565, 3572, 4250]	1.B.11.	100
Drumkay	41	113	1938, 1961, 3659-60, [2298]	4.D.13.	15
Dunganstown	43	113	1939, 3661-62, [2299/300]	4.E.2.	16-17
Dunlavin	8	112	1982, 1987, 3773-74, 3792, [2349, 3565, 4251]	1.C.3., 1.F.1.	101-103
Ennereilly	46	114	1940, 3663-64, [2301]	4.F.2.	18-19
Freynestown	16	112	1988, 3793-94, [2350]	1.F.1.	
Glenealy	33	113	1941, 1962, 3665-66, 3718-19, [2302, 2319]	3.D.7., 4.F.4.	
Hacketstown	35	113	1952, 3699-3700, [4239]	1.A.14.	40-41
Hollywood	7	112	1983, 3775-77, [4252]		104-110
Inch	51	114	1942, 3667, [2303]	4.F.5.	
Kilbride	1, 48	112, 114	1943, 3668-69, 3778-80, [2304/05, 4253]	2.D.13. 4.F.6.	111-2
Kilcommon	32, 38	113	1944, 1953, 3670, 3701-03, 3720, [2306, 2320/21, 4240]	3.D.11., 4.F.13., 5.G.2.	42-43,
Kilcoole	27	113	3721-22, [2322]	3.D.13.	50-54
Killahurler	49	114	1945, 3671-72, [2307]	4.G.1.	20
Killiskey	30	113	3723-24, [2323/24]	3.E.8.	55

PARISH/TOWN	TITHES 1823–38 TAB 32/	FILM	VALUATION FIELD BOOKS 1830s OL4./ HOUSE BOOKS [OL5.]	TENEMENT VALUATION 1852–4 FICHE	1841–1851 CENSUS SEARCH Cen /s/32
Kilmacanoge	11	112	1967, 3734, [2336]	3.A.4.	67-68
Kilpoole	42	113	1946, 3673-74, [2308]	4.G.4.	21
Kilpipe	40	113	1954, 3704-07, [4241]	5.B.8., 6.A.3.	
Kilranelagh	21	112	1989, 3795-97, [2351/52]	1.F.3.	127
Kiltegan	22	112	1955, 1990, 3798-99, 3806, [2353/54, 4242]	2.A.6., 1.B.1.	44-45, 128-130
Knockrath	25	113	1949, 1956, 3684-86, 3708, [2312]	5.D.3., 5.B.7.	35-36
Liscolman	52	114	1974, 3752-3756, [2343]	6.C.6.	
Moyacomb	58	114	1975, 3757-3761, [2344]	6.C.7.	88
Moyne			1957, 3709-11, [4243]	6.A.10.	46
Mullinacuff	56	114	1976, 3762-64, [2345]	6.C.11.	
Newcastle Lower & Upper	29	113	1963, 3725/26, [2325/27]	3.F.3., 3.F.7.	56-60
Powerscourt	10	112	1968, 3735, [2337, 4245]	3.A.14.	69-71
Preban	39	113	1958, 3712-13, [4244]	6.B.1.	
Rathbran		112	1991, 3800-02, [2356]	1.F.8.	131-134
Rathdrum	26	113	1950, 3687-90, [2313, 3575/77]	5.D.12.	37
Rathnew	31	113	1964, 3727-30, [2328/29, 3578]	3.G.3.	61-62
Rathsallagh	14	112	1992, 3805-04, [2357]	1.G.2.	
Rathtoole	17	112	1993, 3805, [2357a]	1.G.3.	
Redcross	45	114	1947, 3675-76, [2309, 3579/80]	5.A.1.	22-23
Tober	5	112	3781, [4254]	1.D.8.	
Wicklow Town			[3587/89]		63

TOWNS	VALUATION HOUSE BOOK 1830s [OL5.]
Ballinlea	[3559]
Baltinglass	[3560/63]
Enniskerry	[3568, 3573]
Newtownmountkennedy	[3574]
Stratford	[3581/83]
Tinahely	[3584/86]

GLOSSARY

ACT OF UNION
In 1800, legislation in Dublin and Westminster created the United Kingdom of Great Britain and Ireland, dissolved the Irish parliament in Dublin, and brought Ireland into one parliament at Westminster, effective 1 January 1801. The 1798 Rebellion was the immediate impetus for this legislation. The Act of Union was controversial from the outset, and efforts in Ireland were launched almost immediately to repeal it. The momentum for Home Rule intensified towards the end of the nineteenth century, and led eventually to the **partition** of Ireland in 1922. The term 'Unionist' designates those who support continued political union of Northern Ireland with Great Britain.

Alumni Dublinensis
This provides a list of registered students of Trinity College Dublin from 1593 to 1860, giving place of birth, father's name and profession, teacher or school attended, and degrees taken (G.D. Burtchaell and T.U. Sadleir (eds), two volumes, 1935).

BARONY
A unit used in Ireland between the sixteenth and nineteenth centuries for administrative (census, taxation and legal) purposes. Drawn on pre-existing Gaelic divisions – the *triocha ced* – the baronies consisted of large groupings of **townlands** within a county. They were superseded as an administrative unit by the creation of county councils in 1898. The 1891 census is the last to use the barony as an administrative unit.

BOARD OF GUARDIANS
See POOR LAW UNION.

CATHOLIC CHURCH
The largest of the churches in Ireland and Northern Ireland. More than 90 per cent of the population in the Republic identifies itself as Catholic, as does 45 per cent of the population of Northern Ireland. The Catholic Archbishop of Armagh and Primate of All Ireland is based in Armagh City. *See* CATHOLIC EMANCIPATION.

CATHOLIC EMANCIPATION

From the 1690s through the 1720s, a series of anti-Catholic laws – popularly called the Penal Laws – were passed by the Irish parliament that severely restricted or denied most civil and religious rights to Catholics, including the right to practise their religion freely, buy or inherit land from Protestants, hold public office, travel abroad for education, operate schools, practise law, serve on **Grand Juries** or in the military, and to vote. While these laws may have been applied only regionally and intermittently, their overall effect was to copper-fasten the Protestant Ascendancy and to create the highly unusual situation of religious discrimination against a majority population. Political resistance to these restrictions gradually escalated in the late eighteenth century, and various Catholic Relief Acts were passed towards the end of the century. In the 1820s, under the flamboyant and effective leadership of Daniel O'Connell, the Catholic Association successfully forced the British Government to pass the final Catholic Relief Act in April 1829, conceding the right of Catholics to sit in parliament.

CENSUS RETURNS

The earliest census taken, for which partial records are extant, is the census of 1659, edited by Seamus Pender in 1939. It is a poll tax list, not a true census, but is of historical significance for recording proportions of settler and native families, the names of principal landowners and tabulations of the most numerous Irish families for each barony. In 1749 Bishop Edward Synge initiated an impressively detailed census for his Church of Ireland Diocese of **Elphin**. There are partial returns of individuals of different denominations in the 1766 census. The first modern census in Ireland began in 1821 and has been held every ten years subsequently, though after independence Ireland conducted a census in 1926, 1936, 1946 and thereafter at five-year intervals. Northern Ireland took a census in 1926, 1937, 1951 and every five years thereafter. The decennial census remains the most important, however. The individual returns up to 1901 were largely destroyed, partially in World War I, when they were pulped as part of the war effort, and partially in the Irish Civil War in 1922. However, abstracts were published and those since 1841 provide important information by individual parish on population, religion, housing, occupation, literacy etc. The first full census for which the individual returns survive is that of 1901: its records, with those from 1911, are publicly available for all 32 counties. Arranged by county, district, electoral division and townland, it provides each occupant's name, age, religion, occupation, ability to read or write, marital status, relationship to householder, county of birth or country if not born in Ireland, and ability to speak English and/or Irish. Details of houses are also provided, including the number of rooms occupied by each family, type of roof and number of windows. Many of the institutions listed in this guide hold copies of the returns on microfilm for both 1901 and 1911, in whole or in part.

CHURCH OF IRELAND

The Church of Ireland, affiliated with the Anglican/Episcopalian tradition, was the established church in Ireland from the Reformation in the sixteenth century to its formal disestablishment in 1869, effective in 1870. Members of other religious denominations, notably Catholics and Dissenters, were forced to pay tithes to maintain the Church of Ireland. It is the largest Protestant denomination in the

Republic of Ireland and on the island of Ireland, but second in numbers to the Presbyterian Church in Northern Ireland. The Church's leader, the Archbishop of Armagh and Primate of All Ireland, is based in Armagh.

CIVIL SURVEY (1654)
This mid-seventeenth century survey records the principal property holders in each county.

COUNTY
The county system as a form of territorial division was introduced into Ireland shortly after the Norman Conquest in the late twelfth century. The creation of counties or shires was gradual, however, and did not reach into Ulster until after the **Flight of the Earls** in 1607. The final configuration of 32 counties was not achieved until the early part of the eighteenth century. The Sheriff was the chief administrative officer in the county and was vested with considerable powers, including public safety and administration. In 1898 the primary administrative duties were assigned to county councils, which remain the principal administrative body in the Republic but were abolished in Northern Ireland in 1972 with the introduction of Direct Rule by the British Government. Counties remain a powerful focus of local allegiance, symbolised by the use of the unit as the basis for the organisation of the **GAA** games of hurling and Gaelic football.

DÁIL ÉIREANN
The Irish parliament, first convened in January 1919 to declare Ireland's independence. The Dáil's 166 members, **TDs**, are elected by proportional representation. Each Dáil sits for a term of up to five years.

ELPHIN CENSUS
In 1749 the Church of Ireland bishop Edward Synge (1691–1762) organised a census of the people in his diocese, which at that time covered County Roscommon and a large part of Counties Sligo and Galway. This census encompasses all inhabitants, regardless of religious affiliation.

ENCUMBERED ESTATES RECORDS
In 1849, parliament passed legislation setting up Encumbered Estate Courts to settle claims against the growing number of estates bankrupted by the Famine. The courts freed up complicated land titles and placed thousands of estates on the open market. Their printed sales brochures frequently contain detailed lists of townlands, tenants, and leases. These brochures can be found at various locations in Ireland, including the NATIONAL ARCHIVES OF IRELAND, the NATIONAL LIBRARY OF IRELAND and the PUBLIC RECORD OFFICE OF NORTHERN IRELAND.

FLIGHT OF THE EARLS
On 4 September 1607, Hugh O'Neill, Earl of Tyrone, and Rory O'Donnell, Earl of Tyrconnell, together with a contingent of their followers, sailed from the port of Rathmullen in County Donegal for Spain, but were diverted to France and eventually to Italy. The 'Great O'Neill' (c. 1550–1616) spent the last years of his life in Rome,

where he is buried. The departure of Ireland's greatest chieftains symbolised the end of overt Gaelic resistance and paved the way for the **Ulster Plantation**.

GAA
The Gaelic Athletic Association was founded in 1884 to promote distinctive Irish sports. It is now probably the world's largest community sporting organisation. There is huge grass roots involvement, especially in rural communities, where clubs represent **parishes**. The GAA principally runs Gaelic football, hurling, handball and camogie (the female version of hurling). Today Gaelic football remains the most popular spectator sport in Ireland, and hurling (the fastest filed sport in the world) also attracts huge crowds to GAA headquarters, the impressively rebuilt 80,000 capacity state of the art Croke Park stadium in Dublin. Gaelic football has enough similarity with Australian Rules football for internationals to be played, in which the amateur Irish hold their own against the professional Australians. From its inception, the GAA has been an explicitly nationalist body. Until 1971 members were forbidden to play or watch 'foreign' sports such as soccer ('the Ban'), and until 2001 the security forces in Northern Ireland were barred from membership.

GRAND JURIES
Established in the thirteenth century, Grand Juries were appointed by the High Sheriff in each county and their membership was drawn largely from local landowners. Responsibilities included the maintenance of roads and bridges and the upkeep of courthouses, hospitals and lunatic asylums. The Juries, which kept minute books and presentment books, had their administrative functions transferred to county councils in 1898.

GRIFFITH'S VALUATION (1848–65)
Compiled by Richard Griffith, the purpose of this undertaking was to value house and land holdings to determine the payment of rates, i.e. property taxes. Tax receipts were administered by the Poor Law Guardians, who oversaw the administration of workhouses and certain public projects, such as road maintenance. The meticulously detailed document, more formally known as *The Primary Valuation*, is arranged by **townland** or street within **barony**, or **Poor Law Union** within county. This survey – of the utmost genealogical significance – is held on microfiche and covers the 32 counties. Most institutions listed in this guide hold at least a copy of Griffith's *Valuation* for their region.

HEARTH MONEY ROLLS
In 1662 the Irish parliament enacted legislation levying a tax of two shillings on every hearth, firing place and stove in Ireland, with exemptions, mostly for the indigent, including widows. Tax evasion was common. The rolls record the names of householders arranged by **parish** or **townland**. Few original rolls survive, but some copies are available. The Public Record Office fire destroyed the originals, but many copies had been transcribed and are still available.

INCUMBERED ESTATES RECORDS
See ENCUMBERED ESTATES RECORDS.

INDEXES TO WILLS
Published indexes to wills, compiled before the destruction of the Public Record
Office, providing important information on wills that are no longer extant.

INDOOR WORKHOUSE REGISTERS
Registers often included the following information: date of admission; first name and
last name; sex and age; marital status; occupation; religion; name of spouse and
number of children; electoral division or townland of residence; date the person left
the workhouse or died; and date of birth if born in the workhouse.

IRISH FOLKLORE COMMISSION SCHOOLS SCHEME PROJECT
Over a period of 18 months between 1937 and 1938, the Irish Folklore Commission,
founded in 1935, organised a project that involved Irish schoolchildren in collecting
and documenting a wide range of Irish folk material, including folk tales and folk
legends, riddles and proverbs, songs, customs and beliefs, games and pastimes, and
traditional work practices and crafts. The stories and information collected have been
preserved on microfilm and offer a good deal of useful historical and genealogical
information.

KING'S INNS ADMISSION PAPERS
This printed volume lists legal students who were admitted to the King's Inns from
1607 to 1867, giving name of father and maiden name of mother, place of birth and
qualifications gained. See THE HONORABLE SOCIETY OF KING'S INNS.

METHODIST CHURCH
The Methodist Church is the third largest Protestant denomination in Ireland, with a
total membership of about 60,000, most of whom reside in Northern Ireland. A
chairman is elected annually.

ORDNANCE SURVEY
Though inaugurated in England in the early 1790s for military purposes, the mapping
of Ireland commenced in 1825 for civil purposes, in anticipation of *Griffith's
Valuation*. More than 2,000 workers carried out the survey, county by county,
completing their work in 1841. In all, some 1,900 maps were drawn, the most detailed
mapping of an entire country ever carried out up to that time, and an invaluable
record of the state of the Irish landscape on the eve of the Great Famine. From 1825
until 1841, all of Ireland was mapped at the intimate scale of six inches to the mile.
At this scale field fences and houses are marked. These are particularly useful for family
research, as they help locate holdings listed in *Griffith's Valuation*.

ORDNANCE SURVEY LETTERS AND MEMOIRS
As the country was being mapped, John O'Donovan and other members of the
Ordnance Survey teams sent erudite and entertaining letters back to headquarters
describing the countryside, monuments, placenames, big houses etc. These were never
published, but are held in typescript copies. They are arranged by county. For much
of Ulster and some of the counties that border it, detailed memoirs were also compiled
for each parish, and these have now been published in a 40 volume series by the

Institute of Irish Studies, Queen's University, Belfast (Angélique Day and Patrick McWilliams, eds). See www.qub.ac.uk/iis/publications.html.

PALMER'S INDEX TO THE TIMES 1790–1905 ON CD-ROM
This index provides a wealth of information about Irish affairs in the nineteenth century. It is especially useful for genealogists wishing to glean information about people, places and social events.

Parish
This territorial division refers to both civil and ecclesiastical boundaries. Civil parishes largely follow the pattern that was established in medieval times, drawn largely along ecclesiastical lines. Ecclesiastical parishes do not always coincide with civil parish boundaries, however. Following the Reformation in the sixteenth century, the Church of Ireland maintained the pre-Reformation arrangement, but low populations forced it to expand its parishes into large groupings of civil parishes. When the Catholic Church began its institutional re-emergence in the late eighteenth and nineteenth centuries, it had to construct an entirely new network of Catholic parishes. The Irish system of parishes is therefore very complex indeed.

PARISH REGISTERS
See Appendix: Karel Kiely's 'Tracing Your County Kildare Ancestors'.

PARTITION
The Government of Ireland Act, passed by the British parliament in 1920, created two separate Home Rule parliaments, one based in Dublin for the 26 counties in the south and north-west, the other based in Belfast for the six north-eastern counties that were to become Northern Ireland in 1921. The latter area is often referred to as Ulster, but in fact includes only six of the nine counties in the province of Ulster, namely Antrim, Armagh, Derry or Londonderry, Down, Fermanagh and Tyrone. The three Ulster counties that came under Dublin's jurisdiction were Cavan, Donegal and Monaghan. The south rejected Home Rule, and in 1922 became the Irish Free State, with dominion status.

PENAL LAWS
Starting in 1695, the Irish parliament passed a series of draconian measures that were intended to limit not only the civil and religious rights of Catholics, but also the rights of all Dissenters, i.e. those who did not belong to the Church of Ireland. Catholics, however, suffered the most severe restrictions. *See* CATHOLIC EMANCIPATION.

PENDER'S CENSUS (1659)
See CENSUS RETURNS.

PLANTATION
See ULSTER PLANTATION.

POOR LAW UNION
Under the Poor Law Act of 1838 Ireland was divided initially into 130 Poor Law

Unions, each administered by an area Board of Guardians, responsible in turn to the Poor Law Commission. The Boards were chiefly responsible for supervising the running of the workhouses and administering poor relief in their unions. Later health services were added to their responsibilities. In 1898 the Local Government Act removed health matters from the Boards and assigned these to Rural District Councils. The Boards of Guardians and the Rural District Councils were abolished in 1930.

PRESBYTERIAN CHURCH
The second largest Protestant denomination in Ireland. Its membership is largely concentrated in the northern counties of the Republic and in Northern Ireland, where it slightly outnumbers the **Church of Ireland**. Its leader is the Moderator, elected annually by the General Assembly of the Church.

PROVINCES
There are four provinces in Ireland: Ulster in the north, Leinster in the east, Munster in the south, and Connacht or Connaught in the west.

REPUBLIC OF IRELAND
Formally established in 1949 as the successor to the Irish Free State of 1922, it consists of 26 counties in the south and north-west. The Irish Constitution of 1937, Articles 2 and 3, laid territorial claim to all 32 counties, but this claim was revoked by referendum as part of the Good Friday Agreement of 10 April 1998.

RIC
Royal Irish Constabulary. Founded originally in 1836 as the Irish Constabulary, the RIC was a national, armed force that took on a distinct military character for much of the nineteenth century. It was disbanded in 1922 and replaced in the Republic by the Garda Síochána and in Northern Ireland by the Royal Ulster Constabulary (**RUC**). The latter was disbanded in 2001 and replaced by the Police Service of Northern Ireland.

ROMAN CATHOLIC CHURCH
See CATHOLIC CHURCH.

RUC
Founded in 1922 with the establishment of Northern Ireland, the Royal Ulster Constabulary was controversial from the outset. Overwhelmingly Protestant and Unionist in composition, it was widely distrusted by the Catholic community. The Good Friday Agreement of 10 April 1998 specifically called for its reform. The subsequent Patten Commission recommended sweeping changes, and the Police Service of Northern Ireland replaced it in 2001.

RURAL DISTRICT COUNCILS
See POOR LAW UNION.

TAOISEACH
Prime Minister of Ireland.

TD
Teachta Dála, i.e. member of the Irish parliament or Dáil.

TITHE APPLOTMENT BOOKS (1823–37)
The tithe books were compiled for each civil parish to assess payment of tithes to the Church of Ireland, the established church in Ireland until 1869. All occupiers of land, regardless of their religious affiliation, were required to pay these tithes. Recorded is the name of the occupier, the acreage and quality of his holding and the amount of tithe payable. The landlord's name is also listed. These records, with variable degrees of detail, are held on microfilm and cover the 32 counties.

TOWNLAND
This is the smallest administrative territorial unit in Ireland, varying in size from a single acre to over 7,000 acres. Originating in the older Gaelic dispensation, townlands were used as the basis of leases in the state system, and subsequently to assess valuations and tithes in the eighteenth and nineteenth centuries. They survive as important markers of identity and as postal addresses.

ULSTER PLANTATION
Following the **Flight of the Earls**, the British crown set about 'planting' British loyalists, mostly Scottish Presbyterians, on the confiscated lands of the Gaelic lords such as the O'Neills and the O'Donnells, who had made Ulster the most autonomous and rebellious province in Ireland. Ulster attracted the largest group of newcomers in seventeenth century Ireland, contributing to a distinctive identity for the province. The first Plantation took place in 1609–10, followed by others, the most ambitious of which was the Cromwellian Plantation in the middle of the seventeenth century. At the beginning of the seventeenth century, Protestants constituted only about two per cent of the population of Ulster. By the end of the century, they were a majority.

WORKHOUSES
See POOR LAW UNION
and INDOOR WORKHOUSE REGISTERS.

For more detailed information on these and other terms, please consult such works as S.J. Connolly's *The Oxford Companion to Irish History* (second edn, Oxford, 2002); William Nolan's *Tracing the Past* (Dublin, 1982); and Donal Begley's *Handbook on Irish Genealogy: How to Trace your Ancestors and Relatives* (sixth edition, Dublin, 1984).

BIBLIOGRAPHY

A select list of general books and monographs only is included here. Monographs primarily of a local interest or serial-type publications, such as Parnham's *1911 Census Ireland References*, or memorial inscriptions of cemeteries, are not included because of space considerations. For articles and CD-ROMs, as well as monographs dealing with local history, consult bibliographies in works listed above, especially James Ryan's works, as well as the catalogues and websites of major distributors of genealogical publications, such as the Ulster Historical Foundation (www.ancestryireland.com), the New England Historic and Genealogical Society (www.newenglandancestors.org), Kennys Bookshop and Art Galleries (www.kennys.ie), and the Genealogical Publishing Company (www.genealogical.com).

ALLEN, F.H.A., KEVIN WHELAN, and MATTHEW STOUT. *Atlas of the Irish Rural Landscape.* Cork: Cork University Press, 1997.

ANDREWS, J.H. *A Paper Landscape: the Ordnance Survey in Nineteenth Century Ireland.* Oxford: Oxford University Press, 1975; reprint Dublin: Four Courts Press, 2001.

BARDEN, JUDITH, ed. *Directory of British and Irish Law Libraries.* 4th edn. Hebden Bridge: Published for the British and Irish Association of Law Librarians by Legal Information Resources Limited, *c.*1992.

BARDON, JONATHAN. *A History of Ulster.* Belfast: Blackstaff Press, 1992; new edition, 2001.

BAXTER, ANGUS. *In Search of Your British & Irish Roots: A Complete Guide to Tracing Your English, Welsh, Scottish, & Irish Ancestors.* 4th edn. Baltimore, MD: Genealogical Publishing Company, 2000.

BEGLEY, DONAL F. *Handbook on Irish Genealogy.* 6th edn. Dublin: Heraldic Artists, 1984.

Irish Genealogy: a Record Finder. Dublin: Heraldic Artists, 1981.

BLESSING, PATRICK J. *The Irish in America: A Guide to the Literature and the Manuscript Collections.* Washington, DC: Catholic University of America Press, 1992.

BOYLAN, HENRY, ed. *A Dictionary of Irish Biography.* 3rd edn. Dublin: Gill & Macmillan, 1998.

BRIGGS, ELIZABETH. *Access to Ancestry: A Genealogical Resource Manual for Canadians*

Tracing Their Heritage. Winnipeg: Westgarth, 1995.

Calendar of Fiants of the Tudor Sovereigns 1521–1603, with Index of Personal and Placenames. 4 vols. Dublin: E. Burke, 1994.

Calendar of State Papers Relating to Ireland. 24 vols. London: 1860–1912.

CARROLL, FRIEDA, comp. *Ireland School Registers, 1861–1872; 1891–1939.* Irish Genealogical Source No. 6. Dún Laoghaire: Dún Laoghaire Genealogical Society, 1998.

Church of Ireland Parish Register Series. Dublin: Representative Church Body Library, 1994–2001.

CONNOLLY, S.J. *The Oxford Companion to Irish History.* 2nd edn. Oxford: Oxford University Press, 2002.

DAY, ANGELIQUE, and PATRICK MCWILLIAMS, eds. *The Ordnance Survey Parish Memoirs of Ireland.* 40 vols. Belfast: Institute of Irish Studies, Queen's University, in association with the Royal Irish Academy, 1990–1998.

DE BRÚN, PÁDRAIG, and MÁIRE HERBERT. *Catalogue of Irish Manuscripts in Cambridge Libraries.* Cambridge (UK), New York: Cambridge University Press, 1986.

DELANEY, ENDA. *Demography, State and Society. Irish Migration to Britain, 1921–1971.* Liverpool: Liverpool University Press, 2000.

DONOVAN, BRIAN C., and DAVID EDWARDS. *British Sources for Irish History, 1485–1641: A Guide to Manuscripts in Local, Regional and Specialised Repositories in England, Scotland and Wales.* Dublin: Irish Manuscripts Commission, 1997.

DOOLEY, TERENCE. *Sources for the History of Landed Estates in Ireland.* Dublin: Irish Academic Press, 2000.

ELLIOTT, MARIANNE. *The Catholics of Ulster: A History.* London: Allen Lane, 2000.

FANNING, CHARLES, ed. *New Perspectives on the Irish Diaspora.* Carbondale, IL: Southern Illinois University Press, 2000.

FOSTER, JANET, and JULIA SHEPPARD. *British Archives: A Guide to Archive Resources in the United Kingdom.* 3rd edn. London: Macmillan, 1995 (reprinted 1996); New York: Stockton Press, 1995.

FOSTER, R.F. *Modern Ireland, 1600–1972.* London: Penguin, 1988.

FOWLER, SIMON. *Tracing Irish Ancestors.* Richmond, UK: Public Record Office, 2001.

The Genealogical Office, Dublin. A Guide. Dublin: Irish Manuscripts Commission, 1998.

GIBBEN, ARTHUR, and RUTH-ANN HARRIS, eds. *The Great Famine and the Irish Diaspora in America.* Amherst: University of Massachusetts Press, 1999.

GLAZIER, MICHAEL. *The Encyclopedia of the Irish in America.* Notre Dame, IN: University of Notre Dame Press, 1999.

GRENHAM, JOHN. *Tracing Your Irish Ancestors: The Complete Guide.* 2nd edn. Dublin: Gill & Macmillan, 1999.

GRIFFIN, WILLIAM D. *The Book of Irish Americans.* New York: Random House, 1990.

HANDRAN, GEORGE B. *Townlands in Poor Law Unions: A Reprint of Poor Law Union Pamphlets of the General Registrar's Office with an Introduction, and Six Appendices Relating to Irish Genealogical Research.* Salem, MA: Higginson Book Company, 1997.

HARTY, PATRICIA, ed. *Greatest Irish Americans of the 20th Century*. Dublin: Oak Tree Press, 2001.

HAYES, R.J. *Manuscript Sources for the Study of Irish Civilisation*. 11 vols, plus supplement (3 vols). Boston: G.K. Hall, 1965–79.

HELFERTY, SEAMUS, and RAYMOND REFASUSSÉ, eds. *Directory of Irish Archives*. 3rd edn. Dublin: Four Courts Press, 1999.

HERITY, MICHAEL. *Ordnance Survey Letters* [of John O'Donovan, 1830s], Counties Donegal, Down, Dublin, Kildare, Meath. Dublin: Royal Irish Academy, *c.*1999–

HOUSTON, CECIL J., and WILLIAM J. SMYTH. *Irish Emigration and Canadian Settlement: Patterns, Links, and Letters*. Toronto: University of Toronto Press, 1990.

JACKSON, ALVIN. *Ireland, 1798–1998*. Oxford: Blackwell, 1999.

KEANE E., E. ELLIS, and P.B. EUSTACE. *Registry of Deeds, Dublin, Abstracts of Wills*, vols. I–III (1708–1832). Dublin: Stationery Office, 1954–1984.

KEANE, E., P.B. PHAIR, and T.U. SADLIER. *King's Inn's Admission Papers, 1607–1867*. Dublin: Stationery Office, 1982.

KENNY, KEVIN. *The American Irish: A History*. Harlow, UK; New York: Longman, 2000.

KILLEN, JOHN. *A History of the Linen Hall Library, 1788–1988*. Belfast: Linen Hall Library, 1990.

MCCAFFREY, LAWRENCE J. *The Irish Catholic Diaspora in America*. Washington, DC: Catholic University of America Press, 1997.

MCCARTHY, TONY and TIM CADOGAN. *A Guide to Tracing Your Cork Ancestors*. Glenageary, Co. Dublin: Flyleaf Press, 1998.

MAC CONGHAIL, MÁIRE, and PAUL GORRY. *Tracing Irish Ancestors: A Practical Guide to Irish Genealogy*. London: Harper Collins, 1997.

MCKAY, PATRICK. *A Dictionary of Ulster Placenames*. Belfast: Institute of Irish Studies, Queen's University, 1999.

MACLYSAGHT, EDWARD. *The Surnames of Ireland*. 6th edn. Dublin: Irish Academic Press, 1985. (Originally published in 1957 as *Irish Families*, followed in 1960 by *More Irish Families*, and in 1964 by a *Supplement to Irish Families*.)

MCREDMOND, LOUIS, gen. ed. *Modern Irish Lives: Dictionary of 20th-century Irish Biography*. Dublin: Gill & Macmillan, 1996.

MCTERNAN, JOHN C., ed. *Sligo: Sources of Local History: A Catalogue of the Local History Collection, with an Introduction and Guide to Sources*. New edn. Sligo: Sligo County Library, 1994.

MCWILLIAMS, PATRICK, ed. *The Ordnance Survey Memoirs of Ireland. Index of People & Places*. Belfast: Institute of Irish Studies, Queen's University Belfast, in Association with the Royal Irish Academy, 2002.

MASTERSON, JOSEPHINE. *Ireland: 1841/1851 Census Abstracts* (Northern Ireland). Baltimore: Genealogical Publishing Company, 1999.

MASTERSON, JOSEPHINE. *Ireland: 1841/1851 Census Abstracts* (Republic of Ireland). Baltimore: Genealogical Publishing Company, 1999.

MAXWELL, IAN. *Tracing Your Ancestors in Northern Ireland*. Edinburgh: Stationery Office, 1997.

MAXWELL, IAN. *Researching Armagh Ancestors: A Practical Guide for the Family and Local Historian.* Belfast: Ulster Historical Foundation, 2000.

MITCHELL, BRIAN. *A Guide to Irish Parish Registers.* Baltimore: Genealogical Publishing Company, 1997.

MITCHELL, BRIAN. *A New Genealogical Atlas of Ireland.* Baltimore: Genealogical Publishing Company, 2001

MOODY, T.W., F.X. MARTIN, and F.J. BYRNE, eds. *A New History of Ireland.* Vol. III. *Early Modern Ireland, 1534–1691.* Oxford: Oxford University Press, 1976.

MOODY, T.W. and W.E. VAUGHAN, eds. *A New History of Ireland.* Vol. IV. *Eighteenth-century Ireland, 1691–1800.* Oxford: Oxford University Press, 1986.

MOODY, T.W., F.X. MARTIN, and F.J. BYRNE, eds. *A New History of Ireland.* Vol. IX. *Maps, Genealogies, Lists.* Oxford: Oxford University Press, 1976.

MORRIN, JAMES, ed. *Calendar of the Patent and Close Rolls of Chancery in Ireland, Henry VIII–Elizabeth.* 2 vols. Dublin, 1861–2.

MOSCINSKI, SHARON. *Tracing Our Irish Roots.* Santa Fe, NM: J. Muir Publications, 1993.

NOLAN, WILLIAM. *Tracing the Past.* Dublin: Geography Publications, 1982.

Ó CÉIRÍN, KIT, and CYRIL Ó CÉIRÍN. *Women of Ireland: A Biographic Dictionary.* Newtownlynch, Kinvara, Co. Galway: Tír Eolas, 1996.

O'CONNOR, JOHN. *From The Workhouses of Ireland: The Fate of Ireland's Poor.* Dublin: Anvil Books, 1995.

O'CONNOR, THOMAS, MARIE DALY, and EDWARD L. GALVIN. *The Irish in New England.* Boston: New England Historic Genealogical Society, 1985.

O'FARRELL, PADRAIC. *Irish Surnames.* Dublin: Gill & Macmillan, 2002.

O'FARRELL, PATRICK. *The Irish in Australia, 1788 to the Present.* Cork: Cork University Press, 2001.

O'NEILL, ROBERT K. *A Visitors' Guide: Ulster Libraries, Archives, Museums & Ancestral Heritage Centres.* Belfast: Ulster Historical Foundation, 1997.

PENDER, SEAMUS, ed. *A Census of Ireland, circa 1659. With Supplemental Material from the Poll Money Ordinances (1660–1661).* 1939, reprinted 1997 by Clearfield Publishing Company, Baltimore, MD.

PHILLIMORE, W.P.W., and GERTRUDE THRIFT, eds. *Indexes to Irish Wills.* London: Phillimore & Co., 1909–20, reprinted 1997.

QUINN, SEAN E. *Tracing Your Irish Ancestors.* Bray: Magh Itha Teoranta, *c.*1989.

RADFORD, DWIGHT A., and KYLE J. BETIT, *A Genealogist's Guide to Discovering Your Irish Ancestors: How to Find and Record Your Unique Heritage.* Cincinnati: Butterway Books, 2001.

REFASUSSÉ, RAYMOND. *Church of Ireland Records.* Dublin: Irish Academic Press, 2000.

RYAN, JAMES G. *A Guide to Tracing Your Dublin Ancestors.* 2nd edn. Glenageary, Co. Dublin: Flyleaf Press, 1998.

RYAN, JAMES G., ed. *Irish Church Records: Their History, Availability and Use in Family and Local History Research.* Glenageary, Co. Dublin: Flyleaf Press, 2001.

RYAN, JAMES G., ed. *Irish Records: Sources for Family and Local History*. Rev. edn. Salt Lake City, UT: Ancestry, *c*.1997.

RYAN, JAMES G., comp. *Sources for Irish Family History: A Listing of Books and Articles on the History of Irish Families*. Glenageary, Co. Dublin: Flyleaf Press, 2001.

VAUGHAN, W.E., ed. *A New History of Ireland*. Vol. V. *Ireland under the Union I: 1801–1870*. Oxford: Oxford University Press, 1989.

VAUGHAN, W.E., ed. *A New History of Ireland*. Vol. VI. *Ireland under the Union II: 1870–1921*. Oxford: Oxford University Press, 1996.

VICARS, SIR ARTHUR. *Index to Prerogative Wills of Ireland: 1536–1810*. 1897, reprinted 1997.

INDEX

Printed in the United Kingdom
by Lightning Source UK Ltd.
122625UK00001B/1-36/A